A PI

THIS MACHI

ANDY GREENBERG is a staff writer f ocusing on technology, information security, and dig civil liberties. His *Forbes* story on WikiLeaks and the future of information leaks in late 2010 was the first magazine cover story to feature Julian Assange. He lives in Brooklyn, New York, with his wife, filmmaker Malika Zouhali-Worrall.

Praise for *This Machine Kills Secrets*

"Fascinating and well-researched." —*Wall Street Journal*

"*Forbes* magazine journalist Andy Greenberg takes readers on a terrific and revealing—if considerably unsettling—investigation into the shadowy war rooms behind our computer screens." —*The Cleveland Plain Dealer*

"Computer hackers haven't been made into heroes like this since Stieg Larsson created Lisbeth Salander—and luckily Greenberg shares a bit of Larsson's flair for suspense, too." —*Slate*

"Greenberg delves eloquently into the magicians of the all-powerful technology that shatters the confidentiality of any and all state secrets while tapping into issues of personal privacy." —*Publishers Weekly*

"While lawmakers and law enforcers struggle with the philosophy and practicality of these issues, the people Greenberg profiles have made up their minds, and they are a few steps ahead. If you're wondering who they are and why they feel so strongly, look no further than this book."

—*New Scientist*

"Greenberg masterfully portrays a new reality. Radical transparency for firms and governments is not just a decision but a technological fact of life."

—Don Tapscott, bestselling author of *The Naked Corporation* and *Macrowikinomics*

"A must-read for those seeking to understand the decades-long struggle between openness and secrecy, anonymity and attribution—and why that might be the most important struggle of the modern era. Meticulously researched, Greenberg provides firsthand accounts of the eccentric pioneers who are coding around censorship, repression, and even traditional law. He also captures the relentless distributed nature of the movement that's powering it all."

—Daniel Suarez, *New York Times* bestselling author of *Daemon* and *Kill Decision*

"Andy Greenberg shows us why cryptography has to be the marrow of the Internet. People who have no technical knowledge along with those who live and breathe bytes will gain a new vision of an invisible army of characters. . . . This book will be one of the most important books of the decade."

—Birgitta Jónsdóttir, member of the Icelandic Parliament and chairperson of the International Modern Media Institute

"This is the story of a revolution in societal transparency. It's an exposé of the characters who have put secrets in peril. For those who seek transparency, it's a riveting tale. For those who must keep secrets, be warned: This book holds up a mirror to your worst fears."

—Hugh Thompson, founder and CEO of People Security, adjunct professor in computer science, Columbia University

"Greenberg's vivid storytelling makes the forces that culminated in WikiLeaks—the people, the politics, and especially the technology—come alive."

—Bruce Schneier, author of *Liars and Outliers* and *Applied Cryptography*

"Andy Greenberg tells a vivid story that weaves together compelling characters and powerful technology that could change politics more profoundly than any technology since the printing press. By the time I was finished, I was both inspired and terrified."

—David Bacon, IBM, Watson Research Center

"Points to a future in which few corporate and government secrets are safe. This is the book you must read to understand the WikiLeaks phenomenon and the growing struggle over the most sensitive institutional secrets."

—Stephen Solomon, director of the Business and Economic Reporting Program, New York University Arthur L. Carter Journalism Institute

"A globe-trotting exploration into the heart of the contentious world of brilliant, eccentric, and erratic game changers who have taken the tools at hand and turned them into powerful weapons that can—and have in some cases—altered the course of history . . . Greenberg went looking for a story and nailed it."

—*Paper* magazine

"A series of moving and deeply complex portraits . . . In all, Greenberg has created a seriously riveting read."

—*Capital New York*

"Gripping . . . For all the technical detail (which Greenberg excels at explaining), this book is still about human feats and failings, idealism, trust, and betrayal.

—*The Irish Times*

. ... -- .- -.-. .... .. -. . -.-
. ... -- .- -.-. .... .. -. . -.- .. .-.
.. -- .- -.-. .... .. -. . -.- .. .-.. .-
- .- -.-. .... .. -. . -.- .. .-.. .-.. .
- -.-. .... .. -. . -.- .. .-.. .-.. .... .
... .. -. . -.- .. .-.. .-.. ... . -.
. -. . -.- .. .-.. .-.. ... ..-. . -.-. .-
-.- .. .-.. .-.. ... . -.-. .-. . -
.- .. .-.. .-.. ... . -.-. .-. . - ..
-.. .-.. ... . -.-. .-. . - ... - .
-.. ... . -.-. .-. . - ... - .... .
.. ... . -.-. .-. . - ... - ....
.. . -.-. .-. . - ... - .... --
-.-. .-. . - ... - .... -- .- -.
-. .- ... - .... -- .- -.-. ..
- ... - .... -- .- -.-. .... .
.. - .... -- .- -.-. .... .. -.
. ... -- .- -.-. .... .. -. . -.-
. ... -- .- -.-. .... .. -. . -.- .. .-.
.. -- .- -.-. .... .. -. . -.- .. .-.. .-
- .- -.-. .... .. -. . -.- .. .-.. .-.. .
- -.-. .... .. -. . -.- .. .-.. .-.. ... .
.. .. -. . -.- .. .-.. .-.. ... . -.
. -. . -.- .. .-.. .-.. ... . -.-. .-
-.- .. .-.. .-.. ... . -.-. .-. . -
-.. .-.. ... . -.-. .-. . - ... - .
.. . -.-. .-. . - ... - .... --
- ... - .... -- .- -.-. .... .. -. .
. ... -- .- -.-. .... .. -. . -.- .. .-.. .-..
.-.. .. .-.. .. -. . -.- .. .-.. .-.. ... .
-.- .. .-.. .-.. ... . -.-. .-. . - ...
-.. ... . -.-. .-. . - ... - ....
.-.. .-.. . - ... - .... -- .- -.-. .
. ... -- .- -.-. .... .. -. . -.- ..
- .- -.-. .... .. -. . -.- .. .-.. .-.. ... .
. -.- . -.- .. .-.. .-.. ... . -.-. .-. . .
-.. .-.. ... . -.-. .-. . - ... - .... .
.. . -.-. .-. . - ... - .... -- .-

THIS MACHINE KILLS SECRETS

Julian Assange, the Cypherpunks, and Their Fight to Empower Whistleblowers

ANDY GREENBERG

A PLUME BOOK

PLUME
Published by the Penguin Group
Penguin Group (USA) LLC
375 Hudson Street
New York, New York 10014

USA | Canada | UK | Ireland | Australia | New Zealand | India | South Africa | China
penguin.com
A Penguin Random House Company

First published in the United States of America by Dutton, a member of Penguin Group (USA) Inc. 2012
First Plume Printing 2013

THE LIBRARY OF CONGRESS HAS CATALOGED THE DUTTON EDITION AS FOLLOWS:
Greenberg, Andy.
This machine kills secrets : how WikiLeakers, cypherpunks, and hacktivists aim to free the world's information / Andy Greenberg.
p. cm.
Includes index.
ISBN 978-0-525-95320-3 (hc.)
ISBN 978-0-14-218049-5 (pbk.)
1. Computer hackers—Political activity. 2. Secrecy. 3. Official secrets. 4. Whistleblowing. 5. Computer crimes. I. Title.
HV6773.G74 2012
364.16'8—dc23

2012004309

Printed in the United States of America
10 9 8 7 6 5 4 3 2 1

Set in FairfieldLH
Original hardcover design by Alissa Amell

For my father, Gary Greenberg, and
the memory of my mother,
Marcia Gottfried

CONTENTS

THIS MACHINE KILLS SECRETS

CHARACTERS

(IN ORDER OF APPEARANCE)

JULIAN ASSANGE

Founder of WikiLeaks, former hacker, cypherpunk, and activist who demonstrated the power of digital, anonymous leaking by publishing record-breaking collections of secret corporate and government material.

DANIEL ELLSBERG

Military analyst who from 1969 to 1971 exfiltrated and leaked the top secret Pentagon Papers to *The New York Times* and seventeen other newspapers.

BRADLEY MANNING

Army private who, at the age of twenty-two, allegedly leaked a trove of secret military and State Department documents to WikiLeaks that would become the largest-ever public disclosure of classified materials.

ADRIAN LAMO

A former hacker and homeless wanderer to whom Manning confessed his leak. Lamo turned Manning in to army investigators.

TIM MAY

Intel physicist, libertarian, and crypto-anarchist thinker who would cofound the cypherpunks in 1991 and create a thought-experiment prototype for cryptographically anonymous leaks called BlackNet.

PHIL ZIMMERMANN

Applied cryptographer whose Pretty Good Privacy program (PGP) brought free, strong encryption to the masses. His investigation by the U.S. Justice Department from 1993 to 1996 ignited a debate over users' right to uncrackable encryption.

DAVID CHAUM

Inventor and academic whose anonymity systems, including DC-Nets and Mix Networks, would inspire the cypherpunks and lead to tools like anonymous remailers and Tor.

ERIC HUGHES

Mathematician, cryptographer, and cofounder of the cypherpunks who ran one of the Internet's first anonymous remailers.

JOHN GILMORE

Former Sun Microsystems programmer who would cofound the cypherpunks as well as the Electronic Frontier Foundation.

JOHN YOUNG

Architect, activist, and cypherpunk who founded Cryptome.org in 1996, a leak-focused site that has published thousands of names of intelligence agents and their sources, along with hundreds of secret encryption- and security-related documents.

JULF HELSINGIUS

Finnish systems administrator and privacy advocate, Helsingius created the Penet anonymous remailer and faced legal pressure from the

Church of Scientology that demanded he turn over the identity of one of his users.

JIM BELL

Engineer and libertarian whose 1997 essay "Assassination Politics" described a system of using encryption to facilitate anonymous, untraceable, and crowd-funded contract killings.

JACOB APPELBAUM

Activist, hacker, and developer for the Tor anonymity network who befriended Julian Assange and became the WikiLeaks' primary American associate.

PAUL SYVERSON

Logician and cryptographer in the Naval Research Laboratory who is credited with inventing the anonymous communications protocol known as "onion routing."

NICK MATHEWSON AND ROGER DINGLEDINE

Two MIT researchers who worked with Syverson to develop onion routing into a usable tool and then a nonprofit known as the Tor Project.

PEITER "MUDGE" ZATKO

Former "gray hat hacker" who served as a spokesperson for the hacker group the L0pht. Now leads the cybersecurity division of the Pentagon's Defense Advanced Research Projects Agency, including its program to find a method of rooting out rogue insiders known as CINDER or Cyber Insider Threat.

AARON BARR

Former chief executive of HBGary Federal, a small D.C. security firm that touted his methods for unmasking anonymous hackers and leakers.

THOMAS DRAKE

National Security Agency whistleblower who was threatened with prosecution under the Espionage Act for communicating with a reporter regarding alleged financial fraud and waste at the agency.

BIRGITTA JÓNSDÓTTIR

Icelandic member of parliament, poet, and activist who worked with WikiLeaks and is pushing a collection of radical transparency bills through Iceland's legislature known as the Icelandic Modern Media Initiative.

DANIEL DOMSCHEIT-BERG

German former WikiLeaks associate who worked closely with Assange but was pushed out of the group in the fall of 2010. He has since engaged in a bitter feud with Assange and founded his own digital whistleblower group known as OpenLeaks.

ATANAS TCHOBANOV AND ASSEN YORDANOV

Two Bulgarian investigative reporters who founded the independent media outlet Bivol and were inspired by WikiLeaks to create the Bulgaria-focused leak site BalkanLeaks.

ANDY MÜLLER-MAGUHN

Former member of the board of the German hacker group the Chaos Computer Club. Müller-Maguhn worked with WikiLeaks and served as an intermediary in the dispute between Assange and Domscheit-Berg.

THE ARCHITECT

Secretive and pseudonymous engineer who worked with Assange and Domscheit-Berg to set up a revamped submission system for WikiLeaks in late 2009 and 2010. After a falling-out with Assange, he joined Domscheit-Berg at OpenLeaks.

PROLOGUE

THE MEGALEAK

On a rainy November day in a garden flat in London, Julian Assange is giving me a lecture on the economics of leaking.

"To put it simply, in order for there to be a market, there has to be information. A perfect market requires perfect information," he says, settling his six-foot-two-inch body, clothed in a sleek navy suit, into the couch, a coffee mug in hand. His voice is a hoarse, Aussie-tinged baritone. As a teenage hacker in Melbourne its pitch helped him impersonate IT staff to trick companies' employees into revealing their passwords over the phone, and today it's deeper still after a recent bout of flu. His once-shaggy white hair, recently dyed brown, has been cropped to a sandy leopard print of blond and tan. (He's said he colors it when he's "being tracked.")

"There's the famous lemon example in the used car market. It's hard for buyers to tell lemons from good cars, and sellers can't get a good price, even when they have a good car," he says in a professorial tone. "We identify the lemons."

Assange, today, has a particular lemon in mind. He's just told me that WikiLeaks plans to release tens of thousands of internal e-mails from a major American bank in early 2011, just a few months away from our meeting. He won't say which bank, or exactly what the e-mails will reveal, but he promises they will expose corporate malfeasance on a massive scale, enough to "take down a bank or two."

"You could call it the ecosystem of corruption," he says. "But it's also all the regular decision making that turns a blind eye to and supports unethical practices: the oversight that's not done, the priorities of executives, how they think they're fulfilling their own self-interest."

This is Assange at the height of his power. When I report his words later that month in *Forbes* magazine, speculation that WikiLeaks' target would be Bank of America shaves off $3.5 billion from the company's stock market value in a matter of hours. The thirty-nine-year-old WikiLeaks founder had gotten accustomed to the feeling of his thumb on the eject button for the world's institutional information. In the last four months, his group had already spilled 76,000 secret documents from the Afghan War and another 391,000 from the war in Iraq, entire shadow histories of the two wars, the largest public classified data breaches of all time. "These big package releases. There should be a cute name for them," he says with a stern look.

"Megaleaks?" I offer tentatively.

"Megaleaks. That's good," he says. "These megaleaks . . . they're an important phenomenon, and they're only going to increase."

A few hours later, after I've turned my recorder off, Assange has donned his gray parka and he and his assistant are packing up to leave. That's when he lets slip that WikiLeaks is planning another megaleak in the near future, speaking about it as if it were an embarrassing technicality he mentions only out of necessity.

A big one? I ask, sweating a little. He responds that it's seven times the size of the Iraq War document dump.

"Does it affect the private sector or a government?" I try to subdue the panicked feeling that after three hours of talking to a man who dispenses secrets to reporters like Christmas gifts, I'm somehow only now getting the real story.

"Both," he says.

"Which industries?" I ask, thinking of my editors' interests at the business magazine I work for.

That's when Assange's professional dispassion seems to crack, and he allows an unrestrained, full schoolboy grin to spread across his face, complete with his usually hidden overbite. "All of them," he says.

A minute later, he's out the door and disappeared down the rain-shined sidewalks of London.

Cablegate changed the world. Three weeks after my meeting with Assange, 251,000 once-secret State Department Cables began flowing out of WikiLeaks and would continue for the next year. The documents had too many connections to too many world affairs to draw straight lines between cause and effect. But when a sidewalk vendor named Mohamed Bouazizi set himself on fire in front of the governor's office in the Tunisian town of Sidi Bouzid, the country's citizens responded by taking to the streets to overthrow their government. Many of them cited WikiLeaks' revelations about the U.S. State Department's disdain for Tunisian president Ben Ali as giving them the courage to oppose their dictator of the prior two-and-a-half decades. If they stood up to him, it was now clear, America wasn't coming to his aid.

As populist anger spread to Egypt, Libya, Syria, and elsewhere, Muammar Qaddafi warned Libyans in a televised speech not to read "WikiLeaks, which publishes information written by lying ambassadors in order to create chaos." Nine months later, that revolutionary chaos had overwhelmed his military, ousted him from power, and killed him.

When President Obama announced that all American troops would be leaving Iraq by the end of 2011, CNN reported that WikiLeaks had cratered negotiations that might have kept them there longer. U.S. generals had asked for guarantees of legal protection for any remaining soldiers in the country. But thanks to leaked cables that revealed a massacre of Iraqi civilians and a subsequent cover-up, the Iraqi government had refused, and sent the American forces on their way.

But even as Assange's ultrascoop percolated around the globe, the bank leak he had foretold to me failed to appear. For the next year, the Australian carefully dodged all questions about the nonleak, offering veiled excuses and eventually seeming to pin the blame on a rogue staffer who WikiLeaks would claim deleted the files. Assange's brash vows to "take down a bank or two" only contributed to the banks' vicious retaliation against WikiLeaks: Bank of America joined an informal coalition of payment firms including Visa, MasterCard, PayPal, Western Union, and others who refused to process donations to the world's most controversial website, choking it to the point of paralysis.

Today, WikiLeaks is on life support. Assange faces questioning for alleged sex crimes in Sweden, with more American legal foes waiting in the wings. Revelations by the prosecutors of WikiLeaks' alleged source Bradley Manning suggest Assange may have actively coached the young army private, potential grounds for his own indictment. His organization's work has stalled as it struggles to raise cash. Some of its most ardent supporters have become its most bitter critics, and its releases have dropped sharply in frequency and impact. Assange seems more interested in hosting a TV talk show on the Russian government–funded network RT than in rebuilding his organization, and WikiLeaks-watchers from Evgeny Morozov to Richard Stallman argue that the group's fate holds dark lessons. With WikiLeaks, they say, the Web turned out to be less the free, anarchic realm we once imagined than a restrictive platform tightly controlled by corporations and governments.

But it would be a mistake to focus only on how WikiLeaks has been contained, muzzled, punished, and sabotaged while ignoring a larger lesson: how the group has inspired an entire generation of political hackers and digital whistleblowers. That story didn't begin or end with Julian Assange, or even with his institution-eviscerating group. Instead, it tracks the ideals, the means, and the movement that WikiLeaks represents, extending from its predecessors decades earlier to the ideological descendants it has radically mobilized.

Since my meeting with Assange that rainy day in London, that thread has taken me from one edge of the Western world to the other as I sought out the history and future of an idea: digital, untraceable, anonymous leaking. And the line of thought I followed remains stronger in many ways than ever before. The activists and fellow travelers I've met have no illusions about WikiLeaks' and Assange's weaknesses and failures. But they share the same spirit that drove Assange: to build a better secret-spilling machine than the last one.

This Machine Kills Secrets is a book about the forces that coalesced to make WikiLeaks happen. And it's also about how those forces are working to make it happen again.

The insider's drive to expose institutional secrets—to conscientiously blow the whistle or vindictively dump a superior's dirty laundry—has always existed. But the technology that enables the spillers of secrets has been accelerating its evolution since the invention of computing. With the dawn of the Internet, the apparatus of disclosure entered a Cambrian explosion, replicating its effective features, excising its failed components, and honing its methods faster than ever before.

The state of the world's information favors the leaker now more than ever. In 2002, the amount of digitally recorded data in the world finally matched the amount of analog recorded information, according to a study by the University of Southern California's Annenberg School for Communication and Journalism. Just five years later in 2007, the most recent year the study included, digital information already accounted for 94 percent of the world's recorded information. And all of that information is *liquid:* infinitely reproducible, frictionlessly mobile—fundamentally leakable.

Just what fraction of that vast digital swamp remains secret is tough to gauge. But Harvard science historian Peter Galison, taking printed files as a proxy, estimates that there are five times as many pages being added to the world's classified libraries as to its unclassified ones. Despite Barack Obama's promises of a more transparent government, 76.7 million documents were classified in 2010, compared with 8.6 million in 2001 and 23.4 million in 2008, the first and last years of George W. Bush's administration.

The numbers of people who have access to that material are just as unfathomable. Four million Americans have some form of clearance to read classified information. Of those, about 1.2 million have top-secret clearance.

But the abundance of widely shared secrets is hardly the only factor pushing the leaking movement forward. Anonymous whistleblowing remains a game of skirting surveillance, and WikiLeaks' key advancement in the science of spilling information has been in separating the leaker from the leaked information. Cutting the data trail to a leak's source was the crucial trick that emboldened ever-greater disclosures from whistleblowers leading up to the Cablegate blowout.

That's why the story of leaked secrets, from the days of Daniel Ellsberg and the Pentagon Papers to the growing brood of sites hoping to reproduce WikiLeaks' work, has not been driven merely by digital disclosure, but by digital anonymity. And true digital anonymity requires cryptography.

The craft of cryptographic leaking that WikiLeaks brought to light seems like a paradox: A movement focused on divulging secrets depends on a technology invented to keep them. But anonymity technologies represent a special kind of encryption: They reveal data itself while hiding certain metadata *about* the data. Specifically, anonymity tools hide that one metadatum that counts most, the IP address that can be linked immediately to a user's location and device. Protecting that one fact is a harder trick than it sounds: In the end, strong anonymity tools have taken more than a decade longer than mere strong encryption to make their way into the hands of the average Internet user. But that strong anonymity, as it slowly matured over the course of two decades, was the lever WikiLeaks used to upend the world.

Today, a schizoid hive-mind of Internet pundits and social media theorists claims, simultaneously, that everyone knows no anonymity exists on the Internet ("These Days the Web Unmasks Everyone," states a *New York Times* headline from 2011) and that everyone knows no *identity* exists on the Internet—that "no one knows you're a dog," as the *New Yorker* cartoon caption reads. Half of security gurus preach about the Internet's invasion of privacy, while the other half bemoan the Internet's lack of authentication, which they say makes the task of identifying bad actors—what they call the "attribution problem"—nearly impossible.

Forget these conflicting parallel realities. The Internet is neither fundamentally private nor fundamentally public, anonymous or onymous. Those who behave a certain way online and use certain services will have no privacy, while those who behave another way and use other services can be very, very hard to identify—harder to identify now, in many ways, than ever in communication's history.

The public and private paths on the Internet have been diverging. Today users have the option to use a service like Facebook, which is designed to learn your real name and attach it to all your actions, preferences, locations, and even thoughts. Or they can use a service like WikiLeaks' now-defunct submission system, which was designed to learn absolutely nothing about them—in fact, to provably demonstrate to users, by using modern anonymity software like Tor, that it *can't* learn anything about them.

All of which is to say that WikiLeaks wasn't a one-off fluke, a brilliant hacker's lucky break, or, as digital pundit Clay Shirky has characterized the press's image of WikiLeaks, a "series of unfortunate events." It was the *inevitable* outcome of the changing nature of information and advancements in cryptographic anonymity, catalyzed to an explosion by Assange's actions.

The first two parts of this book will tell the story of how leaking has been transformed over the last forty years by generations of cryptographers and revolutionary activists of all stripes. The third part tours the post-WikiLeaks world, following the same movement of radical hacktivists as they seek to systematize, replicate, and evolve the craft of disclosure.

As I traveled from San Francisco to Iceland to Berlin to Bulgaria to report this story, I was searching not so much for WikiLeaks' methods, its influences, or its sequels as I was trying to write the story of an ideal that drove this hidden movement. It was on a street in my own neighborhood in Gowanus, Brooklyn, that I saw a busker sitting on a curb, strumming a guitar with the same words scrawled across it that once were written across the one Woody Guthrie played: *This Machine Kills Fascists*. That sentence, to me, brought to mind the ideological arrow I see from Ellsberg to Assange and beyond: a revolutionary protest movement bent not on stealing information, but on building a tool that inexorably coaxes it out, a technology that slips inside of institutions and levels their defenses against the free flow of data like a Trojan horse of cryptographic software and silicon.

But the machine that kills secrets isn't merely WikiLeaks, or the photocopier that duplicated the Pentagon Papers, or the anonymity network Tor, or even the Internet. It's a living idea—one that continues to evolve in the minds of all those who aim to obliterate the world's institutional secrecy.

PART ONE

LEAKER PRESENT, LEAKER PAST

"The mice will win in the end. But in the meantime, the cats will be well fed."

BRUCE SCHNEIER

CHAPTER 1

THE WHISTLEBLOWERS

When Dr. Daniel Ellsberg decided to violate thirteen years' worth of security clearances, embark on the largest public breach of top-secret documents in the twentieth century, and likely spend the rest of his life in prison, he faced a problem: how to duplicate seven thousand pieces of paper many times over using 1969 technology.

RAND, the California military think tank where Ellsberg held a position two steps removed from the president of the United States, didn't have a Xerox machine. The technology was twenty years old, but still not widely used. And it presented some obvious security issues for an agency dealing with ultraclassified materials. So Ellsberg, a thin, thirty-eight-year-old man with wiry dark hair and features that resembled a more Semitic Paul Newman, needed help. He contacted Tony Russo, a mildly subversive Virginian former co-worker, and Russo soon became the only other analyst who knew about and sympathized with Ellsberg's leaking plans.

Russo found one of the newfangled photocopiers in the advertising agency of a friend who shared their antiwar agenda. Over the next year, Ellsberg would spend countless nights hauling RAND's papers out of the building in an inconspicuous briefcase, then standing in front of that primitive copier in a dark office reproducing a secret history of America's involvement in Vietnam: the Pentagon Papers.

It was tedious work. At first Ellsberg tried to copy two pages at a time from one of the forty-seven bound volumes. But he found that the words near the spine were faded and distorted. So he resorted to disassembling the binder and photocopying the pages one by one. "I tried to program my motions," he wrote in his memoir, *Secrets:*

> One hand picked up a page, the other fit it on the glass, top down, push the button, wait . . . lift, move the original to the right while picking another page from the pile. . . . This is all very familiar now, but it was a new technology then. It took a little extra time to put the top down and up, and I didn't know why it had to be done. Did it have to do with the copying quality, or was the light bad for the eyes? Was it dangerously bright? How did it work, anyway? Was that peculiar green color some kind of radiation?

There were complications: Ellsberg intended to give portions of the papers to several senators, and if necessary, the news media too. To make multiple copies, he would have to hand the papers over to a professional copying office, where they'd be subjected to the curious eyes of who-knew-how-many clerks. Inconveniently, the papers were marked with glaring "Top Secret" stamps across their tops and bottoms, with more classified signifiers peppered throughout the margins of the monstrous classified tomes.

So at first Ellsberg cut off the heads and feet of the pages with scissors, later upgrading to a paper cutter. Then Russo suggested he tape strips of cardboard over the top and bottom of the photocopier's glass face, what Ellsberg would later refer to as "declassifiers." Even then, some words were cut off by the declassifiers, and small, randomly interspersed "Top Secret" markings lingered on the edges of the pages. Ellsberg had to comb through the encyclopedia-size pile to excise them. When he thought he was ready to hand the first briefcase-size fraction of the stack over to a New York copy shop months into his project, he riffled through the papers one last time and was startled to immediately find another page with an obvious, unsheared "Top Secret" marking. He left the copy shop and retreated to a lunch counter where he surreptitiously pruned more "Top Secret" remnants out of the papers while attempting to nonchalantly consume a sweet roll and a cup of coffee over the course of several hours.

The process was punctuated with a couple of visits by the local police. Russo's friend in advertising wasn't particularly skilled at manipulating her office's security system, and the result was multiple silent alarms—an average of three a week—that brought in bored policemen to check on the distinguished-looking man who always seemed to be photocopying late at night. Ellsberg would casually cover the classified documents on the desk beside the copy machine, greet the policemen politely, and carry on his work as soon as they left.

Ellsberg recruited Russo to help with the endless task, along with Russo's advertising friend, even his two thirteen- and ten-year-old children from his first marriage. (Why did Ellsberg involve his children? He writes that he expected to spend the next decades talking to them only through a pane of glass in a federal prison, and he wanted them to at least understand exactly what he had done, and why.)

Even with his ragtag team's help, it took the Harvard- and Cambridge-educated analyst nearly a year of on-and-off grunt work to create a full set of the papers and duplicate them at commercial copy centers, eventually creating an eight-foot-tall stack of breached classified documents. At ten cents a page in those shops, the process also required Ellsberg to spend several thousand dollars. (The equivalent of more than twenty thousand dollars today, accounting for inflation.) Once, when he sent a batch of papers off to Senator William Fulbright, Fulbright's aide politely offered to reimburse him. But when Ellsberg named the price—$345 including postage—the aide hastily rescinded the offer. Fulbright, who had told Ellsberg he would launch congressional hearings based on the documents, would later rescind that offer too.

The data leaks that would earn army private first class Bradley Manning the alleged title of the world's most prolific whistleblower weren't merely orders of magnitude larger than Ellsberg's Pentagon Papers. Compared to photocopying seven thousand pages several times over, Manning's leaks were also phenomenally easier—the difference between spending months harvesting a season of crops and playing a few hours of FarmVille on Facebook.

In the midst of his work as a low-level intelligence analyst in Iraq, Manning slipped a rewritable CD marked with "Lady Gaga" into the tray of his work machine, a PC connected only to the military's high-security Secret Internet Protocol Router Network, or SIPRNet. The SIPRNet was "air-gapped": It wasn't connected to the Internet through any plug or wireless signal. But Manning could simply copy the CD's music to the computer, delete it from the rewritable disc, burn whatever top-secret data he wanted to the piece of plastic, and walk away with it minutes later. "[I] listened and lip-synced to Lady Gaga's 'Telephone' while exfiltrating possibly the largest data spillage in American history," Manning would write a few months later. "Pretty simple and unglamorous."

The data caches that Manning replicated, allegedly, included 91,000 files from the war in Afghanistan, 392,000 from the Iraq War, 779 files of inmates in the Pentagon's Guantánamo prison, and a quarter of a million memoranda from the U.S. State Department, which also shared its data with troops via SIPRNet.

If the Ellsberg of 1969 could have seen the size of those leaks and the ease with which Manning extracted them, he might have cried at the unfairness of technological progress. One of Manning's Lady Gaga CDs offered enough capacity to have stored the Pentagon Papers about fifty times over, and the laser head that wrote to those discs could have accomplished in a minute or two what required a year of off-and-on work for Ellsberg and his photocopier.

To turn that comparison around, how long would it have taken Ellsberg to copy a leak the size of Manning's using only his 1969 technology? On a modern copier, I found I could only achieve a pace of around eight pages a minute. Assume that Ellsberg was able to photocopy for eight uninterrupted hours out of every twenty-four—say, from nine at night to five in the morning to avoid suspicion and keep his demanding job at RAND. At that rate, and even with a 2011 photocopier magically transported to 1969, it would have taken Ellsberg six months of straight work to reproduce just one copy of the 261 million words included in the State Department Cables—not even considering the Afghan or Iraqi files—that Manning effortlessly transported onto his Lady Gaga CD.

In fact, Ellsberg never worked steadily at that eight-pages-a-minute pace. If he had, he would have finished copying the Pentagon Papers in a week or less. But at the more realistic pace that Ellsberg set, factoring in the need for sleep, fear of being caught, his much slower copier, distractions, a high-level military job that often required late nights and travel, breaks to maintain his sanity, the need to make secondary copies, and the niggling task of manually scissoring out any evidence of the files' classification before turning them over to a professional copying service, he didn't finish his photocopier work for close to three months of solid work interspersed over a year.

Adding in the textual data that filled the smaller but still massive files from two data-flooded wars and Ellsberg's need to make multiple copies, and it's possible to roughly extrapolate how long a Manning-size leak would have realistically taken at Ellsberg's rate: about eighteen years. Suffice it to say that by then, his revelations would have belonged in a history book rather than *The New York Times*. And therein lies the clearest of so many differences between the act of leaking in the twentieth century and the twenty-first.

Daniel Ellsberg was born into an upper-middle-class Chicago family in 1931, in the depths of the Great Depression. Though his parents were the children of Russian-born Jews, they had converted and raised Ellsberg as a strict Christian Scientist. Ellsberg's father was trained as an engineer but, like many men in that decade, spent years without work. Although Ellsberg would later come to admire his father, the rosy-cheeked boy with dark, close-cropped hair first found a different hero: his father's brother, Ned Ellsberg, the navy admiral and writer. Admiral Ellsberg had risen to fame as a member of the navy's submarine salvage team, invented an underwater torch for cutting through the steel of sunken ships' hulls, and wrote a dozen fiction and nonfiction books with titles like *Men Under the Sea*, *Ocean Gold*, and *I Have Just Begun to Fight!* The young Ellsberg devoured the books and looked up to their author.

Ellsberg's father found work first in Chicago, Illinois, and later in Detroit in 1937, and the family moved to the middle-class Highland Park suburbs. Ellsberg, an intensely intelligent child with few friends, won a scholarship to attend the prestigious Cranbrook private school, just as World War II began to rage in Europe. Despite his reverence for his military uncle, Ellsberg's early memories of war itself were of a vague and evil specter. One of his elementary schoolteachers passed around a model of a magnesium bomb of the kind capable of penetrating buildings and remaining alight continuously no matter how much water was poured on it. "A particle . . . , we were told, would burn through flesh to the bone and wouldn't stop burning even then," he wrote. "It was hard for me to understand people who were willing to burn children like that. It still is."

Ellsberg was a top student in his classes. But his mother wanted her son to be the next Vladimir Horowitz or Arthur Rubinstein, and it was to the piano that she committed nearly all his time. He was expected to practice for six to seven hours a day. Reading was considered a vice and a distraction, and Ellsberg remembers his mother quietly hiding his books to keep him at the keyboard.

As obediently as Ellsberg followed his mother's ambitions, he was less willing to blindly accept the religion that his parents lived by. At Sunday school, he peppered his teacher with tough theological questions. Later, in his teens, he read and deeply absorbed an exposé of plagiarism in the works of Mary Baker Eddy, Christian Science's founder, that shook the faith his parents had tried to instill in him.

One summer day in 1946, much of the influence that Ellsberg's family held over his life suddenly, violently vanished. On a road trip to a party in Denver, Ellsberg's father fell asleep at the wheel of the family's sedan. He awoke just seconds before the car plowed into the concrete structure of an overpass, demolishing the right side of the vehicle. Ellsberg's mother was killed instantly. Though the details were initially kept from him, Ellsberg later learned she was beheaded. His father received facial injuries but survived. Ellsberg awoke thirty-six hours later. His sister never did.

When Ellsberg gained consciousness, his father had gone back to Michigan, leaving him in a Denver hospital with his mother's family. For months after the accident, the elder Ellsberg felt too guilty to face his son. Daniel, for his part, was overcome with a strange emotional numbness. He once said that his first thought after his mother's death was simply "I guess I don't have to play the piano anymore."

When Ellsberg did return to Michigan, he was suddenly freed from the obligation of piano practice and began to hungrily consume books. Two years later, he won a scholarship from the Pepsi-Cola Corporation to attend Harvard. One evening early in his time at the university, while sitting on a bench with a beer and a Hemingway novel, he had an epiphany. "It felt so strange, I couldn't figure out what it was," he told a biographer. "Then I realized: I felt *free,* for the first time in my life."

Ellsberg married his college girlfriend, Carol Cummings, graduated from Harvard, and won a Woodrow Wilson fellowship to spend a year studying at Cambridge University. When he returned, he was more than ready to join the war in Korea, a conflict he saw through the simple Cold War lens of a Communist aggressor pushing into a would-be democratic state. He enlisted in the Marines, prepared to fight alongside his brothers at the forty-ninth parallel. But instead, he spent the next year in officer's training in Quantico, Virginia, long enough that when he emerged, the fighting was over. He had graduated, again, near the top end of his class of a thousand soldiers.

Three years into his military career, Ellsberg was handed his first top-secret security clearances, and a few years after that, clearances that extended beyond top secret.

Several promotions and layers of privileged knowledge later, Ellsberg would have a conversation about those rites of passage with Secretary of State Henry Kissinger, one that he documented in his memoir. Kissinger was about to receive his own beyond-top-secret clearances, and Ellsberg wanted to prepare him for the heady effects of that rarified information. So he described for Kissinger the experience of entering a world of secrets.

At first, Ellsberg said, he'd felt exhilarated at the enormous bounty of incredible facts that flooded into his intelligence. But that initial feeling soon gave way, and instead he felt like a fool for having worked for so long without those secrets, under such a veil of illusions and ignorance. A couple weeks later, he began to see everyone *else* as fools, watching them labor under that same malformed knowledge he had suffered from for years.

It would take years more, Ellsberg recounted, before he finally began to see the limits of his ultra-classified information, the ways that it blinded him and led him astray with the sense of omniscience it offered. In the intervening time, he says, those secrets often prevented him and other secret keepers from learning anything from anyone who didn't have their clearances. Knowing secrets, Ellsberg told Kissinger, requires a person to lie to and distrust everyone who advises him.

"I ended by saying that I'd long thought of this kind of secret information as something like the potion Circe gave to the wanderers and shipwrecked men who happened on her island, which turned them into swine," Ellsberg wrote of his warning to Kissinger. "They became incapable of human speech and couldn't help one another to find their way home."

If Ellsberg's path to becoming the most prolific leaker of his age began with a steep upward trajectory fueled by Ivy League ambition, Bradley Manning set out from far more common circumstances: destitute, middle-American aimlessness.

Manning grew up in Crescent, Oklahoma, a tiny conservative town that had one stop sign and fifteen churches, "more pews than people," as Manning would later write. He was a bright child who could read at three, built his first website at ten, and won the top prize at his school's science fair three times. He also had a rebellious streak that led him to ask hard questions of religious neighbors, argue with Sunday school teachers, and even remain silent during the Pledge of Allegiance in school to avoid its "under God" doctrine. But those from his hometown described him to the local magazine *This Land* as a quiet, good-natured boy, small for his age, who studied hard, played saxophone in the school band, loved video games like the military simulation *Command and Conquer*, and talked sometimes of joining the army one day.

Manning's father, Brian, had a more mixed reputation in the neighborhood where Manning grew up. A gruff former navy computer analyst who worked as an IT manager for Hertz car rentals, he was also a strict and unforgiving father. One neighbor has described him as "demeaning," another as simply "a dick." Brian Manning would leave on business, sometimes for months at a time. His wife, a woman named Susan Fox, whom Manning had met while stationed in the United Kingdom in the late seventies, couldn't drive, and they lived four miles from town. So the older Manning would stock up the house with food and supplies and leave them largely isolated. Fox filled the void of her loneliness with alcohol, starting with vodka in her morning tea.

When Manning was thirteen, his father announced one evening that he was separating from Manning's mother. Fox would bring Manning back to her hometown, the Welsh village of Haverfordwest, not much larger than Crescent.

If growing up as the only American in a small British community hadn't been alienating enough, Manning now faced another new emotional challenge: Just before leaving Oklahoma, he had announced to friends that he was gay.

Manning never publicized his homosexuality in Wales, but he was treated as an outsider nonetheless, teased for his accent, his effeminate mannerisms, his small size—even as an adult, Manning would only measure five feet two and 105 pounds. Manning's inability to fit in wasn't helped by a fierce sense of American patriotism that he inherited from his father. One friend from Crescent described him as "basically really into America," particularly Americans' sense of political and economic liberty—not often an outlook shared by the residents of parochial ends of the United Kingdom.

Alienated from most of his peers, Manning turned to the outlet of so many other young men: computers and the Internet. He spent his lunch periods in the school's computer lab, coding a website that functioned like a primitive version of Facebook, allowing users to create communities and find local news. In the process, he learned about the basics of Web servers and Internet routing.

When he graduated from high school, Manning's strong connection to the United States brought him back to Oklahoma to live with his father and now two stepbrothers in Oklahoma City. He put his computer skills to use at a software start-up called Zoto. The tech firm was a more politically liberal setting than Manning had ever been exposed to, and co-workers remember him speaking out loudly against the deteriorating war in Iraq and criticizing President Bush. In his work, he was a competent coder, but his loneliness and angst sometimes hampered his productivity: One manager, Kord Campbell, has recalled Manning's "thousand mile stare" and described him as "quirky as hell." Manning developed a reputation as odd and unreliable. After a shouting match with his boss, he was fired.

At the same time, the young man's relationship with his restrictive father and new family was fraying quickly. Manning would say years later that he was kicked out of his home because he was gay. But his father told a PBS *Frontline* reporter that he had always accepted his son's sexuality. And a 911 recording of a call from Manning's father's second wife describes Manning throwing objects and threatening her with a knife. "I have been telling him he needs to get a job and he won't get a job!" Manning's stepmother says frantically in the recording. "He said he thinks he should just be able to take money from us." Manning wasn't arrested, but he was escorted from the house by police. Days later, he left in his Toyota pickup truck and drove to Tulsa, homeless, directionless, and largely alone in the world.

For the next months, Manning slept first in his truck and then later in the room of a friend from Crescent, Jordan Davis, hiding in the bedroom from Davis's father until he could find a bare-bones apartment in town. He flitted between menial jobs, working first in a Chucky Cheese–style entertainment center called Incredible Pizza as a waiter, later at a music and video game store. He drifted to Chicago and then to Maryland, working retail jobs at Guitar Center, Starbucks, and Abercrombie & Fitch before finally moving in with his aunt near Rockville and enrolling in a local community college.

Manning had learned the exhaustion of life without a degree. He writes that he was "in desperation to get somewhere in life." But he couldn't afford a four-year university. When he turned to his father for help, the elder Manning told him to take a well-worn path for resourceless and lost young men: the military. Despite Manning's patriotism and admiration of the armed forces years earlier, his opposition to the war in Iraq left him conflicted. Brian Manning, years later, would say of his son that he "twisted his arm."

"He didn't want to join," Manning's father would tell the PBS show *Frontline*. "But he needed structure in his life, he was aimless. I knew in my own life that joining the navy was the only thing that gave me structure."

The army, as promised, swiftly imposed direction on Manning's career. After Manning enlisted in August 2007, he spent the next year in basic training and then, when his superiors recognized his computer skills, specialized education in intelligence analysis. In October 2009, he shipped out to Iraq, a twenty-two-year-old soldier—slight of frame and short on experience—inducted suddenly into wartime's wealth of secrets.

Daniel Ellsberg read as much paperwork on the war in Vietnam as practically any Pentagon analyst. For one stretch in his first years at the Department of Defense, he requested that all new classified documents on the war be sent to his in-box, and he spent practically every waking moment digesting thousands of pages. But his real education on the war would come later: in the passenger's seat of a jeep, traveling the roads of the countryside around Saigon with a rifle in his hand and a grenade in his lap.

In 1962, Ellsberg had completed a doctorate at Harvard in economics, focusing on decision theory. His dissertation homed in on what would come to be known as the Ellsberg Paradox, a strange glitch in the way that humans make choices: Show someone two opaque jars with ten stones in each, one with five black stones and five white ones and one with an unknown number of white and black stones. Then tell the test subject he'll be rewarded for picking a white stone. Experiments show that he'll tend to choose from the jar with a known, equal number of black and white stones. But tell him a second later that he'll be rewarded for choosing a black stone, and he'll *again* choose the jar with known numbers of black and white stones. In both cases, most humans act as if the uncertain jar is less likely to have a favorable ratio of stones, even when those assumptions contradict each other from one second to the next.

When Ellsberg arrived at RAND as an analyst, the White House was already making its choice about which opaque jar it would rather gamble on: armed conflict in Vietnam, or the seemingly riskier idea of letting it fall to Communism and increase the red blotch spreading across half the world map.

Ellsberg spent years at the Pentagon-tied think tank RAND and then as a military analyst in the Pentagon itself, inhaling war files and occasionally digging up documents to justify President Lyndon Johnson's moves to slowly widen the war in Vietnam. But he sensed that the paperwork he was sifting through wasn't the real war, and in 1965 he took a new job at the State Department. Soon he shipped out as a boots-on-the-ground analyst, eager to see the war for himself. He was entrusted with go-anywhere-see-everything status on the irregular banana-shaped landmass known as South Vietnam, and within weeks he was in the field, accompanying troops on operations.

Ellsberg found that he was considered a liability if he didn't carry a firearm or even if he hesitated to use it in combat situations. So despite his State Department civilian observer status, he started carrying a Swedish K submachine gun alongside the soldiers he accompanied, even as he took notes and photographs as an analyst.

The former soldier was soon adopted by John Vann, a seasoned retired lieutenant colonel in the army who had also come to Vietnam as a civilian official. Vann became Ellsberg's roving guide, mentor, and driver. That was no common privilege: Wheels were a risky way to see the country, and most officers didn't even dare to drive the roads through the swamps and jungles that Vann frequented, instead flying between bases by helicopter. At one point, the utility vehicle that Ellsberg and Vann traveled in momentarily broke down in the same spot where, three months later, Vann's assistant would be captured by Vietcong and kept as a POW in a cramped bamboo cage for the next seven years.

But Vann believed that driving was the only way for an officer to understand the real truths of the war, and he had learned that a single, nimble jeep could evade a Vietcong ambush. He taught Ellsberg the roadside clues that the VC firmly controlled certain areas, despite official reports to the contrary. Ellsberg learned to see freshly cut barbed wire fences, dug-up roads, and destroyed buildings just a few feet away from outposts supposedly held by U.S.-friendly Vietnamese.

As Ellsberg interviewed more advisers on the ground, he found more wishful thinking on the part of the U.S. forces: American bureaucrats were told, for instance, that pro-U.S. militias patrolled their territory at night. In reality, much of South Vietnam was handed over to the Vietcong from sundown to sunrise.

When Ellsberg stayed at a base in the town of Long An on Christmas Eve 1966, a very drunk South Vietnamese major began ranting about American arrogance and stupidity. Later, outside, he took several shots with a pistol at Ellsberg and his companions, missing them in the dark before other soldiers could restrain the enraged major. When Ellsberg quizzed a Vietnamese lieutenant about the incident later, the younger man reluctantly admitted that the resentment against American intervention wasn't unique. In fact, many of the other officers felt the same way.

But Ellsberg's notion that Vietnam was an unwinnable war wasn't confirmed for him until New Year's Day 1967, the day he first came face-to-face with Vietcong soldiers. Or rather, face to back. As Ellsberg and three other soldiers walked ahead of a platoon of troops, they suddenly heard firing behind them. Three Vietnamese boys in black shorts had hidden in the grass just feet from where the four men's boots passed, popping up to fire their AK-47s at the troops behind Ellsberg's group. The four Americans didn't dare fire back toward their own men, and instead had to take cover from the hail of bullets sent back from the American platoon.

The three Vietcong boys disappeared into the jungle brush, only to hide and jump up fifty meters behind Ellsberg's forward group and pull the same trick again before vanishing. Three half-naked kids had shown a kind of fearlessness, cunning, and mastery of the terrain that an entire platoon couldn't counter. Later in the day, a pair of Vietcong outfits performed an even more wily maneuver against Ellsberg's platoon, alternately firing on the Americans and then fading into the jungle, first from the left, then from the right, then from the left again. Each burst dragged the platoon toward their imagined attackers to counterattack, and they found themselves moving in a futile zigzag shape as they sought an efficient and ghostly enemy. "I was very, very impressed," wrote Ellsberg in *Secrets*. The "morning's work had sown in my guts a thought that had been only in my head before: These opponents were going to be very hard to beat. Or to put it another way, we were not going to defeat them."

Over the next months, Ellsberg's feelings were reinforced with impossible missions, disappointing interviews with officers, and repeated glimpses of corruption among the military regime the United States supported. When he returned to RAND in the middle of 1967, he had decided: He would work within the system to end this futile war.

Ellsberg became a hard-nosed critic against the war effort within the think tank's walls. But his arguments merely convinced most colleagues that his experiences had destroyed his objectivity. Despite now working under Special Assistant for National Security Kissinger and others at that near-presidential level, he found that his pessimistic comments regarding Vietnam fell on deaf ears.

Still, his time in Vietnam served a purpose beyond grim education: It made him one of the few RAND analysts chosen to work on a landmark study on the evolution of America's involvement in the country, a classified history that would trace the story of Vietnam's endless wars back to the French occupation and the Japanese invasion that preceded it. At the time, it was known as the McNamara study, named for Secretary of Defense Robert McNamara, who launched it before leaving government to become president of the World Bank. Today, that report is known as the Pentagon Papers.

Ellsberg agreed to help write a portion of the study because he hoped that the assignment would also provide him the access to read the entire report, a multivolume, comprehensive effort with the full analytic weight of RAND's brains behind it. And what he found, as he dug into historical documents and then got his hands on the first volumes of the papers in the following months, put his antipathy toward the war in a new light: The American quagmire in Vietnam wasn't an honest mistake, or even a mistake at all. It was the result of a decades-long policy, the tip of an ugly iceberg older and more trenchant than the Cold War itself.

To summarize seven thousand pages in a few words, the United States had controlled and incited the war in Vietnam—and it was a single war, not a series of wars against different regimes—for nearly twenty-five years. And its motives had always been those of geopolitical empire, never the democratic well-being of Vietnamese citizens.

It started in the mid-forties, when the United States had financially and militarily supported France's control of Vietnam as a colony, and then backed its bloody reconquest of the country after French forces were temporarily interned and pushed aside by Japanese invaders. Despite pleas from Vietnamese president Ho Chi Minh to recognize Vietnamese independence, America's motivation was always, simply, to support its Western ally as a colonial power.

Only after the rise of McCarthyism and the Maoist takeover of China did any question of Communism versus democracy in Vietnam arise. And by then it was too politically painful for any president to retreat from the country and allow the Communist hemisphere of the globe to grow one sliver larger. Meanwhile, as every president from Truman to Kennedy to Johnson to Nixon sank deeper into the widening war, they had *known* that the conflict was inherently imperial from the start, and even seen State Department reports that showed that Ho Chi Minh had the majority support of the population.

Vietnam had never been a true civil war. It was a war of conquest, initiated and perpetuated for more than two decades by the United States, fueled by presidential secrecy and lies. It was no catastrophic accident. As Ellsberg wrote, it was simply "a crime."

After his time on the ground, Ellsberg didn't need much convincing of the war's folly. But the Pentagon Papers put the stamp of historical confirmation on his determination to end it. And in 1969, that education as a leaker would be capped by a fateful trip he took to a Haverford College peace conference.

For Ellsberg, simply attending a meeting full of peaceniks was a radical step. After the first day at the small Quaker school, he found himself on the sidewalk in nearby Philadelphia handing out antiwar pamphlets to passersby, a tactic that at first felt awkward and ridiculous for a high-level insider who had vowed to end the war through his influence in Washington's power structure.

The second day on Haverford's campus, a young man named Randy Kehler stood up to speak to the crowd. Like Ellsberg, he had attended Harvard, then graduated from Stanford. Ellsberg was impressed with his poise and levelheaded intellect, and remembers thinking that Kehler was "the best that we've got" as a country.

In a strong and steady tone, Kehler explained that he had become the last remaining male member of the War Resisters League in San Francisco. All the others had been imprisoned for violating the draft. As Kehler's voice cracked onstage, he told the audience how proud and happy he was that he would soon be joining his friends in prison.

The crowd at first seemed stunned at the thought that the young man in front of them was about to be treated as a criminal. Then thunderous applause broke out.

But Ellsberg couldn't stand. He was emotionally devastated. The senior military analyst stumbled out of the auditorium and into an empty bathroom, where he collapsed and sobbed for an hour. "It was as though an ax had split my head, and my heart broke open," he writes. "But what had really happened was that my life had split in two."

When Ellsberg recovered, he made a promise to himself: He would do whatever he could to end the war. Even if it meant going to prison.

Two essential traits of a leaker are an abundance of knowledge and a lack of power. And Bradley Manning both had access to far more information and wielded far less power than Ellsberg ever did. As the young soldier would later write, he was "smart enough to know what's going on, but helpless to do anything."

Manning's army career would quickly become as troubled as his premilitary life. By the middle of 2010, he had been demoted for hitting another soldier and shouting down a superior, assigned to hauling around boxes in the supply closet and working at events like a sparsely attended barbecue for a visiting team of cheerleaders. On one occasion, an officer found him curled in a fetal position on the floor. On another, he was found sitting alone with a knife, the two words *I want* carved into a wooden chair. Fear for his safety and his mental state had led a superior to remove the bolt from his rifle. Even then, he retained his classification privileges.

Manning's demotion may have also been linked to the fact that he now made little effort to conceal his homosexuality, even attending demonstrations against California's anti-gay-marriage Proposition 8 while stationed in upstate New York. He told a reporter that he had been kicked out of his home and lost a job because of his sexual orientation. He said that the military's don't-ask-don't-tell policy was forcing him to live "a double life."

His Facebook statuses referred to a Boston boyfriend, Tyler Watkins, whom he had met while on leave there prior to shipping out to Iraq. "Bradley Manning is glad he is working and active again, yet heartbroken being so far away from hubby," read one status update. And another: "Bradley Manning is in the barracks, alone. I miss you, Tyler!" Manning would write later of his decision to "transition" to becoming a female named Breanna Manning. On one of his leaves, he spent days dressed as a female in public, and had begun planning for electrolysis and other sex change procedures after his discharge.

But the moment that Manning would cite as setting him on the path to become his era's most prolific leaker didn't come during his social struggle in the army's ranks. It occurred during his work as an analyst, one of the hundreds of thousands with access to the army's endless classified troves of information. And it happened far more quickly than Ellsberg's long-burning transformation from hawk to dove.

Fifteen detainees had been taken in by the Iraqi Federal Police for printing "anti-Iraqi literature," and Manning was assigned to investigate the situation. He soon determined that the prisoners hadn't advocated violence, but had simply written what Manning described as a "scholarly critique" of Prime Minister Nouri al-Maliki, looking into possible corruption in the prime minister's cabinet. "I immediately took that information and *ran* to the officer to explain what was going on," Manning would later write. "He didn't want to hear any of it . . . he told me to shut up and explain how we could assist the [police] in finding *more* detainees. . . ."

"I had always questioned the way things worked, and investigated to find the truth. But that was a point where I was a *part* of something. I was actively involved in something that I was completely against," he wrote. "Everything started slipping after that. . . . I saw things differently."

Manning dug deeper, browsing the State Department database he would later be accused of spilling to WikiLeaks: 251,000 memoranda describing the intimate dealings of the world's leaders in candid terms. He described "crazy, almost criminal political back dealings, the non-PR versions of world events and crises, all kinds of stuff like everything from the buildup to the Iraq War during Powell, to what the actual content of "aid packages" is.

"There's so much . . . it affects everybody on Earth. Everywhere there's a US post, there's a diplomatic scandal that will be revealed. . . . Iceland, the Vatican, Spain, Brazil, Madagascar, if it's a country, and it's recognized by the US as a country, it's got dirt on it," Manning wrote. "It's open diplomacy . . . world-wide anarchy in CSV format. It's beautiful, and horrifying."

Finally, he writes of a video shot from the cockpit of an Apache helicopter, showing a group of men being killed by the aircraft's heavy weaponry. "At first glance, it was just a bunch of guys getting shot up by a helicopter. No big deal, about two dozen more where that came from," wrote Manning. But the video was being stored in the file of the Judge Advocate General, implying that it was being used in some sort of military justice proceeding.

So Manning tracked down the video's date—a day in July 2007—and its coordinates, a Baghdad suburb called New Baghdad. And he linked those facts with a story in *The New York Times* that revealed two Reuters journalists had been killed in the helicopter airstrike, along with nine insurgents on the ground and in a black van, who the military said had been firing on U.S. soldiers.

Manning knew that the men on the ground hadn't, in fact, been firing on anyone. The Apache helicopter had mowed down the group from above without any evidence that they were insurgents. And the black van that had pulled up beside the wounded and dying men to help them had similarly been mere civilians, a family hoping to save the lives of a group of strangers who lay dying on the street and sidewalk. But the helicopter had rained down bullets on the van, too, wounding two children and killing their father. "Well it's their fault for bringing their kids into a battle," one soldier quipped in the clip's audio track.

"I kept that in my mind for weeks . . . probably a month and a half," says Manning. Then he decided: He would hand it over to WikiLeaks, where it would become the prologue for a classified exposé to dwarf all others in history.

Adrian Lamo seems to have fallen asleep. His head hangs suspended over his lunch, a plate of salmon, plantains, and vegetables next to a cup of coffee that he has filled to the brim with cream and five packets of sugar.

We're sitting in a restaurant that serves Colombian food, a few blocks from his home in a dreary town that he's requested I not name. Instead, the thirty-year-old hacker has asked me to write only that we met on "an island," a taunting clue to the legions of angry supporters of WikiLeaks and Bradley Manning who would like to locate Lamo and harass or harm him. Those pursuers aren't a figment of Lamo's imagination. Just days before, a news crew from Al Jazeera posted a TV interview of Lamo that included a momentary shot of his computer. One of his many online stalkers quickly spotted an Internet protocol address on the screen, performed a Whois lookup to find a registered location in Carmichael, California, and posted screenshots of the information online. Luckily for Lamo, it was an old address.

Still, Lamo hasn't shaken his paranoid compulsions, partly residual from his years as a hacker and homeless drifter. When we sit down at the restaurant, he insists on switching seats "to face the door," despite the fact that both of our seats are perpendicular to the exit.

The question that seems, a few minutes into our meal, to have had such a soporific effect on Lamo is this one: Now that Bradley Manning has been placed in an isolated cell in a Quantico, Virginia, brig awaiting trial, largely deprived of exercise and visitors and forced to strip and wear nothing but a coarse smock every night to prevent him from committing suicide with his underwear's elastic band, does Lamo regret having turned Manning over to authorities? Looking back, would he still have drawn him out in online conversations that stretched over days as Manning confessed every detail of his leaks, and then allowed those incriminating logs to be used as evidence against him?

Lamo has responded by closing his eyes and allowing his head to bob and sink slowly for several seconds. I consider reaching over to tap him on the shoulder. Before I do, he suddenly looks up and answers me.

"The man is the equivalent of a spy. He's our next Aldrich Ames or Robert Hanssen," Lamo says, naming two convicted double agents who sold information to the USSR over several decades. Lamo's speech is a robotic slur, a result of the cocktail of psychoactive prescription drugs he takes daily. But his hazel eyes have opened wide and he's now staring at me with surprising lucidity. "The only difference is that instead of giving information to the Soviets, he's giving it to an antisecrecy organization. In another country, he'd get a bullet in the head. Here, he gets donations and approbation."

Lamo's hair is slicked back away from a pudgy, almost feminine baby face. In his pierced left earlobe is a small screw he wears as an earring. He wears a blue shirt tucked into his jeans over a potbelly that's likely another side effect of his medical regimen. Earlier, Lamo listed five names of drugs he says he takes to treat his Asperger's syndrome, a form of autism. But when I consult with a doctor after our meeting, I learn that the drugs are generally used for treating chronic pain, depression, and schizophrenia. There is no prescription drug for the treatment of Asperger's.

Lamo goes on to argue that the story of Manning's mistreatment comes from just the few supporters that have managed to visit him: Manning's friend David House and his lawyer, David Coombs. "Manning is being treated as any maximum security detainee would be treated," Lamo slurs. "It's being played up as a sideshow to garner sympathy."

But House and Coombs aren't the only ones to point out Manning's mistreatment. Just the week before, P. J. Crowley, the State Department public affairs official, called Manning's treatment by the military "ridiculous, counterproductive, and stupid" before resigning his government post. Later, a UN torture investigator would also speak out after being barred from visiting Manning.

The waitress comes over, and Lamo, who spent part of his childhood in Colombia, makes her laugh with a few words in slurred Spanish. Then he takes a sip of coffee, but his mouth doesn't seem to function properly, and he moves the liquid around in his cheeks for several seconds before swallowing.

I continue: Doesn't it open Lamo to charges of hypocrisy that he turned Manning in for the same information-wants-to-be-free attitude that Lamo himself preached during his years as an illegal hacker?

Lamo looks down into his plate, closes his eyes, and his neck muscles seem to relax. After a few seconds I fear again that he's finally passed out in his chair. When he looks up suddenly, this time I twitch in surprise. "I know that saying this isn't going to make me very many friends," Lamo says. "But had Manning released just that video and nothing else, I wouldn't have told anyone about it. I would have even exfiltrated it myself if I were him." Lamo pauses, as if to let this sink in.

"He should have gone through the files," he continues. "Instead, he said, 'Here are a million documents. I've read one millionth of a percent of them, but I've established there's no harm in releasing them.'"

Lamo goes through a convoluted arithmetic he says he used to make his decision, first weighing the good of the victims of the helicopter strike and their families versus the good of the soldiers who carried out that strike—

and then the good of Manning versus that of the secrecy of the entire United States military and State Department. And since the moment that he committed to handing over his instant messenger chat logs to the authorities, Lamo says he hasn't doubted the conclusions of his moral calculus.

Lamo's lids fall to half-mast. "He wanted to make the world a better place. He just didn't know what he was doing," he intones flatly. "I wish there could have been some other resolution. I actually suggested to the agents that they keep him around and feed him disinformation. Instead, they chose to grab him."

This is the stranger, of all possible strangers, to whom Bradley Manning chose to confess a leak that may put him in prison for the rest of his life.

When Manning sought out Lamo as a confessor and friend, he had some reason to believe that the older hacker was a kindred spirit. For several years at the beginning of the last decade, Lamo was one of the media's favorite digital deviants: the so-called "homeless hacker." Traveling back and forth across the United States by Greyhound, fueled by amphetamines and painkillers, sleeping in abandoned buildings and on friends' floors, Lamo would stop into twenty-four-hour Kinko's to use their computers for marathon hacking sessions.

Lamo avoided traditional network intrusion, which uses unpatched vulnerabilities in the victim's software. Instead, he often exploited misconfigured proxy servers, meant for use by outsourcing firms and other corporate partners, as hidden gaps in corporate firewalls. Using Internet Explorer as his only tool, Lamo would pry open those gaps and enter forbidden networks.

Once, he tells me, he could have transferred the entire cash pool set aside for bonuses at the telecom giant MCI WorldCom to any account he chose. On another occasion, he found a bug in AOL's network that allowed hackers to hijack users' instant messenger accounts, and he later hacked a Yahoo! website to insert a dig at President Bush into a news story. He carried a stun gun on his travels and used it for electrocuting various objects like electronic locks and vending machines, which sometimes responded by spitting out change or food.

In 2002, Lamo dug up a flaw in *The New York Times'* corporate password system, and exploited it to add his name to the paper's list of op-ed contributors beside the former head of the NSA, Robert Redford, and Rush Limbaugh. On that same field trip inside the *Times'* network, he also used the paper's account to run the equivalent of three hundred thousand dollars in searches on the paid research service Lexis-Nexis.

Lamo made a point of minimizing the damage from his hacks and alerting the administrators of the systems he exploited, going so far as to walk them through the necessary steps to close their security holes. But in the case of the *Times* adventure, Lamo's victim didn't see his intrusion as a favor. The company turned his case over to the FBI, which put out a warrant for his arrest and tracked the twenty-two-year-old's itinerant wandering for five days before he surrendered himself to police in Sacramento. After a yearlong trial, Lamo pled guilty and was sentenced to pay sixty-five thousand dollars in fines and spend six months under house arrest at his parents' home.

After the *New York Times* case, Lamo became a poster boy for the well-intentioned hacker misunderstood by society. He starred as the central character in a documentary film titled *Hackers Wanted* that focused on his mistreatment at the hands of federal law enforcement. In the final message of that film, Lamo gives a soliloquy on digital ethics that transcend what's legal or illegal, delivered at fast-forward pace that sounds nothing like his drug-swamped speech today:

> I hoped and believed that I could [hack systems] in a way that would set a precedent that would allow people to come forward in good faith to try to do the right thing, to let them believe that maybe motives did matter, that it wasn't all black-and-white. I think this is symptomatic of something we're seeing in the government today. In many ways they're eliminating shades of gray. They want to polarize people. It's important to our national agenda today to see good guys and bad guys. Because as soon as we start to believe that maybe it's not all black-and-white, that someone can do wrong for a good reason, that not every action of law is inherently infallible, it strikes a very dangerous precedent for the government the way it wants to operate today.

After the documentary's filming was completed in 2003, *Hackers Wanted* went unreleased for seven years until it was finally leaked in May of 2010 onto copyright-flouting BitTorrent file-sharing networks, where it became a modest hit in the world of hackers and information security. Lamo insists he wasn't the source of the leak.

When fans wrote to Lamo and the film's director, Sam Bozzo, asking how they could support the film with donations, Lamo wrote on his Twitter feed on May 20 that donors should give their money instead to WikiLeaks, the whistleblower organization that one month before had released Manning's Apache helicopter video to an explosive response.

For a young, conscience-stricken soldier who had just completed a massive leak of secret documents, everything would have pointed to Lamo as a sympathetic confidant.

Just a day later, Lamo says he began receiving e-mails from Bradley Manning. The text of the messages was encrypted, and the public key encryption Manning had used was designed so that only Lamo could decrypt it. But Lamo couldn't find the key that would unlock those messages, so they remained hopelessly scrambled. Lamo wrote back suggesting they simply chat over instant messenger.

On May 21, Lamo received the following message, this time encrypted using the Off-the-Record chat protocol:

"Hi. How are you? I'm an army intelligence analyst, deployed to Eastern Baghdad, pending discharge for 'adjustment disorder' . . . I'm sure you're pretty busy," the message from a user named Bradass87 read. And then before even waiting for a response, it continued: "If you had unprecedented access to classified networks fourteen hours a day seven days a week for eight plus months, what would you do?"

After a year of shuttling briefcases of documents out of RAND and standing over photocopiers for nights on end, Ellsberg was ready to spill the Pentagon Papers. His next problem: finding someone to take them.

Ellsberg's Plan A was to have a legislator read the papers into the *Con-*

gressional Record or hold a hearing based on them, an avenue to the public that still played within Washington's rules. But Ellsberg's first choice in the Senate, William Fulbright, balked. After some initial enthusiasm, Fulbright read a portion of the documents and eventually performed an about-face after he realized just what kind of political maelstrom might surround the report's release. "Isn't it after all only history?" he asked Ellsberg dismissively when they met a year later.

Ellsberg moved on to the Democratic presidential hopeful Senator George McGovern, who at first seemed even more gung-ho about airing the papers. McGovern offered to read the study on the Senate floor, which would make it fair game for the media. "I want to do it. I will do it," Ellsberg remembers the Democratic legislator declaring in their meeting.

A week later, he called Ellsberg on the phone. "I'm sorry, I can't do it," McGovern said. His campaign for the presidency, it seemed, would have been hamstrung by the controversy of a political pipe-bomb like Ellsberg's leak.

So Ellsberg turned to Plan B, a whistleblowing outlet he felt was almost sure to result in his spending many years in prison: the press. A few years earlier, Ellsberg had experimented with several single-document leaks to *The New York Times* aimed at chipping away at Vietnam policy. So he knew a political reporter there, Neil Sheehan. Ellsberg had moved to Cambridge after resigning from RAND to protect his former colleagues from whatever backlash might follow the papers' leak. And in his apartment near Harvard Square, he showed Sheehan a copy of his stolen bounty. Sheehan took some notes, but told Ellsberg his editors still hadn't decided whether to go ahead with publication.

In fact, Sheehan's pretense of dallying over the study was designed to prevent the *Times* from being scooped by another publication. A few weeks later, Sheehan used a key Ellsberg had loaned him to sneak into the Cambridge apartment, have the papers photocopied in a nearby shop, and return them. The newspaper had already rented out a portion of the New York Hilton and begun frantically, secretly, building its story on the study.

On June 13, 1971, the story splashed across the front page of the *Times*: VIETNAM ARCHIVE: PENTAGON STUDY TRACES 3 DECADES OF GROWING U.S. INVOLVEMENT.

And how long did it take for the leak to be traced to Ellsberg? In fact, some RAND analysts already suspected him even before the *Times'* presses started rolling. The newspaper had called former Pentagon official Leslie Gelb to give him a chance to comment on the story, and according to Ellsberg biographer Tom Wells, Gelb immediately fixated on Ellsberg as the source. How many high-level analysts, after all, had both access to the papers and such a fierce opposition to the war?

The White House didn't take long to finger Ellsberg either. In archived White House recordings, Nixon names Ellsberg, Mort Halperin, and Leslie Gelb as the only three analysts who had access to the study. Within days, Ellsberg—or "Ellstein" as Nixon called him with crude anti-Semitic humor—was being discussed as the assumed perpetrator of the leak.

When the *Times* hit newsstands, it immediately launched a free-speech battle that would redefine the First Amendment. The White House, arguing that the *Times* had violated the Espionage Act, successfully convinced a federal court to file an injunction against the newspaper to prevent it from publishing any articles on the study. But Ellsberg had already given another copy to *The Washington Post,* which picked up where the *Times* left off.

The *Post* was injuncted too. But Ellsberg stayed a step ahead of the government's censors, distributing copies of the study to *The Boston Globe,* the *L.A. Times, The Christian Science Monitor,* the *St. Louis Post-Dispatch,* and others, avoiding wiretapped phones and staying in friends' houses to dodge arrest until all the papers could be distributed. Faced with an endless game of injunction Whac-A-Mole, the White House would eventually give up on preventing the papers' publication.

Meanwhile, any illusion Ellsberg may have had of remaining anonymous quickly collapsed. A legislative aide to McGovern and congressman Pete McCloskey—another legislator to whom Ellsberg had given the Pentagon Papers but who had failed to bring them to light—both told *News-*

week that Ellsberg had offered them classified documents. The FBI soon extracted an affidavit from Ellsberg's ex-wife, whom he'd told about the leak to prepare her for the possibility that he would soon be in prison and unable to pay alimony. In exchange for a grant of immunity, Tony Russo's advertising friend—the one who had offered Ellsberg her photocopier—testified to the bureau's agents too.

Every element of Ellsberg's leak—from his access to narrowly shared information to that information's copying to its distribution to countless reporters—had left fingerprints for the feds. The press certainly had no doubts: By the time that Ellsberg turned himself in to federal authorities in Boston, *Time* magazine had already put his face on its cover below the words "The War Exposed."

With no anonymity tools or cryptographic protections at his disposal, the whistleblower had also exposed himself.

In Baghdad's forward operating base, Hammer, where Manning was stationed as an intelligence analyst, security was shockingly lax—"physically, technically, and culturally," as Manning would tell Lamo. He sat among rows of other young analysts watching car chases, music videos, clips of buildings exploding, and often writing data to CDs and DVDs. Even the locks on the doors weren't properly implemented. Though they were secured with electronic codes, soldiers would simply knock and be let in. "The culture fed opportunities," he wrote.

And then there were the networks. Although SIPRNet wasn't connected to the Internet, it lacked sophisticated monitoring. Manning would tell Lamo that he once asked an NSA agent at the base if the network was capable of detecting local suspicious activity. Manning says the agent responded that it "wasn't a priority" and returned to watching the Shia LaBeouf film *Eagle Eye* and eating Girl Scout cookies. On another occasion, Manning says he asked the agent specifically about a hypothetical mass internal leak. Manning says the agent responded that he doubted "anyone could figure it out. . . . Resources are strained."

"Weak servers, weak logging, weak physical security, weak counter-intelligence, inattentive signal analysis," Manning listed to Lamo. It was, all told, a "perfect example of how not to do infosec."

In a Senate hearing in early 2011, Senator Susan Collins would grill military and State Department officials over those exact vulnerabilities. "How could it be that a low-level member of the military could download such a volume of documents without it being detected for so long?" she asks in a slow, exasperated tone. "That truly baffles me."

Thomas Ferguson, the deputy undersecretary of defense for intelligence, answers her, sounding distinctly like the teacher's pet who finds himself in the assistant principal's office. "The situation in the theater was such that we took a risk," the gray-goateed official responds flatly, trying to get his confessional over with as quickly as possible. "We took a risk that by putting information out there . . . to provide agility and flexibility of the military forces there, they would be able to reach into any database on SIPRNet, download that information, and move that information using removable media."

And why weren't there at least network forensics to catch Manning after his epic data dump? Here the heat can almost be felt building under Ferguson's collar. "A lot of the systems there are, for lack of a technical term, cobbled together," he continues with a tight chest. "It's not just like Bank of America where it's one homogeneous system and they can insert things and take them out. They have multiple systems and putting in new intrusion software or monitoring tools, you have to approach each system differently."

The military, he adds, "took on the risk. . . . These people are cleared, they go through background investigations."

And then finally, the remarkably honest kicker: "Frankly, most of our focus was on the outside intruder threat, not the inside threat."

Manning, by all indications, was the quintessential insider threat, and he fluidly negotiated the network's vulnerabilities. In fact, until he sent his fateful, encrypted missive to Adrian Lamo, he performed most of his epic data breach as if he were following a leaker's best practices handbook.

As Manning told Lamo, the two SIPRNet machines that linked to troves of classified information lacked most of the forensic monitoring tools that might have detected his abnormal searches and his repeated copying of that data to his camouflaged rewritable disks. But even after collecting that contraband, Manning didn't dare leak it over Internet-connected military networks to WikiLeaks. The timing of his leaks suggests he waited until he was able to return to the United States on leave, and upload it from his MacBook's connection to a nonmilitary network—perhaps from his aunt's house in Rockville, Maryland. Like Ellsberg, in other words, he walked his leak out through the Pentagon's front door.

From there, Manning described to Lamo how he used a combination of security tools to cover every link in the leaking chain that led from WikiLeaks to his MacBook. He connected to WikiLeaks' Web servers that deployed Secure Sockets Layer, or SSL, the Web encryption commonly used to hide e-commerce or banking sites' data from any network snoops looking for passwords or credit card numbers. Then he used Secure Shell File Transfer Protocol, or SSH FTP, a method of creating a tunnel of encryption between two remote systems to allow them to securely share files. Finally, and most significantly, he ran Tor, an anonymity tool that took his path to WikiLeaks' drop site through a series of hops around the Internet, each new address in the series encrypted to prevent anyone from piecing together his final destination and his origin. With that hidden, trace-resistant connection set up, Manning proceeded to siphon out the military's secrets, through Tor's tangle of obfuscating blind alleys around the world, and out to the WikiLeaks server at a data center in Stockholm, Sweden.

A year later, after Manning's loose lips had led military investigators to his name, they confiscated every machine that might have been involved in his leak, from the SIPRNet computers to the MacBook that had by then been shipped back to his aunt's home in Maryland. With access to those specific computers, the game was over. Investigators found plenty of evidence stored on his hard drives to tie Manning to the leak: He had attempted to expunge all the evidence on his MacBook by overwriting the files with junk data, but his laptop had somehow aborted the process. There were Guantánamo detainee files, ten thousand State Department Cables, and—significantly—chat logs between Manning and Julian Assange in which

Assange seemed to help Manning crack into an administrator's account to access the military network while covering his tracks. (Assange had wanted to know as little about Manning as possible, and their communications likely remained pseudonymous. "Lie to me," he had told Manning.)

Investigators even found a "readme" file on Manning's MacBook that he had submitted to WikiLeaks along with his megaleak. "This is possibly one of the more significant documents of our time, removing the fog of war, revealing the true nature of 21st century asymmetric warfare," it read. "Have a good day."

But it's important to remember that none of those fingerprints initially led the investigators to Manning's name. Adrian Lamo, not digital detective work, put the army on Manning's scent: All appearances indicate a forensic trail from WikiLeaks to Manning's identity was never found. Before Lamo handed the investigators Manning's name on a platter, they could hardly have confiscated every machine on SIPRNet—not to mention every possible laptop used by every intelligence officer on leave in every home in America. Manning, after all, was just another of the 1.2 million Americans with a top-secret security clearance, a well-concealed needle in the towering military-industrial haystack.

All of which means that if the young army private hadn't detailed his entire leaking process to a stranger he had met online just minutes before, step by incriminating step, he might never have been found out.

Ellsberg's leak was such a blow to President Nixon's ego and sense of executive power that the White House overreacted in spectacular fashion. "Goddammit, someone has to go to jail!" Nixon was recorded saying, pounding on his desk with a fist. "That's all there is to it!"

Later, the administration's attack methods broadened: "We've got to get him," the president said to Kissinger and Attorney General John Mitchell, referring to Ellsberg. "Don't worry about his trial. Just get everything out. Try him in the press. . . . We want to destroy him in the press. Is that clear?"

What came next must be considered some of the most absurd and shameful tactics in presidential history. One group of Nixon's operatives followed Ellsberg's psychotherapist, Lewis Fielding, disguised with wigs, pipes, and, for one agent, a shoe insert to create a fake limp. Later they broke into Fielding's office to dig up Ellsberg's records. The burglars hoped to find dirt on his personal life, or even a connection to a foreign government or subversive group. They found nothing: Fielding hadn't stored any notes on Ellsberg in his office.

The break-in was followed by an attempt to drug Ellsberg with LSD before a speech he planned to give in Washington. Cuban hotel workers in Miami were recruited by a team led by G. Gordon Liddy to infiltrate the event, spike Ellsberg's soup with acid to "befuddle" him, and "make him appear to be a near burnt-out drug case." But by the time it was all approved, the Miami waiters couldn't be flown to Washington in time. The plan was scrapped.

In the Watergate trial, prosecutors would find that a team of twelve Cuban men had also been hired to assault and "totally incapacitate" Ellsberg at a peace rally. Members of that team later said their mission had been variously to punch Ellsberg in the face or break his legs. But the crowd around the newly famous whistleblower had been too thick, and the twelve goons decided to instead beat up random, unlucky protesters at the event's edges.

Much of that criminal behavior didn't become public until after Ellsberg's trial. But in the meantime, Ellsberg's defense team found that investigators had illegally wiretapped Ellsberg and Mort Halperin without a court order and, even worse, neglected to share those files with the defense. Finally, it emerged that the judge in the case, William Byrne, had been approached by a Nixon aide and offered nothing less than the directorship of the FBI.

That mountain of improprieties added up to a mistrial. "The totality of the circumstances of this case . . . offend a sense of justice," wrote Byrne in his decision. "The bizarre events have incurably infected the prosecution of this case."

Ellsberg was free. The same day, newspapers reported that Nixon's attorney general, John Mitchell, who had indicted Ellsberg, had himself been indicted on charges of conspiracy, obstruction of justice, and perjury.

It was the beginning of the end of the Nixon presidency—and, eventually, the war in Vietnam.

When Manning and Lamo first began their exchange of encrypted messages, Lamo made two promises of confidentiality. "I'm a journalist and a minister," he told Manning. "You can pick either, and treat this as a confession or an interview (never to be published) and enjoy a modicum of legal protection."

In fact, within forty-eight hours of first contact with Bradley Manning, Lamo says he was already mulling the possibility of turning his newfound friend in to authorities. He contacted Tim Webster, a former army counterintelligence agent and friend, and later Chet Uber, an ex-intelligence contractor who worked with Lamo in a volunteer cybersecurity research group called Project Vigilant.

Webster put Lamo in contact with army counterintelligence officers who soon telephoned him at his home. They were skeptical, and asked for proof of Lamo's claims. It hardly seemed credible that a private first class had accessed and stolen gigabytes of some of the world's most sensitive information and then confessed it casually over instant messenger to a stranger. Lamo says he responded by referring to a code-named secret project that Manning had mentioned to him. There was a long silence. Then one of the agents asked Lamo never to repeat that code name. "They told me to forget that I'd ever even heard the word," he says. The feds didn't question Lamo's credibility again.

The call with the Criminal Investigation Division (CID) led to a meeting with FBI agents. Uber would remember that at this point Lamo was conflicted and even called Uber in the middle of his sit-down with the G-men. "I'm in a meeting with five guys and I don't want to do this," Uber says Lamo told him. The older man says he responded, "You don't have any choice, you've got to do this."

For the next two days, Lamo continued to chat with Manning, now with the knowledge that federal agents would be looking over his shoulder at their conversation. They discussed religion, Lamo's legal history, and the "crazy white-haired Australian" Julian Assange, with whom Manning had been communicating. At one point, Manning began to wax lyrical about the victims and perpetrators of the Apache helicopter video he had helped to expose, which WikiLeaks had used to send shock waves around the world just a month before. Manning mentioned that he'd recently added several of the people involved as friends on Facebook. Those individuals included thirty-three-year-old ex-soldier Ethan McCord, who had been racked with guilt over his involvement in the highly publicized Apache helicopter attack and would later speak out against the war. "They touch my life, I touch their life, they touch my life again . . . full circle," Manning wrote.

"Life's funny," Lamo responded.

Then Lamo abruptly changed the subject. "*random* Are you concerned about [army counterintelligence] looking into your Wiki stuff?" he asked. "I was always paranoid."

Manning responded that there was "no open investigation," a sign that he had likely been doing some investigations of his own—counter-counterintelligence. In later conversations, Manning went on to describe how all records of his leak had been "zerofilled"—irreversibly deleted—and to describe the arsenal of anonymity and privacy tools he had used. Lamo asked him what he would do if his cover was blown anyway. "Try and figure out how I could get my side of the story out . . . before everything was twisted around to make me look like Nidal Hasan," Manning replied, referring to the army major who quietly became a radical Islamist and went on a shooting spree at Texas's Fort Hood in 2009, killing thirteen and wounding twenty-nine.

"I don't think it's going to happen," Manning added. "I mean, I was never noticed."

Near the end of their series of chats, Manning seems to be contemplating more existential questions: "I'm not sure whether I'd be considered: A type of 'hacker,' 'cracker,' 'hacktivist,' 'leaker' or what . . ." he mused. "I'm just me . . . really."

"Or a spy," Lamo wrote back, adding a smiling emoticon.

On May 26, less than a week into his chats with Lamo, Manning was arrested by army criminal investigators. He was charged with more than two dozen crimes, including violating the Espionage Act and aiding the enemy. The second of those crimes is punishable in the military justice system with death. But Manning's prosecutors have stated that they don't plan to argue for Manning's execution. Only a life sentence in a military prison.

In March 2011, ten months after Manning's arrest, Daniel Ellsberg stood in front of the White House wearing a navy blue suit and tie, along with hundreds of others protesting Manning's inhumane confinement in a Quantico, Virginia, military jail.

In July, Manning had been moved from a brig in Kuwait to the Quantico base, where he was kept with virtually no contact with other prisoners, allowed an hour of walking exercise a day and just a few hours of visits a week. One of the few friends who managed to see him on a regular basis, a researcher at MIT named David House, describes Manning's deteriorating mental condition over the next months, as a bright twenty-three-year-old eager to discuss physics and sociology slowly devolved into a medicated, near-"catatonic" state. When House saw Manning in February, he says it was as if Manning "had been sleeping hard for days, and needed hours to fully wake up."

At the March protest, the seventy-nine-year-old Ellsberg was asked by police to leave the street in front of the White House, as protesters chanted, "This is what hypocrisy looks like!" He politely declined to leave and was put in handcuffs and taken away in a police van. When he and the other 112 arrested protesters were released later, he promptly traveled to Quantico, where he had trained as an officer in the Marines decades earlier. Outside the base there, he staged another sit-in and was arrested again.

In interviews with reporters around that time, Ellsberg said that he identifies with Manning "more than anyone else I've seen in the last forty years."

"I was that young man," he told a CNN reporter. "I was Bradley Manning."

President Barack Obama disagrees. After a fund-raising event a month later, the president was confronted by a protester doggedly asking him about Manning's confinement. Obama didn't shrink from offering his views, which were caught on camera and soon posted to YouTube. "We're a nation of laws," the president says with a smile to the Manning supporter questioning him. "We don't let individuals make their own decisions about how the laws operate. He broke the law."

"Isn't that just the same thing as what Daniel Ellsberg did?" Obama's interlocutor asks.

"No, it wasn't the same thing," Obama responds dismissively. "Ellsberg's material wasn't classified in the same way." The president turns away, and the conversation is over.

Obama is right, of course. It wasn't the same thing. The materials that Ellsberg leaked were actually of a *higher* top-secret classification. But the president was right on a deeper level too. Ellsberg, despite his sympathy for Manning, is not "that young man."

Daniel Ellsberg's story is that ultrarare conversion of an elite Pentagon insider into a radical dissident. Only a handful of officials had the authorization to read the Pentagon Papers. For Ellsberg to both have had the privileged access to the documents that he leaked and to actually have leaked them required a unique combination: a highly distinguished career that brought him to the pinnacle of Pentagon secrecy and a complexity of conscience that allowed him to execute a 180-degree turn in his loyalties near the peak of that career.

Manning, by contrast, was one of the millions of Americans with security clearances. He fitted the profile of a leaker from the moment he entered the Pentagon's employ: disaffected, powerless, strong-willed, and antiauthority.

In comparing Manning to himself, Ellsberg cites Manning's statement in his chats with Lamo that he "wouldn't mind going to prison or being executed." "I never thought, for the rest of my life, I would ever hear anyone willing to do that, to risk their life, so that horrible, awful secrets could be known," Ellsberg told the CNN reporter. "Then I read those logs and learned Bradley was willing to go to prison. I can't tell you how much that affected me."

But Ellsberg generously overlooks the fact that although Manning says he was *willing* to go to prison, he never *expected* to. Everything in Manning's conversations with Lamo indicates he felt that the anonymity and privacy tools he had used—along with the army's negligent lack of security precautions—had rendered him immune from punishment. Ellsberg, by contrast, assumed he would spend much if not the entire rest of his life in prison, and even made practical preparations for the day when he would be separated by bars and razor wire from his wife and children.

The conclusion to this story, that today Ellsberg is free while Manning is shuttled between jail cells and courtrooms to potentially face a life behind bars, might be misleading. In fact, while the technical play-by-play of each leak shows the evolution of leaking technology and methods, the outcome of those cases is a counterintuitive fluke. If not for his ill-fated conversation with Adrian Lamo, Manning's high-tech leak would likely have gone unpunished. And if not for Nixon's flubbed attacks on Ellsberg, the older man might still be in prison even four decades later.

The barriers to modern megaleakers like Manning have crumbled: They needn't spend a year photocopying. They needn't be Eagle Scouts or war heroes who penetrate the government's most elite layer only to go rogue—just one of the millions of Americans with access to secret government documents or the many, many uncountable millions more with access to secret corporate information. And perhaps most important, they needn't risk reprisal by exposing their identities to the journalists they hope will amplify their whistleblowing.

The forces that caught Manning are real and significant: The greatest vulnerability for any leaker remains his or her human connections. But the lesson of Manning's story for a generation of digital natives will be, above all else, that *he nearly got away with it.* Use the right cryptographic tools, keep your mouth shut, and you, too, can anonymously, frictionlessly, eviscerate an entire institution's information.

There may not be many Daniel Ellbergs in the world, ready to push through the twentieth century's stubborn barriers to leaking. But the twenty-first century would be wise to expect more Bradley Mannings.

PART TWO

THE EVOLUTION OF LEAKING

"Insiders know where the bodies are."

JULIAN ASSANGE

CHAPTER 2

THE CRYPTOGRAPHERS

Tim May stewed in his apartment complex's outdoor Jacuzzi in Sunnyvale, California. He had recently split with his girlfriend, but the burly six-foot-one, bearded physicist wasn't the type to dwell on female troubles. His gray matter was plagued with a more vexing problem: the mystery of the failing semiconductors.

In 1974, May had joined a small computer chip company called Intel. The little-known firm was gambling on using metal oxide semiconductors or MOS in its memory chips instead of the bipolar transistors used in traditional chips from IBM or Fairchild Semiconductor. That new approach was designed to squeeze more tiny gates containing ones or zeros of information onto a single chip, and it had recently won the microprocessor maverick an eight-figure contract from the AT&T division Western Electric to provide the memory chips in its Denver data center PBXs, the boxes that still serve as network hubs for phone systems inside of large companies.

The deal was an enormous windfall for a three-thousand-person firm competing with much larger chip giants. But it had hit a potentially fatal snag. Western Electric's PBXs were crashing frequently and unpredictably. Because the problem had arisen only after its switch to new chips, the AT&T execs put the blame squarely on Intel. And when Intel engineers were dragged in to check on the PBX malfunctions and monitored the PBX's memory for errors, they confessed: As often as every hour, a single bit would flip on their chips—one unit of data switching from a one to a zero or vice versa seemingly of its own accord—leading to maddeningly random software glitches.

Intel's engineers tried every test they could think of to find the source of that bit-flip. But they couldn't even reproduce the problem, much less solve it. They even hypothesized that the magnet from a janitor's floor buffer's motor might be causing the errors as it swept past the PBXs. The theory didn't pan out. As a task force of engineers was assigned to the problem, AT&T's patience was starting to wear thin.

Twenty-five-year-old May wasn't meant to be working on the problem. But one of May's colleagues, knowing the young engineer had a background in particle physics, had stuck his head in May's office and passed on a new theory that none other than Intel founder Gordon Moore wanted May to check out: Perhaps cosmic rays—subatomic particles bombarding Earth from space at near-light speeds—could knock chips' electrons out of place, causing the same sort of problems that were now leading to AT&T's PBX debacle.

May whipped out his trusty Hewlett-Packard calculator and did the math. Some quick operations showed that even at Denver's altitude, not enough cosmic rays could be reaching the chips to explain Western Electric's errors. The ray theory was bunk.

But Moore's question had gotten May thinking. And as he basted in the hot tub that spring evening, he looked down at the granite walls of that outdoor tub and experienced his own bit-flip of intuition. Granite and other stones, May knew, give off extremely low levels of radioactive alpha particles due to their hundredths-of-one-percent thorium and uranium content. And Intel had recently switched its chips' casing to a new type of ceramic material to save a few extra bucks per chip.

On an atomic scale, alpha particles are big and clumsy boulders that plow into objects' surfaces, compared to the cosmic rays that hit Earth from space. Perhaps the radiation necessary to knock those chips' data off kilter wasn't coming from the cosmos. Instead, May thought, what if it came from a source as close to the vulnerable computing jewels as May's skin to the granite hot tub wall at his back?

Drying off and pulling out his calculator, he determined that an alpha particle would be five times the size necessary to affect the distinction between a 1 and a 0 as stored on one of AT&T's chips, corrupting a semiconductor's data storage like a tennis ball crammed into bathroom piping. The next day at Intel's lab, he put a handful of the chips' ceramic material into a radiation-measuring counter chamber, left it there for twenty-four hours, and measured the results. Sure enough, the material was throwing off so much radiation that it maxed out the chamber's meter.

Later, he pulled the chunk of radioactive americium out of a smoke detector and attached it to the test chips with only a strip of masking tape in between, a barrier thick enough to stop the progress of any alpha particles. No errors. Then he stripped the tape away, and sure enough, the radiation reproduced AT&T's problem many thousands of times over in its silicon victim. He saw the problem plaguing Intel's chips laid out before him in all its radioactive simplicity. "When that chip lit up like fireflies," says May, "it was a peak moment in my life."

Intel responded to May's breakthrough by creating a new chip design that used less radioactive materials and more shielding. The entire semiconductor industry, from IBM to Fujitsu, followed suit—an astounding coup for an upstart like Intel. Even years later, the chip giant would hold up May's work as an example of the company's groundbreaking spirit from the start. "Creative, innovative, brilliant, all of the above. Tim May had imagination," former Intel CEO Craig Barrett told a journalist twenty-five years later. "He . . . wasn't encumbered by history. He went off and did something wonderful."

For May, nothing at Intel was ever quite so much fun again. His alpha particle glory earned him his own lab and several promotions. But Intel was growing from a gritty start-up to a corporation full of middle managers and stove-piped divisions. May had no stomach for management, especially under the rise of the gruff Hungarian immigrant chief executive Andy Grove, where the bottom 10 percent of each division continually feared for its jobs.

As the years went by, May occasionally performed a calculation with his well-worn HP calculator based on his stock options, Intel's ballooning share price, his cost of living, and projected interest. Unlike colleagues in Silicon Valley who spent their wealth on boats and beach homes, May lived a largely ascetic life, avoiding restaurants, skipping travel, and saving almost everything he made. By 1986, the results of May's arithmetic showed he had enough money for roughly the rest of his life without ever working again. In July 1986, four months after a critical performance review, he quit.

At thirty-four, May was retired. And he was altogether unsure what to do with the majority of his life that still lay ahead of him. But Intel's Barrett was right: May had imagination, and he wasn't encumbered by history. A few years later, he would list his new interests in the signature of his e-mails: "Anonymous networks, digital pseudonyms, reputations, information markets, black markets, collapse of governments."

One spring afternoon in 2010, close to a year after the release of Bradley Manning's Collateral Murder video, I rented a Volkswagen in San Francisco and drove it south over the nearby hills and down California's treacherously winding Highway 17 to Santa Cruz into a region that harbors two of the great figures in the subversive crypto-history that led to WikiLeaks.

One of those men was Tim May. But I had little hope of actually tracking down that controversial crypto-anarchist and anonymity innovator. Several contacts had already warned me that he didn't take kindly to visits from journalists. One laughed at the mere idea of my trying to find him. A 2003 article I'd read in the German newspaper *Die Zeit* described rumors that May had become a long-bearded hermit, living in a well-fortified redoubt in the mountains. A WikiLeaks associate alluded to claymore mines planted in trees around May's home, a final line of defense should the jackboots finally come for him. I resigned myself to the conclusion that he had achieved the ultimate trick of untraceable anonymity: disappearing completely.

Instead, I'm meeting with a different Santa Cruz crypto-activist, one whose work also helped to spark a movement of anarchist code freaks—and to nearly land him in jail: Philip R. Zimmermann.

When I step into Zimmermann's dining room, a few blocks from the city's rocky coastline, he's wearing a PRZ-monogrammed dress shirt untucked over his round hobbit's torso and drinking tea out of a mug from the annual Black Hat hacker conference in Las Vegas. The trim-bearded, wide-featured, and perpetually grinning programmer takes great pleasure in handing me the NSA mug he bought in the gift shop of the Fort Meade cryptology museum.

As we sit down, he offers a short commentary about how restaurants don't understand that handing someone a lukewarm cup of water and a tea bag isn't an acceptable way to serve Earl Grey. Then we wait for him to eat some microwave noodles before he's ready to begin the interview. "My brain will work better after I've eaten," he says slowly.

When I start to ask him questions, he reminds me, still grinning, that he won't answer them until he's finished his lunch. It occurs to me that this is not a man who would have adjusted well to prison life.

As we sit in silence punctuated by the sound of noodle slurps, I peruse his shelves. One wall is covered in awards from civic organizations and privacy groups, the other with books on nuclear history, novels by Isaac Asimov and Neal Stephenson, and below them a mass of cryptography textbooks.

It's only when I mention one in particular, titled *PGP Source Code and Internals,* that Zimmermann immediately sets aside his lunch and switches into war-story-telling mode. "As soon as they decided to prosecute me," he says in a mischievous tone, "that book would have been Exhibit A in my defense."

But we're getting ahead of ourselves. So now that I have Zimmermann's attention, I ask him to start at the beginning. And he begins with a different war story, the one about Dr. Daniel Ellsberg.

One dusty 1987 morning in the middle of the Nevada desert, as Zimmermann remembers it, Ellsberg, Zimmermann, and a crowd of 430 protesters filed two-by-two through the gates of Nevada's most-active nuclear test site, where waiting guards calmly fitted them with riot handcuffs, led them off to a nearby bus, and trucked them forty miles to the tiny nearby town of Beatty to be detained by local police in a community center and then released.

Ellsberg wore a suit, the better to illustrate with his arrest that even men who wear suits have a duty to practice civil disobedience. Zimmermann abided by a similar principle. "I wanted to show that we weren't just a bunch of hippies protesting," he says in his slow Midwestern cadence. "The message was that we were respectable Americans just like anybody else, only willing to go to jail to stop the nuclear tests."

For Zimmermann, the Nevada protest was the culmination of a decade of following Ellsberg's activist lead. Growing up in the era of the Pentagon Papers and Watergate, Zimmermann had been alarmed by the United States' insistence on maintaining the world's largest, most advanced stockpile of first-strike nuclear warheads. He'd been moved by Robert Scheer's essay *With Enough Shovels,* on the government's callous attitude toward nuclear war. (Scheer quoted a high-level Pentagon official as saying that with enough shovels, every family in America could simply build their own nuclear bomb shelter by digging backyard trenches and covering them with the detached doors of their homes.) Thinking of their newborn son, Zimmermann and his wife made plans to escape the doomed United States for New Zealand, one of the world's most strongly antinuclear nations.

Still in the process of applying for immigration papers, Zimmermann and his wife had attended a Nuclear Weapons Freeze Campaign conference in Denver. The highlight of the event was a speech by Daniel Ellsberg himself. Ellsberg described the millions-strong protest in the Vietnam Moratorium of 1969. At the time, the press had reported that Nixon ignored the marches and watched a football game. In fact, Ellsberg told the Colorado crowd, Nixon had been wringing his hands in the White House situation room, looking at crowd estimates and aerial photography. Though they didn't know it at the time, Vietnam's grassroots activists had convinced President Nixon not to use nuclear weapons in the war.

The conference's message of hope, and particularly Ellsberg's speech, swept away Zimmermann's pessimism. When he and his wife returned to

Boulder, they had made up their mind: They would stay in the United States and fight. "It was like I had been in an airplane that I knew was crashing, trying to get in the back seats to increase my chance of survival," he says. "Instead, I decided to get into the cockpit."

Zimmermann began inhaling books on atomic history, spending forty hours a week at his job as a computer engineer and another forty educating himself on the nuclear age. Within a few months, he was teaching a class in military history at the Free University in Boulder and speaking out publicly against the Reagan administration's policies.

In 1985, Gorbachev came to power and declared a unilateral moratorium on nuclear testing. Now, Zimmermann and his peacenik cohorts hoped, America's aggressive regimen of vaporizing cubic miles of dirt and rock with hydrogen bombs under the Nevada desert could finally end.

But the nuclear tests continued unabated. Under pressure from his generals, Gorbachev warned in 1986 that if the United States exploded just one more nuclear weapon, the USSR would be forced to begin testing again too. And it was that one, crucial nuclear warhead, deep under the Nevada sands, that brought Zimmermann, Ellsberg, and more than four hundred others to Las Vegas, where they piled into buses bound for the desert.

The Pentagon had bumped up its schedule and already exploded its underground bomb the day before. Over the next years, Gorbachev, not Reagan, would end the world's nuclear standoff with the dissolution of the USSR.

But the protest had a different significance: Zimmermann's first experience with civil disobedience locked in his resolve to grapple with unjust authority. And although he didn't know it then, the unassuming geek was entering a new conflict where he, not his activist hero Ellsberg, would take center stage. As the Cold War was winding down, the Crypto Wars were about to begin.

Ten-year-old Tim May sat in his bedroom with the lights turned off. He held a jar-shaped device called a spinthariscope that came with his Gilbert chemistry set, essentially a can with a small piece of radioactive radium at one end, a lens at the other, and in the middle, a thin, whitish screen of zinc sulfide. Zinc sulfide is a scintillator: When alpha particles hit its surface, it gives off light. So May allowed his eyes to adjust to the darkness of his room, and then watched tiny radioactive asteroids flare into stars as they collided with the luminescent material at thirty-three million miles an hour.

Science's ability to generate everyday miracles was a given in May's young life. His earliest memories are of his childhood in the early 1950s, growing up in a suburb of San Diego. Thirty miles north was the Mount Palomar Observatory, with its world's-largest telescope, and another short drive west led to the Scripps Institution of Oceanography. Jules Verne's books fueled his scientist's imagination. Once, he remembers looking out of the window at his family's ranch-style house and seeing a bizarre, smooth wing roar by, a plane without a fuselage. He later learned it was a Northrop prototype for the air force's stealth bomber. One of his neighbors, across his backyard fence, was an aerospace engineer who had worked on some of the first intercontinental ballistic missiles, and when the Soviets launched Sputnik, May remembers looking up with the old man in his backyard one night and watching Sputnik orbit overhead, an artifact of human power in the sky.

Despite his glimpses of the wonders of science, May's upbringing wasn't all innocence and whimsy. Though May's father was a naval officer, he had first been an enlisted man in the South Pacific and drove a bulldozer in World War II. And May's father didn't spare him the grisly tales of war, how he had been ordered to use the machine to push sand over pillbox bunkers full of Japanese soldiers, burying them alive.

After May's father was transferred and the family resettled in Washington, D.C., it was also May's father who encouraged his twelve-year-old son to join the local gun club. They would shoot .22 rifles together, and May learned to feel comfortable carrying and soon owning weapons. (Later in life he would slowly accumulate more of them: a .22 revolver, a .357 Magnum, an AR-15 assault rifle, a Ruger, a pair of Sig Sauers, and many others that he declines to name.)

Just a few years after that first move, May's father was transferred again, shipping out on the day of Kennedy's assassination to the town of Villefranche-sur-Mer on the French Riviera. It was a fantastical setting, with Jacques Cousteau's ship, the *Calypso,* often anchored in the harbor, and looming above the town the hill that Nietzsche climbed while writing *Thus Spoke Zarathustra*.

A newcomer in a foreign country, May had few friends. As he would throughout his life, he replaced much of his social interaction with reading: physics, computers, chemistry, and science fiction, from Asimov to Bradbury. In the seventh grade he put together a hundred-page report on the design of atomic weapons in World War II, complete with explanations of the workings of nuclear fission, diagrams of how Fat Man and Little Boy's chain reactions were triggered, and the effects on their targets, including graphic pictures of Japanese burn victims from Hiroshima and Nagasaki. "It was clear to me then," he says, "I wanted to work in nuclear physics."

When May's family returned to Washington, D.C., he was years ahead of his classmates in his autodidact's understanding of science. He won every high school science fair, with projects demonstrating the radio frequency emissions of ionized gases in magnetic fields and quantum tunneling. And in the summer of 1968 he discovered Ayn Rand.

May read Rand's *Atlas Shrugged* as just another science fiction novel. But this one was about politics, not technology or science. The thousand-page manifesto spoke to him about the hypocrisy of altruism and the exclusive virtue of selfishness. It explained in stark terms why anyone who seeks to oppose the profit motive and take from the rich to give to the poor is a "moocher" or a "looter" and a temporary hurdle to human progress. And most resonant with the young physics wunderkind, Rand imagined a fantasy world, what the book calls "Galt's Gulch," a hidden place in the mountains where the extraordinary and hypercompetent can escape the neediness and regulatory clutches of the masses—a Shangri-La devoted to science, progress, and human greatness.

In the novel's climactic monologue, the heroic John Galt explains to the world that its best thinkers and doers have disappeared to his elite haven. "Do not attempt to find us. We do not choose to be found," he says. "Do not cry that it is our duty to serve you. We do not recognize such duty. Do not cry that you need us. We do not consider need a claim. Do not cry that you own us. You don't. Do not beg us to return. We are on strike, we, the men of the mind."

By the time May reached college, he had already stopped reading Rand, and says he would look back on her books as flawed and smug. But her ideas stuck with him. In the 1972 presidential campaign, May's first as a legal voter, he wrote in John Hospers, the first Libertarian to make it onto some states' ballots. He would continue to vote Libertarian for the next forty years. Today he still throws hints of her ideas, interpreted in their harshest tones, into his speech and writing: He speaks of the "clueless 95 percent," "the dirt people clamoring for more handouts," or predictions that "in the next decades, we're going to see a massive burn-off of useless eaters."

"My political philosophy is keep your hands off my stuff," he says. "Out of my files, out of my office, off what I eat, drink, and smoke. If people want to overdose, c'est la vie. Schadenfreude."

May was accepted to MIT, Stanford, and Berkeley, but chose to attend the University of California at Santa Barbara after the provost of its honors school explained that he could take graduate level classes as an undergrad. He arrived just as the late sixties revolution was in full swing. Anti-Vietnam War protesters burned down the Bank of America in the neighboring college town of Isla Vista. But May largely went about his work, graduated, and took a job beside his fellow physics geniuses at Intel.

May's time at Intel was less a career than a few years' detour from his ideological wanderings. After his alpha particle victory and disillusionment with the world of business, he would retire and retreat from Silicon Valley, over the hills to his own personal Galt's Gulch, a two-story house a mile from the beach in Aptos, California, with only his cat, Nietzsche.

In his new life of aimless intellectual exploration, May would walk down to the beach every day with a stack of business, science, and technology magazines, academic papers, and science fiction novels, and greedily consume them until the sun set. "I never had any interest in horseback riding, boating, hiking, or whatever it is people do," he says. "Instead, I just read and read and read."

The young ex-physicist became a technical and nontechnical intellectual omnivore, consuming science fiction and philosophy with equal literary gluttony. He read John Brunner's science fiction novel *The Shockwave Rider*, about a world where identity is digitally defined and one rebel group allows anyone to anonymously spill their secrets over the phone lines. He read Orson Scott Card's *Ender's Game*, with its pseudonymous characters, Demosthenes and Locke, who are actually genius elementary school–age children influencing global politics on the Internet with their untraceable ideas. He read James Bamford's *The Puzzle Palace*, a history of the National Security Agency and its shadowy work, and Vernor Vinge's *True Names*, a novella about a cyberspace where hackers are elevated to gods and their only weakness is the identity that ties them to their frail bodies.

Soon May discovered the Usenet, the Internet's nascent bulletin board system. He would wait until night to switch on his 1200 baud modem and log on, the better to save money on bandwidth and avoid the traffic jams that plagued the early information networks. "It was slow, and poor and primitive, but it opened up a new world," he said. "I let my magazine subscriptions lapse."

In 1987, May's fellow techno-libertarian Phil Salin came to him with an idea Salin had been turning over in his mind for years: a market for selling information. He would call it AMIX, the American Information Exchange. Long before eBay, Salin imagined an ethereal version of that auction system, where users could pay for answers to their queries or offer up packets of knowledge to the highest bidder. In later years, big-name technologists like Mitch Kapor and Esther Dyson would advise Salin on the project.

But May says he immediately pointed out a fundamental flaw in his friend's vision. AMIX, he told Salin, would inevitably become a black market for stolen knowledge. "Someone asks if anyone knows how to solve the charge buildup problem during ion implant of n-type wafers," May posits. "How long before a guy who works for a chip firm offers to sell his company's tens of millions of dollars in research for a hundred thousand dollars?"

Salin countered that companies and government agencies would prevent their employees from accessing the market and selling out their secrets. But May had an intuitive sense that there was no way that such protections could stop the leaking of expensive information. Motivated individuals would find some way—any way—to anonymously access the site and spill the guts of the companies or government agencies that employed them.

Then, as the idea rolled around the darker edges of May's imagination, he began to reconsider. Perhaps this concept of an information market could be quite interesting after all.

..- -- -- - -..- -.-. --.. .-. .--. --- .. .- -... . -.-. --

Phil Zimmermann was born in 1954, in Camden, New Jersey, to alcoholic parents. His mother was a homemaker, and his father drove a cement truck. Their drinking meant that the family often struggled to pay rent, and Zimmermann remembers frequently moving out of houses in the middle of the night, many times leaving most of his childhood possessions behind them. The Zimmermanns were homeless often enough that their father began to refer to the family car as "the Buick Hotel." Before Zimmermann was eighteen, he says, he had attended twenty-five different schools.

As a rootless kid, Zimmermann took refuge in a secret world of codes. When he was in the fourth grade, then living in Miami, he watched a Saturday morning show called *M. T. Graves and the Dungeon.* Every week it would pose a secret message and tell the audience that for just two dollars, they, too, could buy a decoder and unscramble the cipher. But Zimmermann, who rarely had two dollars of allowance money to squander on such hobbies, cracked the code without the decoder. It turned out to be a simple substitution scheme: 1 for A, 2 for B, and so on. Intrigued by how easily he had outsmarted the show and obtained its two-buck secrets, Zimmermann graduated to more complex codes: Before the age of ten he had learned Morse code, semaphore, and Braille.

It was around that time that the budding cryptanalyst discovered one of the most influential books of his young life, Herbert Zim's *Codes & Secret Writing.* Zim's code book went deep enough into the hidden arts of cryptography to captivate Zimmermann for months with simple cryptanalysis—the science of decrypting codes without knowing the key—fashioning his own encryption systems from scratch, and cloak-and-dagger craft like writing invisible messages with lemon juice or vinegar. (The acid breaks down the paper's cellulose to sugar where the juice has been applied, so that it caramelizes and turns brown when heated with a lightbulb.) Using what he learned from Zim, Zimmermann would challenge a friend to create an encoded message, asking him to make the message as long as possible to make it "harder." Then Zimmermann would use a simple frequency analysis to crack the cipher, counting the proportions of every letter in the encoded text and matching them up with the statistical frequency of letters in the English language to produce a solution in minutes.

Zimmermann's cryptographic dreams always took a backseat to his greater ambition of becoming an astronomer. But when he left high school, Zimmermann faced a tough reality: He was several IQ points short of being a math savant. At Florida Atlantic University—hardly MIT—Zimmermann could never put his foot on the same intuitive grounding in multivariable calculus that he had found in the pleasant logic of codes. He found it, instead, in computer science classes. One of the first programs that Zimmermann wrote outside of class in his nascent coding career was a stab at implementing the simple cryptographic codes he'd loved since childhood. His first project: a digital version of one-time pads—one of cryptography's simplest encryption schemes, and one that's theoretically unbreakable.

One-time pads are a deceptively straightforward tool: Assume Alice wants to send Bob a message (Alice and Bob being the two stand-ins in every cryptographer's explanation of a theoretical scheme) and both have a copy of a pad with random numbers, one through twenty-six. That list is the one-time pad, so called because it's meant to be used for one message and then destroyed. Alice converts every letter in her message using the same A equals 1, B equals 2 substitution scheme that *M. T. Graves and the Dungeon* taught Zimmermann in elementary school. But then Alice goes down the list of numbers on her one-time pad, adding each number from the pad in order to every number from her substitutions and subtracting twenty-six from any number above twenty-six. She sends the resulting gibberish—what cryptographers call "ciphertext"—to Bob. No one who intercepts those numbers can make any sense of them. But Bob uses his copy of the one-time pad to subtract the same series of random digits, adds twenty-six to any negative numbers, reverses the substitution scheme, and, voilà, reads the message in its original form, what crypto types call "plaintext."

If the numbers on a one-time pad are truly random, and if it's used just one time, that simple scheme is mathematically proven to be impossible to crack. But those are significant "ifs." As early as 1942, for instance, U.S. intelligence found that the Soviets were carelessly reusing one-time pads for communication with different countries, and analyzed the multiple examples of the scrambled text to find patterns that allowed them to remove the pads' random noise, breaking the ciphers.

The digital one-time pad that Zimmermann programmed as a hobby project generated its random numbers with FORTRAN's random number generator. Never mind that FORTRAN actually used a *pseudo*random number generator based on a math operation known as a linear congruential equation. Zimmermann thought he'd created an uncrackable encryption program before his senior year of college. "It was very simpleminded crypto, but I believed it was fiendishly clever," Zimmermann says. A few years later, he would find that same scheme he had "invented" in the homework section of a textbook by Georgetown cryptography professor Dorothy Denning. The assignment, Zimmermann discovered to his embarrassment, was to break the code, and it was considered a relatively easy problem.

Zimmermann, a good-natured and humble crypto devotee, took that intellectual blow in stride and lost none of his gusto for the science of scrambling data. And in 1977, he read an article in the *Scientific American* written by Martin Gardner that would change the course of his life as swiftly as Ellsberg's speech in Colorado.

Gardner's article explained a revolutionary new breed of encryption called public key cryptography. And it solved a problem that had plagued cryptographers since the birth of codes: how to share secrets between two people who have never met.

With traditional encryption, or what's known as private key or sometimes symmetric key cryptography, the individuals communicating must somehow both have the secret bit of data, known as the key, that locks and unlocks the encryption on their messages, just as a one-time pad can be added to or subtracted from a message to scramble or unscramble it. If Alice in New York wants to send a private message to Bob in London, she uses a private key to encrypt her message and Bob uses the same key to decrypt it.

But there's an inherent Achilles' heel in that scheme: If Bob has never met Alice, how does Bob get Alice's key securely? She has to send it to him somehow. But they can't encrypt the message that carries the key—they come up against the same problem of how to send a key that decrypts *that* message. If Alice gives up and mails Bob an unencrypted key, on the other hand, any sinister man-in-the-middle could intercept it, copy it, send it on its way, and then decode all their future messages. Unless Alice and Bob have already met in some dark alley and shared their key, private key encryption is hardly private at all. (In fact, it's called "private key encryption" precisely because the key *must* be kept private, which is what makes actually using it so tough.)

Public key encryption, on the other hand, uses some mathematical tricks that vaporize that private key problem as thoroughly as a used one-time pad in a burn bag. In the public key cryptographic scheme, Alice doesn't need to use a private key to encrypt her message and then messenger a copy of the key to Bob. Instead, Bob performs some computational sleights of hand that generate *two keys,* one known as the *public key* and one as the *private key.* That public key isn't for decrypting secrets. It's only for encrypting them. And it has the unique, almost magical property: What's encrypted with that key can only be decrypted with Bob's private key.

Suddenly the conundrum of how Alice mails the private key to Bob disappears. Bob already has the private key, and he can send his public key—the key Alice needs to encrypt messages that only Bob can unlock—to Alice on a postcard from London to New York. The sinister man-in-the-middle can read that postcard all he likes. Not only that, Bob posts his public key on his website, prints it on his business card, and even adds it to the signature of his e-mail. In fact, Bob wants everyone to see the public key, because it's used for harmlessly *scrambling* secrets, not unscrambling them. Bob's private key, meanwhile, remains cozily stored on his hard drive, and never has to be shipped across the Atlantic Ocean. Using Bob's widely available public key, Alice can now send Bob messages that only he can read. Mission accomplished.

In his article, Gardner quoted a dictum from Edgar Allan Poe, that "human ingenuity cannot concoct a cipher which human ingenuity cannot resolve." Poe, in other words, believed no seemingly unbreakable cipher exists that can't be outsmarted by some other, cleverer cryptographer. But Poe had been proven wrong, Gardner wrote, by the implementation of public key encryption invented by three MIT scientists, what would come to be known as RSA. He concluded that the scheme was no less than potential proof that just such a practical, unbreakable form of encryption was possible.

"If the M.I.T. cipher withstands [cryptanalysts'] attacks, as it seems almost certain it will," he wrote, "Poe's dictum will be hard to defend in any form." By Gardner's calculation, cracking MIT's code would take about forty quadrillion years. (In fact, that was a few zeros too many. But even so, requiring somewhere between twenty and forty times the age of humanity to crack meant the scheme remained fairly secure.)

Here was an invention as boundlessly powerful, in its own way, as the atomic bomb, but one that could shield dissidents instead of arming despots. All that was needed was a tool to bring public key encryption out of the realm of academics and spooks, and into the hands of political troublemakers. Zimmermann, naturally, aimed to build it.

Tim May read Martin Gardner's column the same year as Zimmermann, and its promise of unbreakable cryptography planted a seed deep in his science-fiction-fueled imagination. "I came to see [encryption] as a kind of force shield, where the energy to pierce it is more than the entire energy of the universe," May says in the hurried tone that he adopts when building toward something that excites him. "It was a truly impenetrable bubble of privacy."

The seed was still there in 1987, when May learned of Phil Salin's AMIX information exchange plan. Salin would die of stomach cancer several years later, with AMIX still unrealized. But May's obsessive mind never let go of the idea's subversive potential. If encryption could hide not only *what was said,* but *who was saying it,* he realized, that new flavor of secrecy could transform Salin's innocent information market into a guerrilla bazaar for buying, selling, and distributing all the world's secrets.

With those inchoate thoughts of anonymous security breaches whispering in May's ear, he discovered the article whose ideas would finally make his crypto-libertarian dreams possible. It was a 1981 cover story in the journal *Communications of the Association of Computing Machinery,* already years old when May came upon it. Its author: David Chaum, a man who would come to be known as the prophet and godfather of digital anonymity.

Chaum, a bearish, bearded, and white-maned academic, today heads a foundation devoted to secure voting, and spent a decade pitching an anonymous transactions system called eCash. Despite signing up a few major banks, Chaum's crypto-currency never quite caught on, a result of what some say is bad luck and others say was Chaum's overly controlling style of doing business, which may have quashed many of his company's attempts to find mainstream partnerships. But few in the computer security world doubt Chaum's sheer cryptographic brilliance—his patents range from physical locks to software security systems to anonymity and pseudonymity mechanisms that would secure his reputation as a computer science and information security powerhouse.

Growing up and attending high school in an L.A. suburb, Chaum lived the rebellious life of a child who understands he is smarter than everyone he knows. He would show up for shop class and then play hooky the rest of the day, crossing town to sneak into computer science classes at UCLA. He ordered technical manuals for IBM and Fairchild Semiconductor chipsets, and read them the way other kids read comic books. Since no engineers at tech firms would answer the questions of a teenage upstart, he even incorporated a shell company—Security Technology Corporation—and would use it as a front to call up firms and ask questions. "I sensed that secrecy was this powerful mechanism," he says. "I was fascinated by all of it: dead drops, document security, burglar alarms, safes and vaults, locks, flaps and seals."

Attending the University of California, San Diego, in the early seventies, he breathed in the era's liberal sense of privacy and left-wing distrust of power. Chaum later left a four-year graduate fellowship at UCLA after just one quarter, disgusted with the program's military funding. Escaping to Berkeley, he focused on privacy and security features in computing, technologies that he argued were needed in a world where personal data would be ubiquitous and governments could mine it endlessly to track citizens.

The department head at Berkeley, Manuel Blum, chastised Chaum for taking such a focused view of his work's social goals—no scientist should attempt to predict the effects of his or her research, Blum warned. Chaum responded with a dry thank-you note in the introduction to his master's thesis, writing that the urge to prove his adviser wrong had been a central motivating factor in working on the paper.

Later, as a professor at New York University and the University of California, Chaum became obsessed with the problem of anonymity and its political implications, neglecting his teaching for a year to pore over the entire literature of the social benefits and evils of protecting individuals' identity, works by thinkers like Thomas Kuhn and Lewis Mumford. He came out of that personal study surer than ever of his views on privacy, and it was soon after that he unleashed the article that would ignite an entire generation of crypto-focused anonymity advocates.

It was titled "Security without Identification: Transaction Systems to make Big Brother Obsolete." And to a reader like May, it must have seemed like one brilliant gift to the world of ideas after another.

It began with a prescient description of how the digital world would allow surveillance and manipulation of normal people on a terrifying scale. "New and . . . serious dangers derive from computerized pattern recognition techniques: even a small group using these and tapping into data gathered in everyday consumer transactions could secretly conduct mass surveillance, inferring individuals' lifestyles, activities, and associations," Chaum wrote. "The automation of payment and other consumer transactions is expanding these dangers to an unprecedented extent." Big Brother was no longer a character in *1984*. Data tracking and surveillance was an immense societal problem looming just over the newly formed Internet's horizon.

And then, over the next fifteen thousand relentlessly logical words, he offered a collection of semimagical solutions, what he intended to be a comprehensive system for ensuring both the security of information from abuse and safeguarding civil liberties in a digital era.

First, Chaum outlined a method of using "card computers"—tiny machines that resembled credit card–size calculators, as he described them. They would work as virtual wallets, holding a database of encrypted ID credentials and allowing users to spend and receive digital currencies, unique numbers cryptographically protected to prevent forgery or double-spending of the same dollar or deutschmark.

Those crypto-card computers would enable encrypted transaction tricks that wouldn't be possible with mere cash: One such mathematical feat was what Chaum called a "blind signature." A typical cryptographic signature allows anyone to put their personal stamp on a message in a way that no one else can forge. Alice's signature can prove to Bob that a message to him came from Alice and only Alice. That concept had been proposed in the same 1976 paper that first suggested public key cryptography. In his paper, Chaum took the idea a step further, showing a "blind" method of applying that unforgeable stamp—that is, now anyone could put their one-of-a-kind cryptographic signature on a chunk of encrypted data without ever decrypting its contents.

Why does that blind stamp matter? Because, as Chaum described it, now a bank or store could put an unforgeable cryptographic signature on a piece of digital currency without being able to identify and trace each individual virtual coin. Consider the analogy of a money order in a carbon paper envelope. In Chaum's system, someone could write a money order for ten dollars, put it in a sealed cryptographic envelope, and take it to a bank that would remove ten dollars from the user's account and apply Chaum's blind signature function to certify the money order without opening the carbon paper envelope, like a stamp that leaves its unforgeable signature on the paper inside.

When the money order is spent, the user opens the envelope and hands it to the cashier, who checks the now-visible signature on the money order with a bank that verifies the money order is real and worth ten dollars. But because the order was sealed when the bank initially signed it, the financial institution can't put together who withdrew the currency and who finally received it. The result of all that sealing, stamping, and unsealing of envelopes, made effortless by Chaum's card computers, would be a usable digital currency that can't be traced. Strike one against Big Brother.

Chaum intended his system of card computers and blind signatures to be used for more than money. A credentialing organization—say, the department of motor vehicles—could similarly put a blind stamp on the card computers' digital equivalent of a driver's license. The DMV wouldn't ever see the user's full identifying information, but a cop that pulls over a driver could be shown the signature to see that the driver was certified. The necessary credentials of daily life could be split from identification just as easily as financial transactions. Strike two for ubiquitous privacy.

But Chaum wanted to go beyond merely hiding the path of transactions or the personal details on credentials. He aimed to hide the source of *any* communications from *any* snoop. And the third major idea in his paper would be the most elegant blow yet against any would-be surveillance society: a compact method for a group of people to communicate without ever exposing who was doing the talking at any time, a force shield around the identity of a message's sender even more powerful than the one that public key encryption provided for the content of that message. A foolproof cloak of anonymity. Chaum called his privacy panacea the Dining Cryptographers Network, or DC-Net.

Imagine that three cryptographers are having dinner at a restaurant. At the end of the meal, no bill arrives. The three diners want to know if the check has been paid, but out of discretion, none wants to directly ask a waiter or either of their fellow diners if some generous friend among the three secretly paid it.

So instead, they play a game. Two of the cryptographers flip a coin behind a menu to prevent the third from seeing whether it lands heads or tails. Then they go around the table, repeating the secret coin flip between each pair of cryptographers, always keeping the coin toss behind the menu to hide the result from the third friend.

When all that coin flipping is done, each cryptographer gives a thumbs-up or a thumbs-down: up if the results of the two coin tosses he or she saw were the same, and down if the results were different. But there's one important exception: If one of the three paid the bill, that magnanimous cryptographer flips his or her thumb in the opposite direction.

If the total number of thumbs up is even or zero, everyone knows the bill has been paid, and no one's secret generosity has been violated. If it hasn't been paid, the sum of thumbs up will be odd, and the three stingy cryptographers can start arguing about which cheapskate's turn it is to pick up the check.

Silly as that dining cryptographers parlor game sounds, it represented a groundbreaking new idea: that a group of people can communicate among themselves without ever identifying who's doing the talking. In more academic-focused papers, Chaum would show that his DC-Net system was capable of much more than anonymously determining whether a bill had been paid among three friends. Just as it could communicate a single binary "yes" or "no" question in the bill-paying case, it could be expanded to any number of people and any digital message—all computer communications are composed of ones and zeros, after all—whether it be a financial transaction or the launch codes for nuclear missiles.

For an interloper like the NSA who watches the network and tries to locate a message's source, a DC-Net isn't just hard to break. Chaum wrote that it was "unconditionally untraceable." He could mathematically prove that when a DC-Net is properly implemented, there is no evidence whatsoever available to a snoop hoping to find the source of a payment, letter, or leak. In Chaum's world, mathematically perfect anonymity was as real and achievable as a flipped coin behind a menu.

Chaum's paper set Tim May's mind racing. He immediately saw the ideas' darkest implications—ones that Chaum says he never intended to enable. (One cryptographer would tell me that it was as if the crypto-anarchist movement Chaum inspired came upon the advanced technology of an alien civilization and "chose to take only the weapons.")

If financial transactions could be rigorously anonymous, May realized, they could fund anything: illegal drugs, assassinations, everyday transactions shielded from all taxes. If communications could be wholly split from identification, state secrets could be traded like pie recipes. Protected data havens could be created to store and allow anonymous access to illegal or taboo information: massive troves of stolen financial data and intellectual property, incriminating credit reports supposedly erased under the Fair Credit Reporting Act, the purposefully forgotten scientific results from horrific Nazi medical experiments.

The epiphany came to May, he says, like a slow motion version of his alpha particle discovery. Fundamentally, anything that could be done digitally could be done without oversight. For those who understood cryptography, Big Brother could be rendered a toothless nanny. May's imaginary force shield of cryptography could be extended beyond personal messages to entire communities.

The libertarian's dream of an anarchic hideaway in the mountains or on a remote island was obsolete. Galt's Gulch was on the Internet.

The partnership that would result in the revolutionary, populist chunk of crypto-code known by the three letters PGP began with a cold sales call. In 1983, Charlie Merritt, an Arkansas programmer and entrepreneur, was desperately searching for any computer maker who might be interested in reselling what seemed at the time like an obscure invention: his implementation of MIT's public key crypto-system that could run on a desktop computer. When he dialed up Metamorphic Systems, a tiny Boulder, Colorado, start-up specializing in porting Apple software to Intel chips, the man on the other end of the line responded with so much excitement that Merritt thought he might have been planted by a friend as a prank. As he later told an encryption historian, his first impression of Metamorphic's founder, one Phil Zimmermann, was "the most gee-whiz-whoopie enthusiastic character I had run into."

Since his college days, Zimmermann had gotten married, moved from Florida to Colorado to escape his native land's mosquitoes, and founded a less-than-stellar business porting Apple programs to run on Intel chips. But he had never lost his obsession with cryptography. Since reading Gardner's article, he had begun to imagine crypto as an increasingly *necessary* tool for grassroots organizing and international freedom-fighting. Like many of his fellow hackers, Zimmermann shared David Chaum's pessimistic vision that the rise of digital technologies threatened to render personal privacy extinct. The new medium of e-mail was essentially a digital letter without an envelope, readable by any snoop who laid eyes on it. Governments would be able to spy on their citizens like never before.

But strong, universally available encryption could flip that trend to the opposite extreme. Zimmermann envisioned Chinese democracy protesters, South American rebel groups, and radical American antinuclear activists e-mailing one another with impunity, free from the watchful eye of snooping Big Brother. In the early eighties, the FBI had raided the Committee in Solidarity with the People of El Salvador, sweeping up as much private information as the agents could grab or copy. Imagine, as Zimmermann did, if instead of walking out with armfuls of useful intelligence on those activists, the bureau had found only encrypted files, uncrackable by any known computer in the world. To a rebellious mongrel-disciple of Herbert Zim and Daniel Ellsberg, it was an exhilarating thought.

But as elegantly simple as the MIT researchers' public key encryption scheme seemed, Zimmermann still couldn't manage to implement it on his home computer. The PC's processor, a Z80, simply wasn't powerful enough. At one point Zimmermann even called Ron Rivest, one of the three professors who had invented MIT's public key scheme, to ask his advice, only to find that MIT was running the program on a mainframe using LISP, an artificial intelligence language beyond Zimmermann's means.

Merritt, on the other hand, could perform the sorcery of public key encryption on a mundane microcomputer, the equivalent of assembling a three-mast model ship inside a perfume bottle. After their first conversation, Zimmermann began to call Merritt weekly to interrogate him for more details of how to pull off the miniaturized functions of the MIT cryptographers' system. While Merritt had a long head start over Zimmermann, Zimmermann could program in C, a language that worked on everything from IBM computers to Ataris. Eventually Merritt gave up on explaining mathematical operations over the phone and flew to Boulder, and the two men spent a week at his whiteboard hashing out crypto-programming.

Merritt quickly gave up on making any substantial money from his partnership with Zimmermann. But he appreciated Zimmermann's antiauthoritarian bent. For the last several years, Merritt had been repeatedly dogged and threatened by the National Security Agency. The secretive organization would pay visits to his office, pairs of serious-faced spooks in suits, and politely warn Merritt about a certain legal issue that might affect his company: the International Traffic in Arms Regulations, or ITAR.

To the U.S. government's mind, cryptography was the realm of soldiers and spies, not common entrepreneurs like Merritt. Ever since the British encryption genius Alan Turing had broken the Nazis' Enigma encryption engine at Bletchley Park, it had been clear to the military that codebreaking and code-making were as important for winning wars as missile guidance systems, bomber blueprints, and nuclear warheads. And when it came to deciding who could legally access which tools, ITAR painted military hardware and software with the same broad brush. Exporting encryption was just as illegal as hawking uranium to the Libyans.

That meant Merritt could only sell his pint-size crypto-system in the United States and Canada. And because his customers were mostly concerned about maintaining their privacy from regimes less friendly than the U.S. government, ITAR was choking his business. Zimmermann, on the other hand, wasn't concerned about export controls. After all, he only planned to give away any tools he created as grassroots political tools, not sell them. Why would customs agents bother him over his insignificant, do-gooder hobby?

By 1987, Zimmermann had pulled together much of his newfound crypto-programming know-how into an article published in the well-regarded technology journal *IEEE Computer*. The prestige the paper won for Zimmermann allowed him to start calling other cryptographers around the world for advice and coding contributions without coming off as just another paranoid cipher-nut. Thanks in part to those volunteers, Zimmermann's encryption mini-engine was making steady progress. He decided to give it a name, one as folksy and humble as Zimmermann himself: Pretty Good Privacy. (The reference was to Ralph's Pretty Good Grocery, a fictional store on the Garrison Keillor National Public Radio show *A Prairie Home Companion.*)

Soon, Zimmermann also had a new deadline, supplied by the U.S. government. The omnibus crime bill of 1991, known as S.266, contained an inconspicuous paragraph inserted by none other than Delaware senator Joe Biden.

> It is the sense of Congress that providers of electronic communications services and manufacturers of electronic communications service equipment shall ensure that communications systems permit the government to obtain the plain text contents of voice, data, and other communications when appropriately authorized by law.

Congress, like the NSA, could see that the U.S. government was losing its monopoly on uncrackable encryption. It needed a trump card against the Phil Zimmermanns and Tim Mays of the world who might try to subvert the government's authority through the power of perfectly private information. That trump card, Biden's addition to the bill made clear, would be the ability to decrypt any communication traveling across a telecom firm's network.

The U.S. government, after all, saw encryption very much as Tim May saw it: a mathematically rigorous method of castrating law enforcement and intelligence agencies. In a Senate hearing in 1997, FBI director Louis Freeh would put it this way: "Uncrackable encryption will allow drug lords, spies, terrorists, and even violent gangs to communicate about their crimes and their conspiracies with impunity. We will lose one of the few remaining vulnerabilities of the worst criminals and terrorists upon which law enforcement depends to successfully investigate and often prevent the worst crimes."

With encryption running rampant, who knows what evil would lurk within the scrambled messages racing across the Internet? Biden's S.266 was designed as a preemptive strike in the struggle for control of secrecy, the first shot fired in the Crypto Wars that would shake the worlds of privacy and national security for the next decade and beyond.

Zimmermann read about the surreptitious addition to Congress's crime bill on a Usenet bulletin board, and alarms went off in the antiauthoritarian lobes of his brain. A former consultant to the NSA added a bit of prophetic commentary to the Usenet discussion: "I suggest you begin to stock up on crypto gear while you can still get it."

Zimmermann felt he had to finish PGP before that bill became law. So he dropped everything and worked day and night to develop his crypto embryo and deliver it into the world. He neglected his day job and consulting gigs so thoroughly that he missed five mortgage payments. "I really honed my negotiation skills with banks," Zimmermann says.

Within hours of posting it to Usenet, PGP began spreading like a prairie fire, fueled in part by fears of a government crypto crackdown on the way. It was passed among encryption enthusiasts around the world with the message that every copy distributed was another point scored against the government's efforts to smother the populist privacy movement. One encryption activist became PGP's paranoid Paul Revere, riding around California's Bay Area in his car with a laptop and an acoustic coupler and using pay phones to log on and upload copies of the program to message boards without revealing the program's source. Within hours of its creation, PGP had jumped over U.S. borders and multiplied itself around the globe, directly violating ITAR's ban on cryptographic exports.

PGP fulfilled Zimmermann's dream as a political weapon almost immediately. Activists in Myanmar used the encryption program to hide communications from a brutal military junta that would kill its citizens for even owning a fax machine. A Bosnian user sent Zimmermann a message to say that during the siege of Sarajevo, his father had used PGP to encrypt e-mails to his family during the hour or two of occasional electricity in the war-torn city. Finally he received a PGP-encrypted message that would make all of Zimmermann's missed mortgage payments worthwhile. It came from a user in Latvia, where fear still ran high that the newly independent nations and former satellite states of the crumbled USSR would be swept under a new repressive regime.

> Phil, I wish you to know: let it never be, but if dictatorship takes over Russia your PGP is widespread from Baltic to Far East now and will help democratic people if necessary. Thanks.

Shortly after the release of his second version of PGP in 1993, Zimmermann received a call from a U.S. customs agent in San Jose. She asked him for more information on his humble invention, and Zimmermann cheerfully answered her questions, thinking that she had perhaps encountered PGP on a computer the agency was investigating and was merely curious about it. But when the agent told Zimmermann she planned to fly all the way to Boulder to pay him a visit, Zimmermann began to get nervous.

Zimmermann was aware of Charlie Merritt's export warnings, and he had always known that distributing cryptography across foreign borders was illegal—he had simply never thought the government would take notice of his modest hobby. A few months later, a formal notice arrived in the mail. Zimmermann was the subject of a grand jury investigation. His potential crime: sharing his beloved PGP with the world.

The news put Zimmermann into a state of shock. Spending an afternoon or even a night in a Nevada jail swapping activist war stories with his fellow pacifists was one thing. The thought of years in federal prison for simply writing software and putting it on the Internet was more than a pudgy computer programmer could handle.

He called a criminal lawyer, Phil Dubois, a former public defender known in Boulder for being scrappy and cheap—Zimmermann was still catching up with his mortgage payments, and could hardly afford a crack defense team.

On his first visit to Dubois's office, he spotted some files in a box on the floor marked "Michael Bell discovery documents." Bell was a notorious

Colorado murderer who had killed four people and then hidden in the mountains before being tracked down by the largest manhunt in Boulder history. This, Zimmermann thought, was how the government saw him. He had become America's first crypto-criminal.

Tim May had finally figured out what he wanted to do with his post-Intel life. He would write a science fiction novel that expressed the full power of David Chaum's inventions, how they could subvert institutions and empower individuals. It would be a techno-libertarian call to arms, Ayn Rand on public-key encrypted steroids.

May began wading into academic cryptography papers and even came up with a title for his science fiction brainchild: *Degrees of Freedom,* a play on a thermodynamic physics term that also referred to the new political flexibilities that would be opened on the anonymous digital frontier.

In 1988, May took his first crack at putting his ideas on paper, though in nonfiction form: "The Crypto-Anarchist Manifesto." It was a short document, but its Marxist-parodying language carried all the weight of a history-shaping treatise:

> A specter is haunting the modern world, the specter of crypto anarchy.
>
> Computer technology is on the verge of providing the ability for individuals and groups to communicate and interact with each other in a totally anonymous manner. Two persons may exchange messages, conduct business, and negotiate electronic contracts without ever knowing the True Name, or legal identity, of the other. Interactions over networks will be untraceable, via extensive re-routing of encrypted packets and tamper-proof boxes which implement cryptographic protocols with nearly perfect assurance against any tampering. . . .
>
> The State will of course try to slow or halt the spread of this technology, citing national security concerns, use of the tech-

> nology by drug dealers and tax evaders, and fears of societal disintegration. Many of these concerns will be valid; crypto anarchy will allow national secrets to be traded freely and will allow illicit and stolen materials to be traded. An anonymous computerized market will even make possible abhorrent markets for assassinations and extortion. Various criminal and foreign elements will be active users of CryptoNet. But this will not halt the spread of crypto anarchy.
>
> Just as the technology of printing altered and reduced the power of medieval guilds and the social power structure, so too will cryptologic methods fundamentally alter the nature of corporations and of government interference in economic transactions. Combined with emerging information markets, crypto anarchy will create a liquid market for any and all material which can be put into words and pictures. And just as a seemingly minor invention like barbed wire made possible the fencing-off of vast ranches and farms, thus altering forever the concepts of land and property rights in the frontier West, so too will the seemingly minor discovery out of an arcane branch of mathematics come to be the wire clippers which dismantle the barbed wire around intellectual property.
>
> Arise, you have nothing to lose but your barbed wire fences!

May photocopied a few hundred copies and drove down to the crypto-conference in Santa Barbara, convened by none other than his newfound guru, David Chaum. He passed out the flyers at the conference, though the academics largely ignored him. "They weren't thinking about the political implications yet," he says.

But Thomas Paine–style pamphleteering aside, May was struggling as a writer: He couldn't translate his overactive imagination into characters and stories that captured his technical ideas. Meanwhile, he began to get the panicky sense that the concepts he had thought were prescient and futuristic were appearing in the real world faster than he could put them into fiction. He read press reports about an airline bugging its business class seats to acquire corporate intel, the NSA wiretapping Wall Street firms, and New York mafiosi busted after cops figured out the gangsters were using their wives' AOL accounts as dead drops for incriminating communications. It was all happening much too fast.

After nearly three full years of writer's block, May came to a realization: Instead of telling the story of how encryption and anonymity were changing society, he would simply be the protagonist. "I didn't want to work on this stupid novel," he says. "I wanted to actually build this elaborate world that I was imagining."

Around that time, a mathematician and programmer friend named Eric Hughes had come to Berkeley to look for a place to live in the Bay Area while he applied to graduate school. A wayward Mormon who grew up near Washington, D.C., and in Salt Lake City, Hughes shared May's frontier style of cowboy hats and leather, though instead of a beard he wore a blazing red goatee. He also shared May's libertarian ideals, and the sense that cryptography would help to keep the government's tendrils safely hogtied. The pair had met at a party thrown by their libertarian hacker friend John Gilmore, a ponytailed and balding software developer whose sad eyes hid a fiercely independent streak. As the fifth employee of Sun Microsystems, Gilmore had struck it rich in software just as May had in hardware, and retired from the world of Silicon Valley to pursue his digital whims and libertarian ideals.

Since Gilmore's party, Hughes had gone off to work as a coder for none other than the grandmaster of anonymity, David Chaum, at the anonymous transactions start-up he had created in Amsterdam. The gig hadn't worked out. "I'll never work for him in any context ever again," Hughes says flatly when I ask about his time with Chaum in the Netherlands. "At this point I should say that if you can't say anything nice about someone, you shouldn't say anything at all."

Hughes may not have jibed with Chaum's personality, but he was almost as obsessed with Chaum's ideas as May was. So when May suggested Hughes use his home as a base for a few days while looking for a place to live, the pair hit it off like Marx and Engels. Hughes neglected his real estate search to wander with May through Santa Cruz's redwood forests and beaches while the older ex-scientist unloaded several years' worth of bottled-up ideas. "We spent three intense days talking about math, protocols, domain specific languages, secure anonymous systems," says May. "*Man,* it was fun."

Just a week after Zimmermann released PGP 2.0, Hughes and May invited forty of their favorite coders and cryptographers to Hughes's newly purchased home in Oakland. About twenty of them showed up, and the group, mostly wearing its de facto uniform of beards and ponytails, crowded into the furniture-free living room and sat cross-legged on his floor. Tim May, a larger man and a louder personality than Hughes, presided. He distributed a fifty-seven-page handout of background materials and began by reading his "Crypto-Anarchist Manifesto," to great approval.

Then Hughes and May moved on to a game they'd invented—more or less on the spot—called Crypto Anarchy. It was based, like many of May's fantasies, on an idea from David Chaum. This one was called a Mix Network. The concept of a Mix was a simple one from years before Chaum's seminal Big Brother paper with its crypto-card computers and networks of dining cryptographers. It would also become by far the most influential of Chaum's ideas, and one that would reshape anonymity technologies for decades to come.

Users of a Mix Network give the slip to anyone who might be tracking them the same way they would in the real world: by getting lost in the crowd. If someone is being tailed, she might go into a movie theater, find a seat in the dark, and then reemerge in a crowd of people. But a Mix Network gives the followed a much larger head start over the follower: To extend the same analogy, it ushers a crowd of people into a theater, *all* of whom want to avoid being followed, gives them a chance to remove their hats, wigs, sunglasses, and clothes and put on new ones, and then releases them again. Then the crowd disperses to mix with other crowds of disguised people who enter other theaters with other crowds, change their disguises, and repeat the process until no stalker has any hope of keeping up with his target.

Chaum came up with Mixes two years after Martin Gardner's article on public key encryption, and it cleverly applied the MIT researchers' idea of a cipher that only one intended recipient could unscramble. But Chaum took the encryption idea another step: He imagined encrypting the message multiple times in layers. The first layer of encryption would use the public key of the intended recipient as usual. But then that encrypted message would be encrypted *again,* only this time using the public key of an intermediary. That middleman's job would simply be to decrypt the outer layer of encryption with his or her public key. Inside would be a forwarding address and the rest of the message, still encrypted with that first layer of scrambling.

If that middleman—what would come to be known as a *remailer*—collected enough messages before decrypting them and forwarding them out in a large batch, there would be little way for anyone eavesdropping on the network to know the origin of any of those messages. Not even the recipient would necessarily know. If the message contained no information about the sender, it would show up at its destination, encrypted specifically for that recipient, but with no evidence of who had sent it. Or it could contain an encrypted return address, but suggest that the recipient reply through another remailer so that no snoop would be able to know that the two were communicating.

Chaum had taken encryption, which masks the *content* of a message, and applied it to create anonymity, which protects something else altogether: the *identity* of the people communicating.

His Mix idea didn't end there. If a message could be wrapped in two layers of encryption and routed through a remailer, why not encrypt it three times and send it through two relays? Or encrypt it half a dozen times and bounce it through five remailers, each of which has the key to remove just one layer of encryption before forwarding it? With multiple ricochets, not even the remailers themselves need to be trusted. Each one would know only the next recipient, not the entire chain from sender to recipient. And even if a large number of those remailers betrayed the users and collaborated to try and link the ends of the chain, just one trustworthy link—one remailer who refused to spill the beans—would ensure that the identities of the two ends of the chain couldn't be matched up.

In their game of Crypto Anarchy in Hughes's living room, May and

Hughes split their hacker friends into two teams, one of ambassadors, corporations, and rebels trying to communicate anonymously and securely, and the other acting as spies, trying to eavesdrop on those communications. The communicators wrote messages on slips of paper and hid them in envelopes to represent PGP, putting those envelopes inside of other envelopes and addressing them to remailer friends—including some members of the spy team posing as trusted remailers—to try and route secret anonymous messages to each other. In their simulated game of spying cats and crypto-rebel mice, Chaum's ideas came through clearly: With enough layers of encryption and just a few trustworthy friends, the mice could actually win the game.

The meeting's drafted hackers were soon infected with all the same excited sense of encryption's potential as May and Hughes themselves. They talked late into the night, slept on Hughes's floor, and dreamed of crypto-anarchy.

The next morning, May and Hughes went out to buy bagels and brainstorm about the potential of the group that had begun to coalesce around their meeting. Why limit the club to the physical world, for instance, when the real mass of potential cryptography fanatics was online? As May had years earlier realized, cyber-utopias would have to be created on the Internet, not in someone's living room. They later asked John Gilmore if he would host an e-mail list on the server of his personal site, Toad.com, and he eagerly agreed.

But it was Jude Milhon, Hughes's girlfriend several decades his senior, who provided the group's name. At the time, science fiction authors like William Gibson and Neal Stephenson had adopted the "cyberpunk" genre, stories of bohemian hackers fighting steely megacorporations in virtual worlds. But Milhon, a writer for the early technoculture magazine *Mondo 2000,* told Hughes that the group he and May were creating wasn't composed of mere cyberpunks, but a new species of hacker: "cypherpunks."

So Gilmore's e-mail forum was christened the Cypherpunk Mailing List. As it blossomed to nearly a thousand subscribers over the mid-1990s, its physical meetings would expand too. Within a year the group had moved out of Hughes's house and into a spare conference room at John Gilmore's software company, Cygnus, in Mountain View, in a building that bordered an herb farm and was permeated with the scent of fresh basil. The cypherpunks would assemble there monthly, eat burritos, and then sit through talks from invited academics and hobbyist crypto-rebels on their latest schemes, coded contraptions, and diatribes about secrecy politics. The group kept its strong libertarian strain: One adjunct group called the Cypherpunks Shooting Club even organized trips to rifle ranges to teach each other to shoot .22s and semiautomatic weapons, the final resort should the government ever come after their electronic and physical freedoms. (Tim May, an avid gun enthusiast himself, didn't attend. "I don't give free lessons, especially not to clueless software people," he says.)

Shortly after the group's first meeting, John Gilmore and another cypherpunk named Hugh Daniel had bet Hughes that he couldn't write an anonymous remailer system for stripping the identifying traces off e-mail messages within a single month. The next weekend, Hughes dropped all his other projects and cranked out a script in the software language Perl in just two days. It became the first official Cypherpunk Remailer, and would be copied and improved upon by a dozen others in universities and basements around the world to form a growing, living implementation of Chaum's Mix Network.

Around the same time, Hughes answered May's "Crypto-Anarchist Manifesto" with an updated "Cypherpunk's Manifesto," laying out the group's common mission and the tenets of its newborn subculture. It included a sentence that would become a philosophical maxim for the group: "Cypherpunks write code." The slogan represented action instead of rhetoric, writing tools that would shape the world of technology so that when the government belatedly arrived to regulate it, the feds would find an untamable landscape populated by crypto-wielding civilians.

> We know that someone has to write software to defend privacy, and since we can't get privacy unless we all do, we're going to write it. . . .

> We don't much care if you don't approve of the software we write. We know that software can't be destroyed and that a widely dispersed system can't be shut down. . . .
>
> Even laws against cryptography reach only so far as a nation's border and the arm of its violence.

That antiregulation note was a prescient message. Within a month, the U.S. government would test the cypherpunks' resolve.

As Zimmermann polishes off his noodles, I pull a tome off the shelf in his dining room, the one that changed the course of his life fifteen years earlier: *PGP: Source Code and Internals.* As the title suggests, it's literally a printed copy of PGP's code, hardly legible to humans, not to mention the nongeek members of a jury deciding Zimmermann's fate. But as Zimmermann explains, it wasn't any argument or fact written in that volume, but rather the book's mere existence—the fact that PGP's source code was represented in ink on slices of pulped tree between two sheets of cardboard—that made it a crucial weapon in the Crypto Wars.

In 1993, two years before that book was printed and shortly after Zimmermann had been formally notified about a grand jury assembled to decide whether he would be prosecuted, he had been summoned to Washington to testify in a congressional hearing on the future of cryptography. Word of his case spread quickly through the legal community, and by the time he arrived in Washington, lawyers from the Electronic Frontier Foundation and the American Civil Liberties Union were ready to represent him in his upcoming trial.

All of them, to his dismay, believed he had absolutely no chance of winning. In a meeting after his congressional testimony, his pro bono lawyers sat around a conference table and told Zimmermann that there was little doubt that he had done exactly what the law prohibited: created a program that included military-grade encryption, and distributed it across U.S. borders.

"To have ten lawyers all tell me almost unanimously that it was hopeless . . . it was a ton of bricks. It was the worst day," he says.

Only one lawyer seemed optimistic: Phil Dubois, the cut-rate criminal lawyer that Zimmermann had hired in Boulder.

Dubois clashed with Zimmermann's other counsel on the strategic question of taking his case to the press. As a peace activist, Zimmermann instinctively felt he should publicize his pending indictment. And against the advice of all of his other lawyers, Dubois agreed. After all, Zimmermann wasn't an accused drug dealer or murderer like some of Dubois's other clients. He was a soft-spoken, suit-wearing nerd whose crime was only to have written a privacy-preserving piece of software. "Phil was just delighted to have a client who didn't have a spiderweb tattooed on his face," Zimmermann says.

Their media strategy mattered, because Zimmermann's case was about to become especially newsworthy. Shortly after the grand jury was assigned to investigate him, the prophecy of Joe Biden's S.266 finally came true: The newly elected Clinton administration unveiled a new invention called the Clipper Chip, and brought to life every cypherpunk's nightmare.

The chip, designed by the NSA, was meant to solve the government's crypto dilemma. It aimed to offer strong cryptography to the public without giving up the government's ability to decrypt any message it wished to. The Clipper Chip would be made available to private industry so that eventually every computer or phone that offered encryption would use its new, classified scheme known as Skipjack. But in return for that NSA-created scrambling technology, there was a catch: The U.S. government would keep a copy of a backdoor key to every chip in a database, ready to step in and unlock any message.

To May and Hughes's crowd, the chip was stark confirmation: The government feared cryptography because of its subversive power and was determined to cripple it. Who was the NSA kidding? Encryption becomes useless the moment anyone other than you has a copy of your private key. And when that someone is none other than Big Brother, the entire idea is a sick, deceitful parody.

When the plan became public in a front-page *New York Times* story, the cypherpunks held an emergency meeting on a Saturday that packed Cygnus's conference space. They brainstormed about possible schemes to undermine the dreaded chip, from boycotts of AT&T, which had signed on to put the Clipper in an encrypted phone it had begun selling, to injecting negative stories into the press.

Tim May drew the "Intel Inside" logo created by his former employer on the whiteboard at Cygnus, replacing the words with "Big Brother Inside." The cypherpunks later printed that logo on stickers and would sneak into electronics stores to plant it on any machine infected by the hated Clipper spy bug. (A cease-and-desist letter from Intel threatening a suit for trademark infringement eventually kiboshed that guerrilla sticker campaign.) Privacy groups from the Electronic Privacy Information Center to the Electronic Frontier Foundation railed against the idea in the press, and even tech titans like Bill Gates spoke out against what they saw as the government putting its clumsy hands into Silicon Valley, the greatest economic engine of the 1990s.

But it was Phil Zimmermann who embodied Hughes's maxim: "Cypherpunks write code." And there was no better response to the threat of the Clipper Chip than ubiquitous PGP.

The man who had populated the Internet with free, uncrackable crypto had remained at a remove from the cypherpunks—he viewed their gun-toting, ponytailed culture as counterproductive compared to his suit-and-tie, mainstream approach. "I saw them as angry young men in leather jackets, without children and with too much testosterone," he says.

Several times Zimmermann ran into May during trips to the Bay Area and pleaded with him to tone down his antigovernment rhetoric. After all, PGP's inventor was the one facing incarceration for the crypto cause, not May, and he felt that May's movement painted him as another techno-insurgent hell-bent on destroying the government—exactly the image he needed to avoid. May being May, he firmly refused to tone down a word of his anarchist philosophy.

Meanwhile, Zimmermann had been drafted by the media as the face of the Crypto Wars, the man who had put his freedom on the line to fight for the right to privacy. And against the advice of all his lawyers except Phil Dubois, he assumed that role with Ellsberg-like gusto, taking dozens of interviews a week from newspapers and magazines. The resulting articles almost universally came out against crypto-export laws and the Clipper Chip. "Every last article was sympathetic to me," says Zimmermann. "Not ninety-nine percent. One hundred point zero percent."

Though he wasn't one of them, the cypherpunks held Zimmermann up as a folk hero. And it was a cypherpunk, the Qualcomm researcher Phil Karn, who followed Hughes's maxim that code, not mere words, would prove the best way to undermine the government's regulations and keep Zimmermann out of prison.

The cypherpunks, with their eagle eye for vulnerabilities in security software, also had a knack for finding legal loopholes. After one astute subscriber to the mailing list found a clause that allowed munitions like Stinger missiles to be exported if they were in fact being fired at an enemy country, there was some discussion of strapping a copy of PGP to a missile and shooting it at Mexico, just to prove a point.

But Karn found a better trick to undermine those export laws, with all the subtleties of a cryptanalytic attack. The State Department allowed Americans to apply for permission to export goods if they weren't sure about whether they qualified as munitions or other contraband. So Karn bought a copy of Bruce Schneier's book *Applied Cryptography* and sent it to the State Department to ask for export permission. In one of its appendices, the textbook contained the source code for the Digital Encryption Standard (DES), the NSA's declassified encryption scheme for military and civilian uses. Some unwitting official at the State Department took a look at Schneier's book and quickly rubber-stamped the request.

Then came the second stage of Karn's multipronged maneuver. He sent the same DES code to the State Department with the same exact request. But this time it was stored on a floppy disk. "When they got that one, I can imagine the blood draining from their faces," Zimmermann says gleefully.

The State Department had figured out Karn's game by this point, and denied his floppy disk request. He appealed and was denied again. So Karn sued them in a federal court.

While that lawsuit was under way, Zimmermann ran into an editor at MIT Press while attending a privacy conference. The editor wanted to publish the PGP user's manual that Zimmermann had included with PGP 1.0. Zimmermann was willing, but he asked for a favor. "I'd like you to also publish the source code to PGP," Zimmermann said. "All of it."

The code added up to close to eight hundred pages, and MIT printed it in a font that was designed to be easily readable for scanning software, so that it could be converted from ink to bits with minimal effort. Zimmermann was playing with the distinction highlighted by Phil Karn's trick: rendering the line between words—protected by the First Amendment—and ITAR-banned code as blurry as possible.

MIT Press played along, and enacted the final piece of Phil Karn's pincer attack. The publishing house mailed its bound, legitimate-looking textbook filled with PGP's source code to the State Department's export approval office. The department, caught in its own contradictions, never responded to MIT's request for export permission. So with only silence from the U.S. government, MIT Press went ahead and shipped the book to European bookstores along with all its other textbooks. PGP had been exported right under the government's nose.

It's doubtful many Europeans ever scanned that book to implement its code. PGP was already being used across the world, after all. But now Zimmermann's legal team could wield that bound chunk of paper—the one, today long out of print, sitting on Zimmermann's shelf—as a logic bomb planted under the feet of Zimmermann's prosecutors that they would detonate as soon as he was indicted.

In the end, the Justice Department dropped its investigation into PGP, with no explanation. Zimmermann never found out whether it was his public support, Karn's export trick, or simply a lack of political will behind his prosecution that saved him.

The government's crypto fearmongers were busy, anyway, trying to rescue their failing Clipper Chip scheme. Public opinion had swung violently against the plan, with 80 percent of Americans opposing it in one CNN poll. Silicon Valley didn't want to touch it. And to add to the Clinton administration's perfect storm, an encryption researcher at Bell Labs named Matt Blaze had found a vulnerability in the scheme that made it trivial to crack. By 1996, Clipper was sunk. Zimmermann and the cypherpunks had taken on the government and won the first great battle of the Crypto Wars. Cryptography, in all its applications from grassroots activism to child pornography to terrorism to untraceable whistleblowing, belonged to the people.

As I wrap up my interview with Zimmermann and he puts his PGP source-code book back on the shelf, I ask, almost out of a sense of obligation more than hope, whether he has any idea of how I can get in touch with Tim May, or whether he's truly become the well-armed and misanthropic mountain hermit he's described to be.

"Let me see," Zimmermann says. He picks up his iPhone and in a few seconds, he and May are discussing the nuclear disaster at the Fukushima Daiichi power plant in Japan and the potential of thorium reactors to replace uranium reactors in future generators. Then Zimmermann passes the phone to me.

May apologizes for not getting back to me earlier, and as we talk, he checks his e-mail's draft folder to find that he somehow forgot to push send on his response to my message to him. In fact he's less than a mile away, at a bookstore in downtown Santa Cruz. "Everyone always calls me the 'elusive Tim May,'" he says into the phone, sounding flabbergasted. "I'll talk to any reporter who calls me!"

--- -. .--- -.- .--. ..- --.. -.-. ....- ..- ... -.-. .-.. - --

When I find May in the Bookshop Santa Cruz, he's just finished flipping disinterestedly through a copy of a book by former WikiLeaks staffer Daniel Domscheit-Berg, a tell-all memoir of his time at the secret-spilling group. May's beard has expanded in the years since the 1990s, and his arched eyebrows have spiked upward like coarse dark feathers. He's wearing a leather brimmed hat and a pink shirt with white studs, and generally looks much like the mad-scientist frontiersman recluse that *Die Zeit* described. But as we walk down the street to a café, he's practically rupturing with ideas he's ready to share: He quizzes me excitedly about a lattice-based scheme for fully homomorphic cryptography that I barely understand, and then tells me about his own ideas for lattice-based data structures, which I don't understand at all. But when we sit down, he settles into the matter at hand, the idea that was, to many, the most influential and controversial thought he produced in his role as what John Gilmore calls "the Thomas Jefferson of the cypherpunks." That idea was BlackNet.

BlackNet was a thought experiment, the fruit of Chaum's anonymity ideas applied to Phil Salin's online data market, and it aimed to prove that combination's full potential in a wholly imaginary setting. It was also the primordial, evolutionary ancestor to WikiLeaks.

In 1993, May had learned about the Democracy Wall, a brick wall in the Xidan neighborhood of Beijing where late 1970s democracy dissidents had left poetry and antigovernment messages for each other and for the public. The government eventually cracked down on that wall-based messaging system, moving it to a park where visitors had to show identification papers to enter.

May fantasized about a true Democracy Wall online, one without restrictions, where public key cryptography would defeat the government's identification efforts and let anyone post a message that only the recipient could retrieve. "When you licked that envelope and sent it to this site, no one in the *whole fucking world* would know who had sent it or who retrieved it," May says, his voice perceptibly shaking with excitement.

In the summer of that year, May wove together his untraceable message board ideas with Phil Salin's dream of an online information market. And he sent the following unattributed statement to the Cypherpunk Mailing List, routing it through anonymous remailers to shroud it in mystery.

> Your name has come to our attention. We have reason to believe you may be interested in the products and services our new organization, BlackNet, has to offer.

> BlackNet is in the business of buying, selling, trading, and otherwise dealing with information in all its many forms.
>
> We buy and sell information using public key cryptosystems with essentially perfect security for our customers. Unless you tell us who you are (please don't!) or inadvertently reveal information which provides clues, we have no way of identifying you, nor you us.
>
> Our location in physical space is unimportant. Our location in cyberspace is all that matters. . . . We can be contacted (preferably through a chain of anonymous remailers) by encrypting a message to our public key (contained below) and depositing this message in one of the several locations in cyberspace we monitor.

The message went on to list types of information in which BlackNet was particularly interested, including buyout or merger rumors, trade secrets, and confidential product designs ranging from "children's toys to cruise missiles." And it offered to pay for them with CryptoCredits, an untraceable digital currency.

BlackNet spread through the cypherpunks and on to other mailing lists and Usenet groups like a nuclear chain reaction. May says he later learned that it reached several labs working on confidential projects, and Oak Ridge National Laboratories even issued a warning to staff to report any contact with the shadowy organization.

Just a couple of weeks after his first anonymous message, he sent out another e-mail, this time taking credit for the scheme and declaring the game over. Of course, CryptoCredits never existed. Neither did the underground cabal behind the purported digital black market. But with technologies that existed even then, they could have.

BlackNet, May wrote, was a demonstration of

> "Classified classifieds," so to speak. "No More Secrets." At least, no more secrets that you don't keep yourself! (A subtle point: crypto-anarchy doesn't mean a "no secrets" society; it means a society in which individuals must protect their own secrets and not count on

> governments or corporations to do it for them. It also means "public secrets," like troop movements and stealth production plans, or the tricks of implanting wafers, will not remain secret for long.)
>
> To the governments of the world, facing these and other threats to their continued ways of doing business, the existence of strong encryption in the hands of the population is indeed a mortal threat.
>
> In any case, it's too late. The genie's nearly completely out of the bottle. National borders are just speed bumps on the information highway.

Even in the short time before May called off his BlackNet experiment, it proved its purpose. Just before he sent his e-mail taking credit for the ruse, a message encrypted with BlackNet's PGP key appeared on one of the Usenet groups that May had said BlackNet would monitor. It promised to offer evidence that the CIA was spying on ambassadors in Washington from a Central African country and to expose internal corruption in the country's government.

As May tells it, he decrypted the message with BlackNet's private key. He read it. Then he put it in an archive folder and never responded.

Why? May says that he had shown that BlackNet could serve its intended purpose. But he argues, a little defensively, that trying to set up a WikiLeaks-like system to distribute or publish black market information required operational security he couldn't handle. Even if he had kept BlackNet's source secret, he was clearly the cypherpunks' prime suspect for enacting such a scheme. And he points out that the message may have also been a honey trap designed to ensnare him and put him in prison.

But more frankly, May says, he simply didn't care. He was, and remains, a hard-core libertarian looking out for his own Randian self-interest, not a whistleblower advocate trying to expose corruption. "I'm not concerned about things like that. Let the Africans kill each other," he says flatly. "I don't have those kinds of political interests."

When I later ask Jacob Appelbaum, one of the only Americans to associate openly with WikiLeaks, about his thoughts on BlackNet, he sees things more simply. "Tim May is a fucking racist," he says. "And it's really a shame. Because if he weren't, he could have created WikiLeaks himself and made a real difference in the world."

When I repeat Appelbaum's comment to May, he chuckles. "I call 'em as I see 'em," he says. "If I see blacks driving themselves into the gutter, I call it as it is."

May pauses for a moment. "I had the opportunity to either light a candle or teach people how to make candles," he says. "I had the ideas. But the idea of trying to be Julian Assange gives me the creeps."

John Gilmore and I are looking out onto the shiny wet streets of San Francisco's Mission District as the entire Cypherpunk Mailing List archive, all 345 megabytes spanning nearly a decade of hacker rants, attacks, critiques, and announcements that once lived on his server, is siphoned onto my thumb drive. When the bits have finished flowing from his tiny laptop to my stick of solid-state memory, Gilmore opens up the first folder.

Since the days of the cypherpunks, his long wispy beard has shifted to the whitish gray of a caricatured martial-arts master, and his manifold brow has extended to cover his eyes with hoods that wrinkle as he cracks open the cypherpunks' dusty archives.

The first messages are introductions from Tim May, Eric Hughes, and John Gilmore, along with Eric Hughes's declaration of the first cypherpunk remailer, built on Gilmore's dare. And then comes another message containing only an article from *The Sydney Morning Herald* in August 1992.

It seems to have been sent, strangely, by the list itself. In fact, Hughes explains bemusedly, the sender used a fast and dirty trick to protect his or her anonymity, one that didn't require any remailers or other fancy methods. The message's header was spoofed to resemble the cypherpunk list's, and then ricocheted off a random nonexistent address so that it would bounce back with an error message to its fake return address.

The news article details how corporations in Australia, including National Australia Bank and Citicorp, bought proprietary information about citizens from government agencies for millions of dollars, often using it to track down debtors. Gilmore looks over the text thoughtfully and turns to me.

"It seems some anonymous person has posted an article from an Australian newspaper about the government leaking information," he says, with a smile. "I wonder who that could have been?"

CHAPTER 3

THE CYPHERPUNKS

The forty-first issue of the Melbourne University Mathematics and Statistics Society's quarterly magazine, *Paradox*, contains a short but telling anecdote about the society's most well-known former vice president.

One day during his three-year career as an undergraduate student of math and physics, Julian Assange was walking through Melbourne University's campus when he spotted a mysterious valve protruding from the University Chemistry Building's brick wall. He decided, spontaneously, to open it. When he did, the metal sphincter let out a deafening noise and a cloud of smoke. And for a few delightfully chaotic moments, as Assange told a fellow student later that day, the man who would advance the evolution of leaking more than anyone in the twenty-first century "was in heaven."

A lanky, six-foot-two-inch, very pale, white-haired thirty-two-year-old, Assange cut a strange figure among the tanned teens and twentysomethings at the University of Melbourne. He was known to work at his computer for days on end with no sleep and little food. He spent much of his time camped out in the university's Mathematics Society meeting room, usually wearing a dark gray trench coat over a T-shirt and his corn-silk hair in a ponytail. Sometimes he would stand up from his computer and perform a set of twenty or so jumping jacks, explaining to anyone present that short bouts of physical activity served a certain neurobiological function that made stimulant drugs unnecessary.

He spoke rarely about his past, and few asked. He was often accompanied by an entourage of strangers whom he declined to introduce to anyone in the room. And he mysteriously refused to let the society put his photo on its website, citing "security" reasons and insisting that it be replaced with an image of an alien.

Assange no doubt felt like an extraterrestrial among the university's more traditional students. He described the academic physicists at one conference as "snivelling fearful conformists of woefully, woefully inferior character" and wrote that "for every Feynman or Lorentz, [there are] 100 pen-pushing wretches scratching each other's eyes out in academic committees or building better bombs for the DSTO (Defence Science & Technology Organisation), who had provided everyone with a bag, embossed with their logo, which most physicists pathetically lugged about with pride and ignorance."

At the time, as Assange later recounted to *The Age*, the Applied Maths program at the university had received funding from the U.S. Defense Advanced Research Projects Agency (known as DARPA). Assange believed (inaccurately, according to the department's staff) that money would ultimately go toward improving the design of the Grizzly Plow, a military bulldozer used in the first Iraq War and designed to sweep away barbed wire and sand at more than thirty-five miles per hour. The plow, as Assange described it, filled the trenches inhabited by enemy troops, rolling over them and burying them alive like an accelerated version of Tim May's father's bunker-burying bulldozer from World War II.

Assange was disgusted by what he saw as the military's influence on campus and bored by formal education. If his classmates had asked about his past, they would have realized how little he had in common with them: In his three decades, he had already gone toe-to-toe with major corporations and the Pentagon as one of the world's top pseudonymous hackers, been convicted of digital felonies, wandered Australia as a homeless vagrant, traveled to dozens of countries, run a business on the early Internet, co-written a memoir, devised an innovative crypto-system, and, perhaps most significantly, received an education as valuable as any degree: nearly a decade of close reading, writing, and debate on the Cypherpunks Mailing List.

So, perhaps chiefly to entertain himself during his time in college, Assange invented a game: The Puzzle Hunt. Following a model invented by MIT for its venerable Mystery Hunt, the Puzzle Hunt was an elaborate campus-wide scavenger hunt punctuated with dozens of math and logic problems that drew in hundreds of students and still takes place annually on the University of Melbourne's campus.

One of the puzzles Assange generated for that competition—and he created more of them in his first year than any other student—involved a long quote from Shakespeare's *Julius Caesar,* with each letter written backward. Seemingly random gaps appeared throughout the chunk of text, and collecting the letters following those anomalies revealed a clue for the next puzzle. Another conundrum involved factoring large numbers into primes—a procedure that would have seemed natural for anyone familiar with RSA's public key encryption tricks.

Each set of puzzles in the hunt began with a quote. One, from the Koranic figure Ja'far as-Sadiq, captured Assange's playful love of obscurity: "Our cause is a secret within a secret, a secret that only another secret can explain; it is a secret about a secret that is veiled by a secret."

A year after Assange left the university—he's described quitting as a "forced move," as in chess, "when you have to do something or you'll lose the game"—he sent an e-mail to many of his former colleagues in the Melbourne University Math and Statistics Society asking for their participation in a new project as exciting and intellectually challenging as the Puzzle Hunt.

It was called WikiLeaks.

"Are you interested in being involved with a courageous project to reform every political system on earth—and through that reform move the world to a more humane state?" he wrote to his old classmates. "We have only 22 people trying to usher in the start of a world-wide movement. We don't have time to reply to most reporters' emails, let alone the interview requests—and I leave for Africa in under a week! We need help in every area, admining, coding, sys admining, legal research, analysis, writing, proofing, manning the phone, standing around looking pretty, even making tea."

A year later, he would write to his university math colleagues again, this time posing his project directly as an offshoot of the Puzzle Hunt's whimsical mind games.

> Hello Puzzle Hunters.
>
> I am looking for good people, courageous people, intelligent people to help develop and run an international leaked document analysis & essay competition.
>
> Wikileaks is only new, but we have already broken major stories in the international press that have achieved significant reforms likely to save tens of thousands of lives. Our problem? We're drowning in leaked documents.
>
> Across the world there are other notable analytical, mooting and essay competitions. Competition in most of these cases is what we might describe as 'mere competition'; the motivational elements extend to social and professional standing, competition camaraderie and the pleasure of discovery and creation, but together we can create a much more interesting competition; a competition where teams of bright people form an engine for justice, a competition where:
>
> 1. The basis is of real substance and interest in the form of never before released leaked documents of potentially significant political importance.
>
> 2. Discovery and creation are augmented by the nature of the material and its moral calling. These are real puzzles with real discoveries to be found.

> 3. In addition to traditional or academic honors, there is the ultimate honor: to have a positive impact on civilization through one's labours and for this to be internationally recognised.
>
> Each team will receive a previously unanalyzed leaked document or series of leaked documents. . . . Proposed awards: over-all winner, lightning (24 hour), best analysis, best critical analysis, best news story. Where 'best' is defined as 'whose insights contribute most to humanity.'

"I think it would be fair to say that he saw Wikileaks, in some ways, at some times, as a political version of the Puzzle Hunt, with great social implications," Daniel Mathews, one of Assange's college friends and an early volunteer for WikiLeaks, would tell an editor of *Paradox*. Like the hackers and code rebels playing games of Crypto Anarchy with nested envelopes on Eric Hughes's living room floor, Assange approached WikiLeaks as a great game, an elaborate cypherpunk puzzle of leakers, friends, and adversaries playing by rules laid out in the landscape of cryptography.

But for all his talk of "an engine of justice" and "reforms likely to save tens of thousands of lives," the other goal in WikiLeaks' game—or perhaps just a bonus perk for a fire-starter like Assange—was its potential for explosive chaos. The rebellious young Australian felt the same yearning to outsmart and tear down the corrupt establishment as Tim May expressed in his earliest crypto-anarchist dreams.

Four years later, after the firestorms of Bradley Manning's alleged record-breaking, world-shaking releases, the science fiction writer Bruce Sterling wrote of WikiLeaks: "At last—at long last—the homemade nitroglycerin in the old cypherpunks blast shack has gone off."

The denizens of the Cypherpunk Mailing List drew the blueprints for that massive improvised explosive device, refining the recipe not just with theory but with years of trial and error, testing the limits of anonymity and antigovernment provocation. And it was Assange who watched the experiments, studiously mixed the chemicals from their notes, and then opened the fateful valve.

John Young knows something about how to stage a dramatic rendezvous. On an April afternoon, he's asked me to come to Carl Schurz Park on the Upper East Side of Manhattan and wait for him in front of Gracie Mansion. With the precision of his architectural training, he's sent me an aerial still from Google Maps that shows a semicircular bulge in the promenade where I'm to stand, overlooking the East River with a view of the Roosevelt Island lighthouse and the Robert F. Kennedy Bridge.

It's raining, and Young has not been as precise with time as he is with location. So I'm left alone in the eerily empty park, standing under an umbrella by the guardrail holding a briefcase and feeling like a character out of a John Grisham or Tom Clancy novel, which I imagine is exactly what Young had in mind.

Ten minutes later he walks out from behind a row of bushes, a stooped figure with his head down, wearing large black galoshes and holding a closed umbrella at his side while the rain pours down onto a limp fishing hat. He shakes my hand gravely, and as we walk out of the park I ask him why he doesn't carry a cell phone, which makes a useful tool for changing meeting locations from outdoors to indoors on rainy days. "Horrendous spying machines," he answers simply.

Young brightens as we reach East End Avenue. "How about we go find someplace warm and dry to talk," he says. Then, just as quickly, his eyes narrow and he gazes ruefully down the street. "This neighborhood is full of *shitty* restaurants."

Sitting in one of those shitty restaurants a few minutes later, Young lays down some ground rules: "You're interviewing me, but I'm interviewing you too," he says in a grumbled voice so low that I have to lean forward to hear him. "This interview goes both ways."

Fair enough, I agree. But a few questions in, it's clear that his idea of this bidirectional interview is significantly more adversarial than mine. "Where are you from originally?" I ask genially. Young pauses, and seems for a moment to be holding his breath.

"I take umbrage at that question. That is a stupid question, and it's the kind of question asked by stupid people," he says in the same whisper, so soft that I can't tell if he's inhumanly calm or holding back enormous anger. "And it shows me that you're not serious. So let me tell you that if you ask another question like that I will walk out that door."

I must appear so flabbergasted by this response that Young seems to feel the need to explain. "We need more friction in this interview."

Young's strange style of conversation shouldn't come as a surprise; it's no stranger than the equally conspiratorial tone of his singularly strange website, Cryptome.org. In his sixteen years of running Cryptome, Young has become a kind of paranoid twenty-first-century newspaperman, a collector of leaks, curios, raw data, and clues to mysteries that often only he and perhaps his less visible partner, Deborah Natsios, understand.

In the days before our meeting in Manhattan, for instance, Cryptome published archival footage of Hiroshima in the days after its bombing: dazed survivors walking around makeshift shelters and children collecting stones amid the rubble. Another post shows the immigration papers for Barack Obama Sr., perhaps a clue related to Obama's birthplace conspiracy theories. A third shows the finances for WikiLeaks over the year 2010, as collected by the German Wau Holland Foundation. Few of the half a dozen documents that Young and Natsios put online daily are accompanied by any analysis or even an explanation as to why the reclusive couple chose to publish them.

"My mentor, Jean-Paul Sartre, said that imagination is the only thing you can trust," says Young, after I've smoothed out some of our friction. "Facts are not a trustworthy source of knowledge. Cryptome is not an authoritative source. It's a source of imaginatory material. Don't trust Cryptome, we lie to you helplessly. Don't believe anything you see there."

But as much as John Young tries to give the impression that Cryptome is a schizoid lunatic's collage, it's nothing so simple. Since launching the site fifteen years ago, Young has published the names of 2,619 CIA sources, 276 British intelligence agents, 600 Japanese intelligence agents, and internal documents from every company from Microsoft to Cisco to AT&T

revealing their policies for secretly handing users' data over to law enforcement.

Many were leaked to Young by unknown sources. And despite threats, legal attacks, and even maneuvers by Microsoft to remove his site from the Internet in 2010 after he published what he calls the company's "spying guide," Young has never—with a few exceptions to protect private individuals—taken down a document.

The FBI first visited Young in 2003—he describes the pair of agents in typically precise fashion as having "trim haircuts and dark suits, healthy-looking young Caucasians, no facial hair, shined shoes, clean teeth, no noticeable mouth or body odor"—and offered a polite warning about "threats to the nation" that might result from Cryptome's postings of intelligence names and sources. Later, when he extended his repertoire to posting selections from databases of aerial photography, the Department of Homeland Security began calling him and politely asking him to stop. Young ignored all of them.

When Cryptome subsequently published detailed maps of Dick Cheney's secret bunker in March 2005, the site was featured in a *Reader's Digest* section called "That's Outrageous!" The article was titled "Let's Shut Them Down: These Sites Are an Invitation to Terrorists." The interviewer asked Young if there was anything he wouldn't publish—say, a security flaw in the president's Secret Service detail. "Well, I'm actually looking for that information right now," Young answered.

Four years later, when Yahoo! asked Young to unpublish a manual that showed how it complied with law enforcement requests for users' private information like search history and e-mail content, Young referred the company's lawyer to the same *Reader's Digest* story, which includes the words of former NSA counsel Stewart Baker. "If material is leaked to you, you can probably publish that," Baker is quoted saying. "Unfortunately, it's not illegal to be a jerk."

And how did Cryptome obtain those leaks? Not through any promises of high-tech security. The website includes an e-mail address along with a PGP public key. There's also a postal address, as well as a number to a telephone that no one answers.

The site's privacy policy, as far as it even has one, promises that Cryptome doesn't collect user data and deletes its logs several times a day. But its protections for the privacy of its leakers end there. The policy reads:

"As you know there are many, many ways to snoop on traffic, so much that Cryptome asserts there is no trustworthy privacy policy, not for Cryptome, not for anybody else. . . . Those who promise the most protection are out to skin you alive, those who promise the most privacy are selling your most private possessions. Cryptome is not trustworthy, and lies. It's a free site, what else could it be but up to no good?"

Young doesn't recommend that his secret-spillers use Anonymous remailers, like Tim May's BlackNet, or Tor, like WikiLeaks. Cryptome doesn't endorse any specific anonymity technologies, or make promises about safeguarding any identity information it does receive: The leaker's anonymity is wholly his or her own problem. "Do not identify yourself, jerk," says Young. "That's our policy. Don't send us stuff and think that we'll protect you."

But since the days of the cypherpunk remailers, tools for anonymous leaking have been in the hands of leakers, and the submissions have kept coming. When WikiLeaks launched in 2006, the site included a reference to John Young as the "spiritual godfather of online leaking." In fact, his influence is more than spiritual; in the earliest days of WikiLeaks, it was Young's name listed on the registration of the site's domain. And aside from Assange himself, he is perhaps the strongest tie that the secret-spilling site has to its ideological roots in the cypherpunks.

After our lunch, the rain has let up and I walk with Young to the Eighty-Sixth Street subway entrance. I start to thank him for meeting me and ask when we can talk again, so that I can hear the rest of his story. He answers with one final point of friction. "I'll talk to you. But until you publish something that puts you in prison, I won't fully respect you," he says, his face blank.

I tell him I'll do my best. Then we shake hands, and he walks away.

- --.- - ..- .. ...- .--. -- --.. -..- .- --- -.. -- .--. -...

In 1988, as Julian Assange tells it, a sixteen-year-old version of himself sat in a quiet room of a temporary refuge house for families in the Australian town of Emerald, on the eastern edge of Melbourne. He turned on the television news. Then he removed the cover from his Commodore MPS 801 printer and set it printing a long document, with its exposed mechanics emitting a noisy clacking rhythm. And then he started reading passages in *Macbeth* out loud from a Shakespeare anthology. Occasionally he would alter the pitch of his voice, ask himself random questions, pause, and answer them, all while periodically stomping around the room. To anyone watching, he would no doubt have appeared in need of antipsychotic medication.

Every epic hacker story has its Great Hack, when the teenage upstart first gains access to a powerful, faraway machine that opens up vast new possibilities. In 1983's *WarGames*, Matthew Broderick unwittingly hacks the WOPR supercomputer, a vast engine of nuclear war analysis. In 1995's *Hackers*, Angelina Jolie and Jonny Lee Miller breach the Gibson mainframe. And in *Underground*, the 1997 nonfiction book written by Julian Assange and Australian journalist Suelette Dreyfus that sketches the early Australian hacker subculture, that digital golden fleece was Minerva, a system of mainframes run by Australia's Overseas Telecommunications Commission in Sydney.

The protagonist of that story? A hacker named Mendax, who only years later Assange would reveal was none other than Assange himself, using the handle that defined his hacker persona for many of his teen years. The name referred to *splendide mendax*, the "nobly untruthful" in Horace's Odes.

Assange was determined to access Minerva, both for bragging rights and to exploit the mainframes' capabilities to run scanning and cracking programs for other netherworld adventures. But he needed a password. And the only way he knew to get one was through what hackers call "social engineering," simply calling up a human being and conning him or her into divulging secrets.

Hence the noisy layers of Shakespearean tragedy, television, and printer that the altogether sane young man was producing. Assange's sound show was for the benefit of his cassette recorder, the better to simulate the background chaos of a busy office. A few minutes later, he had found a valid number within an OTC branch office in Perth. And using his uncannily deep sixteen-year-old's voice while the noise-tape played behind him, he became "John Keller," a trustworthy operator in the Sydney office trying to check a few data points corrupted by a crashed storage drive.

He dialed and a man picked up. Assange introduced himself and began the game. "The backup tape is two days old, so we want to check your information is up-to-date so your service is not interrupted," he casually told the man who answered the phone, not missing a beat.

"Oh, dear. Yes. Let's check it," Assange's mark responded in a concerned tone.

Assange read out a list of easily accessible information for Minerva staff users that he had downloaded, carefully inserting an error into one user's fax number. The voice on the other end interrupted him helpfully.

"Oh, no, that's wrong, our fax number is definitely wrong," he said.

So Assange tried to match his victim's worried tone and explained that they would need to confirm all the user's information. "Let's see. We have your account number, but we had better check your password . . . what was it?"

"Yes, it's L-U-R-C-H—full stop."

Lurch. Assange was in. He politely ended the conversation, gave his target a callback number that rang eternally busy, and hung up, victorious in the greatest hack of his young life.

Assange was born in Queensland, Australia, on July 3, 1971, less than one month after the first publication of the Pentagon Papers. From as early as he could remember, his family was on the move, as Assange's mother, a free-spirited costume and makeup artist, traveled with his bohemian stepfather from town to town. For a time they lived on Magnetic Island, a tropical paradise off the eastern coast of Australia where Assange's mother remembers "living in a bikini" and "going native." She wore a sarong and would trek around the island with Assange on her back, often leaving him to sleep in the shade of a boulder by the sea while she sketched. The young Australian was dazzled by the phosphorescent phytoplankton that emitted an aqua flash as the ocean's waves broke on the shore, and he swung from giant fig tree roots. His mother would slash a path to the front door with a machete and kept rifle cartridges for shooting snakes. On some occasions, opossums ran across their beds in the dark.

One evening, while the Assanges were out having dinner, their house mysteriously caught fire and burned to the ground, with their snake-shooting ammunition combusting like a series of firecrackers in the night. After losing most of their possessions, they lived with near-ascetic simplicity. "You didn't have to have a lot of money to live a privileged lifestyle," Assange's mother told the local news outlet, the *Magnetic Times*. "It was so beautiful . . . at night, when the ferries stopped, we felt cut off from the world and its troubles. There was a sense of safety and security."

Despite that idyllic setting, Assange made few friends in his "itinerant minstrel childhood," as he called it. "I was quick to anger and brutal statements such as 'You're a bunch of mindless apes out of *Lord of the Flies*' when faced with standover tactics were enough to ensure I got into a series of extreme fights," he wrote in 2006. "I wasn't sorry to leave when presented with the dental bills of my tormentors."

Assange's birth father, whom his mother met at an anti-Vietnam rally, was gone before he was a year old. His next father figure, an alcoholic, was divorced from his mother when he was nine. His second pseudo-stepfather, whom Assange's mother has described as a manipulative and abusive character, had fathered Assange's younger half-brother, and when Assange's mother left him, the man and a powerful cult to which he belonged searched persistently for Assange's family. They stayed on the move, now out of fear rather than the innocent wanderlust of Assange's earliest years. In all, Assange moved through fifteen different towns and at least as many schools, when he attended school at all.

Assange's distrust of power was inculcated just as early as his rootless wandering. He remembers his mother driving through an Adelaide suburb late one night, after leaving an antinuclear protest, giving a ride to a friend who held evidence that the British had forced five thousand natives from their land to test nuclear weapons in the Maralinga region of South Australia. When Assange's mother saw that she was being tailed by a car, she dropped off the friend in a back street and continued. The tail turned out to be a plainclothes policeman who pulled over the car, searched Assange's mother, and made a thinly veiled threat that she "get out of politics" or risk being seen as an "unfit mother."

But just as formative as that dark political lesson was his first computer, a Commodore 64 that he used in a computer shop across the street from a house his mother rented. Seeing his interest and skill, his mother bought it for him, a sacrifice that required moving into a cheaper home. Assange began simple coding and cracking software protections, and soon he was hooked on what he described as "the austerity of one's interactions with a computer." "It is like chess," he told one reporter. "Chess is very austere, in that you don't have many rules, there is no randomness, and the problem is very hard."

Not long after his Minerva hack, Assange and two Australian friends whom he met on Usenet formed the International Subversives, and began publishing a zine of hacking techniques and tales. It had a rather limited circulation: to obtain a copy, a hacker had to write an article for it. Therefore its readership remained at three.

But the International Subversives was no mere geek clubhouse. The group developed into elite hackers, and Assange soon became by some accounts the most accomplished practitioner of digital intrusion in Australia, a near-mythic figure across the burgeoning hacker subculture. He writes in *Underground* of gaining access to networks ranging from Melbourne University to Nortel to NASA to Lockheed Martin and the Los Alamos National Laboratory, and, according to comments he later made in a Swedish documentary, installed a back door in the heart of the Pentagon's systems that allowed him and his friends to come and go as they pleased for two years. "For someone who was young and relatively removed from the rest of the world, to be able to enter the depths of the Pentagon's Eighth Command at the age of seventeen was a liberating experience," he once told the art historian Hans Ulrich Obrist.

Mendax's mission was never to steal or destroy, Assange says, only to explore, and he outlined his hacker's ethic in *Underground*: "Don't damage computer systems you break into (including crashing them); don't change the information in those systems (except for altering logs to cover your tracks); and share information."

One of the two other International Subversives, known as Trax, had found enough information in Telecom Australia garbage bins to learn to spoof calls, making them appear to come from a central exchange hub or even from another person's phone. Just as cypherpunk remailers would hide the origin of e-mail in years to come, Trax taught Assange to hide his location and identity by routing his modem's phone traffic through that intermediary.

An incredibly methodical hacker, Assange didn't depend only on that redirection but also erased all logs, and generally avoided any behavior that would remotely raise suspicion. Still, there were slipups. On one occasion, he accidentally rang a thousand phones simultaneously in a Telecom Australia office building at seven A.M. And finally, on another occasion, he was caught in his tracks by a system administrator trolling the networks late one evening. The admin turned out to be so determined to catch the intruder on his network that he drove in to a Melbourne office from the suburbs in the middle of the night to gain higher network privileges.

When it became clear that he couldn't continue the cat-and-mouse game any longer, Assange sent his pursuer a note that appeared in the center of his screen, one that momentarily shocked him into inaction.

> I have finally become sentient.
> I have taken control.
> For years, I have been struggling in this greyness. But now I have finally seen the light.

Assange knew that the surprise value of a suddenly intelligent machine wouldn't last. So he pleaded for understanding.

> It's been nice playing with your system.
> We didn't do any damage and we even improved a few things. Please don't call the Australian Federal Police.

And then he logged off before the call trace could begin.

Assange left his mother's home at the age of seventeen and moved in with a girl whom he later married, and the young couple soon had a son. As he tells it, he also kept a beehive, endlessly delighting in studying the insects' society in all its complexity. To avoid their stings, he writes that he would collect his sweat in paper tissues and dissolve it into a sugar water solution that he fed the bees as nectar. The trick was meant to associate his odor with the bee-friendly taste of flowers, a clever biological hack.

But the hive also served another purpose. Assange used it as a hiding place for the floppy disks that stored his hacker's booty, data like stolen passwords and logins, and records of the open pathways and security vulnerabilities he had mapped out across the Internet. After every hacking session, he carefully secreted them away among his beloved bees.

With one exception. In October 1991, just as the Crypto Wars were beginning in the United States, his wife of three years left him, taking their young son with her. Assange was emotionally destroyed. He moped around the house for days in fits, and fell into a state of careless lethargy.

When the Australian Federal Police finally knocked on his door one night soon after and showed him a search warrant on suspicion of computer crimes, all of his incriminating disks were strewn across his desk, with one in his PC's disk drive.

Mendax's career was over.

It was the fourth day of the Columbia University Occupation of 1968, and the one hundred radical young men and women who had seized Avery Hall were pissed. Not simply angry that their school had obliterated a huge, tree-covered patch of land in a public park to build a new gym, with its back door facing their Harlem neighbors in a reincarnation of Jim Crow. Or even about the hellish, unjust Vietnam War and the fact that their own university had been shown in newly revealed documents to be secretly tied to the military's Institute for Defense Analyses.

No, the architecture students in Avery Hall were frustrated because the student body's protest, a full-blown strike that had taken control of most of the major buildings on campus, wasn't working. The administration showed no sympathy to their pacifist and progressive demands, and wasn't willing to bargain. Most of the Columbia faculty had refused to stand with them, choosing instead to mediate between the students and the administration. And they could sense that a police crackdown was coming. The mood was tense in Avery and sheer pessimism was threatening to crumble the students' control of the building.

Then John Young spoke up. A thirty-two-year-old widower and graduate student, Young had been so quiet in the activists' meetings until that point that some students had suspected him of being a police spy. But one of those present described the short speech he gave that night as having an easing and profound effect on the group, his Texas-tinged grumbling coming out as "a cross between a mutter and the Oracle of Delphi."

Young began by congratulating his fellow students on having created a true anarchist democracy within the walls of Avery. And then he urged the group to stop moping and push forward with its work, to reach out to the outside world to make their demands heard, and to use its architectural training to build a fairer and more democratic city.

Finally, he told everyone to quit arguing and sulking, and get to work. It was a simple statement, over in five minutes. But it had its intended effect. Thanks to Young's prophetic mumbling, as the historian Richard Rosenkranz wrote in his chronicle of the Columbia protests, "the Avery Commune was once again a functioning organism."

In the end, the Columbia protests did end in violence, with students pulled out of buildings by police who brutally beat them with blackjacks, flashlights, and batons, cracking ribs and splitting scalps.

But the Avery occupation would set Young on a course toward radical, progressive libertarianism for the next forty-odd years. "I knew it was more than a student demonstration and that something extraordinary was going on," he said a few years later. "In a few days, we had sped up our lives, approached a condition of human relationships that can usually be found only in the realm of ideas."

Young had grown up in a poor family, the son of a wandering jack-of-all-trades, traveling around Texas with his father and occasionally to Oklahoma or New Mexico, to find jobs washing dishes, painting, canning, picking cotton, and driving trucks. He described his father's philosophy as "antiorganization, antigovernment, basically antiauthoritarianism, very pro letting the people do it for themselves." But he bristles at the idea that his bottom-rung background drove him toward radicalism. "It would be easy for you to say, 'That poor man from that disadvantaged childhood. He's just striking back because he was denied,'" Young told Columbia protest chronicler Rosenkranz. "Well, that's bullshit. I didn't suffer from being denied, and I think my childhood was just great."

At seventeen, Young shipped out to Germany with the army and spent the next three years as an engineering supply clerk in "a vast storage depot, waiting for the next war." When he returned to the United States, the GI Bill paid for a bachelor's degree at Rice, and he double-majored in architecture and philosophy, mixing Sartre with the knack for building that he'd inherited from his father. After college he worked as a construction engineer, renovating the nineteenth-century Winedale Inn for the unfortunately named grand dame of Texas, Ima Hogg. ("She cracked jokes about her name. You did not.")

The work was meant to match the pre-Civil War–era building, and Young and his workmen scoured the woods for local materials like cedar, oak, and stone. "I learned the idea of being passive in the face of a building, rather than aggressive," he says. "You let the building tell you what to do, rather than tell it what to do."

That approach to architecture wasn't en vogue among the modernist architects at Columbia, where Young enrolled in a master of science program. But the 1968 occupation was his real education. After the strike, the students formed Urban Deadline, a nonprofit that aimed to bring the sensibility of the 1968 protests to architecture, education, and politics. It had no leaders. "Even anarchism was too organized for us," says Young.

As a part of Urban Deadline's architecture group, Young renovated storefronts to turn them into sidewalk schools, an alternative to the "prison-like" school system offered to kids in poor parts of Harlem and Brooklyn.

The group fought to create historic districts and derailed the construction of highways through poor neighborhoods. And Young functioned as the city's architectural gadfly. He once took out an ad in *The New York Times* attacking one of the world's most famous architects. "I. M. Pei," it read: "Why so many bad buildings?" When Young was invited to speak at the Museum of Modern Art, he deadpanned, "I've just had a chance to look around briefly, but if you move that Rubens and the Rembrandt and store them down in the basement, we could put thirty-two units of housing in here. We're prepared to start right now."

In the meantime, Young supported his work with a for-profit architectural firm. But even there, Young says his focus was often to report wrongdoing: corner-cutting and incompetence that led to unsafe buildings. On multiple occasions, he was hired for renovations, and instead pointed out violations like blocked exits, cracked supports, fire-prone ducts meant for air-conditioning but used instead for exhaust. When he was ignored, he reported the owners, losing clients and future work. Young says he considered that watchdogging nothing more than an architect's job. The city's regulatory commission usually ignored his complaints. "Buildings are more dangerous than guns. But real estate is such a powerful interest in New York that no one wants to hear it," he says. "The owners browbeat you into submission. They're willing to fucking ruin you, so they usually win."

It would be another two decades until Young rediscovered the same spirit of excitement, activism, and uncompromising antiauthoritarianism that had swept him up in 1968. He found it, finally, in the cypherpunks.

Assange's friends hadn't been as careful as he had. The third member of the International Subversives, a hacker who went by the handle Prime Suspect, couldn't use Trax's untraceable calling method due to a difference in the telephone exchange connected to his home. And as *Underground* tells it, he had been tracked on Nortel's network on the same fateful night that the network administrator had played cat and mouse with Assange: Prime Suspect breached its firewall during the thin window of time between when Assange had escaped but before he could call his fellow hackers to warn them that he had tipped off the telecom's security.

In the end, it didn't matter. Trax himself had called up the cops and—almost accidentally—turned himself in. The teen hacker had long been unstable, agoraphobic, and unfit for the immense pressure of illegal hacking. When he called up the police to report a death threat against him by another hacker, he found himself inexplicably confessing his own activities. And soon those of his friends.

The Australian justice system took nearly three years to bring charges against Assange, and two more before he was sentenced. The judge, in the end, was lenient, recognizing that Mendax had never intended to profit from his hacks, only to idealistically seek a world without limits on information. He was sentenced to a two-thousand-dollar fine and a five-thousand-dollar bond depending on his good behavior.

But during the intervening five years, the possibility of impending jail time meant Assange never felt safe taking a real job or making long-term plans. He fell into a deep depression, first checking himself into a mental hospital and then checking out to spend six months on an aimless walkabout, sleeping in the wilderness around Melbourne, frequently waking with his face covered by mosquito bites.

Eventually Assange returned to the city to try and reengage with the world. He created a computer security firm with Trax, but it fell apart when their lead investor faced credit problems. And he began volunteering for nonprofit organizations, lending his computer expertise. He even worked with police in the city of Victoria, helping them to track and take down child pornography rings in two separate cases. But he drew the line at helping to catch his fellow hackers. "I couldn't ethically justify that," he's quoted as saying in *Underground*. "But as for others, such as people who prey on children or corporate spies, I am not concerned about using my skills there."

Assange took a job as systems administrator at an Australian Internet service provider (ISP) called Suburbia that hosted online chats on everything from cryptography to religion. In some ways, he later told me, Suburbia was the prototype for WikiLeaks more than any other project he worked on.

Assange says some discussion rooms on Suburbia became forums for discussions among lawyers and activists claiming corrupt practices by the Australian telecom giant Telstra. But Suburbia also hosted discussions about a topic that would become the ground zero battle for free speech in years to come: Scientology. One of the notoriously censorious religion's critics had been sued under copyright claims and had his computers seized after posting documents on the service. The leaked documents, previously only available to members of the religion who had achieved a certain expensive stature, showed that Scientologists believed in communication with plants.

When the ensuing outrage spilled over to Suburbia, American lawyers contacted Assange to question him about one of his customers who had been an outspoken critic, David Gerard. Assange, of course, refused and instead alerted Gerard. "He had titanium balls," Gerard would tell me years later.

"We were the free-speech ISP in Australia," says Assange. "People were fleeing from ISPs that would fold under legal threats, even from a cult in the U.S. That's something I saw early on, without realizing it: potentiating people to reveal their information, creating a conduit. Without having any other robust publisher in the market, people came to us."

Even as he settled into a new life beyond hacking, Assange's charges hung over him like a bitter cloud. Years later, he would compare the feeling, hyperbolically, to Russian dissident writer Alexander Solzhenitsyn's imprisonment in Stalin's gulags. "How close the parallels to my own adventures!" he wrote in a rather self-pitying 2006 blog entry. "Such prosecution in youth is a defining peak experience. To know the state for what it really is! . . . True belief only begins with a jackboot at the door."

For an information freedom advocate like Assange, the plight of Phil Zimmermann in the United States, who, like Assange, had the threat of prosecution for seemingly harmless digital crimes hang over him for three years, must have felt especially familiar. It's little wonder that he fell in with Zimmermann's most hard-core supporters, the crew who happened to also be radical hackers and antiauthoritarian misfits like himself. Assange became a cypherpunk.

He began posting to the mail list under the nickname "Proff" in 1995. His earliest writings, like most of the conversations on the list, were snarky takedowns of fellow posters' ideas. In his third message he calls one demanding user a "dummy" and tells him to "get a life." He tells another that "some research is in order before you go shooting off your mouth," and then makes fun of a third for hosting a party that ends at ten P.M., calling it an "afterschool Tupperware get-together." Apropos of nothing, he posts a list of National Security Agency anagrams in another message, including "Your testical [sic], again Nancy?" and "National Gay Secrecy Unit."

But "Proff" was no mere cynic or jokester. He would eventually use the list to organize a Melbourne protest against Scientology in retaliation for its attempt to censor Suburbia. "To the Church the battle isn't won in the court room," he posted in his anti-Scientology manifesto. "It is won at the very moment the legal process starts unfolding, creating fear and expense in those the Church opposes. Their worst critic at the moment is not a person, or an organisation but a medium—the Internet. The Internet is, by its very nature a censorship free zone." He then called on all good cypherpunks to come make their voices heard at the Melbourne Church of Scientology building at eleven A.M. the next day. Eleven people showed up.

But more important, perhaps, than what Assange wrote on the Cypherpunk Mailing List was what he and his cohorts read. For the decade that it was active, the list chronicled the long and painful evolution of the cryptographic anonymity that Assange would later harness under WikiLeaks. And that anonymity began, in its most newborn and vulnerable form, with a Finn named Julf.

In 1992, Johan "Julf" Helsingius, a cofounder of Finland's biggest Internet service provider, had witnessed a strange conversation on a Usenet forum hosted on an academic server. Two users were arguing, and one had taken the pseudonym Jesus. The other, a pretentious academic type, was not amused by this use of a humorous handle, and tried to argue that it was "against the rules" of the Internet to hide one's identity on a university server, and downright offensive to hide it with a disrespectful nickname.

Coming from the growing nonacademic side of the Net, the notion that one professorial user would try to declare the rules for online identity deeply riled Helsingius. As part of the Swedish-speaking minority group in Finland, Helsingius had a special concern for protecting the rights of marginalized groups and the vulnerable, and felt that anonymity was an important safeguard for those groups. So he set out to prove that technology, not pretensions, would define the nature of identity on the Internet.

The result was Penet, an anonymous remailer server that ran off a humble PC with a 386 processor in a back room of Julf's home. Users could send Penet an e-mail along with a designated final destination—in his explanation posted to the Cypherpunk Mailing List, he cites Usenet groups devoted to erotic needlework and masturbation as examples—and the message would be relayed on to those endpoints with a newly generated pseudonym. Penet would keep a database of those pseudonyms and the e-mail addresses linked to them, so that if anyone wanted to reply to that handle, it would route back through the server and find the original sender.

Penet used none of David Chaum's crypto innovations, and Helsingius listed so many possible security vulnerabilities in his introduction to the service that it's a wonder anyone used it at all. He warned that users would have to trust him as the server's administrator, that he might be subpoenaed to give up someone's identity, and even that hackers could break in and steal the data. "It wasn't the best, the safest, or the most secure, but it was easy," says Helsingius. "That's how I pitched it, and it seems that's what people wanted."

Soon thousands of users—and eventually hundreds of thousands—were routing their secrets through Penet, enough traffic that Helsingius was paying more than ten thousand dollars a month in bandwidth. "I could have bought some expensive golf clubs instead, I suppose. But no hobbies are free, and this was something I believed in," Helsingius says.

For much of the early nineties, Penet became the best-known anonymity service in the world, channeling discussions ranging from sexual abuse to homosexuality to religious freedom to whistleblowing, along with a load of spam, insults, and flame wars. And Helsingius became a cypherpunk regular, the Nordic king of the remailers.

And then in 1995, Helsingius received an e-mail very much like the one that was sent to Assange at Suburbia. It was from the Scientologists.

The lawyer of the Religious Technology Center, which held the copyright on Scientology founder L. Ron Hubbard's work, was requesting that Helsingius block all messages from Penet to the Usenet group on Scientology, which contained equal parts followers and critics of the movement, on the grounds that Penet users were posting copyrighted Scientology materials to the forum. Helsingius refused, of course.

A month later, he got a call. It was the Scientologists again, and this time they told him they had reported a burglary to the L.A. police and the FBI. Their copyrighted material, they argued, had been stolen via Helsingius's data laundering service by one user with the Penet pseudonym "an144108." Six days later, the Finnish police arrived with a warrant.

Helsingius fought the legal battle for more than a year. But Finnish law wasn't ready for the Internet. A postman was legally protected from having to reveal the secrets of the letters he delivered. But a virtual carrier like Helsingius still had no shield from legal orders that require he snitch on his clients. And when it became clear that he could either do just that or go to jail, Helsingius caved. He told the Helsinki court that an144108 was linked to an alumni account at Caltech. And as the Scientologists moved on to harassing Caltech's administrators for the user's name, Helsingius decided to shut down the service. Penet had gone from a symbol of freedom of speech to a honey trap for exposing exactly the people he had hoped to protect. "When the Church of Scientology won, I knew that would have opened the floodgates for anyone to try the same attack," he says. "So I pulled the plug."

Penet had stuck a toe in the water of the Anonymous Internet, and it had come back a bloody stump. Did Assange, who no doubt followed the issue on the Cypherpunk Mailing List, learn something from the saga of

Julf? "I'm sure he got a few ideas," Helsingius says cheerfully, "About exactly how not to do things."

.-. -. .. - -... ... .--- -.-. .. -.. .- . .-- -.. ...- .-..

> At the Village Pizza shop, as they were sitting down to consume a pepperoni, Dorothy asked Jim, "So what other inventions are you working on?" Jim replied, "I've got a new idea . . . Literally REVOLUTIONARY." "Okay, Jim, which government are you planning to overthrow?," she asked, playing along.
>
> "All of them," answered Jim.

So begins a passage in an essay by James Dalton Bell, a ten-part, sixteen-thousand-word screed that hit the Cypherpunk Mailing List in 1997 like a provocateur's glove slap across the face. It was called "Assassination Politics." And like Tim May's BlackNet, it would mix cypherpunk raw materials into an elaborate, imaginary engine that would agitate the list's conversation for years.

Unlike May, however, Bell wasn't just rehearsing a thought experiment. He hoped—and in fact, still believes—that his system would someday be implemented. Nor was "Assassination Politics" an idea that confined its intended effects to mere bits. As its name implied, it was a kind of cypherpunk political institution. And it was engineered for murder.

Assassination Politics' active ingredient was anonymity. And the cypherpunk drive for untraceable digital pseudonyms had hardly ended with Julf Helsingius and the demise of Penet. In fact, long before the Finnish server's shutdown, remailers had been evolving well beyond the simple name-for-nym swapping system that Helsingius had implemented. Instead, they had started to look more and more like the Mix Network idea outlined by David Chaum more than a decade earlier, and emulated on the floor of Eric Hughes's house with slips of paper and envelopes at the first cypherpunks meeting: multiple remailers sending messages inside nested layers of encryption to prevent anyone from knowing the identities of the sender and recipient, not even the remailers themselves.

After Eric Hughes's first stab at a cypherpunk remailer, others had soon improved on his weekend's worth of Perl coding. Hal Finney, a former video game developer who had worked on pieces of PGP, designed a version of the remailer that would integrate Zimmermann's encryption software. Now a message's destination could be encrypted with a remailer's public key. That was the first step toward Chaum's ideal: No one snooping on the sender's network could see the message's final destination. And Finney's system allowed remailers to be chained together, so that a message could be encrypted with many layers of public keys and slowly unpeeled by one remailer after another until it reached its destination. With a long enough chain of remailers, none of them would be able to connect the endpoint to the source.

Cypherpunks, as Eric Hughes had declared, wrote code: Creating was always more admired within the group than theorizing. But it was Lance Cottrell, a Ph.D. student in astrophysics at the University of California, San Diego, who actually took the time to go back to David Chaum's papers and read how a Mix Network was supposed to work. Chaum had imagined facing off against an adversary no less resourceful than the cunning NSA, so he had thought many moves ahead: If a spy could see enough of the network, for instance, Chaum realized that the spook could watch both ends of a correspondence and recognize a message going in one end and then coming out the other a few moments later. Based on the timing, those messages could be spotted as one and the same.

Worse yet, using multiple layers of encryption to route the message through multiple remailers could make a clever snoop's job easier by revealing clues about how many hops remained until the message reached its destination. If a message was wrapped in multiple layers of encryption, it would get substantially larger. And every remailer that stripped away a layer of encryption and sent the message on to its next destination would shrink it down again, providing more accidental hints to anyone trying to trace the source and destination.

So Cottrell finally built in the solutions that Chaum's genius had long ago prescribed. His remailer program, which he called Mixmaster, delayed the transmission of messages until it had a certain number in reserve, and then sent them out in batches to fool any timing-based attacks. If a remailer didn't receive enough messages to mix them up and disguise their timing, it would even generate fake ones to surround and disguise the real one.

To prevent the trick of counting messages' apparent layers of encryption to predict how many hops until their destination, Mixmaster also relayed messages in packets of exactly the same size. If a message ended up too small after some layers of encryption were removed by the first remailers in the chain, the program padded it with junk data; too big, and it split the message up into equal chunks.

The cypherpunks appreciated the rigor of Cottrell's work, and Mixmaster was a hit. Soon it was running on around two thousand Unix machines around the world, pumping a flow of tens of thousands of anonymous e-mails a day, as close an approximation to Chaum's ideal Mix Network as ever existed.

Meanwhile, anonymous financial transactions were starting to feel like a reality too. Chaum's own company, called DigiCash, had implemented many of the ideas he outlined in his *Communications of the ACM* article. The result was eCash, a crypto-currency that would allow buyers to wire money untraceably to a seller. In the mid-nineties, DigiCash botched a series of deals and replaced Chaum with a new CEO before going bankrupt in 1998. But despite its lack of business success, no one doubted that Chaum's anonymous transactions technology worked—it had even been integrated into a Dutch toll road system that could reliably charge drivers without recording any trace of their identities.

Jim Bell, an engineer and chemist with a round face and large glasses, understood the power of Chaum's tools. He had once worked alongside Tim May at Intel, building early solid-state hard drives long before either of them had developed their interest in cryptography. Like May, he was a libertarian to his core. And for both men, in their own ways, the advent of anonymous messaging and anonymous payments represented not just the possibility, but the inevitability of crypto-anarchy. Bell's path to that end was just a bit bloodier.

Assassination Politics' plan was simple enough: Anyone could place a "bet" with a central organization that some specific person would die at a certain time, date, and place. Gamblers would submit their encrypted guesses by e-mail, scrubbed of identifying information by anonymous remailers and linked with a payment of untraceable digital cash. When a person died, anyone could send in the key to decrypt his or her prediction, and if it turned out that the bet had nailed the exact snuff-time of a certain person, the sender collected all the digital cash on the deceased person's head via another untraceable transfer. It would be an encrypted, anonymous, digital dead pool.

Of course, Bell implied with a wink and a nudge, no one could possibly know the date, time, and place of a certain well-known person's death better than the one who caused it. And with a large enough pile of untraceable money riding on someone's head, there would be little doubt that professional killers would get in on the game.

Suddenly, Bell imagined, the minority of Americans with strong antigovernment leanings would gain incredible power. "If only 0.1% of the population, or one person in a thousand, was willing to pay $1 to see some government slimeball dead, that would be, in effect, a $250,000 bounty on his head," Bell wrote.

> Further, imagine that anyone considering collecting that bounty could do so with the mathematical certainty that he could not be identified, and could collect the reward without meeting, or even talking to, anybody who could later identify him. Perfect anonymity, perfect secrecy, and perfect security. And that, combined with the ease and security with which these contributions could be collected, would make being an abusive government employee an extremely risky proposition. Chances are good that nobody above the level of county commissioner would even risk staying in office.
>
> Just how would this change politics in America? It would take far less time to answer, "What would remain the same?" No longer would we be electing people who will turn around

> and tax us to death, regulate us to death, or for that matter sent hired thugs to kill us when we oppose their wishes.
>
> No military?

Bell described global crypto-anarchy in rosy terms: Sure, there would be no government to protect American borders or punish crime. But the military would be unnecessary in a world where no foreign government would be able to form a military, either, and all aggressive dictators would be immediately eliminated by crypto-funded assassins. "Consider how history might have changed if we'd been able to 'bump off' Lenin, Stalin, Hitler, Mussolini, Tojo, Kim Il Sung, Ho Chi Minh, Ayatollah Khomeini, Saddam Hussein, Moammar Khadafi and various others," Bell wrote. As for fighting crime, he explained, citizens could pool together money to put out anonymous hits on criminals just as easily as politicians.

"Assassination Politics" inflamed the Cypherpunk Mailing List almost as much as the defunct Clipper Chip had. "You gleefully propose to let us all in on the immoral game of murdering those who annoy us sufficiently," wrote one user through an anonymous remailer. "I'll pass."

"Others won't," Bell responded simply.

When one cypherpunk implied that Bell was a loony extremist who thought the government was out to get him, Bell corrected him: "I . . . am out to 'get' the government."

Another scolded Bell that "by resorting to violence you are no better than the ones you purport to protect us against." Bell answered that "Assassination Politics" was only responding in kind to a violation of his own rights. And he shot back the most withering possible question in a mail list populated by libertarians: "Are you a statist?"

As for cypherpunk founding father Tim May, he never criticized Bell's morals, only his methods. May, after all, was the one who had called for a "thermonuclear cauterization" of Washington, D.C., in one essay. But why bother with the silly cover story of "predictions," May thought, when anonymity tools could allow the whole assassination market to function in the open? He had predicted online "liquidation markets" ("You slay, we pay") in the e-mail that followed his BlackNet experiment more than three years earlier.

More important, May felt, Bell lacked discretion. Even attaching his own name to "Assassination Politics" made Bell and everyone associated with him a target for the feds. "He wasn't paranoid enough in distancing himself from the project," says May. "I just stayed away from it. If I got an e-mail from Bell, I dropped it, unanswered. I didn't think he was an original thinker, and I didn't want to get involved with his lame-ass idea."

Phil Zimmermann, who had always considered the cypherpunks too radical and provocative, felt perhaps the strongest aversion of all to Bell's murderous blueprint. "He was so full of violence and anger," Zimmermann says with disgust. At one point Bell wrote to Zimmermann to ask what the inventor of PGP thought of his ideas. "I wrote him back and said that he had managed to do what no one in the U.S. government could ever do: He had made me wonder whether I never should have worked on encryption in the first place."

John Young's eyes almost seem to mist at the thought of the cypherpunks' heyday. "My beloved cypherpunks," he says with a faraway look. "They were disputatious. Endlessly disputatious. You make a point and someone immediately attacks you unfairly, cruelly, mercilessly.

"Weakling, phony, bullshitter! Everywhere they saw authority, they attacked it."

Young and his wife, Deborah Natsios, had discovered the Internet in 1993 and marveled at the massive river of information it represented. They signed up for practically every mail list and Usenet group they could find. "We felt that we had been living in the doldrums, and suddenly we were on the cutting edge," he says.

In June 1994, he discovered the cypherpunks when Tim May, John Gilmore, Eric Hughes, and Phil Zimmermann were featured in a *New York Times* magazine story that quoted chunks of both May's "Crypto-Anarchist Manifesto" and Hughes's "Cypherpunk's Manifesto." For Young, their cause sounded like a struggle for freedom and power as idealistic and critical as the occupation of Avery Hall had been two and a half decades before.

A fifty-seven-year-old architect among graduate students and young neorich Silicon Valley types, he didn't try to insert himself into the mail list's fierce technical debates. Instead, Young became a kind of obsessive cypherpunks news service, transcribing, scanning, summarizing, and posting articles to the list daily.

And there was plenty of news: Phil Zimmermann's battle to stay out of prison, the encroaching Clipper Chip, not to mention the rise of the World Wide Web and the security issues it introduced. Two years into his cypherpunk tenure, Young created Cryptome.org, a Web-based version of the service with prolific news updates and postings. Today it might be called a blog, though the term *Weblog* wouldn't be coined for another year.

Cryptome, as its name implied, was meant to be a repository for crypto-focused materials from any source where Young could grab them. One of its first posts was a publicly available 1985 paper by the Dutch researcher Wim van Eck introducing a method of reading the electromagnetic fields around computing equipment to surreptitiously pick up the data it displayed from a distance, even through walls. With the right equipment, van Eck wrote, it would be possible to snoop on someone's computer screen in a seemingly private location from a distance of more than a kilometer. Every PC with a monitor, in other words, constantly leaked data in all directions.

Worse yet, the dreaded NSA had developed a technique, code-named TEMPEST, to read those signals. Cryptome published everything Young could find about TEMPEST, and it became a leitmotif among the paranoid cypherpunks. At one point in 1996, both Assange and Bell joined in a heated discussion of whether even the water pipes and sprinkler system around a computer might propagate its electric field and spill its data even further.

Soon after "Assassination Politics" hit the list, Young would post that essay, which he still calls a "masterful piece of fiction," to Cryptome. And amid the online shouting match that surrounded the article, it was Young who first took Bell seriously.

"It's hard to tell the difference between 'Assassination Politics' and government-sponsored provocateurism, a well-documented practice to stigmatize anarchical and antiauthoritarian ventures," he wrote. "However, it takes guts and thick skin to advocate overthrow of authority, knowing that reasonable people will think you're a nut seeking celebrity martyrdom."

"Well, it's not like I'm SEEKING martyrdom," Bell responded. "But the possibilities have certainly crossed my mind. Some people have suggested, and only partially in jest, that I may be one of the system's first victims."

In fact, Bell achieved martyrdom through a more common fate. In April 1997, his home was raided by federal agents who seized his computers, his car, three assault rifles, and a .44 Magnum handgun. It turned out Bell had pursued his agenda against the feds through more direct avenues than mere essays. In the criminal complaint filed against him, he was accused of evading taxes, falsifying his social security number, and intimidating federal agents, with "Assassination Politics" as Exhibit A. Agents dug up e-mails in which he had discussed buying the ingredients for the poison ricin, and other messages suggested he was planning to drop nickel-plated carbon fiber down the air shafts of a federal building. Bell believed that the material, which agents found in large quantities at a friend's house, would become airborne, find its way into the building's computers, and short out their wiring.

Finally, he was accused of dumping a chemical called mercaptan on the rug outside an IRS office in Vancouver, Washington. The stink bomb smelled like very potent rotten cabbage.

Despite his various stunts, Bell was charged only with tax evasion and sentenced to eleven months in prison. He was out again by the next summer, but rearrested for violating his probation. Prison darkened his outlook even further. "I once believed it's too bad that there are a lot of people who work for government who are hardworking and honest people who will get hit [because of "Assassination Politics"] and it's a shame," he told *Wired* after being released in 2000. "Well, I don't believe that anymore. They are all either crooks or they tolerate crooks or they are aware of crooks among their numbers."

Eventually he would be tried again for stalking federal agents across state lines and sentenced to another decade in prison, where he spent his days demolishing computer monitors for forty-six cents an hour.

For some cypherpunks, Bell came to represent the first real victim of the Crypto Wars, and Cryptome became a resource for those following the case: It documented every step of Bell's legal ordeals more closely than any newspaper. Young collected media clippings, court documents, even anonymized messages from friends who had received word from Bell during his time in prison. He became so closely involved in the case that in Bell's first trial Young was subpoenaed as a witness, and argued on the stand that Bell had never intended to carry out any of his antigovernment plans so much as trumpet them around the Net.

In 1998, the committee for the Chrysler Award for Innovation in Design contacted Young to ask him, based on his architecture work, to nominate candidates for their annual award. Naturally, he submitted Jim Bell for "Assassination Politics," a groundbreaking work in "government accountability systems."

--- -... -.. ....-. --.- -.- -.- ..- --. .-- -. .- --.

Julian Assange continued to throw occasional jabs and quips into the mail list's discussions of everything from the NSA's TEMPEST project to "Assassination Politics" well into the late nineties. When Bell was sentenced to his first prison term and a copycat wrote up a new flavor of his murder-for-hire project aimed at celebrities, Assange posted it with the subject "Jim Bell . . . lives . . . on . . . in . . . Hollywood!"

Contributing to the melee of controversial ideas offered some light amusement for a wayward ex-con crypto-savant. But cypherpunks write code. And Julian Assange was a cypherpunk.

The story of Julf Helsingius and the Scientologists had sharply illustrated the human vulnerabilities in any encryption scheme. No matter how strong crypto may be or how cleverly the key is hidden, the cypherpunks had learned a user threatened with jail or bodily harm will cough up the goods. Cryptographers, with typical dark humor, call the method Rubber Hose Cryptanalysis: Rather than try to break an encryption scheme, simply imprison the user and beat the key out of him or her with a length of heavy tubing.

So a year after Helsingius broke under the pressure of a Finnish warrant, Assange posted a newly coded creation to another cypherpunk-friendly mail list, designed to outsmart rubber hose bullies. He called it Marutukku, after an Akkadian deity of protection, though he and his cocreators, a fellow researcher named Ralf-Philipp Weinmann and coauthor of *Underground* Suelette Dreyfus, would soon rename it, simply, "Rubberhose."

Like Zimmermann's PGP, Rubberhose was designed for activists in repressive regimes to smuggle out controversial data. But where a captured rebel activist with a laptop hard drive encrypted with PGP might be vulnerable to torturous key extraction, Rubberhose offered a clever solution. The keyholder would have multiple secret keys, each of which would appear to decrypt the entire hard drive. But the program could hide volumes of the drive like a false bottom of a box. (In fact, the effect works by spreading each encrypted portion of the data evenly over the entire hard drive to give the appearance that one volume fills the entire capacity, with no room for more secrets.)

When the torturer pulls out the rubber hose, the user simply pretends to give in, handing over a key that decrypts a volume full of decoy data. Thanks to Rubberhose's unique properties, the torturer should believe he's seen the full contents of the drive and grudgingly release the activist.

The program included an antiauthoritarian mission statement: "Entrenched moguls . . . label the activists as trouble-makers or whistle blowers to justify misusing them," it read. "Where there is injustice, we like to upset the status quo too, and to support others who want to do the same. Our motto is 'let's make a little trouble.'"

But there was a darker side to Rubberhose, one that reveals something about Assange's style of cold calculation. Say the torturers know that the user encrypted the hard drive with Rubberhose. Then there's little she (Assange, in cryptographers' fashion, calls her Alice) can do to prove that she's given up all the keys. With the understanding that her torturers will beat her endlessly regardless of what she does, Alice has little incentive to give up information that incriminates her comrades to save herself. Like a cyanide capsule hidden in a spy's tooth, Rubberhose actually motivates users to sacrifice themselves rather than give up their friends' information. As Assange wrote:

> With Rubberhose-style deniable cryptography, the benefits to a group member from choosing tactic 1 (defection) are subdued, because they will never be able to convince their interrogators that they have defected. Rational individuals that are "otherwise loyal" to the group, will realise the minimal gains to be made in choosing defection and choose tactic 2 (loyalty), instead.

Or as he put it more simply in the Rubberhose documentation: "Alice certainly isn't in for a very nice time of it. (Although she's far more likely to protect her data.)"

Despite Rubberhose's cleverness, Assange wasn't content to create mere tools. But it would take him another decade to evolve from the creation of his own equivalent of PGP to his own equivalent of BlackNet. He spent two years traveling the world, shaking off the anger and frustration of his years in legal limbo. In 1999, he registered Leaks.org in a moment of foresight, but had no clear idea of what to do with it and left it fallow for years longer.

When Assange returned to the Cypherpunk Mailing List after his travels, he seemed to have taken on a new political radicalism. The list's popularity was waning and it was choked with spam. In his second-to-last message he posted the following, which seems almost a rebuttal to Tim May's libertarian dismissal of the "clueless 95%." "The 95% of the population which comprise the flock have never been my target, and neither should they be yours," he wrote. "It's the 2.5 percent at either end of the normal that I find in my sights, one to be cherished and the other to be destroyed."

That same liberal radicalism drove him to give up on formal education at military-tinged Melbourne University. And finally it pushed him to write the essay that would become his own "Crypto-Anarchist Manifesto." Fresh from the influence of university, he typed it up in the font and style of an academic math paper and posted it to his blog with the name "Conspiracy as Governance."

The paper described authoritarian regimes as collections of nodes connected by lines of communication that depend on technology for their survival: Internet, phones, fax machines. And the key to toppling those structures was to cut those data-lines, Assange wrote.

> When we look at an authoritarian conspiracy as a whole, we see a system of interacting organs, a beast with arteries and veins whose blood may be thickened and slowed until it falls, stupefied; unable to sufficiently comprehend and control the forces in its environment.
>
> Later we will see how new technology and insights into the psychological motivations of conspirators can give us practical methods for preventing or reducing important communication between authoritarian conspirators, foment strong resistance to authoritarian planning and create powerful incentives for more humane forms of governance.

In fact, "later" never came. The essay gave no explanation of how technology could be used for cutting those communication lines. But it did say, in what seems to be a jab at Jim Bell, that killing conspiratorial leaders wasn't the answer. "The act of assassination—the targeting of visible individuals, is the result of mental inclinations honed for the pre-literate societies in which our species evolved," Assange wrote.

Later that month in his blog, Assange would write the solution to the puzzle of "Conspiracy as Governance," like an answer key at the back of a textbook. The solution was leaks.

> The more secretive or unjust an organization is, the more leaks induce fear and paranoia in its leadership and planning coterie. This must result in minimization of efficient internal communications mechanisms (an increase in cognitive "secrecy tax") and

> consequent system-wide cognitive decline resulting in decreased ability to hold onto power as the environment demands adaption.

Leaks had a twofold purpose in Assange's view: They empowered the regime's enemies with damning facts. But more important, they induced the regime to stop communicating internally, a kind of calcification of its circulatory system more deadly than any outside enemy. "Hence in a world where leaking is easy, secretive or unjust systems are nonlinearly hit relative to open, just systems," Assange wrote.

Which leaves one final, unspoken question: how to make leaks happen? That's a puzzle Assange had worked out years before, hiding the answer in his introduction to the pseudo-autobiographical *Underground*.

He quotes Oscar Wilde: "Man is least himself when he talks in his own person. Give him a mask and he'll tell you the truth."

While Assange theorized about leaks, Young was busy springing them.

After years of merely digging up public documents and reposting news, the anonymous tips began to flow. In May 1999, an anonymous e-mail referred Young to an article, already pulled from the Web at the time of the e-mail, in an issue of *Executive Intelligence Review*, which listed 116 names of MI6 officials sent to the newsweekly, along with locations and dates showing their movements across the globe. Young posted the file to Cryptome and it was downloaded tens of thousands of times within days.

The next year, Young received a UK MI5 report from an anonymous source, detailing the surveillance of a Libyan diplomat in London that British intelligence suspected of being a spy. The paper accused the diplomat of being involved in the murder of a UK-based Libyan dissident. It was marked "TOP SECRET DELICATE SOURCE UK EYES." Young published it in its entirety.

A few months later, Young published a list of six hundred Japanese intelligence agents who were being sent abroad after the failure of Japan's Public Security Investigation Agency to gather sufficient intelligence to shut down the Aum Shinrikyo cult that carried out a sarin gas attack on the Tokyo subway, killing thirteen people. The list was titled "The Most Incompetent Intelligence Agency in the World." Young received the list anonymously at first, but the source, a PSIA agent named Hironari Noda, revealed his identity within days.

The Japanese leak was followed by a list of 2,619 CIA informants from an anonymous sender. Young posted the names alphabetically with every source's address. Within a week the leaker outed himself as the journalist Gregory Douglas, who had been given a trove of files by an ex-CIA agent to be published at his death.

Young's next scoop came from old-fashioned investigative reporting. He filed a Freedom of Information Act request to the NSA that it release all nonclassified data on TEMPEST, the electromagnetic spying trick that allowed intelligence agents to read screens through walls. The NSA first denied his request but gave in on appeal. He published hundreds of pages of detailed descriptions of the mechanisms behind the NSA's epic hack. Much of it was painstakingly transcribed into HTML from the paper documents.

By 2006, Young had received two more leaks outing MI6 agents and was publishing controversial images of secure government facilities on a regular basis. He had gotten the attention of the three letter agencies: NSA programs crawled his website daily to monitor his material, and he'd received visits from the FBI and calls from DHS officials.

At some point, he also got the attention of Julian Assange. The PGP-encrypted e-mail hit Young's in-box in early October 2006: "You knew me under another name from cypherpunk days. I am involved in a project that you may have feeling for. I will not mention its name yet in case you feel you are not able to be involved.

"The project is a mass document leaking project that requires someone with backbone to hold the .org domain registration. We would like that person to be someone who is not privy to the location of the master servers which are otherwise obscured by technical means.

". . . Will you be that person?"

Young agreed, and two months later he found himself subscribed to an internal mailing list for developers on Assange's secretive project. Every e-mail on the list began with the message: "This is a restricted internal development mailinglist for w-i-k-i-l-e-a-k-s-.-o-r-g. Please do not mention that word directly in these discussions; refer instead to 'WL.'"

The list argued over everything from the logo for the site—originally a mole breaking through a wall in front of a phalanx of dark bureaucratic figures—to potential funding sources and figureheads. The group approached Chinese-American dissident professor Xiao Qiang, Ben Laurie, a cryptographer who had developed an open-source version of the SSL protocol for encrypting Web traffic, and perhaps most significantly Daniel Ellsberg, the leaker upon whom all their greatest hopes were modeled.

"We have come to the conclusion that fomenting a world wide movement of mass leaking is the most cost effective political intervention available to us," read the group's e-mail inviting Ellsberg to join their advisory board. "New technology and cryptographic ideas permit us to not only encourage document leaking, but to facilitate it directly on a mass scale. We intend to place a new star in the political firmament of man."

Ellsberg never responded to that message. But the e-mail to the archetypal twentieth-century leaker crystallized everything Assange had learned from the cypherpunks: WikiLeaks would share all of David Chaum's, Tim May's and Phil Zimmermann's beliefs in the power of cryptography to effect political change. It had all the ambitious complexity of "Assassination Politics," with its illegality and violence carefully excised. And it had learned from Cryptome's model of soliciting and anonymizing leaks as a self-propelled weapon against authority.

John Young's tenure as a WikiLeaks adviser was short. Just two weeks after Young joined the mail list, Assange suggested attempting to raise five million dollars from sources like the Soros Foundation. Like my innocuous question about Young's childhood when we met in an Upper East Side restaurant, the notion seemed to flip a switch in Young's unpredictable mind.

The Cryptome founder responded with a series of increasingly angry and sarcastic e-mails, sent too fast to even allow responses from the other WikiLeakers. "The CIA would be the most likely $5M funder. Soros is suspected of being a conduit for black money to dissident groups racketeering for such payola," he wrote bitterly, suggesting that WikiLeaks attempt to raise a hundred million dollars from the CIA instead.

"Fuck your cute hustle and disinformation campaign against legitimate dissent. Same old shit, working for the enemy," Young added, vowing to leak the entire mail list on Cryptome—which he soon did. He signed off, "In solidarity with fuck em all."

Assange responded shortly thereafter. "J., We are going to fuck them all."

Then he unsubscribed John Young from the list.

In February 2011, I e-mailed a request to a Sheridan, Oregon, detention facility to speak with Jim Bell, who was serving the last years of the same sentence for a parole violation that had put him in prison earlier in the decade.

The month after my e-mail, I received a seven-page letter from Bell, single-spaced, written on a typewriter, and virtually free of typos. The letter was focused on two points: First, that Bell had been the subject of a fraudulent show trial, and that he wanted me to request that *Forbes*'s internal counsel help him prove that the Ninth Circuit Court had forged records of an entire appeals case that ruled against him without his knowledge or participation.

Second, Bell wrote that while in the Special Housing Unit, also known as the "hole," in 2009, he had made a "truly phenomenal discovery in the areas of Chemistry, Physics, and Material Science, of total value well in excess of <u>$100 Billion</u>." (The underlining is his.)

Although he didn't remember Assange's comments on the Cypherpunk Mailing List, he expressed his admiration for WikiLeaks, and wrote that after being released from prison and becoming enormously wealthy in the following six months to one year, he planned to donate somewhere between a hundred thousand and a million dollars to the group.

In later letters he would explain that he had invented a new form of fiber-optic cable that would transmit data 33 percent faster than conventional fiber optics, and planned to obtain five thousand patents after he was released, five times more than Thomas Edison. "It will affect virtually every science, every field of engineering, thousands or even tens of thousands of products," he wrote. "You will find this hard, even impossible to believe, yet it is quite true."

Bell was right: I didn't believe him. But I did approach *Forbes*'s counsel to ask her assistance in pursuing Bell's legal case. She read Bell's letter, then checked his legal file, which showed that he had fired practically every court-appointed lawyer ever assigned to him—little wonder that he had botched his appeals. It also showed he had filed fifty-one lawsuits against the government while in prison—nearly all dismissed immediately. She wanted nothing to do with it.

I wrote back to Bell apologizing that I couldn't offer legal help, and asking whether he still planned to pursue "Assassination Politics" when he was released.

He mailed back an even longer letter, mostly chastising me for failing to help him expose the government's fraud and accusing me of being in the pocket of the authorities. "Wake up! Wake up! Wake up!" he wrote. "You need to tell your editorial counsel that I have given you a very specific example of a crime the government committed against me. . . . If he isn't fully behind assisting you in exposing this crime, then he must be part of the problem."

And then he wrote about "Assassination Politics."

> Unfortunately, you reveal a little of your biases by saying, "Do you still hope/plan . . ." Implying I did so, etc. Nope! At the time I wrote AP, I presumed that I wouldn't be the one to implement it, and that is, indeed, WHY I publicized the idea with my own name.

Bell went on to write, however, that he would soon be a "hero of scientific and technological progress," and that his "inventions and technologies will usher in a boom unlike the world has ever seen. I've already probably solved the 'energy crisis' a dozen times over." As the world realized the brilliance of his inventions, "thousands of people" would reassess his ideas, including "Assassination Politics." If no one else were to implement the contract killer system, it would be easy enough for him to do it himself, he wrote.

> It would be as simple as directing a work-group, or (more likely) forming a new division in my set of corporations. The AP system is sufficiently similar to [the] insurance or gambling industry, and a dozen lawyers or two will ensure that it stays within the laws of the region it is sited at.
>
> . . . [T]he government (and those employed by it) should defend their continued existence (life) in the face of what they have done to America's finances.
>
> Interesting benchmark: The French Revolution in [1794] resulted in the guillotining of about 19,000 persons, of a total population in France of 25 million people. Adjusted for a population of America of about 300 million, that would be about 230,000 persons. Do you really believe that those in the [U.S. government] would have run up that $14 trillion debt (actually a lot more, depending on the kind of analysis) if they knew that at some point in the near future, 230,000 of their kind would be killed?

As this book went to press, Jim Bell was scheduled for release from prison on March 12, 2012.

CHAPTER 4

THE ONION ROUTERS

Jacob Appelbaum drops a black, hard plastic container the size of a small suitcase on the conference table in a sterile-chic conference room in MIT's Media Lab, a six-story structure of sleek white walls and glass that resembles a giant iPod. Twenty or so motley hackers sitting around the table and lounging in the corners of the room suddenly look up from their laptops. Appelbaum cracks the box open to show off a large chunk of white, ruggedized hardware encased in foam. The group admires it in hushed tones, slowly drawing closer.

The twenty-seven-year-old stands in the center of the room, six feet tall, with neatly parted black hair, Italian glasses, and tattoos that run up his left arm. His T-shirt is a baseball jersey with the word KINSEY written across the back and the number three, a reference to his position on the Kinsey Institute's sexual persuasion scale. (Zero indicates heterosexual, six homosexual.) "This," he says, chewing a piece of raspberry chocolate with studied nonchalance, "is what I've been working on."

Until that moment in the Tor Hackfest, things had been getting dangerously technical. Tor is one of the world's most widely used and perhaps most secure anonymity programs. And Nick Mathewson, Tor's grinning, round-faced, ponytailed chief architect and codirector, had kicked off the day by dropping the room into the deep end of the cryptographic swimming pool. The geekery had gotten so thick that even some of Tor's modern-day cypherpunks and volunteer coders, loath as they might have been to admit it, might just have gotten lost. Within minutes, Mathewson, wearing a sport jacket over a Tor T-shirt over a dwarfish potbelly, was delving into security issues like "epistemic attacks" and "Byzantine fault tolerances." By the time he sat down, still grinning, a growing fraction of the room seemed baffled or possibly bored.

Appelbaum's presence, on the other hand, is as much guerrilla as geek. He's Tor's field researcher, unofficial revolutionary, and man on the ground in countries from Qatar to Brazil. And he knows the appeal of a sexy piece of hardware. After instantly acquiring the room's attention, Appelbaum explains that the device his small audience is ogling is a satellite modem, one that he's just rented with the aim of figuring out how to make Tor accessible to those in the Middle East who need to use satellite connections to access the Internet.

The project is not theoretical. For the prior three weeks, an entire civilization has been turning itself upside down. The wave of revolts that overthrew the government of Tunisia and ousted President Hosni Mubarak from Egypt has just spilled into massive protests in Morocco, Libya, and Bahrain. And while the rest of the world has been lauding the power of Twitter and Facebook to organize and catalyze those movements, the digerati in this room know that the protesters' connection to the Internet has a more sinister side. Unless they use anonymity tools like Tor, every dissident who plugs into those online services can have his or her information perpetually monitored by governments that don't hesitate to knock down doors and haul away political enemies on a whim. Hence Appelbaum's latest science experiment: He aims to shield the identities of dissidents and journalists who use satellite connections to get online even when the government has locked down, throttled, and surveilled their bandwidth.

But there's a problem, Appelbaum says. Tor hides a user's IP address, but a satellite modem's communication protocols reveal its location to the satellite provider. "Even if you use Tor, someone can still find all the users in a given country," Appelbaum cautions. "That means you need to connect to the network and then drive fifty kilometers, or you get the cruise missile."

"If you need GPS spoofing, my people in Zurich can help with that," offers one clean-cut researcher with expertise in hacking pacemakers and cardiac defibrillators.

"OK," Appelbaum says in an unimpressed tone that implies spoofing GPS is about as difficult as microwaving a burrito.

The gaggle of hackers pepper him with questions about the modem's specs and the company he rented it from. "I gave them your information, Mike," he says, turning to another Tor programmer with a mock-sheepish smile. "Sorry."

No one needs to ask why Appelbaum wouldn't hand out his own personal data. Even among Tor's security-conscious crowd, Appelbaum is an exemplar of privacy paranoia in its purest form. And lately, for good reason. Because aside from his day job as a programmer and evangelist for Tor, Appelbaum moonlights as a freelance Internet freedom fighter, one that many governments, including America's, might like to see disappear.

Just the night before the MIT gathering, for instance, the young hacker was probing the digital infrastructure of Libya, where the military was busy firing live ammunition at defenseless crowds that included women and children. Muammar Qaddafi's dictatorship had shut down most of the Internet, leaving only its military and government connections online. So Appelbaum used a tool he created called BlockFinder to list which branches of the country's networks remained online and broadcast their IP addresses to any and all hacker allies. "Systems that are online in Libya are probably worth scanning; those are the systems required or used by the current government oppressors," he wrote on Twitter. He suggested digging into one connection in Palermo, Italy, that connected North Africa with the Internet at large, what he identified as "the Arab dictator's favorite uplink."

"Now is the time for all good black hats to come to the aid of humanity," he added, throwing in a riff off a line from the film *Full Metal Jacket*: "I wanted to visit exotic Libya . . . I wanted to meet interesting and stimulating people of an ancient culture . . . and own them."

"Black hats," of course, are hackers who engage in usually illegal tactics of intrusive or destructive hacking. And to "own" a target is hacker jargon for penetrating or taking control of its systems. As in a message Appelbaum had posted just a few hours earlier: "Shooting unarmed protesters in the head? Bahrain's government has demonstrated that they are over the line. It's ethical to own them."

During the protests in Egypt a few weeks earlier, Appelbaum had put out another call for help in tracking down President Hosni Mubarak to prevent him from fleeing the country in the midst of the revolution there. "I'm looking for Mubarak or his handlers' cell phone numbers—if you've got them, I'll track them," he wrote.

"Mubarak is trying really hard to not end up like Nicolae Ceauşescu," he added, referencing the Romanian dictator who was executed by a firing squad after a two-hour trial during the country's 1989 revolution. "Good luck with that, you son of a bitch!"

Appelbaum later explains to me that a technique known as an HLR query can approximate a user's location on a carrier's network. Did he ever successfully use that trick to pin down Mubarak's location? The young hacker smiles and changes the subject.

But organizing penetrations of Libyan Internet infrastructure and tracking dictators' cell phones, as legally questionable as those feats may be, aren't the most pressing reason for the young hacktivist's privacy obsession. Appelbaum has ties to WikiLeaks. Not simply as a nameless volunteer, but as one of its most die-hard supporters and its most prominent American face. In late 2010, Julian Assange told *Rolling Stone* that "Tor's importance to WikiLeaks cannot be understated" and that "Jake has been a tireless promoter behind the scenes of our cause." In late 2010, when Assange seemed to be on the brink of long-term jail awaiting questioning for alleged sex crimes, one WikiLeaks staffer told me he hoped Appelbaum might even be the favored successor to Assange in WikiLeaks' hierarchy.

None of which is news to the U.S. government. Several months earlier, Twitter revealed that the company had been directed by the Department of Justice to hand over Appelbaum's data, along with that of two others associated with Julian Assange's secret-spilling group, likely part of a larger dragnet to build a conspiracy charge against WikiLeaks staffers. Since then, the threat of an indictment that could put Appelbaum in prison for a significant portion of the rest of his life has been hanging just a few inches above his neck.

Even here at the MIT Hackfest, that threat makes its presence felt rather awkwardly when, as Appelbaum tells it, he runs into a State Department official later in the day, a clean-shaven man dressed in a gray fleece. Appelbaum greets him politely. "You probably want to shoot me in the head," he says with a wary grin.

"We have other people who do that," the official says, also smiling.

Neither of them seems quite sure whether this is a joke.

At least twice now in the evolution of leaking, it was the U.S. government, specifically the U.S. military, and even more specifically the Defense Advanced Research Projects Agency, or DARPA, that built the machine that would ultimately hemorrhage the government's secrets.

DARPA, after all, created the prototype for the Internet, that massive secret-siphoning neural network. And along with the State Department and the Naval Research Laboratory, DARPA would also build and fund Tor, the tool that WikiLeaks would use to effect the largest-ever public data breaches against the military and the State Department, exactly the institutions that created it.

Stranger yet is that even after Tor was allegedly used by Bradley Manning and potentially many others to anonymously leak massive troves of highly secret U.S. government documents, government agencies haven't withdrawn their support for the tool any more than they've withdrawn from the Internet. Because just as government agents can't survive without the Internet's information-sharing powers, they also sometimes need the ability to be completely anonymous online. Not simply private, but strongly, cryptographically anonymous.

Tor offers that cryptographic anonymity to its users with the same principles as David Chaum's Mix Network, but stripped down and built to function at Web speed. Like a Mix, the software doesn't necessarily prevent anyone from seeing what a Web user is writing or reading. Instead, it's designed to prevent anyone from knowing who is doing the writing or the reading. That's because if a CIA informant in Iran is visiting the agency's website to drop a tip, the government spying on the informant's connection doesn't need to know what information he's passing on: Even if the data he shares is encrypted, just the knowledge that he was talking to American spooks is likely to earn him a knock on the door from the country's secret police.

The State Department funds Tor to communicate with political dissidents from Iran to Myanmar and to help them access the unfettered Web, a key element in Secretary of State Hillary Clinton's mission of so-called "Internet Freedom." The U.S. military uses Tor for open-source intelligence, gleaning foreign policy or military strategy from other countries' websites without tipping them off to a spook's presence. Corporations use Tor to facilitate industrial espionage or, in some cases, prevent it. One example offered by Tor's executive director Andrew Lewman: IBM hosts a copy of the U.S. Patent and Trademark Office database. If someone at Hewlett-Packard wants to browse sensor designs in that database without tipping off its biggest competitor, it had better use a thick cloak of anonymity.

But Tor can also work in reverse: A website implementing a Tor feature called a Hidden Service can mask its location and allow users to find it in the Web's ether without anyone knowing where the site is physically hosted. To access a Tor Hidden Service, the user has to run Tor, too, so both the visitor's physical location and that of the site are completely masked. Neither reveals anything other than the information they're sharing, like two trench-coated men handing off a briefcase in a dark parking structure.

And like any setting where packages are exchanged in the shadows, crime has found its way in too. It's no secret that Tor is used by child pornographers and black hat hackers. Seconds after installing the program a user can untraceably access sites like Silk Road, an online bazaar for hard drugs and weapons, or one of several sites that claim to offer untraceable contract killings. But Tor is also used by the FBI to infiltrate those lawbreakers' ranks without being detected, and for cybersecurity researchers to test websites without tipping them off that they're being patrolled by

McAfee or Symantec. "When I'm speaking to a law enforcement crowd and someone complains that Tor is used for crime, I find an agent who uses Tor every day for fighting crime, and I try to get those two to talk to each other," says Tor's director, Roger Dingledine.

Technically, Tor faces the same tricky paradox Chaum aimed to solve in 1981: Location equals identity. If someone can locate your computer, they know where you live or work, which is a trivial step from knowing who you are. So Tor needs to accomplish the Internet's main task—mapping out connections between people so that data can travel to and fro as quickly as possible—without letting anyone in the system know where those two ends lie.

Like its users, Tor operates in a state of functional paranoia. It assumes that its network of messengers is littered with traitorous spies, and no single node can be trusted. So taking a cue from Chaum's original Mix idea, the data is triple-encrypted. No one node can figure out the entire route. Each node unscrambles one of those three layers, as if each of the series of messengers removes one opaque skin from an onion to find the address of their next contact written on the surface underneath. Hence Tor's name, an abbreviation for "The Onion Router."

Since Tor employs the uniquely targeted scrambling of public key encryption, each layer of onion skin is wrapped in a way that can be unwrapped only by the next node. All the messengers have keys to a layer of the onion, but they can only open the layers specifically addressed to them. So that first node in the chain might see that an Iranian informant wants to visit a website, but it can only open the layer of encryption that tells it to pass the rest of the onion on to a node in Cupertino. Even if Iran's secret police control that relay, they'll never know that the data jumped from California on to Berlin and finally to the CIA website in Langley, Virginia.

But is Tor secure enough to stymie the CIA itself, along with its brainier cousin, the NSA? The typical answer to that question is one I hear from Chris Soghoian, a Soros Foundation fellow who lives in Washington, D.C., and spends his days fighting for stronger privacy and anonymity regulations. "Have you got a better alternative?"

Tor, as Soghoian and most other security researchers will tell you, is not secure. For those who have watched the world of cryptography long enough, nothing is. Every crypto-system has hidden weaknesses that another cleverer cryptographer will ferret out. And almost any scheme can be cracked with enough time and computing power. But "Tor has been torn apart and banged on for years," says Soghoian. "Every year flaws are found and fixed. Because of that, it's better than the rest. It's the only solidly peer-reviewed anonymity system for real-time communications."

In fact, Tor has been shown to be vulnerable to a slew of brilliant attacks, most found by Tor staffers themselves. One, for instance, involves a website feeding the user a sequence of data that can be recognized coming out the other side of the network to match up a user with his online activities. Another uses flaws in common file-sharing programs to reveal the IP addresses of the programs' users and then extrapolate the addresses of others. A third depends on the temperature of the servers: Hotter computers run faster, and an attacker can start to recognize and analyze Tor Hidden Services based on fingerprinting those timing differences.

Whether those attacks could be performed at scale to identify a leaker remains an open question. If anyone could perform massive cryptographic and signals intelligence feats on large networks, it would be the NSA. For now, there's no known real-world case of Tor being broken to identify a user. (All signs still indicate, for instance, that it was Adrian Lamo, not the NSA, that ultimately fingered Bradley Manning, the Tor user federal agencies would have liked to have identified more than practically any other.) Even many of those who are most skeptical of Tor's security suggest that users seeking absolute anonymity should still use the tool along with other, commercial proxy services to create extra layers of defense.

But it can't be denied that Tor has a fundamental flaw, and one that is also its greatest strength: Any agency or individual can set up a Tor node on a computer. By subtly starting up hundreds or thousands of nodes around the world, the U.S. government might be able to get access to a large enough fraction of the comings and goings of Tor users to map out their communications and find their endpoints. To do so, of course, would mean ingeniously disguising the nodes and competing with every other government that seeks to track the network, many of whom might not be keen on sharing their intelligence.

In fact, Tor's community-built properties are fundamental to its functioning. They were, in some ways, the seed that germinated from an idea deep inside the military's institutional mind into the public Tor Project as it exists today. And if onion routing's inventors hadn't needed to share the technology beyond the walls of the Pentagon to make that volunteer system work, it might never have become a software Frankenstein's monster, directing mayhem directly back at the agencies that created it.

. ...- . -.. .-. --- -.- . .--. -- .... - .--- .... -.- .--.

When Paul Syverson, the researcher known by many today as the "father of onion routing," arrived at the Naval Research Laboratory in 1989, most of his degrees were in philosophical logic, not mathematics or computer science. As an undergraduate bumping up for the first time against ideas from epistemic logic—a field that seeks to rigorously answer formalized questions about what can be known—he pored over the puzzle books of Raymond Smullyan, the eccentric writer, pianist, and magic performer. (Smullyan once dazzled the audience on Johnny Carson's *Tonight Show* with questions like this one: Say you have three opaque containers of coins, one full of nickels, one of dimes, one of both types of coin mixed together. All three have been mislabeled with one of the others' names. How many coins do you have to pull at random from each jar to properly rearrange the labels? The surprise answer: just one coin from the container labeled "mixed." Late night television audiences were clearly more entertained by epistemic logic puzzles in 1982 than they would be today.)

Smullyan would later sit on Syverson's dissertation committee at Indiana University, and often wandered into the young graduate student's office to pull cards out of Syverson's ears or rehearse logical scenarios with the younger researcher. Smullyan's books permutated ever-more-complex versions of a type captured by a well-known riddle, the one about asking directions from two men, one who always tells the truth and one who always lies. His increasingly tangled conundrums were populated by vampires who always lie, humans who always tell the truth, insane humans who think they're telling the truth but lie, insane vampires who think they lie but actually tell the truth, and some in-between actors whose truth-telling is utterly unpredictable.

So it's fitting that when Syverson approached the problem in 1995 of how to route the Web's information anonymously, his solution would depend on tolerating many thousands of untrustworthy characters.

Syverson, with fellow NRL researchers David Goldschlag and Michael Reed, was determined to build a Mix Network for the Web. But they faced the same challenge that inspired Lance Cottrell's Mixmaster e-mail anonymity program: Clever spies can correlate messages going in and going out of a network based on timing. "The bad guy watches three bytes go in and three bytes come out," says Syverson. "When the data is moving in real time, it's an analysis that's easy to perform, and hard to defeat." Lance Cottrell had solved that problem in Mixmaster by designing the program to collect individual messages for hours or even days, the better to obscure their timing. On the Web, where users hardly tolerate a second's delay, that approach would fall flat.

So the researchers suggested a less-than-elegant fix: a network so big, with data going into and coming out of thousands of nodes, that matching up the head and tail of every connection in real time becomes a matter of finding two ends of a needle in a haystack full of bits of needles. "If your adversary is in a position to watch both ends of the communication, he wins," says Syverson. "But if the adversary can't see those ends, he doesn't even know where to start looking."

And the most practical way to expand the network? Invite everyone to join it. The NRL team imagined a volunteer network run by a diverse crowd of hosts, each controlling its own piece of the mix of relay nodes. In that populist system, no user can trust every node. But every user can be relatively sure that no single host—not even the system's creator, the navy—is watching the entire network and tracing users' paths. (Today Tor has more than three thousand nodes, each receiving and sending off data packets in unpredictable paths, and Tor's organizers hope to someday broaden the network of relays to tens or even hundreds of thousands more.)

To work, that volunteer mix didn't just need to be big. It needed to be diverse. Lots of unlikely bedfellows hosting nodes—everyone from the U.S. intelligence agencies to cypherpunks—attract a motley network of users. And without a diverse set of users, an anonymity network is hardly anonymous; if only the navy used Tor, it wouldn't take much Smullyanian logic to figure that anyone using Tor would be part of the navy. For Tor to offer meaningful anonymity, the military had to set it free, to be both maintained and used by everyone from hackers to revolutionaries to criminals to G-men.

In that sense, even though Tor was first created behind government walls, there could never be the sort of debate over the public distribution of the strong anonymity tool that took place over the public access to strong encryption in the 1990s. Even if the government had sensed that the software it was funding for masking users' identities was a dangerous weapon, it couldn't keep that program to itself. To be effective, Tor had to be shared with everyone—even those who would use it against the very institutions that created it.

The Naval Research Lab's idea of recruiting a volunteer network wasn't Tor's cleverest trick—just a formalization of what Mix Networks had already been doing since the early cypherpunk days. But to work at Web speed, Tor also needed a new, faster way to route data at Web velocity through its three-stop circuit. Chaum's original idea used public key encryption to scramble the data it sent from one node to the next, a process that took as much as a thousand times too long for real-time traffic.

So the NRL team suggested a shortcut. Old-fashioned symmetric key encryption, where the same key is used to encrypt and decrypt data on both ends, is far faster than the public key encryption invented by MIT's cryptographers in 1977. But symmetric key encryption is less secure, in that the keys have to travel to their destination and might be eavesdropped.

If, however, those symmetric keys are themselves encrypted with public key encryption and only decrypted once they reach the nodes in the network, they can be securely set in place, well guarded and ready to decrypt data far faster than public key encryption keys.

In Syverson's system, each node would use slow, secure, public key encryption to generate public keys for encrypting and private keys for decrypting. Then the user's software would triple-encrypt the first parcel of data with the public keys of three randomly selected nodes in far-flung places around the globe, just like any Mix Network. But the first message sent along that triple-bounce path wouldn't be any real communication from the user. It would simply hold three more keys, of the old-fashioned symmetric key encryption sort. Only once those new, speedy private keys were placed safely in the three nodes around the globe, laying out a path to their destination, would the user start sending packets of real content bundled in three layers of symmetric key encryption that the relays could peel off, one after another, at blinding Web speed. (In fact, Tor today repeats that entire preparatory process every ten minutes, repeatedly laying down new paths with public key encryption to offer one more safeguard against surveillance.)

Syverson coined the term *onion routing* because the first data package to travel across the network was less like a triple-wrapped rock with a hard center of information than an onion, with nothing but layers all the way down. It would be a carefully wrapped envelope with no message inside. The crucial data held by that envelope, like the sweetness of a Georgia Vidalia, was in the skin itself.

.-- -.. .--- -.-- -. . -..- -.- .- .--- - ..- .... ..- ... .-.

Even with the navy's innovations, Tor was still just an idea. But it bounced around Syverson's brain for years like so many triple-encrypted data packets, well after Goldschlag and Reed had moved on to other research topics. So when Syverson received a grant from DARPA to revive the project in 2001, he needed help: The father of onion routing, despite his logical prowess, had never quite learned to code.

Syverson had met Roger Dingledine a year before at the Privacy Enhancing Technologies conference in Berkeley, where the recent MIT graduate was presenting his own digital-freedom-focused brainchild, a project Dingledine called Free Haven. Dingledine, a ponytailed and apple-cheeked savant with strangely unblinking eyes and a robotically logical manner of speaking, explained that Free Haven would function as a distributed, uncensorable publishing system. He pointed to examples like the property records that had been destroyed in the Kosovo refugee crisis in the late nineties: Kosovars displaced by Serbian attacks returned to their land to find that no one had any formal proof of who owned what. "Someone didn't want those records around," says Dingledine. "If Free Haven had existed, there might have been an archive of that data. And it wouldn't have been vulnerable to political, social, or corporate pressure."

Dingledine's project, outlined in his master's thesis at MIT, depended on distributing information among many anonymous volunteer publishers and constantly grading how reliably each node served up data. To Syverson, it sounded like a project near to Tor's heart.

By the time Syverson found Dingledine, the young hacker had joined a Cambridge start-up called Reputation.com and was using ideas analogous to his Free Haven reliability system to grade the reputation of suppliers in business-to-business commerce. The system presaged the reputation network used by eBay to rate buyers and sellers, and offered plenty of intellectual challenge. But it lacked the political drive of Dingledine's anticensorship work. So when Syverson asked Dingledine to help him implement a real-world tool for creating total anonymity, Dingledine was ready to jump. Syverson was soon using DARPA's money to contract work from the younger researcher, and then convinced him to leave Reputation.com outright.

It wasn't long before Dingledine's role at Tor started to exert a gravitational pull on his closest college friend and co-worker at Reputation.com, Nick Mathewson.

A few years earlier, Mathewson and Dingledine had immediately bonded as freshmen at MIT. Mathewson had grown up watching and rewatching *Tron* on VHS, fiddling with PGP, and reading the Cypherpunk Mailing List archives. Dingledine, raised in North Carolina, had found early dial-up access to the Internet through the University of North Carolina at Chapel Hill's VAX system and created an architecture for networked, text-based dungeon worlds where users could meet, talk, and embark on fantastical quests.

The two teenage hackers moved into MIT's Senior House, a dormitory with a legendarily bizarre culture, captured best by its official emblem: a star-spangled-banner-emblazoned skull with the words "Only life can kill you" in its teeth and the motto "Sport Death" written below. That two-word phrase, once found written in pen in the MIT library copy of Hunter S. Thompson's *Fear and Loathing on the Campaign Trail '72*, denoted an attitude of pushing life to its limits, whether in politics, recreation, or hacking. "Sport Death" culture mixed MIT nerdery into a stew of anarchism, leather jackets, drugs, and polyamorous sex. Music blared at all hours, boxes of computer components often littered the hallways, and sleep was generally considered an occasional nuisance.

Mathewson painted the larger two walls of his room bright red, and the other two black. His theory was that the red walls' psychosomatic effect would keep him alert and reduce his sleep requirements, with the black ones offering enough contrast to shock his brain into hyperactivity again every time he returned his gaze to the red. Mathewson and Dingledine spent much of their college lives in their rooms, hacking away at a half-dozen computers, each kept running constantly. Dingledine named his flock of PCs and servers after *Lord of the Rings* characters, while Mathewson named his after personae from the songs of Frank Zappa. "Most of the interesting things I did in college, I did in software," says Mathewson.

Mathewson and Dingledine subscribed to Sport Death's antiauthoritarian politics, and they lived by the mantra embodied by Tim May and Eric Hughes: "Cypherpunks write code." Don't spend your time arguing with politicians in the physical world about the rules of the digital one. Create the digital world and, with it, your own rules. "Network protocols are the unacknowledged legislators of cyberspace," says Mathewson. "We believed that if we were going to change the world, it would be through code."

So when Reputation.com suddenly found itself sinking into the quicksand of the dot-com bust, Mathewson was ready to join his comrade in digital progressivism at Tor. Funded by the navy and DARPA for the next three years, Dingledine and Mathewson took apart the tangled code-base developed by the NRL and rebuilt it from scratch. By 2004, there were still only about a hundred nodes on the nascent Tor network, mostly researchers who were curious about the project—Mathewson and Dingledine, perhaps still living in an MIT-like bubble where everyone was an adept hacker, were distributing Tor as raw source code, tough to use for nongeeks.

The civil liberties group, the Electronic Frontier Foundation, on the other hand, saw Tor's potential for mass adoption: They injected another round of funding for Tor to create Windows, Mac, and Linux versions that anyone could install, and Tor's network quickly mushroomed out to several hundred more relays.

But it was only in 2006 that Tor's value suddenly left the realm of computer science theory and jumped onto the world stage. That year, Dingledine and Mathewson started to get e-mails from users in countries like Iran and China, regimes that filter their Internet and monitor it to spy on opposition groups. Tor, unbeknownst to the hackers who created it, had accidentally become one of the world's most effective censorship circumvention tools. By encrypting traffic and routing it indirectly to and from websites via foreign nodes, Tor stymied the digital filters in countries that weed out sites with antigovernment messages and pornography. And unlike other services that promise to skirt censorship—programs like Freegate, Ultrasurf, Hotspot Shield, and Psiphon—it doesn't merely give users access to verboten content while potentially allowing the regime to track their online activity. Tor offers a portal to the Web that's both censorship- and surveillance-free.

The Broadcasting Board of Governors, a little-known U.S. government agency responsible for U.S.-run media outlets like Voice of America, Radio Free Europe, Radio Free Asia, and the Persian-language Radio Farda, contacted Dingledine and asked whether he'd be interested in financial backing to make Tor sleeker and more usable for its censor-skirting audience. The State Department followed up with its own infusion of cash. The result was enough funds to pay the project's entire small staff and develop a new incarnation of Tor known as the Browser Bundle, a program that can be installed with more or less two clicks. Tor incorporated as a nonprofit. Since then, both its number of nodes and users have exploded. The service added thirty-six million users in 2010 alone.

But Tor's tens of millions of new friends came with powerful enemies. In a gesture to the transparency of its inner workings, Tor publishes the IP address of every relay in its network. To prevent a government from simply blocking all those addresses, it maintains some semipublic relays that it calls "bridges," publishing them on chat networks and social media sites. In 2009, China began crawling the entire Chinese-language Web looking for Tor node addresses and blocked nearly all of them.

Since then, Tor has been playing a game of cat and mouse with the authorities who seek to strangle it. And it's often winning by only a move or two. That's not enough to satisfy Dingledine. "We need to take big steps if we're going to stay ahead," he says grimly. "We need to win this arms race for a while."

Tor has two aces up its sleeve. One is a plan to build a Tor home Wi-Fi router. The Wi-Fi hot spots, in theory, would sell for less than a hundred dollars each and run Tor by default, automatically pushing all the users' traffic through the anonymity network. In exchange, it would function as a Tor bridge relay. Tor's staff hopes those little boxes might add as many as ten thousand nodes, vastly strengthening its network.

Its other secret weapon is a small army of globe-trotting developers. One of them is Jacob Appelbaum. Since Appelbaum joined the nonprofit as a staffer in 2008, the young anarchist has served as one of Tor's primary coders as well as one of its international evangelists, preaching the gospel of anonymity wherever he goes. In a one-month span just before we met in Boston, for instance, Appelbaum had traveled to Brazil, China, Turkey, Poland, Germany, and England, as well as several U.S. cities, giving talks, rallying like-minded hackers to run Tor nodes and volunteer for the organization, and distributing copies of Tor and bridge relay addresses.

If the users or developers he meets worry that Tor's government funding compromises its ideals, there's no one better than Appelbaum to show the group doesn't take orders from the feds. He refers to capitalism as a "system of violence," and in spite of Tor's early navy funding, he speaks disdainfully of those who work with the military as "war profiteers." In his role as an auto-mythologizing hacktivist, Appelbaum looks the part: His hair has taken the form, variously, of sculpted black spikes, a shaggy side-mop, or a bleached blond crop. His face is studded with piercings that periodically migrate, and tattoos have staked out a growing portion of his body. The largest, on his upper left arm, is a symbol of a peacock taken from the symbology of a group of Satan-worshipping animists he met while traveling in war-torn Iraq. (Several of his personal stories of radicalization—including a few from that trip—were, fittingly, unverifiable.)

But Appelbaum's best evidence of Tor's purity from Big Brother's interference, perhaps, is his very public association with WikiLeaks, the American government's least favorite website. In a surprise speech at the Hackers on Planet Earth conference in July 2010, Appelbaum gave a keynote address on behalf of WikiLeaks after Julian Assange decided that traveling to the United States spelled legal trouble. Since then, the U.S. government has expressed its displeasure with him by tasking Customs and Border Protection agents with harassing him every time he crosses the border, where the Fourth Amendment's restrictions on searches and seizures abandon citizens. According to Appelbaum's accounts, he's often detained for hours, searched in intrusive bodily detail, and forced to miss any connecting flight.

In those detainment sessions, Appelbaum is separated from any phones, computers, or storage devices that he may be carrying, a painful security breach for a privacy-conscious cypherpunk. After abandoning several computers that he considered compromised, he no longer travels with a hard drive in his machines. How does that work? I ask. "Not very well," he says.

He takes the harassment with a dose of humor, often live-blogging his run-ins with customs on Twitter and at least once leaving a spring-loaded snake inside a fake can of nuts for a customs agent to find. But the intimidation as he tries to reenter his own country serves as a constant reminder to Appelbaum of the looming threat of prosecution. When the agents interrogate him, he says the questions are always the same: "What's your relationship to Julian Assange? What's your association with WikiLeaks?"

Appelbaum usually responds to those questions with stony silence, and he won't answer them for me either. But when I ask Appelbaum if Tor is in fact the powerful tool for anonymous whistleblowing that Assange and others believe it to be, he smiles. Then he quotes Assange quoting Oscar Wilde.

"Give a man a mask," he says, "and he'll tell you the truth."

Appelbaum was born in Northern California to two poor, freewheeling, secular Jews who never married. To call the environment of his early childhood a dysfunctional family wouldn't capture just how rarely it functioned at all: Appelbaum describes his mother as a paranoid schizophrenic who split with his father before Appelbaum was born—he would later hear stories that she believed his father had molested him while he was still in her womb. Appelbaum's father was a heroin addict and, in the eyes of the court, was hardly more fit than his mother to care for their newborn son. The couple's custody fight would last a full decade of his life.

During that prolonged legal battle, Appelbaum lived with his mother's sister, but he says she wasn't ready for parenthood. At the age of eight she sent him to live at the Sonoma County children's home. One of his only happy memories of the next lonely years, he says, was a night when an older child at the home taught him to hack the building's combination keypads by blowing chalk dust onto them, revealing the entry pattern in finger oils. Appelbaum remembers slipping out into the night and wandering an empty baseball diamond, for a moment free and in control of his life.

Appelbaum would spend another two years in the home and in foster care before his father won custody of him. Despite seeing him rarely for the first ten years of his life, Appelbaum still paints his father in heroic terms. An actor, director, and member of a band called the Tattooed Vegetables, Ricky Appelbaum ran in the same circles as Frank Zappa and the Lithuanian-American sculptor and dancer Vito Paulekas and was known to have sported half a beard on one side of his face and half a mustache on the other. According to his son, he also became a serial burglar for several years in the 1970s, mostly robbing pharmacies to feed his addiction.

The stories Appelbaum shares of his father's exploits are legendary, if unconfirmable: how he learned to lift fingerprints from random surfaces, set them in latex, and plant them at the scenes of crimes; how he stole police cars, went joyriding, and crashed them; how, the night he was finally caught by the cops, he'd had a nervous breakdown and lain down behind the counter of a store he had broken into. (In fact, no legal records show any convictions.) Soon after moving in with his father, the young Appelbaum says his father showed him how to crack the safe he kept in his office, listening to its inner workings with a stethoscope.

Like his father, the younger Appelbaum slipped naturally into life on the fringes of society, cross-dressing, dying his hair, and begging for change on the street. As much as he idolized his father, living in his drug-fueled, anarchic world was often nightmarish. The family spent much of its time in homeless shelters or moving from house to house. When they did settle down temporarily, Appelbaum's father would sublet most of the rooms of their home to fellow junkies to pay for his own habit, leaving Appelbaum with half of the kitchen as a bedroom and only a hanging sheet for privacy.

Appelbaum remembers the cast of housemates who inhabited that broken home: One lunatic who believed he was Anthony Burgess and spent his time rewriting *The Doctor Is Sick* in blue ballpoint pen. A small balding man who spat on the floor. Two Rastafarian junkies who once used the lightbulbs in Appelbaum's "bedroom" to smoke mothballs; he woke up in the middle of the night to the sounds of their laughter, choking in the dark on the acrid fumes.

One morning, he walked into the bathroom before school to find a woman convulsing in the tub with a syringe in her arm. Another day, Appelbaum came home from school and found his own father overdosing on the couch. He had written a note: "Dear Jake. Life is hard. Goodbye. I love you." Appelbaum woke his father up, walked him around the house, and he survived.

Despite those experiences, Appelbaum doesn't blame his father for his tarnished childhood. Ricky Appelbaum's inability to kick drugs, he believes, stems in part from a childhood accident: The elder Appelbaum was hit by a drunk driver at the age of nine and for the rest of his life suffered from incurable pain. Appelbaum himself was hit by a car while crossing the street at the age of fourteen—he was wearing a black dress, black tights, and a purple wig—and still suffers from chronic back injuries. "We weren't so different," he says. "I chose computers instead of heroin."

Appelbaum's first PC, in fact, was a gift from his father, a Macintosh 7200/90 that was almost certainly stolen. ("Junkies don't acquire things like that by buying them," he explains.) A friend at school and a neighbor's father taught him about networking protocols, the inner workings of operating systems, simple programming. He read the Cypherpunk Mailing List archives and rediscovered its lessons about the power of cryptography to counter authority and violence, how it "shifts the balance of power from those with a monopoly on violence to those who comprehend mathematics and security design." And the digital world at large offered him an abstract realm free of the corruption of his psychotic and drug-addled home, a place unhooked from reality where he could reinvent himself at will.

Appelbaum had a knack for manipulating that world and its tools. But his formal education was cut short. At the age of twenty, he dropped out of Santa Rosa Junior College to take care of his father, who by then was suffering from cirrhosis of the liver, hepatitis C, and diabetes. To pay his bills and those of his ailing father, he took a job working in a nonprofit that refurbished old computers for charity. On the side, he began volunteering for activist collectives and NGOs, groups with names like Resist.ca, and the Ruckus Society.

In 2002, those gigs led Appelbaum to his first real job: an information technology administrator position at Greenpeace. It was a tougher and more practical education than anything he would have found at Santa Rosa Junior College. Appelbaum learned from a combative, grizzled Linux guru at the NGO who went by the hacker handle Shord. His mentor—and the rest of Greenpeace—took information security seriously. The group's radical environmentalists often referenced the *Rainbow Warrior,* a ship Greenpeace used in its antiwhaling activities that was sabotaged and sunk by

French intelligence agents in 1985, drowning one of the group's photographers. "Greenpeace's security issues are real," says Appelbaum. "When things go badly, people die."

Appelbaum's induction into radical activism was also the beginning of his borderless lifestyle, flying around the world to participate in the group's direct actions. He helped perform reconnaissance for a San Francisco stunt in which the group dropped a massive banner over the Wells Fargo building to protest its funding of Appalachian mountaintop-removal coal mining. At one point he flew to Amsterdam to meet the Dutch cypherpunk Rop Gonggrijp and his business associates, who handed over Pelican cases of CryptoPhones. Greenpeace was among the first independent organizations to test those encryption-enabled mobile devices, now widespread among intelligence agencies and those that fear them.

When he wasn't working for Greenpeace, Appelbaum volunteered and contracted his computer skills to groups like the Rainforest Action Network, the Tactical Tech Collective, and the Open Society Institute. He met Roger Dingledine and Nick Mathewson at the Defcon hacker conference at the Bellagio Hotel in Las Vegas, and soon began volunteering for Tor, too, running Tor nodes on whatever PCs he had available. Dingledine, in return, became Appelbaum's educator in all things anonymous. "Roger is the Gutenberg of anonymity. He taught me how to think," says Appelbaum. "They were welcoming. They had a community. I joined it."

Out of his shattered childhood, Appelbaum had assembled a life on the front lines of digital activism. And then it all fell apart again.

Ricky Appelbaum died four days before Christmas in a San Francisco hospital. The younger Appelbaum blames the junkies who had shared his father's home. He says they had withheld his drugs, repeatedly injecting his legs instead with warm water. When Ricky Appelbaum died of cirrhosis and infected abscesses in his legs, they left the apartment with practically everything he owned. The police, his son says, weren't interested in investigating. He claims they told him that "no one cares about junkies" and instead threatened to arrest him for possessing his father's drug paraphernalia.

"My hatred of authority was pretty much solidified," he says.

After his father's death, activism no longer felt like enough. Appelbaum wanted to escape American society, to "stop contributing to a world of bullshit evil," as he would later describe it. He decided to leave the United States and visit an old friend from Greenpeace who had started a wireless infrastructure business in a place as far as possible from San Francisco and the ghost of his father: Iraq.

No military escort or even a visa; he would smuggle himself over the northern border with Turkey. "I guess I was tired of my first-world problems," Appelbaum says. "I decided that I would either come back whole, or come back full of holes."

In the months before Julian Assange dropped out of college in 2005 to pursue his antiauthoritarian dreams, he was plagued by ideas that seemed to have lodged in his mind, so deeply that when they emerged in discussions with fellow students, they burst forth almost as fully formed lectures.

One of the topics over which Assange obsessed was the Bourbaki, a circle of 1930s French mathematicians who all wrote under the name Nicolas Bourbaki. The Bourbakis' goal was to create a new groundwork for mathematics out of solid and apparent first principles. Seeking to delete ego from their rigorous, systematic work, they assumed the Bourbaki name to expel all public identity beyond that of the group itself. Assange dreamed of a group that would apply the same ideas to journalism, building stories out of public documents available to all, and posting them under a single, pseudonymous byline.

Another of Assange's idées fixes, one fellow student remembers, was onion routing. And over beers one evening in an Irish pub called Pugg Mahones at the edge of Melbourne University, he laid out Paul Syverson's elegant idea to that friend in pedagogical detail: a wrapped ball of information shedding skins as it bounced between relays from secret origin to secret destination. The perfect conduit for Oscar Wilde's masked truth-teller.

In 2005, Assange quit school and moved into a nearby house that became a proto-headquarters for what would become WikiLeaks. He covered the walls with blueprints for the site's architecture, code, and mathematical formulas. He worked for long hours, installed a red lightbulb in his bedroom in an effort to regulate his sleep, and ate little. The house filled with fellow hackers and like-minded activists who would crash in the house rent-free in exchange for working on Assange's project.

WikiLeaks, in its original conception, would use a wide variety of tricks to keep the world—and even itself—totally ignorant of its sources' identities. It deployed Secure Sockets Layer encryption like any banking or e-commerce site to scramble its communication with all visitors and obscure its content from snoops. One of WikiLeaks' initial advisers, Ben Laurie, had invented an open-source version of that protocol for the Web server software Apache, OpenSSL, that nearly half the world's websites use today.

Encryption wasn't enough, however. WikiLeaks didn't want to simply hide what sources said, but rather completely obliterate any way of finding out who they were. The server that ran the site would keep no logs of any IP addresses of visitors; Assange would risk no Penet-type subpoena debacle. But WikiLeaks added another, unique trick to that end: a script that launched in the browser of any visitor to the site and generated commands that looked like randomly sized submissions to WikiLeaks' secure server. To anyone snooping on WikiLeaks' visitors, it would be impossible to distinguish between those who had come to the site to read its publications or make a donation and those who intended to drop secrets. Thanks to the cover traffic of spoofed submissions, everyone looked like a leaker.

But it was Tor, of course, that would become WikiLeaks' core tool for protecting the anonymity of both its most sensitive sources and the site itself. The leaking site's submission system would run a Tor Hidden Service, so that users could access it through rendezvous points in its volunteer network of relay nodes. The submissions server's location would be just as hidden as that of the user. In theory, no one who wanted to launch a digital or legal attack on the site would even know where to begin, and sources would have the assurance from Tor that their identity was as anonymous as any Web communication could be.

In the early WikiLeaks developer communications leaked by John Young, Assange also describes physical drop-offs: mailing addresses where sources could anonymously send materials ranging from CDs to thumb drives to paper documents. Some would be "deniable" submissions addresses, in that the material would be encrypted with WikiLeaks' public key, and the drop-off handler wouldn't have the private key to unscramble the material. The uploader would never have any knowledge or responsibility for the leaked content. But other volunteers would accept unencrypted documents by post and even scan in reams of paper submissions and convert them to text files.

The postal system, for anyone careful with fingerprints, has the potential to be more anonymous than any means of digital communication. But aside from its snailish speed, physical mailings with no return address have an obvious bug compared with onion-routed digital leaks: They don't provide a way to write back. In the United States, even setting up a post office box as a return address requires two forms of identification, hardly the ideal feedback channel for an anonymous leaker.

Tor, on the other hand, allows instant feedback. WikiLeaks initially ran a chat room that used the instant messaging protocol IRC. An anonymous source communicating by Tor-protected instant messages could be questioned one second and respond the next with a verifying fact, another crucial document, or simple technical fixes.

For Assange, Tor may have also possessed another unique capability, one that served a far more morally ambiguous purpose—as much an inherent bug in the system as a feature. Anyone who controls a node on the edge of the network, with a few simple tools, can read every unencrypted file that comes out of it. While Tor triple-encrypts all the files it routes as a key step in its anonymity mechanism, that encryption is stripped away in the routing process. Any data that isn't encrypted before it enters Tor's maze of pipes won't be encrypted when it comes out the other end either. The service, after all, is designed to hide who the user is, not the data he or she is accessing or uploading.

Traditional implementations of encryption like SSL and PGP can solve that problem. But as with every security mechanism, users slip up. And much of the Web isn't configured for SSL. The result, apparent to thousands of the hacker types who run Tor nodes, is that a clever relay operator can essentially suck out copies of any unencrypted data that exits the anonymity network through the node he or she controls. Tor's administrators explain as much in the tool's documentation:

"Tor anonymizes the origin of your traffic, and it makes sure to encrypt everything inside the Tor network, but it does not magically encrypt all traffic throughout the Internet," the site warns. "Yes, the guy running the exit node can read the bytes that come in and out there."

And many believe that WikiLeaks did exactly that.

In a June 2010 profile of Assange, *The New Yorker* reported that before WikiLeaks' launch, a member of the project who ran a Tor exit node had noticed Chinese hackers using the relay to hide their tracks. Millions of documents were passing through the computer as the cyberspies went about their daily business of penetrating target servers and exfiltrating vast amounts of data. WikiLeaks' volunteers began to record that traffic, and the immense bolus of information that they collected became a repository of documents that Assange would later tout, in what may have been a less-than-honest bit of marketing, as proof of WikiLeaks' early success. "We have received over 1.2 million documents so far from dissident communities and anonymous sources," WikiLeaks boasted on its site circa 2007.

When that *New Yorker* account of WikiLeaks' origin story became a headline on Wired.com, Assange issued a vague and circuitous denial. "The imputation is incorrect," he told the tech news site The Register. "The facts concern a 2006 investigation into Chinese espionage one of our contacts [was] involved in. Somewhere between none and a handful of those documents were ever released on WikiLeaks."

But in another 2006 e-mail published by John Young on Cryptome after his falling-out with WikiLeaks, Assange described something that sounds very much like hoovering up sensitive data as it spills out of a Tor node. "Hackers monitor Chinese and other intel as they burrow into their targets," he wrote to Young. "When they pull, so do we."

The result, Assange continued breathlessly in that message, was an "inexhaustible supply of material. Near 100,000 documents/emails a day."

The data flood, he wrote, included hacked internal documents from the Council on Foreign Relations, half a dozen foreign ministries, the United Nations, trade groups, the World Bank, even the Russian cybercriminal mafia. Mendax's hacker dream made reality.

"We're drowning. We don't even know a tenth of what we have or who it belongs to. We stopped storing it at one terabyte," he wrote. That data trove would have been thirty times the size of every text article stored on Wikipedia today.

Whether or not those files were ever released, they marked the first seeds of WikiLeaks' power. Assange sounds in his e-mail like a man made practically giddy over the wealth of secrets at his fingertips. "We're going to crack the world open," he told Young, "and let it flower into something new."

When Appelbaum told the guards on the Turkish-Iraqi border that he was a tourist, as he recounts the story, they laughed at him and waved him through, refusing to even stamp his passport. A taxi had taken him from Diyarbakir through the Turkish city of Batman, and crossed into Iraq over a bridge straddling a river Appelbaum describes as "so brown and polluted that you wondered whether, if you fell in it, your bones would reach the bottom."

In the Iraqi city of Zakho, he was picked up by his old Greenpeace friend and his wife in a white SUV, with a Glock, an AK-47, and Browning nine millimeter handgun in the backseat. They drove to the northern town of Arbil, stopping to look in ghostly abandoned buildings along the highway. In one they found children's drawings of helicopters firing on humans, rockets hitting buildings. In Arbil, Appelbaum spent the next days photoblogging and interviewing locals, uploading the results with a satellite modem and the peer-to-peer file-sharing protocol BitTorrent. To any Iraqis who seemed computer-savvy, he distributed copies of the open-source operating system Linux, spreading free software like a hacker Johnny Appleseed.

Appelbaum found in his conversations that the local Kurds, unsurprisingly, were mostly happy with the U.S. invasion and the toppling of Saddam Hussein's regime. But from the Arabs who lived in Arbil he claims to have heard more disturbing stories of soldiers who fired .50 caliber bullets at oncoming cars at checkpoints, killing their drivers and all passengers, rather than aim for the engine block. A man told Appelbaum he kissed his wife every morning before leaving the house, thinking he would never see her again. Iraqis asked him sincerely whether Americans understood that they were normal people with homes and families. "As an American, I found myself feeling pretty awful about what we'd contributed to," he says.

In Kirkuk, the trio's vehicle broke down. While they waited for help on the side of the road, an enormous boom sounded over the hill behind them, and a black cloud of smoke rose from what seemed to be an oil refinery. Minutes later, two truckloads of soldiers, one American followed by one Iraqi, drove by. Appelbaum's group laid low until his friends' co-workers could bring them a new car, and then drove on. But the incident reminded him of how close he was to real harm. When his friends left Iraq for Istanbul, he left with them. "I was not in the greatest headspace, I guess," he says. "But at some point my desire to live started to outweigh my desire to be shot in a war zone."

Appelbaum returned to San Francisco and took a job at a security start-up, building software that automatically scanned code for vulnerabilities. The company was acquired and his entire office was laid off. Soon after, he was at a party in the city's Mission District when news hit that the levees had broken in New Orleans: Hurricane Katrina had left nearly two thousand dead and tens of thousands more stranded in sports stadiums used as shelters. When one of the partygoers tried to turn off the television and lighten the mood, Appelbaum angrily grabbed the remote, turned up the volume, and refused to change the channel.

Days later, he flew to Texas, created a press pass for an obscure news agency, and slipped into the Astrodome to interview Katrina's victims. "I got through the checkpoints the same way you hack firewalls: by identifying and exploiting weaknesses," he says. Inside the makeshift shelter, he reported the inhabitants' stories of prisonlike conditions: A man beaten in the shower. Nightly curfews, women raped. Some of the evacuees believed that the Army Corps of Engineers had blown up New Orleans's levees to preserve more expensive real estate while flooding their parishes. Some other reports disputed those stories. But for Appelbaum, "This American disaster was a lot like the other American disaster I witnessed in Iraq," he says. "The same thing, over and over again. The disconnection. The lack of humanity."

Appelbaum worked with a group of activists that collected radios and distributed them to the Astrodome's inhabitants to provide news for those trapped inside. Then he loaded up on provisions and drove to the Algiers neighborhood of New Orleans, moved into a house organized by the activist collective Common Ground, and helped to set up EVDO wireless Internet connections so that the area's hard-hit inhabitants could register online with FEMA to receive aid.

When Appelbaum returned from New Orleans, his tour through two levels of hell had left him more committed than ever to the liberating powers of technology. But he had yet to find the community that would be his own cypherpunks, the crypto-obsessed peers who would enwrap him in a larger movement and push him to greater feats of crypto-anarchy.

That group would be the Chaos Computer Club.

In many ways, the CCC had progressed years ahead of Tim May and Eric Hughes's crypto-liberation movement in California. Founded by the German hacker luminary Wau Holland in 1981, the Hamburg- and Berlin-based nonprofit had been demonstrating the insecurity of public computer systems as early as 1984, when its hackers used the home terminal system created by the German postal system to transfer the equivalent of $50,000 from a bank to the CCC's accounts. (The money was given back in a public ceremony the next day.) With a true surveillance state looming just over the Berlin Wall, privacy, antiauthoritarianism, and the need for strong crypto had been steeped into the group's core.

Almost exactly a year after his father's death, Appelbaum flew to Berlin to attend the CCC's annual Chaos Communication Congress. The topic of his talk was the same problem that had troubled Julian Assange years earlier, one central to any activist who believes in the power of cryptography: how to keep encrypted data encrypted, even when authorities are standing over the user, rubber hose in hand, demanding the key.

In his talk in Berlin, Appelbaum walked the audience through a series of crypto-schemes, grading various software and taking special pleasure in giving Apple an F. (The user's unencrypted key could be extracted from a file Apple carelessly left on the computer's hard drive.) And then he came to Julian Assange's very own solution to the problem of violent key extraction—Assange's 1997 invention, the crypto-scheme Rubberhose.

"In today's world," Appelbaum told the audience of European hackers, "this is probably going to get you killed."

Appelbaum cited the obvious issue: If the jailer knows his prisoner, Alice, is using Rubberhose, he'll never stop torturing her to try and get more of the data that may be hidden on her hard drive. "I don't think it's a good idea to never be able to prove you don't have any more secrets," Appelbaum told the CCC crowd.

Instead, he offered an idea for a new theoretical solution: MAID, or mutually assured information destruction. In the system Appelbaum suggested, Alice keeps her cryptographic keys on a faraway server, accesses it only with Tor to keep its location obscured, and sets a certain time limit. If that time limit passes without Alice checking in, MAID automatically deletes all her keys. When Alice gives in to her jailer after either suffering through a certain period of torture or legal silence, she can show him that the keys no longer exist. Everything on the server full of secrets becomes permanently, irrevocably encrypted. "You're not obstructing justice anymore," Appelbaum explained. "Justice was just too slow to catch you."

In the questions period following the talk, Ralf-Philipp Weinmann, the researcher who had developed Rubberhose with Assange a decade earlier, stood up and laid into Appelbaum, defending Rubberhose and pointing out flaws in the MAID concept. They debated genially and then agreed to talk afterward.

That conversation drew Appelbaum into Assange's circle, albeit indirectly. Appelbaum became a CCC regular, and Assange would attend the next year to introduce a project he was working on: WikiLeaks.

Friends say they met at that wintry Berlin conference. Their paths must have felt uncannily parallel: broken, wayward childhoods, IQs beyond those of the hated authorities that tried to exert power over their lives, and a belief in the redemptive power of cryptography to defeat those forces. By Appelbaum's fourth year at the conference, they had become close. Appelbaum told me he woke up on New Year's Day after the Twenty-sixth Chaos Communication Congress in bed with Assange and two women. "That was how we rolled in 2010," he says, smiling. (He later clarifies that they had busied themselves the night before with programming, not sex, and slept in different beds. "I can dream," he adds.)

The two never spoke about Appelbaum's critique of Rubberhose. But the CCC conference where Appelbaum spoke on the superiority of cryptography to violence, the young cypherpunk says, was "the start of a good friendship."

Browsing WikiLeaks' archives from 2006 to late 2009—the years before it was catapulted onto the world stage—feels like opening a creaking door onto a dusty museum of badly organized, fascinating secret artifacts: A purported draft of a resignation letter from Venezuelan president Hugo Chavez. A military report on the prevalence of hash-smoking among a group of American soldiers. An internal video from networking tech giant Cisco showing every television and movie scene in which it had purchased product placement. A list of sites to be censored by a Norwegian Internet service provider. A report on incompetence among safety staff at the Rocky Mountain Biological Laboratory. A censored image of the Belgian chief of police photoshopped into a pornographic scene. The handbooks of secret rituals for nine different fraternities.

It all started with a single, unverified document. Whether by sniffing the Tor network, receiving it from a Tor-masked source, or through other untraced means, Assange and WikiLeaks obtained and published its first leak: It was a Somalian government document calling for the assassinations of leaders in two rogue Somali states.

John Young, who at that point hadn't yet broken off from the group, warned that the leak could easily be disinformation or a forgery. "This is not to suggest leaks are not to be trusted, just not blindly so, for they are now standard tools for lying, smearing and stinging by governments, corporations, persons of all demonics," Young wrote on the WikiLeaks mail list.

In the end, WikiLeaks did post the Somalian leak, but with a breathless disclaimer: "Is it a bold manifesto by a flamboyant Islamic militant with links to Bin Laden? Or is it a clever smear by US intelligence?"

As WikiLeaks' profile rose, the answer never surfaced, and hardly mattered. Assange traveled to Kenya, moved into the compound of Doctors Without Borders, and continued to tout WikiLeaks at the World Social Forum, a collection of nonprofits and activists that shadowed the World Economic Forum. Seeking to create a "WikiLeaks advisory board for Africa," he met with Mwalimu Mati, an organizer of Transparency International in Nairobi. "We had tried many online whistleblowing sites," says Mati. "But WikiLeaks' idea of using cryptography to separate the whistleblower and the source . . . that seemed to me to be very useful and clever."

The Kenyan leak that would put WikiLeaks on the map, it turned out, had little to do with encryption. In 2004, the Nairobi government of Mwai Kibaki had taken power after the long reign of Daniel arap Moi, promising an end to the corruption of the Moi regime. Kibaki commissioned a report into the previous regime's embezzlement, suspected to be billions of dollars, that would come to be known as the Kroll Report. But when Kibaki's government started to come under fire for its connections to the Moi indiscretions, the report wasn't released.

Instead, someone printed it out and mailed it to Mati. It confirmed the worst: more than two billion dollars siphoned to Moi's associates' properties in twenty-eight countries, hundreds of millions given to his children, and even reports of currency counterfeiting by the regime's organized crime connections. Knowing that Nairobi's media was hardly independent enough to publish the bombshell report, Mati gave it to WikiLeaks. *The Guardian* picked up WikiLeaks' release and printed the front-page headline "The Looting of Kenya." Mati and Assange followed up with another major leak, again sourced to an envelope that appeared on Mati's desk. It detailed the extrajudicial executions of members of a criminal gang called the Mungiki, a crackdown that led to the indiscriminate police killings of thousands of young men.

After those exposés, "the site's popularity rocketed," says Mati. Leaks began to flow in earnest to the site's submissions system: A detailed account of the Cayman Islands tax shelters administered by the Swiss bank Julius Baer, an internal report from the mining giant Trafigura detailing the effects of its toxic dumping in the Ivory Coast that had been legally prevented from appearing in British media. Icelandic banking documents that would catalog the country's financial meltdown and eventually inspire a transformative legal movement in the volcanic island. And a collection of pager messages from September 11, 2001, that would catch the attention of one young analyst in a dusty base in Iraq.

But for Assange, the most gratifying moment of WikiLeaks' ascendancy may have had a smaller, but more personally meaningful, target: the Church of Scientology. Since the days of Penet and Suburbia, the church's lawyers had continued to intimidate anyone that leaked its manifold secrets, both to traditional media and digital outlets. So when WikiLeaks published a 208-page strategy manual that seemed to have been written by founder L. Ron Hubbard himself and detailed strong-arm tactics for attacking journalists and even tricking airlines into revealing their flight details, the church responded with its usual suppressive methods. A letter from the group's lawyer asked WikiLeaks to remove the documents immediately.

Assange, needless to say, did not. And instead of merely holding an eleven-person protest as he had in his cypherpunk days, this time he fired back with both barrels. "WikiLeaks will not comply with legally abusive requests from Scientology any more than WikiLeaks has complied with similar demands from Swiss banks, Russian off-shore stem cell centers, former African kleptocrats, or the Pentagon. WikiLeaks will remain a place where people of the world may safely expose injustice and corruption," read a letter sent back to the church's lawyer. "In response to the attempted suppression, Wikileaks will release several thousand additional pages of Scientology material next week."

Today, the site has a special Scientology section in its archives. It holds more than one hundred documents, one of the largest collections of the church's internal papers stored anywhere in the world.

In July 2010, three months after WikiLeaks had released a clip of a U.S. Apache helicopter gunning down civilians and journalists in a Baghdad suburb and just days before the group would publish seventy-six thousand secret military documents from Afghanistan, Julian Assange was scheduled to deliver the keynote address to an audience of thousands at the Hackers on Planet Earth conference, a gathering held at the venerable Hotel Pennsylvania in New York. But when the keynote began, it was a young, dark-haired American, not Assange, who walked onto the stage. He wore a T-shirt that read "Stop Snitching," a reference to Adrian Lamo, and was introduced by the conference organizers merely as "WikiLeaks."

"Hello to all my friends and fans in domestic and international surveillance. I'm here today because I believe we can make a better world," Appelbaum told a bewildered crowd that had expected a blonder, more Australian figure. "Julian, unfortunately, can't make it, because we don't live in that better world right now, because we haven't yet made it."

"I wanted to make a little declaration for the federal agents that are standing in the back of the room and the ones that are standing in the front of the room, and to be very clear about this: I have, on me, in my pocket, some money, the Bill of Rights, and a driver's license, and that's it. I have no computer system, I have no telephone, I have no keys, no access to anything. There's absolutely no reason that you should arrest me or bother me. And just in case you were wondering, I'm an American, born and raised, who's unhappy. I'm unhappy with how things are going."

He explained that he worked for Tor, but that he wasn't at the conference to represent his employer. "I'm certain they wouldn't be too unhappy with me speaking here, but they certainly didn't know about it before this moment." Then he explained that he believed in standing up for human rights and social change, for free speech without retribution.

"To quote from *Tron,*" he said, "I fight for the user."

For the next hour and fifteen minutes, Appelbaum railed against the war in Iraq and Afghanistan in steady, simple rhetoric. He lashed out at

WikiLeaks' critics and Lamo, whose name he refused to even utter, for informing on Bradley Manning. He argued against the idea of "speaking truth to power." "You stick it to the man and show the man how it is? Well I think that's stupid. Power knows power because power's in power," he told the crowd. "It's important to take this power and give it to people who are not simply the ones who make the decisions. Give it to the people who vote them in and out of office.

"The people in power cannot issue a denial when everyone knows the truth," he continued. "They can't redact a document when everyone has a copy of it in their heart and in their mind."

And then, he delivered the news: Appelbaum announced that WikiLeaks' submissions system, which had been down the previous months, had been redesigned and relaunched. He displayed the Tor Hidden Services page that any leaker could visit to anonymously feed documents to the site.

And then Appelbaum went further, directly appealing for the audience of hackers, many of whom held day jobs in corporate cybersecurity, to become an army of leakers.

"I never expect to work in the computer security industry again. But that's OK. I think this is far more important than anything like that," Appelbaum said, with a vulnerable note in his voice. "Some of you won't make this choice, and that's OK. And some of you will pretend not to make this choice, and you'll go in deep. And thank you for that."

Appelbaum paused. The audience response began with a few sparse claps, as if the crowd wasn't yet sure about its commitment to the role they were being asked to take on. Then it slowly grew, rippling through the room, and swelled into a steady roar of applause. As his talk ended, Appelbaum exited the stage, and seemed to reappear donning a black hoodie.

In fact, the hoodie wearer was a decoy. Appelbaum had slipped out a back exit to board a flight to Berlin. While he surreptitiously left the hotel, the Collateral Murder video was projected onto an enormous screen. Apache gunfire echoed over a silent throng of hackers: a dark orientation video for the newborn leaking movement.

PART THREE

THE FUTURE OF LEAKING

"Paranoia will kill us."

BIRGITTA JÓNSDÓTTIR

CHAPTER 5

THE PLUMBERS

In an unmarked government building on the edge of a residential Arlington, Virginia, neighborhood, a grinning, suit-wearing official named Peiter Zatko describes the anatomy of a leak.

His eyes flit over a table covered in printouts from a PowerPoint document, representing a blow-by-blow case study of one insider data theft. Zatko explains the example computer network's data breach in a rapid-fire patter, shuffling the papers and referring to visualizations of branching file systems with a fluency polished by repetition. His cheeks, dabbled with a hint of pockmarks, twitch with the nervous energy of someone who is setting up a fantastic punch line.

In Zatko's test case, the suspected leaker searches broadly over the network to find the areas where data related to critical infrastructure is stored, then returns to manually probe a few interesting files. "Then he walked away with enough information to shut down big chunks of the telephone systems in the United States," Zatko concludes flatly, his face blank.

And who was that rogue insider? "That was me," Zatko says. Then he giggles mischievously.

Zatko, a puckishly hyperactive forty-year-old, is not a typical Department of Defense employee. He wears a tie, has cut his once-shoulder-length mane of brown hair into a tidy executive part, and shaved his goatee. But even in his new Beltway digs, he still goes by the nickname "Mudge." That's the hacker handle Zatko used in decades of exploring the dark corners of the Internet and charting the back doors in its labyrinthine alleys, and he prefers his friends and acquaintances, his boss, even his parents, to refer to him by that name.

In the American hacker circles Mudge travels, it's also an identity that elicits a certain amount of worship. Frank Heidt, a former security consultant at MCI and several military contractors, says that when he first read Mudge's security exploit research in mid-nineties hacker zines, he believed that "Mudge" must be the pseudonym of a group. "He was so prolific that I thought he couldn't be one person," Heidt says. Mudge's revelations included fundamental vulnerabilities in software as ubiquitous as Windows NT and Internet Explorer, digital sleights of hand that could humiliate multinational companies with a few lines of code. For an older generation of hacker, his sobriquet calls to mind other bold-faced names in the American digital underground like the L0pht, @stake, and Cult of the Dead Cow, elite hacker collectives where Mudge was often regarded as the most visible and brilliant member.

Lately, Mudge has led a very different sort of group: the cybersecurity research team at the Defense Advanced Research Projects Agency. DARPA, the mad-scientist wing of the Pentagon that built the Internet and funded Tor, hides a Silicon Valley sense of wild technological optimism behind its bureaucratic Washington exterior. For the last fifty years, it's functioned as the Department of Defense's blue-sky Skunk Works, devoted to seemingly science-fictional projects designed to keep America's military forces a decade or more ahead of their foes.

Occasionally the agency's imagination germinates into technologies that disrupt and reshape the world. In 1960, it put the first five GPS satellites into orbit. In 1969, it launched the ARPANET, a system of remotely networked computers that would later be renamed the Internet. In the late 1970s, it developed and flew the first stealth planes. From 2006 to 2008,

DARPA organized a series of races of robotic, driverless cars through the desert. Several of the top scientists in those competitions now work for Google, where they've built autonomous automobiles that have driven between San Francisco and Los Angeles with no human assistance. In 2011, it tested an unmanned plane that can fly twenty times the speed of sound. Other projects that it's funded seek to build flying Humvees, mechanical bats that can suck electricity from power lines, cyborg cockroaches, and roving robots that can switch between liquid and solid form or feed themselves with grass and twigs.

Mudge's new pet project, as outlined in a forty-six-page announcement DARPA released two months before our meeting, may sound less flashy. But it's equally ambitious: He aims to rid the world of digital leaks.

"Leaks," of course, isn't how Mudge describes the problem. He and DARPA use the more general industry term for an enemy within the system: an "insider threat." Since the summer of 2010, Mudge has led a project known as CINDER, or Cyber Insider Threat, a DARPA program that aims to turn the question of information security inside out and look at it afresh: Instead of trying to keep the bad guys out of your system, assume they're already inside and impersonating innocent staffers, whether in the form of malicious software that hijacks an authorized PC or a human leaker. CINDER was conceived to identify and neutralize moles of all varieties.

The telephone system theft case that Mudge dissected for me in an unassuming DARPA conference room was, of course, a mere penetration test, demonstrating that anyone with access to the victim's network could exfiltrate any data he chose without detection, despite all the system's sophisticated security software. Now this hacker's challenge is to fix, rather than merely demonstrate, that epic problem: Like most DARPA initiatives, CINDER functions as an open, X-Prize-style invitation for ideas. While Mudge won't reveal the project's budget, qualifying DARPA-funded projects typically receive anywhere from hundreds of thousands to tens of millions of dollars in government capital. More than fifty entrants, ranging from tiny companies to the defense giant Raytheon, have publicly signed up to submit ideas—many more in secret. Projects at DARPA's intelligence agency counterpart IARPA and other wings of the Pentagon are tackling the problem, too, but few have the mandate that Mudge has, to think years and decades ahead.

"We're looking to everyone from academia to start-ups to large government contractors," says Mudge with a salesman's intensity. "We're not looking for evolutionary improvement. We want to pull the rug out from the problem altogether."

Despite his hacker past, Mudge fits in at DARPA. For years, he's thought eleven steps beyond the corporations and government agencies whose security he gleefully dismantled. Now he's working in the same office building as scientists tasked with equally unreal work, building Iron Man–like exoskeletons that multiply human strength by a factor of ten and surveillance systems designed to watch every moving object in entire cities.

But Mudge has something else in common with the agency that now employs him. Each has played both sides of the secret-spilling game. Without DARPA's money and ideas, the transparency movement as we know it, built on the Internet and enabled by anonymity technologies, wouldn't exist.

And Mudge, for his part, isn't just any hacker-turned-fed. Peiter Zatko, loath though he may be to discuss it, knows Julian Assange.

The two forty-year-old ex-hackers grew up cruising the same primordial Internet of the 1980s and 1990s. They bristled under the same restrictions and shared a friendship through connections that spanned continents. Twenty years ago, Mudge and Mendax were teammates in the same digital free-for-all. Now they've found themselves on opposing sides, vying for the fate of the world's information. And it's Mudge's move.

The Collateral Murder video was only the overture to Assange's magnum opus of leaks.

Just days after Jacob Appelbaum's call-to-arms speech at the HOPE conference, the first wave hit: seventy-six thousand documents from the Afghan War, detailing every significant action over nine years of skirmishes and pitched battles, every casualty and drone strike gone awry.

The Pentagon wasn't surprised by the blowout leak—it had already read the chat logs of its prime suspect and thrown him in a military stockade. But there was little else the most powerful military in the world could do in its escalating battle with WikiLeaks other than issue rhetoric. Admiral Mike Mullen and Secretary of Defense Robert Gates criticized WikiLeaks' release and lack of discretion in failing to redact names of informants, with Mullen stating in a press conference that the group "might already have on their hands the blood of some young soldier." (Later reports from the Pentagon, widely touted by WikiLeaks' supporters, said that the exposure hadn't led to any documented casualties. WikiLeaks claimed it had taken out files with the most sensitive names.)

Three months later, WikiLeaks released 392,000 documents from the Iraq War, another record-breaking classified data breach that exposed American knowledge of torture by Iraqi police, evidence that Iraqi Prime Minister Nouri al-Maliki used "detention squads" in the Iraqi army to harass political rival groups, and another fifteen thousand civilian deaths that hadn't been previously documented. Assange delivered the news in a London press conference, the long hair of his early thirties now cut short, his gray trench coat switched out for a well-tailored suit.

But by this time WikiLeaks' enemies were responding with more than mere words. Prior to the Iraq release, the site faced a digital intrusion by what one WikiLeaks source told me were "very sophisticated attackers," compromising the encryption keys the group used for instant messaging and forcing it to issue new keys and move its chat server from Amsterdam to somewhere in Germany. One British payment provider, Moneybookers, froze donations to the site, claiming it violated the company's terms of service.

But the leak that would give way to an all-out Cold War on WikiLeaks was yet to come. On November 28, seventeen days after Assange had told me of an upcoming data dump that would affect every government and every industry in the world, the data bomb struck on schedule: the first of 251,000 State Department Cables, candid communiqués from American diplomats in every corner of the world, all secret, all utterly exposed.

They included frank insults of world leaders' nepotism, corruption, and sexual appetites, countless stories of America's sticky fingers penetrating into political dealings in supposedly independent democracies, and evidence of filthy practices on the part of multinational corporations, a Leviathan bundle of secrets torn open to feed the front pages of the world's newspapers and magazines for months, even years. The headlines rang out with a force and volume greater than any leak since the Pentagon Papers: "Saudi Arabia Urges U.S. Attack on Iran to Stop Nuclear Program." "China Leadership 'Orchestrated Google Hacking.'" "Did Pfizer Bribe Its Way Out of Criminal Charges in Nigeria?" "Texas Company Helped Pimp Little Boys to Stoned Afghan Cops." "China 'Ready to Abandon North Korea.'" "WikiLeaks Cables on Afghanistan Reveal Monumental Corruption." "Iraqi Children in U.S. Raid Shot in Head." "U.S. Bombs Yemen in Secret." "U.S. Diplomats Spied on UN Leadership." An analysis by the magazine *The Atlantic* five months later would show that close to one out of every two issues of *The New York Times* in 2011 cited a document published by WikiLeaks.

It was a cypherpunk apotheosis, and the greatest hacktivist coup in history.

Detailing the true nature of war was one thing. Massively embarrassing the world's most powerful politicians and companies was quite another. After Cablegate, the counterattacks were immediate and relentless. Vice President Joe Biden said in a television interview that Assange was "closer to being a hi-tech terrorist than the Pentagon Papers." Sarah Palin suggested he should be "pursued with the same urgency we pursue al-Qaeda and Taliban leaders."

Senator Joe Lieberman called the release "an outrageous, reckless, and despicable action that will undermine the ability of our government and our partners to keep our people safe and to work together to defend our vital interests." After receiving a call from Lieberman staffers, Amazon, which had hosted some WikiLeaks Web servers, banned the group. (The company denies the decision was political.) WikiLeaks moved to a new host in Switzerland, where untraced cyberattacks flooded its servers. Its DNS service provider EveryDNS, which allowed the site to use the name WikiLeaks.org, exiled the group as well, forcing it to switch to alternatives like WikiLeaks.ch and WikiLeaks.de. PayPal cut off the site's main faucet of donations. Visa, MasterCard, and then Bank of America followed by ending all payments to the increasingly isolated digital fugitives.

Assange responded to the digital and financial attacks by putting out a call for volunteers to "mirror" the site, setting up an exact replica of WikiLeaks.org. In a show of solidarity, hundreds of clones were set up around the world in a matter of days.

But Assange himself, whether through pressure from the American government or mere coincidence, was coming under fire as well. Interpol issued a Red Notice of arrest for him, not for any data-related crime, but for sex crimes against two women in Stockholm. According to documents from the Swedish justice system that leaked to the Web, both women alleged that WikiLeaks' headstrong founder had unprotected—if consensual—sex with them despite their protests that he use a condom. In one case, a woman said he had sabotaged the condom so that it broke during intercourse. Another woman said he had begun having sex with her in her sleep.

In January 2011, Assange was jailed for seven days in the same Wandsworth Prison cell that, according to his lawyer, once housed the writer of his favorite quote on the power of anonymity: Oscar Wilde. Out on bail and fighting extradition to Sweden, he was confined to house arrest in the Norfolk mansion of a war reporter friend and wealthy heir named Vaughan Smith, on the condition that he wear a tracking bracelet on his ankle and report to the local police station daily—grating restrictions for a man who rarely spent two months in a row living in the same country.

But even as he faced potential financial ruin, humiliation, prison, and death threats, Assange continued to goad the world's superpowers.

When the Australian met with me in London before the Cablegate release, he also told me of plans to publish a leak from a major U.S. bank in early 2011, a new chapter for the group after its series of government exposés. He wouldn't name the bank, or what exactly was revealed in the thousands of documents WikiLeaks had obtained from its servers. But the spilled viscera of this financial institution, he claimed, would expose an "ecosystem of corruption."

"It will give a true and representative insight into how banks behave at the executive level in a way that will stimulate investigations and reforms, I presume," he told me.

All signs pointed to Bank of America: In 2009, Assange had said in an interview with *Computer World* that he had five gigabytes of data from the megabank, too much at the time for WikiLeaks to even know how to publish it in a readable form. But even after I and other journalists started making the connection to the Bank of America statement, Assange wouldn't confirm his target. In an appearance on *60 Minutes,* he poked at the financial industry again. When the show's host, Steve Kroft, asked for more information on the bank leak, Assange revealed nothing, and seemed to delight instead in the anxiety he was causing.

"I think it's great. We have all these banks squirming, thinking maybe it's them," he told Kroft.

As of this book's writing, that leak still hasn't materialized. Perhaps the group was too distracted by the political and digital blitzkriegs that hammered it for much of early 2011, or Assange lost focus when he faced the threat of criminal prosecution. Perhaps, as some have reported, the bank documents lacked the punch of WikiLeaks' previous three megaleaks and Assange felt that publishing them would erode the group's fearsome reputation. Or perhaps, as the group has claimed, the files were lost after Daniel Domscheit-Berg, the group's German spokesperson, defected with a large slice of the group's submissions.

Regardless, by 2011 WikiLeaks had risen to a place in the world's perception where even a mere threat of a leak served the purpose Assange had laid out in his five-years-earlier essay on conspiracies. By Assange's reckoning, it wasn't the leaks themselves, after all, but rather the fear of leaks, that thickens the blood of the giants he hoped to paralyze. Leaks' central purpose, in Assange's original conception, was to sow such internal anxiety that corporations and governments overreacted, freezing their internal communications, or, as in Ellsberg's case, taking their counterattack too far and embarrassing themselves.

Right on cue, Bank of America acted—or overreacted—swiftly. It commissioned an internal team of more than a dozen staffers who worked day and night to track down potential moles. It hired a chief information security officer and brought on the defense contractor Booz Allen Hamilton to audit its security and to review millions of documents in its archive that might damage the firm if they were leaked. It even began preemptively buying up website names like Brianmoynihanblows.com and Brianmoynihansucks.com, references to its CEO, as a defensive measure to prevent the domains from falling into the hands of critics.

The finance giant went so far as to call the Department of Justice for advice about who might be able to help it with its so-far speculative WikiLeaks dilemma. The Department of Justice recommended it consult with the Washington, D.C., law firm of Hunton & Williams, known for handling sensitive Beltway issues.

That law firm, in turn, put out a call to its subcontractors, including one tiny outfit: HBGary Federal.

The year-old start-up, a Washington spin-off of data security firm HBGary, had far more ambition than manpower—it employed only three staffers. But one, its chief executive Aaron Barr, was eager to turn his small company into an online gun for hire, a digital detective firm that could cut through the Internet's most dangerous and powerful weapon: Barr wanted to make a name for HBGary Federal by defeating anonymity. Instead, he would soon become the world's most infamous victim of Anonymous itself.

The e-mail appeared in Aaron Barr's in-box at 3:55 P.M. on December 2. It was from John Hunt, a lawyer at Hunton & Williams. Its subject line: "URGENT—OPPORTUNITY."

> Richard and I are meeting with senior executives at a large U.S. bank tomorrow regarding WikiLeaks. We want to sell this team as part of what we are talking about. I need a favor. I need five to six slides on WikiLeaks—who they are, how they operate and how [your] group may help this bank. Please advise if you can help get something ASAP. My call is at noon.

Barr, a short, tanned forty-year-old with military shoulders, a square jaw, and hints of gray at his temples, read the message on his iPhone while on his way to a meeting with executives of TASC, an intelligence contractor division of Northrop Grumman in northern Virginia. He responded twenty minutes later, before any of the other three staffers from the two other security firms listed in the address field, eagerly promising to take the case. The project would keep him up late. But Barr wasn't in a position to turn down work.

Earlier that same day, Barr had sent a note to the Northrop Grumman executive he was meeting that read like a thinly veiled plea for a job. HBGary Federal, the company he had left Northrop to found a year earlier, was barely treading water, and Barr was looking for a life raft.

The executives at the larger firm HBGary who had hired him to run HBGary Federal and invested in his government-focused offshoot were getting frustrated. They had put faith in his pitch that social media could solve the cybersecurity world's "attribution" problem. Analyzing social connections, he argued, could identify the anonymous hackers plaguing government agencies and corporations. On the Internet, criminals and spies could hide their IP addresses with proxies and pseudonyms. But Barr believed that their human relationships, mapped out through online conversations and social media connections, would reveal hackers' true identities.

As a successful defense contractor executive with a secret clearance, HBGary's execs had taken him on as an "A player" and expected him to "walk the halls" of government agencies, preaching his social media gospel and opening a faucet of lucrative deals, as they wrote in internal e-mails.

But the deals weren't coming. HBGary was starting to consider selling its stake, and Barr was spending sleepless nights pondering the fate of his company and career.

"Everything we are chasing seems to keep getting pushed to the right and it is really causing a strain financially," Barr wrote to the Northrop Grumman contact he was meeting that winter day.

> Ted and I are looking at our books and pipeline and defining some short term gates we need to make it through in order to stay operational. We will likely make that determination soon, and if the outcome is negative I will be actively looking for the right opportunity with an organization that I believe in and trust.
>
> Unfortunate thing is I think the area of our expertise, social media, is going to explode over the next few years, but a lot is about timing. . . . I will keep you posted.

Perhaps this WikiLeaks bolt from the blue, striking the very same day, could be Barr's chance to prove his social media detective methods and spark some cash flow for HBGary Federal.

An e-mail from Matthew Steckman, at HBGary Federal's Palo Alto partner firm Palantir, laid out the details of the assignment:

> They are pitching the bank to retain them for an internal investigation around WikiLeaks. They basically want to sue them to put an injunction on releasing any data. The Department of Justice called the General Counsel of Bank of America and told them to hire Hunton and Williams, specifically to hire Richard Wyatt who I'm beginning to think is the Emperor. They want to present to the bank a team capable of doing a comprehensive investigation into the data leak.
>
> They have a half hour with the general counsel of the third largest bank in the world to plead their case.

Within minutes, Barr was on a conference call with Steckman and staffers from a third security firm called Berico, and then the three companies brainstormed late into the evening. Barr sent Steckman a first draft of his PowerPoint slides just after midnight.

Barr's slides were simplistic, full of typos, and inaccurate in places. (At one point he referenced someone named John Shipton as a WikiLeaks staffer—in an homage or joke, Assange had listed his long-lost biological father's name on the site's registration.) But the presentation got Barr's central points across. WikiLeaks' data was hosted in a French data center, Barr said, and its submissions platform by a Swedish firm called PRQ. The security exec suggested "cyber attacks against the infrastructure to get data on document submitters. This would kill the project. Since the servers are now in Sweden and France putting a team together to get access is more straightforward."

The slides went on to suggest a disinformation campaign against WikiLeaks to sow internal dissension, fake submissions to discredit it, and social media analysis to identify the key players in the group. "Need to attack the organization, its infrastructure, and its people," Barr wrote. HBGary could offer "Computer Network Attack/Exploitation," "Influence and Deception Operations," and "Social Media Collection, Analysis, Exploitation," he concluded.

By the next morning, the team of security firms had added charts that showed the geographic movement of WikiLeaks' servers from Amazon's cloud to a French host to the Swedish Internet service provider Bahnhof, along with a branching diagram of WikiLeaks' supporters and their social connections. With only half an hour before the slides were to be presented to Hunton & Williams, Barr injected some last-minute addenda: "They are under increasing financial pressure because authorities are blocking their funding sources," he wrote to Steckman. "Need to help enumerate these. Also need to get people to understand that if they support the organization we will come after them. Transaction records are easily identifiable."

Finally he put the spotlight on one high-profile WikiLeaks supporter: civil liberties lawyer and Salon.com columnist Glenn Greenwald. "It is this level of support we need to attack," he wrote. "These are established professionals that have a liberal bent, but ultimately most of them if pushed will choose professional preservation over cause, such is the mentality of most business professionals. Without the support of people like Glenn WikiLeaks would fold."

The presentation, essentially offering a mix of illegal hacking, intimidation, and forgery, was packaged up and sent to Hunton & Williams with a title: "The WikiLeaks Threat." And then the firms began the long wait for their go-ahead to act.

Hunton & Williams, it turned out, wasn't ready to start channeling money to its subcontractors as quickly as they had hoped. Another assignment that Barr had worked on for the firm, using social media to track, analyze, and potentially disrupt pro-union enemies of the U.S. Chamber of Commerce, was stalled. Working in partnership with Palantir and Berico, HBGary had originally requested $2 million a month for the companies' services. When the law firm balked, they reduced the cost to $200,000 a month, and eventually to free spec work in the hopes that the Chamber would start paying once their project showed results.

Barr needed to demonstrate that he had digital sleuthing skills that his clients couldn't "push to the right." He needed a test case for his social media strategy that would indisputably prove its brilliance. And so he began looking for a very prominent target.

He would find one in Anonymous, a phenomenon that looked like Tim May's vision of crypto-anarchy come to life.

Anonymous was the name, paradoxically, taken by the world's largest, most active group of black hat hackers and hacktivists. More than a traditional organization, it functioned as a loosely organized movement, or even an elaborate, participatory meme. Those who took part in the group—and anyone could be Anonymous—joined in crowd-sourced swarm attacks on whatever target offended its values, tenets like freedom of speech and anti-corporatism. Anonymous' victims, in the years since the movement emerged out of juvenile online forums and began its politically motivated missions, have included the Tea Party and its billionaire corporate supporters the Koch brothers, the antihomosexual extremist Westboro Baptist Church, Sony Corporation after it sued a hacker who reverse-engineered the PlayStation 3, and the governments of Anguilla, Australia, Brazil, Egypt, Israel, Sweden, Tunisia, Turkey, the United States, Venezuela, and Zimbabwe, among others.

One Anon, as the movement's members call themselves, would post a call to arms online against a certain target, often an institution that seemed to be bullying a smaller entity or acting with corrupt impunity. And then, if the suggestion struck the collective's fancy, hundreds or even thousands more would glom together across international boundaries into an attacking horde, stealing information from the target's computers and posting it online, or flooding their victims' Web servers with fraudulent data requests that paralyzed the machines, like flies choking the mouth and nostrils of an elephant.

And how did participants in Anonymous stay anonymous, even as they engaged in those highly illegal online attacks? By dipping into the cypherpunk toolbag. Anons, in decentralized fashion, use any anonymity tools available to them, including all varieties of proxies. One recruitment handbook of anonymity methods that the group distributed online begins by explaining how to install Tor on any operating system. Then it moves on to alternatives like the similarly structured I2P anonymity network, virtualization software that allows the user to create a cordoned-off sandbox of security on his or her machine, PGP encryption, and commercial services that act as faster but less secure single-hop versions of Tor.

Not every Anon uses those tools effectively. Dozens of the least skilled and most active denizens of the group have been identified, arrested, and imprisoned—some have been revealed to be teens as young as fifteen years old. But every police action only inspires more recruitment and hardens the group's culture of strong anonymity. One typical propaganda poster for Anonymous shows a headless, suited man—the group's central emblem—pointing out in Uncle Sam fashion. "ANONYMOUS WANTS YOU," it reads, "TO GET YOUR ASS BEHIND A PROXY AND JOIN THE RAID!"

Anonymous would soon find common cause with WikiLeaks. In fact, the two groups shared many of their roots in an early enemy: the Church of Scientology.

In January 2008, the church began a campaign of suppression to prevent a leaked video of scientologist star Tom Cruise extolling the church's virtues from spreading around the Internet and traditional media. Anonymous, until then focused on nihilistic pranks like hacking an online epilepsy forum to display blinking lights intended to cause seizures, responded with its first political action.

It began with a two-minute video posted to YouTube, a robotic voice delivering a manifesto as foreboding gray clouds drifted across the sky.

> Hello, Scientology. We are Anonymous.
>
> Over the years, we have been watching you. Your campaigns of misinformation; suppression of dissent; your litigious nature, all of these things have caught our eye. With the leakage of your latest propaganda video into mainstream circulation, the extent of your malign influence over those who trust you, who call you leader, has been made clear to us. Anonymous has therefore decided that your organization should be destroyed. For the good of your followers, for the good of mankind—for the laughs—we shall expel you from the Internet and systematically dismantle the Church of Scientology in its present form.
>
> . . .
>
> Knowledge is free.
>
> We are Anonymous. We are Legion.
>
> We do not forgive. We do not forget. Expect us.

The video received 4.5 million views on YouTube, and was followed by close to two hundred cyberattacks on Scientology websites around the world, in-person protests at Scientology buildings attended by thousands wearing Guy Fawkes masks, and even envelopes of white powder—it turned out to be harmless wheat germ and cornstarch—mailed to dozens of the church's addresses.

When WikiLeaks began posting Scientology documents in record numbers a few months after Anonymous' Scientology campaign, Anonymous' and WikiLeaks' supporters began to blend. And when the attacks on WikiLeaks began in December 2010, it was Anonymous that attacked back.

The requisite manifesto broadcast through the Internet's message board and blogs called for an action titled "Operation Avenge Assange." It appeared shortly after PayPal cut off transfers to the group and quoted John Perry Barlow, a founder of the cypherpunk-affiliated Electronic Frontier Foundation: "The first serious infowar is now engaged. The field of battle is WikiLeaks. You are the troops."

The poster went on to call for boycotts and cyberattacks, mass distribution of the cables online and off, and even a letter-writing campaign to government officials in support of Assange. A wave of digital broadsides followed as Anonymous trained its stream of crowd-sourced junk data, powered by a software weapon called Low Orbit Ion Cannon, at one target after another. PayPal's corporate blog was temporarily blown off the Web, followed by the websites of Visa and MasterCard as well as the Swedish prosecutor's office that was attempting to extradite Assange.

The hackers followed up with another direct action called "Operation Bradical" that focused instead on Bradley Manning, by then languishing in a Quantico, Virginia, brig, kept on suicide watch and forced to strip naked nightly by commanding officers. An Anonymous missive posted online called on Anons to "dox" the brig's officers, digging up their personal information and using it to harass them and their families. They demanded that Manning be given "sheets, blankets, any religious texts he desires, adequate reading material, clothes, and a ball. One week. Otherwise, we continue to dox and ruin those responsible for keeping him naked, without bedding, without any of the basic amenities that were provided even to captured Nazis in WWII."

As Anonymous began to share the media spotlight surrounding Cablegate, Aaron Barr became increasingly preoccupied with the group. It represented a tempting case study for the kind of analysis he hoped to validate: Although Anons fiercely guarded their true names, they openly congregated and planned their actions in online chat rooms and crowd-sourced documents using pseudonyms. Despite all its proxies and masks, perhaps the entire social graph of Anonymous could be infiltrated and charted.

Barr had been planning on giving a talk at the BSides security conference in San Francisco in March, in which he'd use clues built from a Web of online relationships to reveal human flaws in the security of a nuclear facility in Pennsylvania and the army intelligence group INSCOM. He had titled the talk "Who Needs the NSA When We Have Social Media?"

But by January, Barr was determined to make a bigger splash than the usual slide show of security vulnerabilities could generate. He needed one that would get HBGary Federal into the headlines and flush out business leads. So he added a third target.

"I am going to focus on outing the major players of the Anonymous group, I think," he wrote to two other staffers at HBGary Federal in January 2011.

"After all—no secrets, right? :)"

In early 2011, I contacted each of the four dozen companies that had publicly signed up to submit proposals to DARPA's open casting call for anti-leak technologies. And I soon got a taste of the immensely tedious task that Peiter "Mudge" Zatko faces.

About two-thirds of the companies, a crowd of generic-sounding contractors with names like Securonix, IntelliGenesis, Trustifier, IT Solutions Partners, and Applied Visions, didn't respond or declined to talk. Of those that did give me a description of their ideas, deciphering anything unique about their approaches involved wading into bland white-paper-speak filled with phrases like a "solution [that] automatically adjusts weights assigned to user and/or peer group behavior models based on the life cycle of the user" and "a risk-based analysis [of] an abstraction matrix along with a decision model that conforms to a government-, department-, or office-information policy."

Perhaps the most candid response came from a firm called Teledyne that had already bowed out of the program. Mark Anderson, a director of information sciences at the company, complained that without access to past investigations, companies like his had little hope of guessing at a workable way of combing through data for culprits. And he pointed out that the request for proposals seemed to focus on online activities, but ignored the Luddite end of the leaking spectrum. "How would one detect a bad guy exfiltrating data on a memory device using a low tech technique (like swallowing it)?" Anderson wrote to me. "Don't get me wrong, it's a really important problem. I am just skeptical that we can employ cyber techniques instead of old-school human detective techniques."

When I called Alan Paller, the avuncular research director of the cybersecurity education organization the SANS Institute, he began our conversation with a gloomy line. "I prefer to focus on the problems that have solutions."

When I pressed him, Paller admitted that there is indeed a solution to the problem of leaks. "Lock it all up, and don't let anyone read anything. But that flies in the face of everything we know about organizational effectiveness."

In fact, the cybersecurity industry has tried a more practical version of Paller's fix before. Beginning in 2007, practically every major software vendor from McAfee to Symantec to Trend Micro spent hundreds of millions of dollars acquiring companies in the so-called Data-Leak Prevention (DLP) industry—software designed to locate and tag sensitive information on a firm's servers, and then guard against its departure at the edges of the network. "Data-centric security" briefly became a buzz phrase full of promise as companies realized that antivirus and firewalls weren't enough to cure their information ailments. Even in 2010, a study by Forrester Research showed that about a quarter of firms in the United States, UK, Canada, France, and Germany were implementing leak-focused software, and another third were considering the option.

Unfortunately, Data-Leak Prevention never quite worked. In modern companies and agencies, where the will to let employees "connect the dots" between data points has defeated any impulse to wall off various parts of the network, information is simply created too quickly and moved around too often for a mere filter to catch it. Even after the DLP acquisition craze, insider data theft kept flowing: A study in 2009 by the privacy-focused Ponemon Institute found that about 60 percent of employees admit to taking sensitive data before leaving a job.

One reason the bleeding hasn't stopped, particularly in the public sector: Since the 9/11 Commission determined that a lack of data sharing between intelligence agencies blinded the government's counterterrorism efforts, Uncle Sam has kept his focus on stopping the next terror attack rather than preventing the next leak.

In the wake of Cablegate, the White House would issue an order to more closely restrict and monitor who had access to classified materials, and the armed forces would establish new rules about how physical media like CDs could be used on SIPRNet machines. But the Senate's first official reaction to the scandal (after Senator Joseph Lieberman's suggestion of a new law that would make revealing an intelligence source a federal crime) was to hold a hearing not on how to better restrict information, but how to make sure it was *not* restricted. Lieberman's introduction to the hearing began with references to the World Trade Center attacks and the improvements in intelligence in the nearly ten years since.

"Now I fear the WikiLeaks case has become a rallying cry for an overreaction, for those who would take us back to the days before 9/11 when information was considered the property of the agency that developed it and was not to be shared," Lieberman said. "The bulk of the information illegally taken and given to WikiLeaks would not have been available had that information not been on a shared system, some argue. But to me this is putting an ax to a problem that requires a scalpel."

In other words, some in Washington refuse to fall into Assange's trap: The WikiLeaks founder predicted that leaks would halt communications within conspiratorial institutions and paralyze their ability to conspire. But the government, perhaps wisely, would rather let the data leak than stop its flow.

All that information sharing makes Data-Leak Prevention tough to put into practice. How to seal an agency's edges when they're meant to be porous? So the cybersecurity industry has evolved instead to embrace another tactic: Network forensics, the process of constantly collecting every fingerprint on a company's servers to trace an intruder or leaker after the fact—not simply the moment of the leak, but the entire story of the leaker's behavior in the days or even months before and after.

NetWitness, one prominent start-up in that budding field, saw its revenue grow seventy-eight-fold from 2007 to 2010, for instance, before it was acquired by software giant EMC. But even NetWitness's software generally gathers information about network activities and makes it easily available to queries—it doesn't explain it. "There's nothing in current technology that can do this in an automated fashion," says Shawn Carpenter, principal forensic analyst at the company. "You need a Columbo."

Since DARPA tapped Mudge in early 2010, he has aimed to build that leak-sniffing robo-Columbo. Though his role is mainly to function as referee in a global contest of ideas, he's also been reviving the methods he developed years earlier as the chief scientist at an insider-threat-focused security start-up called Intrusic. As he described it to me in our interview, Mudge's project seeks to identify what he calls "malicious missions": That means any insider activity aimed at stealing data from inside a company's firewall, whether it's a Dell PC remotely hijacked by a Chinese cyberspy or Bradley Manning. His system would monitor networks in real time for just the sort of data-stealing behavior he would have performed himself in his years playing digital offense.

Mudge is intensely aware of the potential for false positives: Given that the CINDER system would have to function on networks used by hundreds of thousands of employees, even a 1 percent error rate could lead to mistaken accusations against thousands of users on a regular basis. "It's as if we're trying to come up with a medical test for some kind of super-AIDS," Zatko says with a cheerful inattention to political correctness. "If you incorrectly report that ten thousand people have super-AIDS, they're going to have a very bad day at the office."

To cut down those false alarms, no single act would signal a leak; instead, Zatko says his detection system would link acts in a probabilistic chain that would trigger an alert only if it could put together an entire string of events that pointed to purposeful data theft. "You put all these things together into the different components of the mission," says Mudge. "I'm looking for these new rhythms, new tells, new interrelations and requirements."

The public request for proposals that Mudge released at CINDER's launch lists a series of possible actions, what it terms "dimensions of the mission," any of which could be strung together and add up to a data leak. First comes reconnaissance, exploring file directories or scanning networks to map their architecture. Then comes analyses of files, searching their contents or reading their metadata, the hidden information that describes the files for the operating system and other applications. Then the leaker would need to gather the files together and prepare them for exfiltration, burning them to a CD, printing them, or encrypting them for transmission. And finally comes the leak itself, the moment when the insider walks out of the building with the physical material in hand, pushes it out by e-mail, or spills it onto the Web.

Even after the initial leak, Mudge argues, the "tells" might continue. He points to the case of Robert Hanssen, a former FBI agent currently serving a life sentence in a Colorado supermax prison for giving intelligence information to the Soviets over two decades. In 2002, he confessed to selling the USSR $1.4 million in secrets, from signals intelligence methods to the fact that the FBI had dug an eavesdropping tunnel under the Soviet embassy in Washington, D.C.

Every few days, Hanssen would stop his normal activities and make a single query to a server across the network, a pattern he repeated for almost ten years. That server, Mudge says, held the counterintelligence database. Hanssen was searching for himself, a routine check to see if he'd finally been found out.

In mid-January 2011, HBGary Federal's Aaron Barr set about trying to deanonymize Anonymous.

With a software developer at the security firm named Mark Trynor, Barr had built a tool designed to scrape users' social networking pages and aggregate the data for analysis. Facebook enforces a "real name policy": No pseudonyms allowed. That meant if Barr could map Anons' Facebook identities to the ones used in the group's IRC instant messaging forums, he could pin down their real-world identities. "One of the goals is to tie as many of the IRC nicks to FB profiles as possible," he wrote in a report on his research.

He and Trynor had first used the software to analyze the social media profiles of members of the Colombian insurgent group FARC. But now Barr wanted to apply the same data collection and analysis to the world's most vindictive group of hacktivists.

This time Barr's coder balked. And the two entered into a back-and-forth debate that dragged on for much of that chilly January afternoon.

"Every time you use this it just erodes the American sense of personal liberty for what you believe is security," Trynor wrote to Barr in an e-mail.

"We don't have liberty or security . . . so what is the point," Barr responded.

"Jefferson would be proud of you," the developer shot back, citing Barr's favorite president.

"Jefferson was an idealist that lived in a very different time."

"What's wrong with striving to reach idealist principles?"

"Nothing is wrong with it. But doing it recklessly is as bad as those wanting to squash ideals. The unions started with a good idea and then got corrupted because power does that to everyone," Barr wrote, referencing HBGary Federal's earlier work for the Chamber of Commerce. "With WikiLeaks and Anonymous they corrupted faster. I believed in what WikiLeaks did when they released the helicopter video. I now believe they are a menace."

Trynor doggedly refused to cede the argument to the CEO. "What does it take for evil men to rise to power again?" he asked, paraphrasing the eighteenth-century English politician Edmund Burke in defense of the hacktivists.

"But dude, who's evil?" wrote Barr. "US Gov? WikiLeaks? Anonymous?

> Its all about power. The WikiLeaks and Anonymous guys think they are doing the people justice by, without much investigation or education, exposing information or targeting organizations? BS. It's about trying to take power from others and give it to themselves.
>
> I follow one law. Mine.

In fact, Barr's research was testing the boundaries of morality beyond merely harvesting data scraps from Facebook pages. He had also created a false persona that he used in chat rooms and social networks to infiltrate Anonymous' ranks and gain the hackers' trust: He called himself Julian Goodspeak on Facebook and CogAnon when participating in Anonymous' IRC conversations.

Within days he had identified what he believed were the three "leaders" of Anonymous, who went by the pseudonyms CommanderX, Q, and Owen. (In fact, that trio influenced only a small fraction of Anonymous' activities—the largely anarchic movement had countless subgroups.) In total, Barr prepared a list of a hundred names of Anonymous participants around the world. He believed that CommanderX, for instance, was a Californian named Benjamin Spock de Vries.

But as Barr dug in deeper, his coding assistant began to raise questions about more than the morality of their work. He also started to question Barr's judgment and cast doubt on the social media research's results.

"You keep assuming you're right," warned Trynor. "And basing that assumption off of guilt by association."

"Noooo," wrote Barr. "It's about probability based on frequency. . . . C'mon you're way smarter at math than me."

"Right, which is why I know your numbers are too small to draw [this] conclusion, but you don't want to accept it," Trynor repeated. "Your probability based on frequency right now is a gut feeling. Gut feelings are usually wrong."

"Dude, I don't just go by gut feeling. . . . I spend hours doing analysis and come to conclusions that I know can be automated . . . so put the taco down and get to work!"

"I'm not doubting that you're doing analysis. I'm doubting that statistically that analysis has any mathematical weight to back it. I put it at less than .1% chance that it's right . . . mmmm . . . taco!"

Barr pushed ahead. He was confident enough in his findings that he began to tout them to John Woods, his contact at Hunton & Williams, in the hope of pushing the law firm to move ahead with the two projects it was dangling in front of HBGary Federal's nose. Woods referred Barr to Booz Allen, writing that the defense contractor would likely be interested. Emboldened, Barr contacted the *Financial Times* and a slew of government agencies including the FBI and the director of National Intelligence.

But internally, HBGary Federal's staff was doubting the wisdom of Barr's brazenness. "He's on a bad path," wrote Trynor to HBGary Federal president Ted Vera. "He's talking about his analytics and that he can prove things statistically, but he hasn't proven anything mathematically, nor has he had any of his data vetted for accuracy, yet he keeps briefing people and giving interviews. . . . I feel his arrogance is catching up to him again and that has never ended well . . . for any of us."

"Yeah, my spider senses are tingling too," wrote Vera.

In an e-mail chain among HBGary and HBGary Federal execs on the eve of Barr's meeting with the FBI, they debated the wisdom of releasing Barr's full data set to the public.

"Danger, danger Will Robinson," wrote Vera. "You could end up accusing a wrong person. Or you could further enrage the group."

HBGary's founder, the well-known security researcher Greg Hoglund, on the other hand, believed Barr should go ahead full-bore with his outing of Anonymous. "Jesus man, these people are not your friends, they are three steps away from being terrorists," he wrote. "Just blow the balls off of it!"

The *Financial Times* published a story about Barr's research with the headline "Net Closing Around Cyber Activists." Barr sent a link to the story to his Booz Allen contact and to Hunton & Williams's Woods, who wished him luck with the meetings with federal agencies.

HBGary's own Greg Hoglund e-mailed Barr a congratulatory note. Its subject line read, "You are the dark star," probably meaning the Death Star from the Star Wars films. And he quoted the evil emperor from those movies: "Oh, I'm afraid the deflector shield will be quite operational when your friends arrive. . . ."

If one arbitrary fact of reality separates the fates of the two hackers Peiter Zatko and Julian Assange, it was that Zatko, unlike his Australian counterpart, was lucky enough to have violated the Internet's commandments largely before they were written.

As early as he can remember, computers were a part of Zatko's life as fundamental as food or clothing. His father was a professor at the University of Alabama who studied how the magnetic pull of electrons could help analyze chemicals and spent his spare time obsessing over early home-built PCs. The elder Zatko sanded the sharp edges off of components like circuit boards and nixie tubes and placed them in his son's crib as toys. "He saw very early that there was a schism forming between people who understood computers and those who were afraid of them," says Zatko. "He wanted me to grow up with technology all around me."

Sure enough, by the time Zatko could speak, he was asking questions about his computational playthings. By the age of five, he was tinkering with his father's Southwest Technical Products Corporation 6800 microcomputer, Altair 8800, and Tektronix 4051. Those early PCs had to be assembled from kits, and learning to use them was often inextricable from learning to code. So a kindergarten-age Zatko acquired the ability to write software as naturally as most children learn to write their ABCs. At the same time, his parents introduced him to the violin and later the guitar; his talents on both sets of instruments, digital and analog, developed in parallel.

When the Apple II was released, Zatko's grandfather spent Zatko's father's entire inheritance to buy the sleek new machine for the family's prodigy. Plugging into Steve Jobs and Steve Wozniak's powerful creation, Zatko soon discovered video games, their annoying copyright protections, and the tantalizing task of picking those digital locks. "It's 1978, I'm eight years old, and twenty dollars for a game is a lot of money," says Zatko. "I can't even make a backup copy. So I had to hack the systems, reverse engineer and disassemble them. That became my game."

Soon the allure of piracy gave way to a game with a far wider scope: Zatko discovered the anarchic landscape of connected information systems built by the same agency that would hire him thirty years later: The ARPANET. Zatko would set his modem to cycle through random numbers, a process known as "war dialing," until it found a connection with a faraway Honeywell mainframe in some academic research lab across America. Connecting with those seemingly abstract machines, he'd roam the primitive and sparsely populated networks of a barely discovered digital continent.

Security in the networked world of the early 1980s wasn't merely lax; it was an idea that would have seemed culturally nonsensical, like locking the fridge in your own home. Instead of requiring passwords, common courtesy required that anyone dialing in simply introduce himself or herself, and the local administrator would respond, often asking the visitor to politely avoid certain parts of the network.

Those innocent times evaporated, Zatko says, in 1983, the year that the film *WarGames* hit theaters. In the movie, a young Matthew Broderick demonstrates tricks like hacking into his school's network to change his grades, and eventually war-dials into a military supercomputer known as the WOPR, gaining control of the United States' arsenal of nuclear weapons. Thinking he's merely playing a game, Broderick's character launches a simulated Russian attack that nearly sparks a nuclear apocalypse.

"That Christmas," says Zatko, "every kid in America asked his parents for a modem."

Soon Zatko's silent forays into the unknown were crowded with other, overeager young intruders, many of whom didn't possess the technical knowledge or cultural context to tread lightly on the systems they visited. "The noise versus signal ratio on the networks shot way up," Zatko says. By the time the Computer Fraud and Abuse Act was passed in 1986, making unauthorized intrusions on closed networks illegal, "everything was already locked up," he says.

But Zatko's hobby of breaking the copy protections on video games had evolved into a taste for circumventing security, as it had in the minds of thousands of other kids across the world. They met on bulletin boards and Usenet to exchange tricks—how to crack passwords, make free calls, even get hold of credit card numbers.

The teenaged Zatko, who idolized Frank Zappa and as a teenager met another of his heroes, Abbie Hoffman, felt the same distaste for authority as his networked cohorts. Still, he says his explorations remained a matter of innocent curiosity, and he claims he was granted permission by system administrators to access the same networks that had long been his online haunts. "If you asked, it was amazing how often people would say OK and invite you in," he says.

But Zatko's friends from a decade later tell a somewhat different story, one of a young hacker who saw network defenses as speed bumps, and crossed enough of them to run afoul of the feds before the age of eighteen. In 1999, he told *The New York Times Magazine* that he had once received an informal warning from a "three letter agency." Zatko claims he never knowingly broke computer laws as a teenager; he has no criminal record. The only souvenir that remains of his adventures on the edge of the law would be a long-confiscated Apple II PC that his colleagues say appeared in his office many years later, a well-preserved time capsule from a more anarchic period of Zatko's and the Internet's life.

Fortunately for the young hacker, he also possessed less controversial talents. In 1988, Zatko was accepted to the Berklee College of Music in

Boston and spent the next four years honing his guitar skills and composing music. After graduating at the top of his class, Mudge started work at a Boston computer graphics firm, joined a progressive rock band, and began attending a meet-up of hacker types the first Friday of every month at the Au Bon Pain across from Harvard Square's chess tables. It was a young male scene drawn from an online bulletin board called the Works, where Zatko had made a name for himself under the pseudonym "Mudge." One evening, a co-worker who was known within the group by the handle White Knight invited Mudge into a far more elite world of in-the-flesh hackers, a group that would become as iconic in cybersecurity circles as any rock band: the L0pht.

Leading Mudge up to the second floor of a rough brick warehouse above a woodworking shop in Boston's South End, White Knight opened a door to a hacker clubhouse of every *WarGames*-induced fantasy. The walls were paneled with old motherboards and AT&T signs, and lined with microcomputers from Digital Equipment Corporation, outdated Apple and Commodore PCs, and scavenged pay phones. Cables hung from the ceiling, plugged into modems and half-assembled PCs and strung around salvaged mannequins in sadomasochistic configurations. In later incarnations, the L0pht would add a PC with Web access rigged to the toilet for convenient bathroom browsing. A fifty-foot antenna was attached to the roof. All of it had no purpose other than pure merriment and experimentation.

Even before Mudge arrived, the L0pht had a unique approach to hacking. Instead of seeking out other vulnerable networks for infiltration, the ten or so members of the L0pht's lab acquired and built their own computers and even their own networks, hardly a common feat at the time. Then the band of twentysomethings, split between one room for software hacking and the other for hardware, would systematically and gleefully defeat their own systems' security.

That strategy meant that the members of the L0pht, hackers with names like Kingpin, Weld Pond, Count Zero, Space Rogue, Brian Oblivion, Silicosis, and Dildog, could refine their skills and break ground in digital penetration without ever stepping across the law. The L0pht's misfits adhered instead to a sort of modernized version of the hacker code laid out ten years before by Steven Levy in the book *Hackers*: Don't hack anyone else's machines. Don't break the law. Share everything, both physical materials and information.

Ethics aside, the L0pht was a wellspring of epic mischief. Kingpin, a brilliant baby-faced hacker in his early twenties, had developed a hardware kit to eavesdrop on the unencrypted signals from pagers, a protocol known as POCSAG. Space Rogue, a former army soldier with close-cropped hair, hosted the Whacked Mac Archives, an FTP download site with the world's largest collection of Apple hacking tools. At one point, the group heard that a university in Pennsylvania was giving away a PDP-11 microcomputer. So they rented a Ryder truck, hauled the washing machine–size monster to Boston along with its equally large storage module, got them running, and then tried to digitally penetrate them, simply to see if they could.

The first night Mudge entered the L0pht, the elite group of hackers were struck by his technical genius, his heavy-metal hair, and the onstage charisma and extroversion that he'd learned as a performing musician. "He had that reality distortion field," says Space Rogue. "He could see we needed a front man, and that's what he became."

At the time, the L0pht had a de facto leader in Count Zero, one of the group's two cofounders. But Count Zero was going through a messy divorce that kept him away from the L0pht for months at a time, long enough for Mudge to stake his claim. When the group decided to upgrade to a larger space in Watertown on the outskirts of the city, Mudge suggested a vote on whether to leave the absent Count behind. At an Italian restaurant, the group officially announced Count Zero's exile. Mudge had cemented his role as first among the hacker gang's equals.

As he became the group's public face and dominant personality, Mudge began to push a new exhibitionist strategy for the L0pht: not simply to hack for its own sake, but to hack in public, publishing their work on L0pht.com and online forums. The hacker mantra of free information taken to its logical extreme: They would emerge from the underground and broadcast their digital exploits.

Mudge began to court the media, finding curious reporters first in local trade publications and then later in *Wired, The Washington Post,* and the BBC. They sold T-shirts, attracted groupies, and proudly called themselves "media whores." Taking cues from Mudge's hero Abbie Hoffman and consumer protection icon Ralph Nader, the L0pht provocatively placed the onus for security blowups not on evil hacker bogeymen, but on the IBMs, Oracles, Microsofts, and Sun Microsystems of the world, chiding them for not building safer tools for customers. "Companies were saying their products were secure, with no proof at all. So we ripped them apart," says Mudge with a tinge of excitement. "It felt good to take down corporate giants."

Mudge and the L0pht dug into a new middle ground between villainous "black hat" hackers and milquetoast "white hat" penetration testers: They called it "gray hat" hacking. The group didn't use its skills for evil or illegality. But nor did they hide their uncanny ability to demolish common programs' security. At first, companies tried not to acknowledge them. Soon, they had no choice.

In 1997, for instance, the L0pht members found a vulnerability known as a buffer overflow in Internet Explorer. Exploiting that flaw meant that any user tricked into clicking on a booby-trapped link could have his or her computer immediately hijacked. As Dildog wrote in the advisory L0pht published, "Click on the link. Become aware of what happens to your machine. Freak out and beg Microsoft to make the bad man stop."

The next year, Mudge discovered that the encryption used by Windows NT, the corporate version of Microsoft's operating system, had several fatal weaknesses: It stored passwords without regard for upper or lower case characters, and split them into more easily analyzed chunks of seven characters no matter how long they were. While it used a technique called a "hash" to encrypt those password chunks, it failed to "salt" its hashes, a trick that added another layer of noise into the cipher. Each of those mistakes made it mathematically far easier for a systematic hacker to guess the key.

Mudge called Microsoft's approach "kindergarten crypto." And L0pht-Crack, the tool he built, combined every trick in the code-breaking textbook—dictionary attacks that cycle through huge word-sets, brute force attacks that attempted every possible key, and more technical methods like rainbow tables—to defeat that crippled cryptography in record time. By the time the tool was released, it could unlock a network's entire registry of passwords in around twenty-six days, compared with the five thousand years that Microsoft claimed. "It's big. It's bad. It cuts through NT passwords like a diamond tipped, steel blade," the tool's documentation read. "It ferrets them out from the registry, from repair disks, and by sniffing the net like an anteater on Dexedrine."

Microsoft noticed. At the next Black Hat security conference in Las Vegas, the software megalith's executives took the L0pht out for an expensive dinner, agreeing to patch their security flaws on a rigorous deadline and publicly credit the L0pht if the group's researchers would give them a window of time before going public. Eventually, several of the L0pht's members would be hired to contract for Microsoft as security consultants.

As the L0pht members hacked away into the early morning hours, they'd drink whiskey and beer and shout taunts at one another through the wall separating their hardware and software teams. But they weren't just talking among themselves. They were often communing with hackers around the globe over IRC, the same protocol still used today by Anonymous to coordinate its actions. Then as now, it was the lingua franca of the hacker underground. And it was through IRC that Mudge met Julian Assange.

Assange, then using the handle Proff, took note of Mudge's cleverer hacks and often distributed L0pht's advisories to the Best of Security group that Assange ran on Suburbia's servers. But the two hackers had a mutual regard for the other's alpha geek status that went beyond reading each other's research, and they exchanged ideas over the undersea cables that connected Melbourne and Boston. More than once, they met in the physical world, including at least one meal together at the Chaos Communication Congress in Berlin. "Everyone knew everyone on IRC," says one ex-member of the L0pht. "But when Mudge and Assange met at conferences or had dinner, that seemed like a different sort of connection."

No one besides Mudge and Assange themselves, perhaps, knows the content of their conversations. When I asked Assange about Mudge in 2010, he would only say guardedly that "they were in the same milieu."

I reminded Assange that Mudge today leads CINDER, a military program designed to plug the same leaks that fuel his secret-spilling organization. Assange seemed unwilling to accept that idea. "He's a very clever guy, and a very ethical person. I don't believe that he would build a tool for censorship."

When I asked Mudge about Assange, he warned me that his official role at DARPA meant he couldn't make any comments about the Australian. But he added that he still has "very fond memories of those old days gone by."

In December, *Forbes* magazine published a story I wrote about WikiLeaks, with Assange's face on the cover. It quoted Mudge speaking about his leadership of CINDER and mentioned his friendly connection to the WikiLeaks founder. After the magazine hit newsstands, Mudge never spoke to me again.

If Mudge's career followed the same path as his Australian doppelgänger, Aaron Barr's traced one closer to that of Bradley Manning: an aimless American teenager, tempted into the military by the siren song of a top-secret clearance.

Barr grew up in Hoquiam, Washington, a rough logging community in the same cluster of towns that produced Kurt Cobain. He remembers "hardy, dirty people," drunken fights nightly, and "more bars than churches." His father was an exception: A former mill worker, he had lost two fingers and part of his thumb to an industrial saw. That accident had produced a legal settlement, enough for the elder Barr to return to school and study Nietzsche. He would write poetry and take his son on long drives, quizzing him on history and politics.

As a teen, Barr was given a Commodore 64 and spent hours reading programming magazines to tame its mysterious innards. He played Dungeons & Dragons, took apart and reassembled electronics, and joined his school's computer club.

Then he discovered girls. A confident teen with a talent for sports, he found his focus on technology and education dissolving; by the time he graduated, he had a 2.7 GPA, the lowest of all his friends.

Barr tried a few semesters at the local community college without much enthusiasm. But when a couple of old classmates joined the army and told him about their experiences at boot camp, the eighteen-year-old was intrigued. He spoke with a navy recruiter, who wowed him with talk of code-breaking and privileged secrecy. "It sounded sexy to an eighteen-year-old," he says. "So I joined up."

After a few years at a Florida naval base, Barr's technical affinity and the navy's training had made him a competent practitioner of high-frequency direction finding or huff-duff, the branch of signals intelligence aimed at analyzing the information wrapped up in a radio signal to locate its source. By the mid-nineties he had graduated to advanced signals analysis, what he describes as "big, hard communications." Barr's team would intercept a radio signal, often a multilayered collection of voice and data, unravel the strands of that information rope, and seek to understand it, sometimes breaking Russian and Chinese crypto with techniques unfit for public consumption.

The navy moved Barr to Rota, Spain, near the Strait of Gibraltar. Ships passing on to the Mediterranean Sea, Adriatic, or down the coast of Africa would request analysts for specific stints and Barr would often be helicoptered out to spend weeks on whatever aircraft carrier he was assigned to. He remembers those missions and the leaves between them as some of the best experiences of his life: roasting chicken on an isolated beach in the Ivory Coast, or drinking formaldehyde-tinged beer with locals in an Odessa bar.

In 1998, NATO entered the war in Kosovo. And in 1999, the Marines needed SIGINT analysts to support their incursion into the war-torn region. Barr, then serving on the USS *Kearsarge,* volunteered. "I thought it would be neat," he says. "I'm kind of an outdoorsy guy."

Soon he found himself on a helicopter to Macedonia, then camping in a disused chicken farm near Gnjilane, Kosovo. He and his Marine companions brought what they could carry, ate meals from bags, and went the entire month-long mission without showering. Barr slept under the stars. "I couldn't even stand my own smell, not to mention the four other men in my tent," he says.

Soon his platoon moved into an empty police station in the city's downtown and began its work. Much of the fighting was over: NATO had already been dropping bombs for a year. But the lingering Serbian presence under the command of alleged war criminal Slobodan Milošević continued to attack NATO forces and Albanians continued to retaliate against the Serbs. Barr's group was dispatched to track down and break up pockets of violence.

The signals-analyst-turned-soldier would be sent into combat with two oversize and armored Tadpole Unix laptops strapped to his body, one as a backup, and a pair of transceivers with antennae designed for intercepting and interpreting radio communications. He hadn't been certified to carry heavy weapons, so he was given only a nine millimeter pistol. The Marines joked that if they took fire, he would be the first to be shot, because the weapon made him look like an officer.

In the end, the United States and its allies suffered zero combat casualties in Kosovo. But Barr left the peacekeeping mission with a bitter taste in his mouth. "I was struck by the folly of the exercise, how we had no business inserting ourselves into a battle that had been going on for centuries," he says.

He recalled one Albanian man who was detained by the troops for possessing weapons. "He told the interpreter that the Serbs had killed his wife and kids," says Barr. "What else was he supposed to do, he asked us. It was hard to argue with that."

Barr left the military two years later and took a job for the defense contractor TRW in Unix systems administration. But in 2003 he began a master's degree in cybersecurity at Colorado Technical College in Colorado Springs. With a classmate who would later become a cofounder of HBGary

Federal, Ted Vera, he drove around the town with an antenna, combing the streets for security vulnerabilities in local networks. That process was called "war driving," a modern take on the "war dialing" technique that hackers like Mudge had used decades earlier.

The two applied for a single position as a "cyber warrior" at Northrop Grumman, with the agreement that whichever was hired would try to bring the other on later. Instead, they were both hired together to work as a team.

At the time, the defense industrial base was just beginning to be vivisected by cyberspies, a phenomenon that today has become a full-blown hemorrhaging of data from government and private industry. Just as Barr and Vera were finishing their master's degrees, *The Washington Post* reported the attack on Sandia National Laboratories and the defense contractor Lockheed Martin that would become known as Titan Rain. The advanced intrusion had penetrated some of the military's deepest research secrets, including four hundred pages of proprietary documents and plans for the Mars Reconnaissance Orbiter, a satellite whose technology could be repurposed for military applications.

The culprits were methodical and untraceable, sussing out the target networks, siphoning off sensitive data, and covering their tracks in minutes. The stolen data could be tracked back to servers in the Guangdong province of China. But the thieves themselves hid behind layers of proxies that kept them altogether anonymous.

At Northrop Grumman, Barr taught a class to Department of Defense officials on social media vulnerabilities, scaring them with demonstrations of how LinkedIn and Facebook profiles could be used to case potential target organizations, gleaning information for social engineering attacks. The young defense exec began to wonder if the same attacks couldn't be used against the Pentagon's faceless enemies, too, matching characteristics of the malicious software planted by cyberspies with any personal information they leaked to the world. "It hit me: We could apply social media analysis with a different problem set. Instead of working our way into an organization, maybe we could identify individuals who didn't want to be ID'd," he says.

The military was desperate for any solution to the attribution problem, and Northrop was eager to sell Barr's solution. He rose to chief engineer and then technical director of a division, managing twenty million dollars in annual research budget. Aaron Barr, the humble enlisted man, had become Aaron Barr, the defender of American secrets and slayer of anonymity.

In 1998, Richard Clarke, President Clinton's head of national security, came to Boston on a self-guided educational tour to learn about the growing risk of cyberattacks on American critical infrastructure. A legal counsel to the White House suggested he meet Mudge, whose name had begun to be passed around as a smart, articulate hacker without the taint of a criminal record.

Clarke was told to come alone to John Harvard's Brew House, just a block away from the same Au Bon Pain that hosted the city's hacker underground. He sat, drank a vodka on the rocks, and waited. No one showed up. Thirty minutes later, his drink long finished, Clarke began to pay the bill and leave when Mudge, who had been sitting at the bar sizing up Clarke since he arrived, announced himself. "You were only going to wait half an hour?" Mudge asked.

Mudge had been watching for Clarke to reveal what other agent he had brought with him. He was surprised to see that such a high-level cabinet official traveled alone to clandestine meetings with digital miscreants. Over the rest of the evening, they drank and talked about how to break the Internet and put it back together.

A few weeks later, Mudge invited Clarke back to the L0pht. It was a strange scene: one of the country's top "feds," with four members of the National Security Council at his side, in the digital lion's den. But Clarke's endless curiosity charmed and flattered the young hackers. He pulled out his Palm Pilot and asked what sorts of security flaws it might have. Kingpin plugged it into a device he'd created that could quickly crack the device's password and siphon off its files in seconds.

Clarke quizzed them about vulnerabilities in the country's critical infrastructure. Soon they were deep in a discussion about BGP hijacking, a then-theoretical trick: BGP, or Border Gateway Protocol, is the language used by the routers that connect major carriers like AT&T and Qwest. Taking advantage of a bug in those routers could detour large chunks of the Internet or send it into a black hole. (The same exploit is still possible today, and some researchers believe it was used to mysteriously reroute a significant fraction of the Internet through China for eighteen minutes in April 2010.)

For a moment, Clarke huddled with his NSC colleagues in private conversation. But Mudge interrupted, chiding the feds for excluding him and his hacker friends on their own turf. So Clarke repeated what they had just been discussing: Until his visit, he had believed that only state-sponsored hackers were capable of what the L0pht's members were showing him. "Have any governments asked you to do technical work for them?" he asked.

"No," Mudge said with a smile. "But if you're willing to be the first, we're willing to entertain offers."

Clarke wanted lawmakers to see what he had seen. So in April 1998, he helped arrange for Mudge to be invited to speak at a congressional hearing. Mudge insisted that if the legislators wanted his presence, the entire L0pht would need to testify together. So the eight hackers piled into a rented van with tinted windows they'd outfitted with war-driving antennas and drove to Washington. On the way they stopped at the NSA's Cryptologic Museum and accidentally drove past the guards into the agency's secure facility, before timidly backing out. They visited the museum, played with its Nazi-built Enigma encryption machine, and took turns posing for photos in front of a computer in the museum's exhibition on the rising threat of cyberattacks. It was, in other words, a giddy hacker field trip.

Later, at the hearing before senators that included John Glenn, Fred Thompson, and Joe Lieberman, the group rattled off a terrifying list of flaws in America's digital backbone. Mudge, his mane of hair spilling over the lapels of a gray suit and tie, stole the show and the next day's headlines by explaining BGP hijacking, a trick that he warned the legislators could take down the entire Internet in half an hour.

Before the hackers left the chamber, Senator Thompson told the group that they were "performing a valuable service" to their country. Lieberman compared them to Rachel Carson and Paul Revere. Then the L0pht went off for a tour of the White House situation room and ended their trip hanging out in the same room as Secret Service agents at Archibald's, a nearby strip club.

After the Senate hearing, the L0pht felt like it had overgrown its after-work hacker clubhouse. So Mudge engineered a deal with a young company called @stake (pronounced "at stake"), a venture-capitalist-backed consultancy based in Cambridge that would make the L0pht its research lab. As Hunter S. Thompson would say, the weird were turning pro.

But soon after the L0pht moved into its swanky new building, complete with Aeron chairs and a hundred-gallon aquarium where a new tropical fish was added for each new employee, Mudge began to disappear for long stretches. "Where's Mudge?" became a mantra, eventually a bitter slogan, among the rest of the group.

Then the dot-com crash hit. Budgets were eviscerated, clients evaporated, even @stake's tropical fish began to die. The L0pht's members began to be laid off one by one, starting with Space Rogue and Brian Oblivion.

And where was Mudge? Much of the time, he was in Washington. After the Senate hearing, the rest of the L0pht left the political limelight. But Mudge went in deeper. He was invited to an off-site meeting of legislators in West Virginia, and convinced the politicos to offer him a ride on the congressional bus instead of the one reserved for guests. For the entire drive, he held court with some of the country's most powerful politicians, sharing Internet war stories and fielding questions. In 2000, as cyberattacks began to pound major websites like Amazon and Yahoo!, Mudge was asked to attend a National Security Council meeting on cybersecurity at the White House, where he sat two seats away from the president.

In 2002, Mudge's frequent absence became official—he announced that he was taking a year's sabbatical. Some say he left @stake for personal reasons, others because he was doing sensitive work for the government.

Regardless, he never returned. Eventually, after most of the L0pht's hackers left @stake, the start-up was sold to the security giant Symantec at a price low enough that it didn't affect the antivirus giant's accounting enough to be disclosed. "We had had a clubhouse, and it was communal and close-knit and awesome. And then we threw it all away," recalls Kingpin. "It was a typical sellout."

Mudge wouldn't reappear on the cybersecurity scene for another two years. When he did, it was with a research paper focused on a little-discussed problem: the "insider threat."

Mudge's scenario started with a counterintuitive assumption: that the evildoer was already inside the company's network. Then it suggested ways that malicious insider might get data out, whether it be moving large amounts of information, accessing unusual elements of the company's network, or using obfuscation techniques like "reverse HTTP tunnels," a technique of disguising outgoing data as Web traffic.

"Like a mole in a government agency, the greatest value is achieved through unnoticed longevity in the target environment," Mudge wrote in another late 2003 article for the journal of the Unix-focused group USENIX. "The expected movement and characteristics of information and its handling related to business functions must change in these cases, providing us with the ability to identify such covert activities." In other words, with a constant eye toward mole-ish behavior in your employees and their computers, those moles can be whacked.

The idea grabbed the attention of two brothers, Jonathan and Justin Bingham, who raised nineteen million dollars from venture capital firms and made Mudge chief scientist of a start-up called Intrusic. Intrusic never got off the ground and folded three years later. Mudge blames its failure on infighting and bad business decisions caused by friction between the Binghams. He would spend the next three years before his government appointment at the contractor BBN Technologies.

Why did Intrusic fail? Some say its problems went beyond family tensions. Like the L0pht, it was populated largely by twentysomething researchers. One analyst who worked with the start-up, Jon Oltsik, describes it as lacking "adult supervision," and producing tools that worked for hackers but never had the polish and the disciplined development cycle of business software. "Mudge makes a great evangelist and champion," says Oltsik. "I would never give him execution responsibility."

But the fundamental flaw in Intrusic's business may have had less to do with management than the nature of the eternal problem the company hoped to solve. The company's technology could never provide the easy litmus test for insider misbehavior that customers wanted. Its tools were hardly an automatic mole-whacking machine: Like its competitors', the company's products required humans to monitor and analyze the data they produced.

And just as important, there was a cultural barrier to pushing insider threat software. Mudge himself, in his USENIX journal article, had already guessed at that hard sell: "Perhaps, whether accurate or not, it is too painful for organizations to entertain the notion that they might already be compromised. Being overrun by reverse HTTP tunnels might be an easier pill to swallow than accepting that these reverse tunnels are symptoms of actions initiated from internal machines that are already compromised."

Politically and culturally, companies simply didn't want to accept that they were teeming with leaks.

When the *Financial Times* story about Aaron Barr's research hit the Web, Anonymous quietly moved into action. Strange traffic began hitting the HBGary Federal website. It appeared to be a distributed denial of service attack, Anonymous' usual tactic of clogging a site with phony data requests. "DDOS, fuckers!" Barr wrote to his colleagues. Privately, he was relieved. A mere DDOS attack he could handle.

But Barr had hit at Anonymous' deepest nerve—its anonymity. And the id of the Internet wasn't content merely causing his website some downtime.

HBGary Federal used custom software for managing its website, and the Anonymous hackers quickly combed the site and found a critical flaw in the code. When the software stored data in a database, it didn't always differentiate that information from executable commands—with a trick called SQL injection, a user could pretend to be entering something as innocuous as a username and password, but in fact include characters that triggered actions on the website's back end—even actions like coughing up sensitive data.

HBGary's attackers sussed out the flaw immediately and used it to access the company's password database. But the security firm hadn't been altogether careless: Instead of storing the passwords unprotected, it had scrambled them with a type of encryption called cryptographic hashes.

Hashes are mathematical functions designed to be irreversible. When a user entered a password, HBGary's server would perform a hash that converted it to a unique number and checked whether that number matched the one in the database. But the function couldn't be used in the other direction, to start with the number and reverse the hash to find the password. So storing the numbers instead of the passwords helped protect them against hackers.

In theory, at least. In practice, with a bit of crypto savvy, an attacker can feed every possible password into a hashing function, simply trying them all until one matches. By precomputing hashes of entire dictionaries of passwords, code breakers can use so-called "rainbow tables" to vastly speed up the process. The attack could be prevented by salting the hashes, injecting random numbers to make the operations far more difficult. But like Microsoft in 1998, HBGary didn't use salting.

As Mudge would say, "kindergarten crypto."

The process was made easier still by the fact that Barr's password was short and simple: "kibafo33." The attackers had it in minutes. Barr, being a systems administrator himself as well as HBGary Federal's chief executive, had administrative privileges on HBGary's network. He could reset the password of any other user. So once the attackers owned his account, they owned all of them. Barr had used the same password again and again. So Anonymous soon had access to his Twitter feed and HBGary's home page. And, most crucially, the more than seventy thousand e-mails archived on the company's servers.

For one last laugh, the Anons also decided to hack the personal website of HBGary's Greg Hoglund, rootkit.com. So, like Assange in his Shakespearean phone hack twenty-five years earlier, they set about using a bit of social engineering. The hackers found the name of a systems administrator for the site who worked for Nokia in Finland. Pretending to be Hoglund, they e-mailed the administrator.

"I'm in Europe and need to SSH into the server. Can you drop open up firewall and allow SSH through port 59022 or something vague?" Then they tried two passwords they had found in his mail archive. "Is our root password still 88j4bb3rw0cky88 or did we change to 88Scr3am3r88?"

"It is w0cky—though no remote root access allowed," the Finn answered.

"Just reset my password to changeme123 and give me public IP, and I'll SSH in and reset my pw."

"Your password is changeme123. I am online so just shoot me if you need something."

Anonymous' hackers had utterly disemboweled HBGary and HBGary Federal. They set about defacing the companies' websites and Barr's Twitter account while deleting a terabyte of backup data and research materials. The hackers used Barr's own Twitter account to publish his home address, social security number, and other personal information. Then they posted a long message on HBGary's home page.

> You think you've gathered full names and home addresses of the "higher-ups" of Anonymous? You haven't. You think Anonymous has a founder and various co-founders? False. You believe that you can sell the information you've found to the FBI? False. Now, why is this one false? We've seen your internal documents, all of them, and do you know what we did? We laughed. Most of the information you've "extracted" is publicly available via our IRC networks. The personal details of Anonymous "members" you think you've acquired are, quite simply, nonsense.

. . . You have blindly charged into the Anonymous hive, a hive from which you've tried to steal honey. Did you think the bees would not defend it? Well here we are. You've angered the hive, and now you are being stung. . . .

We are Anonymous.

We are legion.

We do not forgive.

We do not forget.

Expect us—always.

Just who pulled off the epic hack remains unclear. But one hacker named Sabu would later claim in a conversation on Anonymous' elite IRC channel #HQ that he had "rooted their boxes, cracked their hashes, owned their e-mails, and social engineered their admins in hours."

Whoever it was, they seemed to have learned something from the tactics of WikiLeaks. The Anonymous hackers set up their own website, calling it AnonLeaks. Then, partly to prove how little they thought of Barr's work, they published the entire stolen contents of HBGary's mail archive, including his database of Anonymous' purported identities, adding a search feature for easy reading of the executives' most personal messages, the tool that provided me with much of the material for this story.

At first, only the e-mails of executives from HBGary Federal were included. Penny Leavy, Greg Hoglund's wife and president of HBGary, was sent into an Anonymous IRC channel to negotiate by instant message on behalf of HBGary and prevent the release of the rest of the e-mails.

Sabu addressed her immediately. "Penny. Before we get started—know that we have all e-mail communication between you and everyone in HBGary. So my first question would be why would you allow Aaron to sell such garbage under your company name? Did you also know that Aaron was peddling fake/wrong/false information leading to the potential arrest of innocent people?"

"We have no idea," responded Penny. "We have not seen the list and we are kind of pissed at him right now."

"If what you are saying is true then why is Aaron meeting with the FBI tomorrow morning at 11am?" retorted Sabu. "PLEASE KEEP IN MIND WE HAVE ALL YOUR EMAILS."

Sabu demanded that HBGary fire Barr and donate its stake in HBGary Federal to the Bradley Manning Defense Fund. In the bizarre scrum that followed, Leavy debated the morality of Bradley Manning's actions with dozens of angry hackers, and eventually Barr and Hoglund jumped into the Anonymous snake pit and tried to defend their companies' actions. After four hours of arguments, Anonymous decided to publish Greg Hoglund's e-mail too.

AnonLeaks exposed more dirt than the hackers had ever dreamed possible: Barr's plan to unmask Anonymous provided them with humorous reading. Benjamin Spock de Vries, whom Barr had identified as CommanderX, turned out to be a permaculture expert whose anarchist activities only extended as far as home gardening.

But Barr's e-mails also revealed HBGary Federal's spec work online surveilling and tracking enemies of the Chamber of Commerce, the firm's possession of malicious software capable of rooting deep into an unsuspecting user's machine, even Barr's arguments with his wife in which she threatened divorce.

And then there was Barr's attack plan against WikiLeaks. The secret-spilling group immediately posted the slides to WikiLeaks' home page as evidence of the corrupt and illegal conspiracies against it. And as the press and blogs began to pick up the story, HBGary Federal's partners increasingly abandoned Barr to the wolves. While Hunton & Williams declined to comment to the media, Berico, Palantir, and the client that had started the entire chain of events, Bank of America, all released statements disclaiming responsibility for the attack plan and severing relations with HBGary Federal.

The security firm went into damage control mode. Barr canceled his talk at the BSides conference and stopped giving press interviews. Hoglund canceled a talk of his own at the simultaneous RSA conference in San Francisco. As the company went silent, Glenn Greenwald and others wrote excoriating essays on the military-industrial complex's dirty tactics in the digital realm. *The Colbert Report* aired a segment mocking Barr. A few days later, he resigned from his position at HBGary Federal. (A year later, the small company would persist in name alone, without employees or customers. And in February 2012, its parent firm, HBGary, would be swallowed up by the larger defense contractor ManTech for an undisclosed price.)

On the news site AnonNews, frequented by members of the movement, Anons reacted to the news of Barr's resignation with little sympathy. "Anonymous should be as cold as ice and get on to the next operation," wrote one.

"Poor Aaron Barr," added another. "Wait, no, that guy was a dick. At least we destroyed him in anonymous style."

In the months that followed Barr's takedown, several of the pseudonymous hackers who made references to participating in the hack in chat rooms and media interviews were arrested. (An anonymity service called HideMyAss, which some Anons had used in lieu of Tor, admitted it turned over data to law enforcement in response to a court order.) The captured hackers included Tflow, a sixteen-year-old boy from South London, Topiary, aka Jake Davis, a nineteen-year-old who lived in the UK's isolated Shetland Islands, and Kayla, a hacker who claimed to be a sixteen-year-old girl but was actually a twenty-four-year-old man in Doncaster. At the time of this writing, their prosecution is ongoing.

It would be more than a year before the FBI unsealed its indictment against the hacker Sabu, also known as Hector Xavier Monsegur, a twenty-eight-year-old New York man, outed by a single occasion when he had entered an Anonymous chat room without disguising his IP address. Monsegur had pleaded guilty to computer hacking and other crimes in August of 2011. Faced with 124 years and six months in prison, he instead became a government informant, aiding the FBI in its takedown of his friends. In the end, the hacker who humiliated Aaron Barr achieved what Aaron Barr couldn't: He had infiltrated and identified Anonymous' inner circle.

In August 2011, Peiter Zatko walked onto the main stage of the Black Hat hacker conference at Caesars Palace in Las Vegas, wearing a sleek tan sport jacket and jeans, with a room-shaking bass beat announcing his entrance to a crowd of thousands.

He began his keynote address with a kind of acknowledgment that he was no longer Mudge the hacker who headlined Black Hat in 1999, but now Mudge the high-ranking Department of Defense official. "Old Mudge would ask current Mudge, did you sell out? Or are you still doing what you believe in and trying to put a dent in the universe?" Mudge asked himself. Leaving the question unanswered, he launched into a talk on his work at DARPA, focusing on his plan to give small grants to L0pht-style hackerspaces.

In his hour-long talk before Black Hat's assembly of hackers and security researchers, he mentioned CINDER only once, and described it as having "nothing to do with humans."

When I followed up by e-mail with Mudge and his public affairs officer to ask what that meant, they would tell me an entirely different story from the one Mudge had described in his public request for proposals and in our meeting the previous year. "While the CINDER program did not initially preclude the consideration of human insiders, the primary goal of the program has always been to identify future autonomous software insider activities," read an e-mail from DARPA public affairs officer Eric Mazzacone. "The program manager revised and refocused each of the phase I efforts to replace any semblances of human insiders in their missions with software agents while retaining the same mission goals."

Never mind that Mudge had specifically spoken about rogue employees who steal data by burning it to a CD. Or that DARPA's official description of the project posted to its website included an example "malicious mission" of a human printing files and walking out of a building, a description that was never changed, even many months and several revisions of the document later. Or that every contractor who spoke to me about the project—including one who had passed CINDER's first round and remains involved today—described it as including human leakers.

Perhaps Mudge had decided that CINDER would be better off focusing on problems with less controversy than rooting out potential whistleblowers—or perhaps DARPA hoped to make it appear that way. By the time Mudge's public description of CINDER had changed, the project had entered a phase without public documentation, with participating contractors sworn to secrecy.

At the end of his talk at Black Hat, Mudge returned to his original question. "I hope that the old Mudge of 1999 is looking at the current Mudge of 2011," he said. "And other than saying, 'Why are you wearing a pocket square and don't have any long hair,' that, yeah, you're still remaining true to the cause." Then the applause and the bass beat swelled again, and he walked off the stage.

Two hours later I leave the casino's conference center, descend its three-story escalator, and find my way through the lobby to a Chinese restaurant with massive goldfish tanks at its entrance. Waiting outside is a man with an athletic build, wearing a baseball hat, a Pearl Jam T-shirt, and a wary smile that seems to acknowledge that many of the people in the crowded lobby have read hundreds of his e-mails: Aaron Barr.

"It's a bit surreal," he tells me with a self-effacing smile after we sit down. "I hope this doesn't sound overly inflated. But I think I have a small window of what celebrities must feel like, to have so much of your life on public display, even while you're still going on in your own little bubble with all your personal relationships."

Barr's spat with Anonymous has only strengthened his antipathy toward the group. He wants to emphasize that he's not against civil disobedience. He tells me emphatically about how he led a protest against Wal-Mart in 2004, fighting the store's opening on behalf of the small businesses in the Colorado town where he lived.

What Barr opposes, he says, is the abuse of anonymity. "Anonymous believes what they're doing is like holding a virtual sit-in. It sounds good, but it's not equivalent," he says. "If you want to protest unfair or broken laws, get a lot of people together, involve the press, and get arrested. Don't throw rocks from the shadows of an alley. That just looks mean."

And what about anonymity for whistleblowers? "Some amount of anonymity is good," he responds quickly. "You look at countries like Iran and Syria, those folks need to have some ability to have anonymity to get information out."

And what about in a functioning democracy, I ask, like the United States?

Barr pauses. And then he asks for a moment to think. To all appearances, it's not a question he's considered before.

We sit in silence for perhaps a full minute, as Barr looks at the menu. When the waitress comes by our table, Barr still seems preoccupied, and asks for only the same bowl of noodles and cup of coffee that I order.

"In a free and open democracy, it should be attributable," he answers finally. "That's one of my problems with anonymity. In most whistleblowing cases, there's a lot of personal risk and sacrifice. Their name's going to be attached to it. There are personal repercussions. There's pressure to get the information right, to get the perspective right.

"With anonymity," he adds, his uncertainty gone, "there's none of that."

Barr can philosophize about identity and anonymity with me. But for legal reasons, he warns me that he can't talk about his actual work with HBGary Federal to unmask and defeat faceless actors online.

In fact, he doesn't need to. Deep in the thousands of hacked e-mails released by Anonymous sits HBGary Federal's very own proposal to Mudge's CINDER program, Barr's unique contribution to the state of the art for tracking down leakers.

He called it the "Paranoia Meter."

In the document, HBGary Federal offered to build a piece of spyware to be installed on every user's machine in an organization. It would be hidden deep within the operating system to avoid detection, and would communicate with a central server only by weaving its communications into the user's Web traffic, impersonating the exchange of data packets to Web advertising servers.

From its perch inside the potential leaker's machine, it would watch every move he or she made, constantly collecting screenshots of the user's computer, mouse movements, and even using the computer's front-facing camera to watch for suspicious twitches. "We believe that during particularly risky activities we will see more erratic mouse movements and keystrokes as well as physical observations such as surveying surroundings, shifting more frequently, etc.," read the proposal Barr submitted to DARPA.

> Like a lie detector detects biological and physical changes based on sensitivities to specific questions, we believe there are physical changes in the body that are represented in observable behavioral changes when committing actions someone knows is wrong. . . .
>
> Using shoplifting as an example, there are peaks and valleys of adrenaline during the entire theft process. There is the moment the thief puts an item in their pocket (high), then as they walk around the store the adrenaline begins to valley a bit, then they attempt to walk out of the store (very high). It is at these points that we want to be able to take as many behavioral measurements as possible because it is at these points the insider's activity will be as far from normal behavior.

HBGary didn't intend to stop with monitoring only military machines either. It asked to retain the intellectual property of its Paranoia Meter to "transition to commercial products," according to the proposal.

Mudge, it seems, was not impressed. Barr's Paranoia Meter was rejected in CINDER's first round with a form letter from Zatko himself. The note merely thanked the firm for applying and offered no explanation.

Perhaps DARPA was disturbed by the company's unapologetic invasion of users' privacy. Or perhaps by the time of Barr's submission, Mudge had already shifted CINDER's focus to automated software instead of humans, as he would later claim.

Regardless, since the first round of submissions ended in March 2011, DARPA no longer publicizes any of the contractors that have received funding. If a Paranoia Meter has found its way into DARPA's budget, reconceived in a form that better suits the agency's standards, Mudge isn't telling.

For now, the results of his work, like the information it's meant to protect, have become another sealed file in the Pentagon's vault of secrets.

The individuals tasked with rooting out leaks—from Adrian Lamo to Aaron Barr—tend to compare their targets to Robert Hanssen and Aldrich Ames, spies who sold uncountable secrets to foreign empires for millions of dollars. In fact, the archetypal leaker is often more like one NSA analyst named Thomas Drake: a conscientious whistleblower repaid only with crushing legal retribution.

Drake, a thin and severe-looking man with a wisp of brown hair, has the hard stare of someone who has dealt in serious affairs and seen them go very badly. Drake's troubles began on his first full day of work at the National Security Agency: September 11, 2001.

To the NSA, the horrors of that day represented its gaping inadequacies in the new millennium. The agency had intercepted but ignored phrases in the hijackers' communications including "Tomorrow is zero hour," and "The match begins tomorrow." The digital world's vast and messy flood of information had diluted those key warnings into insignificance. The NSA was drowning in data.

Drake's first position at the agency, after a career in air force signals intelligence, was on a project code-named Jackpot. Jackpot aimed to analyze the agency's software to sniff out bugs and inefficiencies. One piece of code came to Drake's attention: a data-sifting algorithm known as Thinthread. The program had been built by the agency's brilliant mathematician Bill Binney to address the Internet's deluge of digital information, and

Drake assessed it as a highly effective, scalable, and elegant tool, one that might have caught the needles in the digital haystack that represented 9/11 if it had only been implemented in time.

Before September 11, Thinthread had been dismissed as too invasive of Americans' privacy. Binney had responded by altering the program to encrypt all its results so that they would only be made available with a court order. But after 2001, the landscape had changed: In the bureaucratic handwringing that followed America's worst-ever terrorist attack, the NSA's leadership was looking for a solution to match the size of its problems, not a single, simple program. It launched a new project called Trailblazer with nine-figure resources aimed at funding private contractors to build new data-combing tools.

Drake would come to see the decision to pursue Trailblazer instead of Thinthread as a corrupt, negligent, and wasteful move. "Trailblazer became a corporate solution," he said when we met in the Washington, D.C., office of the Government Accountability Project, a whistleblower advocacy group. "We disregarded the traditional strength of the NSA, solving problems with the best minds of the private sector and the government, and instead turned the entire project over to industry. You always have to look at alternative options. They chose not to."

Over the next years, Trailblazer doled out massive contracts: Hundreds of millions went to the contractor SAIC, which had hired a former NSA director and formerly employed the NSA deputy director at the time, what Drake describes as "a revolving door refined to an art form." But even as it overran its budget, Trailblazer ran into endless delays and dead ends. By the time the project was canceled in 2006, it had become a $1.2 billion boondoggle.

Drake says he could see the monumental waste in Trailblazer from the start. "It didn't matter if Thinthread was better. They just wanted to spend a lot of money over many years. Corruption had become normalized," he says. "It still chaps my lips today to think about it: the amount of money wasted that never contributed to national security, and no one has ever been held accountable."

In the early days of the program, Drake and three other NSA officials approached one of the agency's budget overseers on the House Intelligence Committee to alert her to the project's overblown costs and ineffectiveness. She passed on the criticisms to others on the committee and even Supreme Court Justice William Rehnquist, but no one acted to rein in the program.

In 2005, Drake faced the last resort of so many ignored internal whistleblowers: anonymous digital communications with the press. He signed up for an account with Hushmail, an encrypted e-mail service, and, using a proxy to disguise his IP address, began sending messages about Trailblazer's alleged corruption to Siobhan Gorman, a reporter at *The Baltimore Sun*. His pseudonym: "The Shadow Knows." With the paranoia of an NSA analyst, Drake took a certain amount of caution in those missives. He installed four layers of firewalls on his home network and used a 256-character password on his encrypted e-mail account, the longest the service would accept.

Even then, Drake eventually decided physical meetings would be more difficult to eavesdrop, and trusted Gorman enough that he believed meeting her in person would be safer. "There is no absolute anonymity electronically," says Drake. "There are means that make it more difficult to identify you. But there's always a digital trail."

Drake says he made certain to never share classified documents in his dealings with Gorman, only testifying to Trailblazer's fiscal waste. In early 2006, as Trailblazer was collapsing, the *Sun* published an award-winning series of articles about the NSA's problems, including one that focused on Trailblazer.

But by then, the agency was concerned about a leak of far larger proportions. A few months before, *The New York Times* had published its story detailing how the NSA had engaged in widespread, illegal spying on Americans. In the post-9/11 era, the privacy concerns that had shelved Thinthread were now an anachronism. According to the *Times'* story, a new project was now hoovering up phone conversations and Internet traffic without the encryption and court-order protections that Thinthread had implemented: warrantless wiretapping. "Every line was crossed," says Drake. "They had turned the U.S. into a foreign nation electronically."

The Bush administration, which had pleaded with the *Times* not to publish the story, was humiliated and furious. A Department of Justice witch hunt set out to find the newspaper's sources.

Drake had participated in official protests against Trailblazer and also provided classified information to Congress during its investigation of intelligence failures before September 11. Those two actions were easily enough to pull him into the Justice Department's dragnet. In November 2007, a team of armed FBI agents arrived at his home.

Drake sensed that the agents had no interest in Trailblazer, and he believed that his communications with Gorman were both legal and insignificant compared to the leak that had exposed the NSA's warrantless wiretapping program. So he decided on the spot to come clean, and spent the day sitting with the agents at his kitchen table, debriefing them on his whistleblowing activities to avoid any confusion with their investigation. He gave the investigators full access to his computers, and they carted away boxes full of his papers.

Eventually, the FBI would identify Department of Justice lawyer Thomas Tamm as at least one source for *The New York Times'* exposé. But Tamm was never prosecuted, likely for fear that his trial would expose too many details of the secret surveillance program that have yet to come to light.

Instead, they indicted Drake.

Drake was accused of illegally taking classified papers from his office to his home under a section of the Espionage Act, the same spy-hunting law used to indict Daniel Ellsberg and Bradley Manning. He faced ten felony charges and thirty-five years in prison, and his case was pursued for more than two and a half years without a trial. The prosecutor in the case argued that Drake should be used to "send a message to the silent majority of people who live by secrecy agreements."

Finally, just days before his court date in 2011, the prosecution admitted that it had vastly exaggerated the classification of the documents Drake had been holding. Drake pleaded guilty to a misdemeanor charge that carried a year of probation and community service. In the sentencing hearing, the judge in the case called the prosecution's behavior in exaggerating the charges against Drake "inappropriate" and "unconscionable."

By that point, Drake had spent eighty-two thousand dollars in legal fees, taken a second mortgage on his house, and been dismissed from his job both at the NSA and as an instructor at the National Defense University. Factoring in his lost pension after decades of military service, he estimates his financial damages in the millions. His Pentagon colleagues cut ties with him. He was separated from his wife for a year. Even his father, a World War II veteran, struggled to understand his actions. Today, he works at a Washington, D.C., Apple store for an hourly wage.

"I worked with the system, and I got fried," he says.

Thomas Drake's story is hardly unique. The Obama administration has pursued more leakers under espionage charges than all other presidential administrations combined. They include Jeffrey Sterling, an ex-CIA analyst who gave information to author James Risen about how the agency had botched an attempt to sabotage Iran's nuclear development plans. Lawyer and FBI translator Shamai Leibowitz pleaded guilty to leaking classified transcripts of bugged conversations in the Israeli embassy to the blog Tikun Olam, in the hopes of stemming Israeli aggression toward Iran. Stephen Kim, an arms expert for the State Department, the military, and Lawrence Livermore National Lab, was prosecuted for leaking a report to Fox News on North Korea's plans to develop a nuclear weapon. Ex-CIA officer John Kiriakou, who had at times defended and criticized the Bush administration's use of waterboarding, was indicted for revealing the name of two of the agency's interrogators to media including *The New York Times*. As of this writing, prosecutions of Kiriakou, Kim, and Sterling continue—as does that of Bradley Manning.

All totaled, that makes six leakers prosecuted under the Espionage Act, compared with three such cases in all previous history—the Obama administration may yet pursue a seventh case with the prosecution of Julian Assange. All of which adds up to an unlikely track record for a president who came to office spouting promises of unprecedented government transparency and proclaiming on his official website in 2009 that whistle-blowing is an act "of courage and patriotism, which can sometimes save lives and often save taxpayer dollars" and "should be encouraged rather than stifled."

Where did that evident hypocrisy come from? Obama has been "co-opted" by Washington's culture of secrecy, argues Jesselyn Radack, a lawyer at the Government Accountability Project who has advised Drake, and who once served as a whistleblower herself, leaking evidence of Justice Department ethics violations to *Newsweek* in 2002. "He wants to curry favor with the national intelligence community, where he's perceived as weak," she says.

But Drake, who has tasted secret information many times over in his career, offers an explanation of Obama's behavior that comes closer to the speech about Circe's potion that Daniel Ellsberg once gave to Henry Kissinger.

"He had never had that kind of access to secrets before," says Drake. "It was a lot of power. He was enamored with it. And it changed him."

CHAPTER 6

THE GLOBALIZERS

Birgitta Jónsdóttir and I are driving away from Reykjavík on a highway that cuts through Iceland's starkly sculpted tundra. Nearly every other car on the road is headed in the opposite direction. And with good reason: Just the day before, the volcanic mountain Grímsvötn at the center of Vatnajökull, a glacier in southeastern Iceland the size of Delaware, spontaneously ejected a twelve-mile-high mushroom cloud of steam and ash into the sky.

Now Jónsdóttir's white Honda Jazz is pointed in the direction of the mass of aerosolized lava rock slowly expanding across the country. "The government put out a warning that you shouldn't drive this way," Jónsdóttir says flatly from behind the wheel, her expression mostly hidden by large black sunglasses covered in glass crystals and framed by black hair cut into a severe fringe. She's wearing a black skirt, stockings with a blue-and-black paisley design, and white leather boots. "I don't care. We're going anyway."

When we arrive in the town of Hveragerði an hour later, the ash cloud has become a thick gray line with vague borders looming on the horizon. By early evening it will have reached the town and blocked out the sun, imposing a biblical darkness that's especially unusual in late Icelandic May, where the sun typically sets at eleven P.M. and continues to illuminate the sky from behind the horizon for the entire night. With a few hours before the ash cloud hits, we drive through the small town where Jónsdóttir lived in her teens, and she points out landmarks: the concrete house with a large garden that her grandparents built; the unassuming headquarters for the neo-Nazi party of Iceland next door; greenhouses heated with geothermal water and sulfurous hot springs that bubble up randomly around the suburban grid. "They're always changing, always changing," Jónsdóttir says in her lilting and staccato English. "A few years ago one opened up underneath a family's living room."

Then we drive by an old schoolhouse, and Jónsdóttir tells me one of her many stories of antiauthoritarian rebellion. In this building, she says, a teacher first cornered her and tried to sexually molest her, threatening to give the fourteen-year-old a low grade in his class unless she let him touch her breasts. She says she responded by threatening to "hang him from his dick if he ever tried to touch me or any girl in the school again."

She drives on, any emotion hidden behind her glasses. But she continues her tale: Over the next days, Jónsdóttir tried to convince other victims who had been sexually bullied by the teacher to press charges or speak out against him. None would. She talked to school administrators, who she says ignored her story and asked her not to repeat it.

A few minutes later in our tour of Hveragerði, we pull up to an art gallery built into a greenhouse. This glass structure, Jónsdóttir says with a dark laugh, was the scene of her first "direct action." In the middle of an art exhibition attended by the teacher who had tried to touch her, the punkishly clad teenager stood on a chair above the crowd and publicly denounced him, calling the man a pedophile and detailing his attempted sex abuses. "My grandparents weren't very happy about this," she says with a thin smile.

Telling uncomfortable truths is a skill that's come in handy in twenty-first-century Iceland, a fishing island turned banking paradise where a mountain of financial and political lies and half-truths have collapsed into a record-setting financial crater. Only in the angry revolution that followed that crisis could a punk, poet, anarchist, and all-around kicker of hornet's nests like Jónsdóttir dream of coming to power as a politician.

Since being elected to Iceland's parliament in 2009, Jónsdóttir has sought to fill the Vatnajökull-size void left by the country's banks with a new national identity: The Icelandic Modern Media Initiative. A series of bills that she and others are still propelling through the Icelandic legislature would turn the island into the world's strongest legal haven for leakers, whistleblowers, and digital truth-tellers of every variety.

The inspiration for the Initiative, known as IMMI, was conceived in the same hacktivist fits of imagination as WikiLeaks. Jónsdóttir, Julian Assange, and other WikiLeaks volunteers crafted it side-by-side, and Jónsdóttir worked with the secret-spilling group during its ascendancy to the international spotlight and its release of the Collateral Murder video.

But Jónsdóttir sees IMMI not as merely a stable foundation for the future of any single transparency outlet. She views it as the next step in a decentralized and global media movement, an arctic anchor for whistleblowers and muckrakers everywhere. "I want WikiLeaks to morph into two things or ten," she told me when we first met in a Reykjavík café six months earlier. "The most important thing is to make it possible for others to do what they're doing. Once IMMI is in place, they can all come here."

IMMI, in its ideal incarnation, would mean that the manifold WikiLeaks of the future wouldn't need to live outside the law and use uncanny technical expertise to stay ahead of their foes. Instead, she envisions a horde of leaking outlets and investigative journalists simply moving their servers and a skeleton staff to Iceland, just as companies incorporate in the Cayman Islands to escape the world's tax system, or Ayn Rand's men of the mind moved to the mountains to escape corrupt government. A Scandinavian Galt's Gulch for the world's secret-spillers.

"WikiLeaks was an important icebreaker," she says, her words accelerating. "It was the tip. IMMI is the rest of the wedge, and it will open up everything."

In September 2010, just as WikiLeaks was ramping up its serial blitzkrieg of leaks, a German spokesperson for the group then known as Daniel

Schmitt gave an interview with the magazine *Der Spiegel.* He told the newsweekly that his real name was Daniel Domscheit-Berg, and that he was leaving WikiLeaks after having been suspended by Julian Assange. His expulsion after three years of work, he said, was due to his having asked too many questions about Assange's focus on America-centric mega-leaks and the group's growing dysfunction. "There are technical problems and no one to take care of them," he told the magazine. "We grew insanely fast in recent months and we urgently need to become more professional and transparent in all areas. This development is being blocked internally. It is no longer clear even to me who is actually making decisions and who is answerable to them."

He hinted at a new post-WikiLeaks project. "I will continue to do my part to ensure that the idea of a decentralized whistleblower platform stays afloat. I will work on that now. It's in line with one of our original shared convictions—in the end, there must be a thousand WikiLeaks."

In the year following that "thousand WikiLeaks" prophecy, copycats began to spring up by the dozens in all flavors and languages, editorial goals, and technological means: BaltiLeaks, BritiLeaks, BrusselsLeaks, Corporate Leaks, CrowdLeaks, EnviroLeaks, FrenchLeaks, GlobaLeaks, Indoleaks, IrishLeaks, IsraeliLeaks, Jumbo Leaks, KHLeaks, LeakyMails, Localeaks, MapleLeaks, MurdochLeaks, Office Leaks, Porn WikiLeaks, PinoyLeaks, PirateLeaks, QuebecLeaks, RuLeaks, ScienceLeaks, TradeLeaks, UniLeaks.

Mainstream media outlets like *The Wall Street Journal,* Al Jazeera, and Sweden's public radio service set up their own experimental leak portals. CommanderX, the "leader" within Anonymous whom Aaron Barr had tried and failed to unmask, created HackerLeaks, a repository for material stolen by hackers. The leaking scene became so crowded that two environmentally focused sites, GreenLeaks.com and GreenLeaks.org, threatened legal action against each other over the rights to the name.

As *Nation* blogger Greg Mitchell noted, only one thing was missing from this newborn leaking movement: Leaks.

Around the time of Domscheit-Berg's departure from WikiLeaks, the site's submission system had disappeared. Assange would tell me in November that the group simply had too much material in its publishing backlog to accept new submissions, a half-truth that hid a much messier explanation, one that would only be revealed by Domscheit-Berg in later months.

But even with WikiLeaks' conduit closed, the new players in the leaking game seemed to be receiving virtually none of those displaced leaks. One reason: They had missed the lessons of WikiLeaks' anonymity protections. Many of the new sites made no mention of Tor and used only SSL encryption or PGP, which fail to hide the identity of the user visiting the site. In some cases they offered no security measures or encryption at all.

Even the mainstream media sites, despite coveting WikiLeaks' trove of documents, seemed to have misunderstood its technical side. Al Jazeera's leak portal, which it called its Transparency Unit, only offered an SSL-encrypted site with a PGP key and suggested users run Tor. It had no Tor Hidden Service, the safeguard that would have not only permitted, but *required* users to be anonymous. It didn't offer cover traffic, and even planted a tracking cookie file in the user's browser.

The Wall Street Journal's leak conduit, called Safehouse, was built so ineptly that the security community declared it dead on arrival. Jacob Appelbaum, who had been supportive of other leaking copycats, pointed out that Safehouse was vulnerable to an attack that would allow a network snoop to easily strip away the SSL encryption it used, and worse, the site wasn't compatible with Tor, despite suggesting that users run the anonymity program. "Pro tip: if you're going to create a document leaking website—have a clue!" Appelbaum wrote.

A legal analysis by the Electronic Frontier Foundation found that both the Al Jazeera and *Wall Street Journal* sites' fine print contained just as many holes. Both stated that if law enforcement asked for identifying information on the user, they could comply and hand over whatever data they might possess. The *Journal*'s site warned users it might share the leaker's information with *any* third party that served its interests. In other words, as EFF attorney Hanni Fakhoury wrote in a blog post, "They reserve the right to sell you out."

With WikiLeaks' submissions offline and no trustworthy alternative, the newborn leaking movement found itself in a drought. With one exception.

In December 2010, BalkanLeaks, the document leaking site for a Bulgarian investigative journalism outfit called Bivol, came online, with a slogan across its masthead: "The Balkans aren't keeping secrets anymore." When I checked out the site, I saw that it used a Tor Hidden Service for submissions, a rare sign of security smarts among the new crop of copycats. But otherwise it resembled all the other obscure and leakless WikiLeaks wannabes from Brussels to Jakarta.

Later that month, BalkanLeaks posted a Microsoft Word file with a note saying that the document had been submitted to the site's Tor server. It was an agreement from the Bulgarian Department of Energy outlining the construction of a nuclear power plant as a joint project of Russia and Bulgaria. Despite the importance of the agreement, the Word file seemed strangely to have been written by an employee of a private firm. But it showed no real evidence of corruption, and the agreement was even available on the Department of Energy's website. Hardly the world's juiciest leak.

Just days later, another document appeared on BalkanLeaks, again obtained through Tor. This one was a letter from one prosecutor to another, including a list of thirty Bulgarian names, all the prosecutors and judges in the highest levels of the country's courts who were also Freemasons. "It is not illegal [to be a Freemason]," BalkanLeaks' note in Bulgarian posted with the document read. "But does their oath to protect the public interest take precedence over their oath to the 'brotherhood'? Perhaps the chairman of the Ethics Commission, Tsoni Tsonev, who is a member of the Masonic lodge, has an answer to this question."

Bulgaria's contribution to the leaking movement was warming up.

The next leak came shortly after, and it was a whopper: one hundred pages of documents. They represented the full transcript of hours upon hours of wiretaps in a bribery case against Bulgaria's former minister of defense, a judge, and the former secretary general of the Ministry of Public

Finance. They contained frank discussions of how much every level of the judiciary demanded in bribes for various matters, so many hundreds of Bulgarian lev for this crime, so many thousands for this contract. "This is the first publication of the full texts of these recordings, which are a true guide to the methodology of bribery in the judiciary," BalkanLeaks' representatives wrote.

The site had its first real scoop. And as dozens of other leaking sites launched over the next months only to produce nothing, the lone Bulgarian trickle of leaks kept flowing. A few months later, the site published a criminal complaint in Greek against a high-level Bulgarian prosecutor, Rossen Dimov. Nine years before his judicial appointment, it turned out, Dimov, his girlfriend, and two Greeks had been charged in Thessaloniki—though not convicted—with smuggling and money laundering.

Then it offered up transcribed, suppressed testimony of a witness saying that he had been pressured by a prosecutor to change his opinion in a Sofia real estate case. Then a list of the partial names and identification numbers of thirty-seven previously unexposed ex-members of the Darzhavna Sigurnost, Bulgaria's brutal secret police during the country's Communist era. BalkanLeaks had arrived: a lone beacon of success in the leaking diaspora.

So in the summer of 2011, I pay a visit to Atanas Tchobanov, one of BalkanLeaks' founders. We meet in front of the roaring Fontaine Saint-Michel in Paris, where he's lived as an expatriate for the last two decades. Tchobanov appears wearing a T-shirt promoting Bivol, the tiny news site that spawned BalkanLeaks, with its logo of a Bulgarian buffalo and its slogan in Cyrillic: "Horns ahead!" He's a smallish man with a shaved head, elfin ears, and a perpetual few days' growth of salt-and-pepper stubble. And after we sit down at a café outside the Sorbonne University nearby, he flashes an impish smile.

"We just got two new leaks, and they're good ones," he says in an accent that has layers of French and Bulgarian. One of those documents is rather tame: the budget for the national Bulgarian railways, showing that they're deeply in debt. The other is significantly more interesting. It's the full transcript of the trial of Angel Donchev, a Bulgarian prosecutor who was recently found guilty of blackmailing another prosecutor, threatening him with a corruption investigation and a raid by the dreaded antimafia police known as the "berets."

The case was sealed in court, but the leak reveals the full thirty-three pages of transcribed phone taps. In those wiretaps, the blackmailed prosecutor mentions that he had a million-dollar home and was taking in ten thousand euros a month, far more than a typical prosecutor makes. Tchobanov believes the case was kept shut to avoid revelations about the plaintiff prosecutor as it revealed the crimes of the defendant. He points out that every prosecutor involved in the case is also shown in the transcript to be a Freemason. "Juicy stuff," says Tchobanov with a tilt of his head and a giggle.

As usual, the two new submissions, like all but the few of BalkanLeaks documents that came through postal mail, were submitted through BalkanLeaks' Tor Hidden Service. Tchobanov attributes the leak site's rare success in part to that religious adherence to strong anonymity—nothing is accepted through e-mail, Facebook messages, or the chat protocol IRC. "Tor is not friendly," says Tchobanov. "We wrote a detailed explanation of how to install it, how to connect, and so on. But it's something pedagogical. We have to teach people to use anonymity, force them to use it."

He admits that the system's inflexibility has likely turned some leakers away. "In the end, we chose less usability and more anonymity. And it worked. We got submissions. In the long run, it pays to have that confidence. We became trusted because we don't give away our sources. Because we don't even know who they are."

But BalkanLeaks' reputation comes from more than its technology. The site and its parent, Bivol.bg, have two public faces among the dozen or so people who work behind the scenes: Tchobanov and another well-known Bulgarian journalist, Assen Yordanov. They make an odd pair: Tchobanov is small, bald, and cheery where Yordanov is bearish, grizzled, and wears a dour expression by default. But they have a rare attribute in common: Both have sterling journalistic records in a country where most of the media functions as a toothless state apparatus. "Reporters in Bulgaria are either scared or bought," says Tchobanov. "Money and fear."

In Bulgaria, newspapers frequently have contracts with government agencies to run notices and advertising on their behalf, a revenue stream that fuels a culture of self-censorship, Tchobanov explains. Many media owners have close ties to the government. According to Reporters Without Borders' rankings, the country has the least freedom of the press of any in the European Union.

And on the darker side of its carrot-and-stick system, journalists are periodically and horrifically attacked. In 2006, TV journalist Vassil Ivanov, who had investigated organized crime in the country, had his apartment ripped apart by a bomb. A writer who covered the mafia, Georgi Stoev, was fatally gunned down in central Sofia in 2008. Another, Ognyan Stefanov, suffered a beating with hammers the same year that broke most of the bones in his body. No one was charged in any of the three cases. The tradition of journalistic intimidation goes back to the dark days of Communist rule, when the Bulgarian dissident writer Georgi Markov, living then in London, was nicked with an umbrella tip carried by a spy posing as an antiques salesman. The tip planted a pellet of the poison ricin in Markov's leg, and he died in a hospital three days later.

Yordanov and Tchobanov live on opposite sides of Europe. By remaining in Paris and stashing BalkanLeaks servers elsewhere in France, Tchobanov and the site's hardware are protected from the government and mafia in his home country. Yordanov, who still lives in the eastern Bulgarian city of Burgas, has no such protection.

Neither is immune from attacks. Tchobanov's family house in southeastern Bulgaria was visited in 2010 by officials who claimed that it was built illegally, what Reporters Without Borders described in a report as a typical intimidation tactic often followed by violence. And in 2008, Yordanov was nearly murdered in his hometown by a knife-wielding hitman.

Like a government- and mafia-sponsored security audit, what hasn't killed the pair has only proved their journalistic credentials, casting them as incorruptible in the eyes of leakers. And the enmity of Bulgaria's powers-that-be may have also helped them gain the trust of their most useful source of all: Julian Assange.

Clay Shirky, a bald and brilliant new media professor at New York University, traces the concepts behind the Icelandic Modern Media Initiative to a time long before WikiLeaks, before science fiction novels like *Cryptonomicon* and *Islands in the Net* imagined havens for contraband data in Grenada, Singapore, or the fictional South Sea island of Kinakuta, before even the invention of the Internet.

He points instead to an agreement made at the end of World War II between the intelligence agencies in the United States, Great Britain, Canada, Australia, and New Zealand. With the war winding down and an elaborate system of intelligence sharing set up, this English-speaking subset of the Allies considered the prospect of giving up the stream of useful data each was receiving from its partners, and instead decided to simply keep pooling that information in the postwar era.

They called it the UKUSA agreement (exotically pronounced yoo-kew-za), and according to a theory that Shirky laid out for the audience at the Personal Democracy Forum in January 2011, it allowed the intelligence services to do more than continue spying on the Germans and the Japanese. Because the UKUSA member organizations were legally prevented from intercepting the communications of their own citizens, they traded off. Canada would spy on Australia's citizens and share its data with the Australian Secret Intelligence Service, for instance, while Australia wiretapped the Canadian populace and handed over its data to Canada's Communications Security Establishment.

In fact, the mutual domestic spying Shirky describes has never been reliably documented, and may be apocryphal. But the converse in Shirky's analogy remains true: Just as governments may have spied on each other's citizens for the last sixty years, citizens are now spying on each other's governments.

"What we're seeing is a pattern of transnational leaking," he told the conference. "WikiLeaks is the first media outlet that is genuinely multihomed. There is no one country's laws that govern how WikiLeaks operates."

Just minutes before, Birgitta Jónsdóttir had spoken to the same crowd via Skype, unable to travel to the United States for fear that her association with WikiLeaks would tempt U.S. authorities to keep her for questioning in its unfolding investigation. In her virtual talk, she outlined her plan for the Icelandic Modern Media Initiative and how she had tasked four ministries of the Icelandic government with changing thirteen laws to make Iceland the most liberated media nation in the world.

Shirky followed Jónsdóttir by describing how the combination of that plan and WikiLeaks functions as the inverse of his UKUSA scenario, a "globalization of citizen oversight." Pointing to the South African government's attempts to control and redact the local press, he suggested that the path of a future leak might be routed from Johannesburg to Reykjavík, through London, and back to Cape Town. Just as WikiLeaks detoured its whistleblowers' documents through Sweden and BalkanLeaks routed its submissions through France, perhaps the future of secret-spilling lay in WikiLeaks' and IMMI's multinational leak-laundering.

"This is an alternate way of leaking that is, in at least its current instantiation, obviously superior from the point of view of the leaker to any previous system," he told the crowd.

And then he ended with a prediction: that this innovation in leaking across national boundaries would lead to leak suppression laws that crossed national boundaries too. "There will be a massive push for globalization of control of secrets. . . . I think we can expect an enormous amount of pressure to be brought to bear against the system we've just heard described," he warned. "I think this will fail. But that is the struggle we're going to see today."

Around the corner from a sunny square on Stockholm's Nytorget Street, where blond youths wear straw hats, eat ice cream, and lounge on the grass, walls of craggy granite spring up and drop the sidewalk into the shadows. A hundred-foot rocky hill rises to a peak overlooking Vita Bergen Park, a large patch of green in Södermalm, the hip neighborhood where Lisbeth Salander lived in Stieg Larsson's Millennium Trilogy. At the summit perches a picturesque nineteenth-century stone cathedral. But, as in Larsson's novels, the darker, more interesting world lies beneath.

Jon Karlung, the gray-stubbled and blue-eyed founder of the Internet service provider Bahnhof, leads me into a tunnel cut into the hill, past a pair of twenty-inch-thick steel doors, and into the White Mountain Data Center, a digital bunker first built as a Cold War nuclear shelter and now converted into one of the world's most secure places to store information.

We walk past two backup power generators originally designed for German submarines, a hydroponic garden, and a network operations center housed in the room that would have been used to run Sweden's civil defense in the event of a nuclear winter. In a cave full of servers cooled by roaring fans, a glass-walled conference room hangs above the racked computers, embedded in the ceiling rock with thirteen-foot steel bolts. Climbing up a set of stairs, through a tiny door that forces the tall Swede to stoop and bend, and past a wall of gallon-size lead batteries, we arrive at our destination in a messy storage room.

On a cluttered IKEA shelf sit the two elongated pizza-box-shaped objects that Karlung has brought me here to see: a pair of Dell servers. From the day of WikiLeaks' October 2010 Iraq War exposé through the first seven months of its Cablegate release, these two machines ran the world's most controversial website.

He picks one up and hefts it into my hands, admiring the computer with a boyish smile. "I like to imagine it's the Ark in the first Indiana Jones movie, a box in a warehouse somewhere that contains all the world's secrets," he gushes.

In fact, even now, a month after WikiLeaks ended its contract with Bahnhof, the data center's staff still hasn't erased the servers' data. "I'm thinking of putting them on eBay. A joke! A joke!" Karlung adds, pronouncing the word "yoke."

Bahnhof's granite walls, Karlung assures me, are strong enough to protect its computers from even a nuclear blast. But that's not why WikiLeaks sought out the data center's pricey services, starting at fifteen hundred dollars a month and steeply rising with power and bandwidth costs. Instead, he says, the underground fortress is "a kind of metaphor." Since 1766, Sweden has had some of the world's strongest protection for journalistic sources and freedom of information, rooted in a constitution written before the United States' First Amendment. Under that constitution, censorship of the press is virtually impossible. And except in cases of national security or treason, prosecutors are prevented from even asking a media organization for the identity of a confidential source.

Despite its subterranean chambers and bulletproof doors, not even Bahnhof pushes the boundaries of those free-speech laws quite as far as another company across the city in a bedroom-size basement of a rundown building in a northwestern Stockholm neighborhood. PeRiQuito AB, also known as PRQ, has no hydroponic gardens or other James Bond villain accessories in its humble server room. But the company served as the central hub for WikiLeaks, including its submissions system, long before it engaged the services of Bahnhof. In fact, since 2004 PRQ has assembled some of the Web's most controversial and legally questionable denizens, and the company brags that it has never once taken down one of their sites.

Before WikiLeaks, the most famous inhabitant of PRQ's racks was undoubtedly the Pirate Bay, the world's most popular source of pirated music and videos. Both PRQ and that iconic piracy site were founded by two Swedish hackers, Gottfrid Svartholm and Fredrik Neij, a pair of neo-libertarian coding savants who were nineteen and twenty-five years old at the time.

The Pirate Bay draws more Web visits than *The New York Times,* the Huffington Post, or Netflix, not simply by maintaining an enormous index of downloadable copyright-violating material, but also with entertaining antics like posting the legal threats it receives, along with its own responses, on its website. Once the Swedes advised lawyers from Steven Spielberg's DreamWorks studio to "please go sodomize yourself with retractable batons." On another occasion they went so far as to suggest a specific model of baton to Apple's attorneys, the ASP twenty-one-inch. In 2007, Neij, Svartholm, and a third owner, Peter Sunde, tried to raise enough donations from their users to purchase Sealand, an abandoned UK military platform in the North Sea that would serve as a home outside of any nation's copyright laws. (Sealand refused to sell to them.)

After Swedish police raided PRQ in 2007 and confiscated servers with the intention of taking the Pirate Bay offline, the file-sharing site left its original home to bounce among a variety of temporary hosts across Europe. But PRQ has kept plenty of other colorful customers. Kavkaz Center, a Chechen rebel media site, was one of the first to take refuge in PRQ's basement in 2005. The site's users regularly post Islamist extremist rants about violent jihad against Russian, American, and Israeli infidels along with uncensored news about the war-torn Caucasus. The Russian ambassador to Sweden demanded Kavkaz be taken down in 2007, but when the Stockholm prosecutor had the server seized, PRQ immediately put up a backup server, fought the decision in court, and extracted fourteen thousand dollars in damages from the government.

PRQ also hosts Perugia Shock, an Italian blog that was banned from Google's Blogger service for allegedly defaming the prosecutor of 2011's Amanda Knox murder trial. It even offers a home to Pedophile.se and the website of the North American Man/Boy Love Association, Web forums where users discuss sex with children but are restricted from posting images of child pornography.

"Even though I loathe what they say, I defend them," says Mikael Viborg, a short, muscular lawyer who was recruited by Svartholm and Neij to become PRQ's chief executive. "We don't cooperate with the authorities unless we absolutely have to."

That absolutist antiauthoritarian policy means PRQ keeps no logs of traffic that could identify site visitors, as little information about its two thousand customers as it can, and that it encrypts the small amount of identifying information that it does obtain. It requires sites to pay up front rather than ask for any personal details that would allow the company to extract payment later, and often receives those funds in envelopes without return addresses or handed over in briefcases of cash. "Generally we don't know who our customers are, and by Swedish law we're not required to," Viborg says.

These two Swedish data companies and the laws they exploit made WikiLeaks possible. But across the Scandinavian Peninsula and the Norwegian Sea, through an unmarked door in a Reykjavík alley and up a flight of stairs, another hosting company may represent the PRQ and Bahnhof for Jónsdóttir's next generation of media.

When I ask 1984 Web Hosting founder Mordur Ingólfsson for some examples of his customers, he gives me a simple and defiant response. "I won't answer that unless you get a court order."

A forty-one-year-old Icelander rendered hairless by the genetic condition alopecia, Ingólfsson says he created the ironically named firm to "prevent thought control." The company has become Iceland's largest Web host, partly by maintaining an attitude in keeping with the island's Viking personalities. "We don't respond to threats, intimidation, manipulation, pressure, or probes," says Ingólfsson. "We will go bankrupt before we break the trust of our customers."

One thing Ingólfsson won't do for his customers, however, is break the law. So instead he's trying to change it, working as the treasurer for Jónsdóttir's IMMI movement. IMMI is designed to not merely imitate the Swedish laws that brought WikiLeaks to PRQ, but to take them much further. It pulls together the best freedom-of-information laws from every country in the world: Source protection from Sweden, safeguards on third-party communications from Belgium that prevent Internet service providers from having their records subpoenaed, and New York state's prohibition on using foreign libel laws to bring local lawsuits, for instance. It revamps the Freedom of Information Act that allows citizens to requisition government documents and even introduces a Nobel-style prize for freedom of expression.

Laws aside, Iceland already sports a few features of a perfect island data haven. The newly built Thor Data Center, for instance, on the outskirts of Reykjavík pipes in cheap, green electricity from geothermal power plants along with free arctic air to cool the racks of computers. Its owners hope IMMI will help expand the dozens of servers in the former aluminum plant to thousands, as controversial data from around the globe flocks to Iceland's protective borders.

Cagey as always, Ingólfsson won't say where 1984's servers are housed, but he assures me they're mostly in Iceland, ready to benefit from Jónsdóttir's initiative. If IMMI can be passed, he says, it won't merely boost his business, but help to redeem Iceland from the shame and economic tragedy of the financial crisis that recently saddled every person in the country with the equivalent of $220,000 in debt. "If we succeed, this will be the new cornerstone of the country's reputation," he says. "In my humble opinion, IMMI is the most important thing to happen to this godforsaken island since the Sagas were written."

Tchobanov, Yordanov, and a circle of other Bulgarian journalists sit around a table at a café in the sunny Bulgarian resort town of Varvara. Tchobanov has been leading a training session on using encryption, Tor, and proxy services for reporters to protect sources and themselves. Now they're drinking beer at noon, eating fried shrimp pulled from the Black Sea nearby, and swapping dirty jokes in Bulgarian. They translate one for me that involves Vladimir Putin, Dmitri Medvedev, and a prostitute.

Tchobanov is sitting next to Yordanov, looking rather tiny beside his heftier, square-bodied partner. The smaller of the two BalkanLeakers is wearing the Bivol T-shirt with the buffalo again. So I ask him why his news site uses the animal as its symbol.

It's Yordanov who answers. The bulkier Bulgarian wears a pair of very scuffed, knockoff Oakley sunglasses, a half-week's worth of thick stubble, a black shirt tucked over a barrel chest into black shorts, sandals, and a leather case for his cell phone on his belt. He looks, to my ignorant American eyes, like a caricature of an Eastern European mafia thug on holiday.

"The buffalo is a very special animal," the forty-eight-year-old reporter intones slowly, with a thick Slavic accent. "It is the most intelligent animal. Much more intelligent than a dog. It has a perfect memory.

"Once, there was a baby buffalo that was beaten very badly by a man," he continues, in a manner that leaves it unspoken whether he is telling a story from personal experience or as a kind of Aesop's fable. "It grew up, and eight years later it left the herd one day. When it was found, it had killed the man and trampled him so that you couldn't recognize him. The buffalo had smelled the man from fifteen kilometers away.

"So in this way we're like the buffalo," Yordanov concludes without expression.

"We do not forgive, we do not forget!" explains Tchobanov with a silly grin, borrowing the Anonymous hackers' slogan.

Tchobanov had mentioned to me in passing that Yordanov had been a cowboy and raised buffalo before becoming an investigative journalist. So I ask how it was that he ended up on that unlikely career path.

There's a long pause. Then Yordanov speaks, and I can sense from the silence around the table that I've now touched on the wrong topic for a sunny lunchtime discussion.

"I was twenty-four years old. And I was married to a woman that I loved very much. And I discovered that my wife, this woman who I loved more than anything in the world, was an agent of the secret police," he says simply. "She was spying on me in my own home. So that's why I left the city and became a cowboy."

I drop the subject, seemingly to the relief of everyone present. But a few hours later, during another break in the training sessions, Assen Yordanov tells me his story.

In the 1930s and 1940s, Yordanov's grandfather was a commandant in the Bulgarian resistance leading guerrilla troops in the country's southeastern mountains against the Nazis and the official Bulgarian government that had allied with them. But even after Bulgaria switched to the Allied side near the end of the war and later became a Soviet satellite state, the Communist government distrusted Yordanov's grandfather's political power.

On the twenty-eighth of March, 1947, Yordanov's grandfather was given what seemed to be a routine medical injection by a Community Party doctor. He died half an hour later, while his twenty-seven-year-old wife and seven-year-old son, Assen Yordanov's father, watched. An autopsy was never performed.

Yordanov's grandmother was asked to sign a statement that cut all ties with her dead husband. She refused. So she and her family remained enemies of the state, shunned and ignored even by their neighbors for close to a decade.

Assen Yordanov grew up with only a shadow of those years hanging over his childhood. His father had become a man of letters and a famous poet within Bulgaria, and the younger Yordanov sailed through school, publishing poems and essays in the local newspaper. He graduated from St. Konstantin Preslavski University with high marks and performed his military service with distinction in the region of the country close to the Turkish border. Yordanov mostly stayed away from politics. But he didn't hide his hatred of the Communist regime. "I knew our society was heading toward a dead end, and I wasn't afraid to say so," he says.

While he worked toward his master's degree in Bulgarian literature and philology, he took a job as an audio and video engineer in the local Burgas theater. It was there he met a petite Turkish actress, a very pretty twenty-four-year-old with short dark hair and brown eyes. He asked her to marry him three days later.

They had been husband and wife for one year when a friend in the government called Yordanov and asked to meet for a walk in Burgas Park. There the agitated friend told him about a detailed report he had stumbled upon, and asked him to promise that he would never reveal his source. The report was written by Yordanov's wife under the pseudonym "Christina." She was a paid informant of the same secret services that had engineered the murder of his grandfather. For the last year, she had monitored and reported every word he and his parents had said. The books he read. The jokes he told his friends.

"When I found out, I didn't know what was real or false, what was true and what was a lie. The thinking in my head turned to marmalade," Yordanov says. He stumbled out of the park in a state of dazed denial.

Yordanov says his wife rejected his accusations, then confessed, then collapsed and cried for forgiveness. She promised to end her work for the secret services, which had begun six years earlier during her years as a student in Sofia. "But I knew that once you're part of this system, you can't get out," he says. "It's not a disease that can be cured."

He felt betrayed by Bulgarian society at the deepest level. So he simply left it behind.

Yordanov divorced his wife and began a period of wandering in the Strandzha Mountains. He passed through communities where only handfuls of people lived, and eventually settled in a village of about thirty people, taking up residence in an abandoned building on its outskirts. He had no access to electricity, carried all the water he used up a cliff face half a mile away, and stopped cutting his beard or hair. He went months without speaking. "I never wanted to see a human face again," he says. "I wanted to live by different laws. To escape the laws of man."

To sustain himself, Yordanov worked as a shepherd in a cooperative farm. With no expenses, he eventually saved enough to buy three cows, a buffalo, and later ten sheep and three goats, and began selling their milk. Feed suppliers who learned that he was an enemy of the state refused to sell to him, so he grew his own oats, beans, corn, and alfalfa, hiring locals to help tend the crops.

After his first year as a cowboy, he left his bare-bones shelter and went into the forest to live with his herd. When the animals wandered wild, he wandered with them, riding horses and sometimes training and riding the buffalo themselves. He slept occasionally in a shack he found in the woods, more often on the ground, in caves or in trees, wherever he was when night fell. Eventually his itinerant farm grew to more than 150 animals.

Yordanov spent nearly five years this way. He would receive mail and occasional phone calls from the nearest village once a week. And then in late 1992 he got word from his seventy-three-year-old grandmother that his father was moving to Sofia. So he sold his beloved herd and returned to the city to take care of her.

Back in Burgas, he found that Bulgarian society was utterly

transformed—on its surface, if not at its corrupted core. The Communist regime that had wrecked his life had been disassembled and reassembled in the hands of several well-connected oligarchs. The Darzhavna Sigurnost secret service had evaporated in name, but many of the same faces had found their way into the new government.

For a year he lived in a state of culture shock, taking temporary jobs in construction and as a dockworker at the Port of Burgas with no ambition or direction. And then a friend told him about a job opening at the *Dneven Trud,* or *Labor Daily,* the country's biggest newspaper. With his father's name and his education in literature, Yordanov got the job.

Within months, Yordanov discovered he had a gift for eliciting bombshell stories from sources. "With me people seem to feel that they can tell me anything without danger," he says simply. He showed unusual fearlessness in publishing articles about mafia murders, government corruption, and the privatization of the country's resources, and soon he was seen as one of Bulgaria's top muckrakers in the eastern part of the country.

During the Yugoslavian wars of the mid-1990s, Serbia had been struck with an international embargo. As a result, Bulgaria's eastern coast across the Black Sea from Russia became a lucrative smuggling gateway. In 1994, Yordanov established through confidential sources that the Burgas airport was being used in a complex scheme involving local mafia and the government, with undeclared tankers arriving laden with oil, cigarettes, weapons, and gold and being registered at the airport rather than the port to hide their cargo. He published the eight-page story in *Standard Weekly* and immediately faced a series of defamation suits. All were eventually dropped, and the chief customs officer of Burgas was indicted on smuggling charges and convicted.

The next year, Yordanov got a tip that a factory north of Burgas was being used for illegal cigarette production. He gained access to the property, took pictures, and published the story. Soon after, he received his first death threat, a letter delivered by messenger that suggested he "reserve a place in the cemetery for his tomb." The police raided the factory and shut it down, and began a two-year investigation against the politicians and businessmen involved, which mysteriously ended without arrests.

Yordanov suddenly interrupts his storytelling. The sun has set, and he's taken off his sunglasses to reveal a pair of deep-set and sad eyes. "I want to stop here and say something," he says. "One of those men involved in this factory that I exposed was Boyko Borisov. Today, he is the prime minister of Bulgaria. And sixteen years ago I showed that he is a criminal."

"A scent of death bleeds into the scent of Christmas," begins Birgitta Jónsdóttir's illustrated memoir, *The Chameleon's Diary.* Sewing together childhood dreams and memories, she tells the story of a small girl with black hair and pale skin in the tiny Icelandic fishing village of Thorlákshöfn, who ran up and down the slippery, rotting black wood at the edges of the pier, using her mother's violin bow as a fishing pole and terrifying the old men who worked on the wharf.

Jónsdóttir's mother, Bergthóra Arnadóttir, had moved to the town of eight hundred Icelanders to escape Jónsdóttir's mentally disturbed birth father, whom Arnadóttir had married at the age of sixteen. The mother and four-year-old daughter soon met her stepfather, a kind, sturdy fishing boat captain with long sideburns and one of the biggest houses in the village. It was the young Jónsdóttir, not her mother, who brought up the idea of marriage. "I proposed to him," she says. "I got down on my knees and asked him to be my father."

Jónsdóttir would remain close to her stepfather even after her parents divorced a few years later, and she says he taught her lessons she would remember: He lived simply and honestly, paid his employees before himself, and carried no debts. She called him "the Fisher King."

Arnadóttir was a well-known folk singer who organized a monthly music night in Reykjavík, and her daughter grew up surrounded by artists, musicians, and writers. Jónsdóttir pored over her grandparents' books on Tibetan Buddhism and the American spiritualist Edgar Cayce. As she grew into her teens, she discovered the punk scene and its roots in anarchist politics. Her mother recorded her first album at the same recording studio as Björk, during the recording of the Icelandic pop star's premiere record. Jónsdóttir remembers that once, while her mother strummed her guitar and sang, the two teenagers whispered secrets to each other in the studio's attic.

Surrounded by uncompromising artists and writers from that young age, Jónsdóttir says she never had much use for conformity. She bought a secondhand tuxedo jacket with long tails, and painted an enormous anarchist symbol on its back in orange. When her mother entered her into a youth modeling competition, she responded by cutting her hair into a towering black Mohawk. She blew the whistle on her sexually abusive teacher. And when a school trip took her class to visit a Coca-Cola factory and then the Icelandic Parliament building, the Althingi, she refused to go inside. Instead, the fourteen-year-old sat on the school bus and wrote a poem about a nuclear holocaust with an eyeliner pencil on a paper bag.

It was called "Svartar Rósir," or "Black Roses," and was later published in the newspaper *Helgarpósturinn*. "I look out the window and see collapsed houses," it reads in English.

I look out the window
and I see streams of blood.
I look out the window
and I see the black ashes
and remains of human bodies.
This is all that's left
of our humanity.

One stormy Christmas Eve just before the traditional six o'clock Icelandic Christmas dinner, Jónsdóttir's stepfather arrived at her grandparents' home in Hveragerði, dropped off her younger brother, then abruptly plunged back into the blizzard, saying he needed to deliver a package to a friend's place.

The next day, he was still missing. The police found his car next to a river, a ten-minute drive away from the village. There was no body or suicide note. But the police concluded that he must have drowned himself in the icy floes. "My father the Fisher King killed himself last night. . . . I pictured him in my mind's eye walking heavily into the river, a little bit bent. A lone dark shadow in a blizzard of white," she would write. "I have to remain strong. I have erected an iron raft in my back, it will not bend."

In the months that followed, Jónsdóttir's mother moved to Denmark in a state of near emotional collapse, and Jónsdóttir followed her there to care for her. The young woman entered a state of self-imposed exile, painting, writing, and reflection that she describes as a walk "through the valley of the shadows." Her first volume of poetry, *Frostdinglar* or "Icicles," was published the next year. When she returned to Iceland to launch the book, she met a handsome, sensitive young Icelandic-American photographer, with large brown eyes and thick black hair that fell over his forehead.

The twenty-two-year-old Jónsdóttir was given a grant by Iceland's government to stay in Reykjavík and write a book a year, an idea that struck her as deathly boring. Her photographer boyfriend, on the other hand, wanted to return to the United States to reconnect with his American father, and asked her to come with him. To avoid immigration hassles they were married, and six weeks after the birth of their son, they moved to West Virginia. After a few weeks there, the new family put their belongings into a trailer and took a road trip across the country, finally settling in Medford, New Jersey, where Jónsdóttir sold Kirby vacuum cleaners door-to-door to pay the bills while writing and painting.

When she had had enough of hawking payment plans to poor suburbanites who couldn't afford them, they returned to Iceland. But back in their homeland, another problem was coming to a head. Before the birth of their son, Jónsdóttir's husband had begun to suffer from grand mal seizures. Doctors diagnosed him with epilepsy and prescribed drugs that left him vacant, deeply depressed, and sapped of creativity.

Early one morning, he told Jónsdóttir he was leaving for work, and disappeared. She found a note from him when she woke up an hour later: "Can you forgive a desperate soul?"

Despite a manhunt that covered much of western Iceland, it would be another half decade before his weathered and smooth bones were found in a field of moss on Snaefellsnes Peninsula to the north of Reykjavík in a suicide that mirrored her stepfather's.

Fifteen years later, when Iceland found itself in one of the deepest financial crises in the world's history, Jónsdóttir would write that the long-smoldering tragedies of her early life had served as preparation for the country's hour of reckoning. "This morning I realized why I had been given these lessons of living in suspense without going quite mad or losing my integrated sense of optimism," she would write in her blog. "I was being prepared for the times we are facing on my nearly bankrupted island."

After her husband's death, Jónsdóttir buried herself in her usual creative outlets for her grief: words, images, and ideas. But she also discovered a new one that tied them all together: the Internet. While working a temporary job at Iceland's first Internet ad agency, she was amused to see that the company's designers had left a typo on its website—in the word "proofreading," no less. When she couldn't get anyone at the firm to fix it, she learned HTML and corrected it herself, then began making her own sites, mixing poetry, paintings, and video.

Soon she and two other early Web obsessives named Gunnar Grímsson and Guðmundur Guðmundsson formed a group called InterOrgan or IO, a kind of Web art collective. "Io is the most volcanically active moon in the solar system. The friction from the forces pulling on it creates all this heat inside. It was a very appropriate name," says Guðmundsson. He, Grímsson, and Jónsdóttir pushed the boundaries of the Internet with some of the Web's first live audio and video. "If it was new, we did it," he says. "If it already worked, we weren't interested." One of Jónsdóttir's sites, at its peak, received enough traffic to account for 60 percent of the country's bandwidth.

When Jónsdóttir wasn't programming, she was protesting. She organized demonstrations against the construction of the Kárahnjúkar Dam in the east of the country, which threatened to swallow up some of the country's most beautiful waterfalls to power aluminum smelters. She found the phone numbers of the handful of Icelandic-Tibetans in Reykjavík and organized a series of Free Tibet protests in front of the Chinese embassy. And in 2003, she led protests against the buildup to the invasion of Iraq, writing poems that vented her frustration at political lies and the mass media's blindness as it stumbled toward a seemingly preordained war.

One was titled "The Horror of War."

mountains of starved children
shiny bones
burning flesh
these are images we should
put in a frame
mount them in our homes
so we never forget
the true horror of war

For Jónsdóttir, protest became practically a way of life, even when her fellow demonstrators could be counted on a single hand.

Then, in October 2008, the whole of Iceland was suddenly protesting beside her.

Iceland's banks had been deregulated in 2001, and privatized in 2003 under the Milton Friedman–influenced leadership of Prime Minister Davið Oddsson. With Viking zeal, the country had adopted some of the most highly leveraged, riskiest banking practices in the world. In a few years, the assets of the country's financial industry grew from 100 percent of the country's gross domestic product to 1,000 percent. And then, at the height of those bankers' hubris, the international credit crisis hit.

As the banks failed to repay their mountains of short-term debt, they collapsed and were nationalized in a panic. The stock market value of Icelandic companies fell 90 percent. Luxury properties being built in Reykjavík with make-believe money were halted midconstruction. Consumers defaulted on the expensive car loans they had taken as their savings winked out of existence. Iceland's obligations to international depositors in one bank alone, Landsbanki, were roughly as damaging to its economy as the reparations Germany had been forced to pay in its crippling Treaty of Versailles after World War I.

Icelanders revolted. The protests began every Saturday outside the Althingi, and grew from hundreds to thousands. They banged on pots and pans, replaced the parliament's flag with that of a corporate grocery store chain, and at one point nearly managed to storm the building. Word of the demonstrations and organizational details spread through Facebook, where almost half of all Icelanders had accounts, more per capita than any other country. "The first Facebook revolution didn't happen in Tunisia or Egypt," says Róbert Marshall, a former journalist who now serves as a member of the Icelandic parliament. "It happened here."

Three months later, when it became clear that the crowds would paralyze the country before they gave up, the government resigned. An election was scheduled.

In the chaos of that interregnum, Icelanders began meeting in small groups to discuss what they wanted from the new government. Jónsdóttir was a regular at one of those makeshift assemblies at the Reykjavík Academy, and it quickly grew into a political party: the Citizens' Movement. It had a handful of goals such as keeping the International Monetary Fund out of Iceland and increasing direct democracy. But it vowed to use a hit-and-run strategy: Whether or not it could achieve those goals, it planned to dissolve after eight years, a short enough time that it couldn't be corrupted.

When Jónsdóttir volunteered to run for parliament as part of that subversive political party, its poll numbers showed that it would receive half of one percent of the vote. "It seemed like a suicide mission," says Margrét Tryggvadóttir, another of the candidates.

The Citizens' Movement was largely ignored by the mainstream media. But through its visibility on Facebook, in blogs and Twitter—and by virtue of the electorate's vast anger toward Iceland's existing parties—it steadily rose in popularity. They finagled their way into the candidate debates, where Jónsdóttir cut a fiery figure. "We used a kind of hacker mentality," she says. "We found the cracks in the system where we could get our voices heard."

In the election that April, more than a third of the country's representatives were replaced with candidates who had never held office before. Seven percent of the vote went to the Citizens' Movement, enough to give the party four seats in the legislature.

One of those seats belonged to Birgitta Jónsdóttir.

Long before Atanas Tchobanov ever thought he could take an active part in the leaking movement, he pioneered another method of hacktivism: text message terrorism.

Tchobanov had known since his teen years that Sofia was simply not a place where his brand of free thinking could exist: He refused to take part in the Community youth movement activities and was fired from the low-level industrial job he had been forced into by the Bulgarian government. When the Iron Curtain parted in 1989, he got a fellowship at Paris Ouest University and moved to Paris's Latin Quarter without hesitation.

Tchobanov went on to get a Ph.D. in linguistics and became a skilled computer scientist, analyzing large databases of spoken and written word to find the fundamental underpinnings of human language. But as Bulgarian news began to trickle across the border via the growing online news media, he found his native country's political problems harder to ignore—and also saw his opportunity to help. In 2004, he created an NGO for Bulgarians living abroad and became the editor of the Bulgaria-focused *Parizhi Vesti,* or *Paris News,* attacking what he calls the country's "slow and stupid" administration and highlighting issues like a wasteful, no-bid, thirty-five-year highway contract proposed in 2006. "It was my small way of fighting for normality," he says.

One of the issues that infuriated Tchobanov most was a health care tax that was applied to all Bulgarians: both the seven million that lived in the country and the one million or so that had emigrated since the fall of the Soviet Union. Even those who paid for health care abroad still had to fork out the equivalent of thousands of dollars or risk paying an accumulated fine if they ever set foot in the country again. The law made less sense than ever after Bulgaria's 2007 accession to the European Union. But despite immense anger from expats, the unresponsive parliament had no incentive to dial down or delete a tax that affected those who couldn't vote against them.

Just before Christmas in 2008, one Bulgarian newspaper made the mistake of publishing the cell phone numbers of every member of the country's parliament in a feel-good invitation to the country's citizens to send them Happy New Year text messages. Tchobanov seized the opportunity, forwarding the list to thousands of Bulgarians around the world, calling on them to send SMS messages demanding the tax be lifted.

Soon more than ten thousand petitioners flooded the parliamentarians' in-boxes with as many as ninety texts each in a day, paralyzing their phones in a legal version of the same attacks Anonymous would use to take down Visa's and MasterCard's websites. Newspapers and lawmakers denounced the tactic and called it "SMS terrorism." One member of parliament, who was pushing a bill to repeal the tax, issued a public apology to the parliament. But Tchobanov won: The anti-tax bill passed. Today he laughs off the use of the word *terrorism* to describe his cell phone subterfuge. "People paying lawmakers' salaries have the right to contact them," he says with a shrug.

Back in Bulgaria, Yordanov was fighting other battles—without the thousand miles of buffer between Paris and Sofia to protect him.

In 2007, he and fellow reporter Maria Nikolayeva at the newspaper *Politika* dug into a political decision that would allow a swath of ecologically protected coastal land twelve miles north of Burgas to have its protections stripped, be bought on the cheap, and turned into a lucrative holiday resort. Other patches of coastline were distributed to public officials, their families, and even the police officer responsible for investigating possible ethics violations by the mayor who had removed the land's protected status.

The two reporters prepared a series of front-page stories for *Politika*, exposing the allegedly corrupt deals, titling the series the "Crusade Against Strandzha." When the first article appeared, Nikolayeva received a visit from two men in the paper's Sofia office. They dropped the day's paper on her desk and made some offhand remarks about the building's security. "You know full well that you shouldn't write things like this," they said. "And you know what happens to curious journalists. They get acid thrown at them."

The two were referring to Anna Zarkova, a reporter for the *Dneven Trud* who had sulphuric acid splashed on her face and body at a Sofia bus stop in 1998 after publishing a story on Bulgarian human trafficking. Her left eye was so badly damaged that it had to be surgically removed.

The paper's surveillance camera caught the license plate of the men's car who had threatened Nikolayeva and the footage was submitted to the police. No arrests were made.

She and Yordanov refused to back down. Instead, Nikolayeva made as many television appearances and gave as many newspaper interviews as possible to try and publicize the threat against her.

After that first installment in the series, Yordanov learned that someone in Burgas was trying a different censorship tactic, purchasing every issue of the paper from the distributor before it could be delivered to newsstands. When the next issue came out, he drove to the distributor early in the morning, filled his car with papers, and handed them out himself to local retailers.

Yordanov's brazenness didn't go unnoticed. It would nearly cost him his life.

. --- .. .-.. .. .. --.- ..- ... .--- .... .--. ...- --.

If John Perry Barlow ever wrote a résumé—and he's probably not the type who ever has—it would list seventeen years of cattle ranching in Wyoming, a few decades of writing lyrics for the Grateful Dead, experimenting with LSD alongside Timothy Leary, and cofounding the Electronic Frontier Foundation. But science fiction author Bruce Sterling once named Barlow's primary profession as that of a poet, in the sense that Percy Shelley once described poets: "the unacknowledged legislators of the world."

When Barlow stood behind the podium at the Icelandic Digital Freedom Society's conference at Reykjavík University the summer before the country's banking collapse, the stubble-jowled rancher looked more like a western priest, wearing a black leather jacket over a black shirt, a black kerchief tied into his collar with a white cross emblem above it. The sermon he offered the assembled Icelandic technophiles was a people's history of communication, from the invention of language to the first printing press, a device he argued had launched a "renegotiation of power" that led to everything from the Thirty Years' War to the Spanish Inquisition.

A half-millennium or so farther down his timeline, Barlow came to his own discovery of the Internet. "And lo, I typed in 'telnet,'" he said, "and I could make a hard disk spin anywhere in the world."

"I had a real holy vision at that point," he continued. "If you're going to take all of humanity and put them in the same social space where they don't have clothes and buildings, or anything to show who they are, they don't have property, they don't have jurisdictional boundaries, they don't have law maybe . . . it could be the biggest thing since the capture of fire."

The Internet represented another "renegotiation of power," he argued, one just as dangerous to the status quo as Gutenberg's invention had been. For the next twenty-five years, he and fellow cyberlibertarians like John Gilmore and Lotus founder Mitch Kapor would spend much of their lives and enormous sums of money fighting the governments and corporations that would seek to neuter or restrain that new "social space."

Birgitta Jónsdóttir was in the audience. And it was one tossed-off idea near the end of Barlow's speech that lodged in her mind. "My dream for this country," he said, "is that it could become like the Switzerland of Bits."

He didn't elaborate.

(When I visited Barlow in his Chinatown apartment in New York a few years later, he was more explicit. "I had thought about the Pirate Bay a lot, and I wanted something more robust than that," he said between drags of a Marlboro cigarette and sips of Red Bull. He had even discussed the transparency haven idea with a government minister in Monaco before thinking of Iceland. "I felt like the answer to sovereignty was sovereignty. To fight them on their own terms.")

A few months later, Jónsdóttir was elected. And then the final ingredient in Barlow's idea appeared: WikiLeaks came to Iceland.

It began when Bogi Ágústsson, a Walter Cronkite-ish anchor for Icelandic national broadcaster RUV, appeared on the evening news and calmly explained that a legal injunction had prevented the station from airing a prepared exposé on Kaupthing Bank, the biggest bank in Iceland. Instead, he said, viewers should visit a site called WikiLeaks, where they could see the source material for the TV segment themselves.

Icelanders who took Ágústsson's advice found a newly leaked summary of Kaupthing's loan book posted on the site, detailing an ugly web of more than five billion dollars in loans from Kaupthing's coffers to its own proprietors and companies they owned, with little or no collateral. Two billion dollars, for instance, went to the bank's main owners, brothers Ágúst and Lýður Guðmundsson. Another billion went to Ólafur Ólafsson, a major investor in Kaupthing who had on his own birthday flown in Elton John from England, along with a grand piano, for a one-hour concert. "The banks had been eaten from the inside out," says Kristinn Hrafnsson, a former investigative reporter in Reykjavík who had worked on RUV's blocked report and later joined WikiLeaks as a spokesperson.

A government inquest began pulling apart the documents to determine if Iceland's anger could be channeled into criminal charges against Kaupthing executives and others. Eleven men, including billionaire brothers Robert and Vincent Tchenguiz, who both took loans from Kaupthing and also held an investment stake in the bank, would eventually be arrested in London and Reykjavík. Neither the Guðmundsson brothers nor the Tchenguiz brothers were indicted, but Ólafsson, the Elton John fan, faces charges of money laundering, and his prosecution is ongoing.

WikiLeaks immediately became a household name in Iceland. And just three months later, Julian Assange and Daniel Domscheit-Berg arrived in Reykjavík, conquering heroes from abroad. They were invited to appear on the talk show of Egill Helgason to discuss their bombshell bank leak, two idealistic young men unable to suppress goofy grins on camera as they basked in some of the first mainstream attention to their work. Afterward, strangers on the street offered them hugs and bought them drinks in bars.

It was on the set of Helgason's talk show that Assange reintroduced a long-smoldering idea, a blend of his love of Neal Stephenson's data haven novel *Cryptonomicon*, his recent work digging into the internals of the Cayman Islands holdings of the Swiss bank Julius Baer, and Barlow's seed of an idea from his talk a year before.

"You mentioned to me this idea that in Iceland we should become a vanguard of publishing freedom," Helgason, a cheery round man with blond curls said to the pair of WikiLeakers in their on-camera interview.

"Absolutely, absolutely," Assange responded. "We see in the Caribbean Islands and the Cayman Islands that politicians create laws to enable off-shore financial institutions to hide the assets of the developing and the developed world," he said. Iceland could pull off the opposite trick, he argued: transforming itself into an island where *nothing* is hidden. He went on to list the world's most liberal freedom-of-information and media laws from Sweden to Georgia. "Why not pull all this together, and become *the* center for publishing in the world?"

Two days later, he and Domscheit-Berg spoke at the same Digital Freedom Society conference that Barlow had keynoted, fleshing out the idea with an even longer list of possible laws Iceland could cherry-pick and emulate. Jónsdóttir spoke at the same conference, and when she left the university building for a cigarette break, Assange introduced himself and said he would join her outside in a moment to smoke a cigar. When he came out the door, he was, instead, carrying a hard-boiled egg, which he ate without explanation. "That's the strangest cigar I've ever seen," Jónsdóttir deadpanned. They liked each other immediately.

Two days later, Jónsdóttir brought Assange and Domscheit-Berg to a late-night meeting with a group of activists at a Reykjavík tapas restaurant. Not to dream any longer about a transparency haven in Iceland, but to strategize about how to actually build one.

For the next months, IMMI commanded the activists' lives. Rop Gonggrijp, an old Dutch cypherpunk friend of Assange's and a longtime member of the Chaos Computer Club, flew in to help manage the research. Smári McCarthy, a half-Irish, half-Icelandic free-information advocate and hacker, taught himself to read the legal codes of countries across the Western world, culling and tweaking a list of laws the group had compiled. By February, the small group had a proposal ready, one that tasked the Althingi with researching and voting on a series of bills over the next years. One dark winter evening, Jónsdóttir read that call to action into the parliamentary record before a sparse crowd of legislators.

"It is hard to imagine a resurrection of our country from financial ruin and widespread corruption due to secrecy, but we intend to offer a business model based on transparency and justice," she said. "We will be the first in the world to market ourselves as a country with a principled, holistic, and modern set of laws fit for the digital age."

The proposal passed unanimously. IMMI had taken on a life of its own. But Julian Assange had other work left to do in Iceland.

A few weeks later, Jónsdóttir and Assange were sitting in the English Pub, a quiet café across a courtyard from the Althingi. Assange asked Jónsdóttir to watch a video, and he turned his laptop's screen toward her. Typically unaware of his surroundings, he had left the volume on full blast without headphones, and a waiter walked over to shush him.

Jónsdóttir looked on as a helicopter circled a group of men on the streets of New Baghdad. Then as it showered the figures with bullets as they ran for cover. Then as it fired again on what remained of their bodies. Then again on the family of bystanders in a black van who tried to help them. And sitting in the middle of that Reykjavík café, Jónsdóttir openly wept.

Later, as WikiLeaks set about tearing two wars open for the world to see, she would think of the poem she had written before the invasion of Iraq in 2003.

these are images we should
put in a frame
mount them in our homes
so we never forget
the true horror of war.

Zlatarov Street in Burgas is a quiet, tree-lined strip of cobblestones just a few blocks from Burgas Park and the beach. It takes its name from a Bulgarian chemist and novelist who famously worked to protect the country's Jews during the Second World War. At seven P.M. on December 20, 2007, the sun had already set, and most of the street's lampposts were in disrepair, leaving the sidewalks nearly dark.

Yordanov was walking to his apartment along that peaceful lane when a man in a black ski mask turned swiftly from a gated alleyway on his left, blocking Yordanov's path. He barely saw the figure in time to jump backward instinctively. The man's knife darted toward Yordanov's chest, cutting through his coat, his sweater, and the skin of his torso. But Yordanov wrested the blade out of the man's hand and punched him in his masked face while holding his shirt. He felt two broad lines of pain suddenly spread across his back. Two other men had come from around the other corner and were beating his torso, arms, legs, with steel bars—one blow struck the back of his head. He dropped the first man and started kicking back at the two others, but they quickly retreated into the dark—a fourth grabbed the incapacitated knife-wielder and dragged him off hastily. Yordanov was too injured to follow, and spent days recovering from dark hematomas covering his arms, legs, the top and back of his head, and spreading into violet wings on his shoulder blades.

In Paris, Tchobanov was working occasionally with Reporters Without

Borders when he learned of the attack. He interviewed Yordanov by phone on behalf of the group, and the two became friends. They would later discover that Tchobanov's grandparents had lived in the same neighborhood of Burgas as Yordanov's. Their grandfathers had known of each other during the war, and Tchobanov's family had been one of the only ones to acknowledge Yordanov's grandmother's existence and visit her after Yordanov's grandfather's murder.

Yordanov told Tchobanov he had no intention of caving to the thugs who had nearly killed him. In fact, he intended to take his journalistic independence even further: He wanted to launch his own news website, free of any corporate or government ties. And he wanted Tchobanov, a computer-savvy reporter with a convenient geographic remove, to help him.

They called it Bivol. And in its first months, the site had immediate impact. Rumiana Jeleva, Bulgaria's foreign minister, was set to be confirmed as a representative of the European Commission. Yordanov and Tchobanov helped uncover her connections to the Darzhavna Sigurnost and financial ties she had failed to disclose, showing that she continued to own a consulting company long after she had claimed to have no interests in it. The story kicked off an investigation of Jeleva that was picked up in foreign media and finally led to her resignation from not only the EU post, but also her ministry position.

Despite their early success, Tchobanov could sense that Yordanov's traditional breed of muckraking was endangered: In September 2008, the journalist Ognyan Stefanov had been stopped outside a Sofia restaurant one night and brutally beaten with hammers and steel bars, left for dead with broken arms and legs and a severe concussion that he barely survived. In this case, the attack had a new twist: The victim had attempted—and failed—to remain anonymous.

Stefanov was secretly the editor of the blog Opasnite Novini—"Dangerous News"—that ten days before had published a story based on a leak that showed officials in the new intelligence agency DANS were involved in a smuggling ring. DANS, whose name translates to "National Security Agency," had been formed the same year, supposedly to fight organized crime. Somehow it had identified Stefanov.

In a government investigation that followed Stefanov's beating and through more anonymous leaks to the press, DANS was revealed to be engaged in mass wiretapping of journalists and government officials. (By 2010, the Bulgarian government would perform around fifteen thousand wiretaps annually, close to two hundred times the number per capita reported in the United States that year.) The mass surveillance and intimidation tactics of the Communist era Darzhavna Sigurnost were alive and thriving.

Tchobanov knew that Bivol needed new ways to protect itself and its sources. So he simply typed "anonymous submissions" into Google. Soon he began to discover the cypherpunks' many gifts to journalists: PGP, Off-The-Record messaging, Tor. And WikiLeaks.

The Bulgarian technophile was immediately fascinated by the site's technical methods and utter fearlessness. He began to monitor its leaks closely, and even experimented with uploading an unverified document that a source had sent him, in the hopes that this mysterious group might be able to authenticate it and publish it to a global audience. The document, written in Bulgarian, never surfaced on the site.

It was only after the Cablegate release that Tchobanov began to consider the full power of WikiLeaks' model—not just to protect journalism, but potentially to advance it. In a Skype chat with a few other journalists and technologists who worked on and off with Bivol, they proposed the idea of a leaking site that would publish locally focused documents that WikiLeaks wouldn't, a leaking syringe targeted at the Balkans and its neighbors rather than a hose aimed at the world at large. Within days, they had registered the URL and set up an SSL-protected site and a Tor Hidden Service in an OVH data center in the French city of Roubaix, the same one that briefly housed WikiLeaks' publications until they migrated to Sweden.

To Tchobanov and Yordanov's delight, the documents flowed in immediately, from the nuclear power agreement to the judicial bribery tapes: solid, irrefutable primary-source evidence obtained with cryptographic anonymity.

But Tchobanov was no Tim May, and BalkanLeaks wasn't BlackNet. The Bulgarian wasn't merely seeking to prove the power of cryptography and anonymity to slice through institutional secrecy; like all good journalists, he and his colleagues were on the scent of the biggest possible stories—and they smelled them hidden deep in the still-unpublished majority of the WikiLeaks cables, a trove of documents that, as Bradley Manning had promised, affected every country in the world.

After the criticism WikiLeaks faced over its dump of the Afghanistan documents, the group had adopted a "harm minimization policy" that sought to redact the names of potential State Department informants or other sensitive individuals who might be endangered by exposure. That meant the small group was dependent on its relationships with media partners like *The Guardian* and *The New York Times* to dig through the immense collection of text and carefully redact names before the cables could be published.

That painstaking process meant the leaks were flowing like molasses. By March, nearly four months after Cablegate began, only five thousand of the quarter million cables had appeared. WikiLeaks had put out a call on its Twitter feed for more media organizations to participate. Tchobanov e-mailed a plea to a WikiLeaks contact to give the 978 cables from the embassy in Sofia to Bivol. No response.

One released cable in particular had tantalized and galled Tchobanov and Yordanov: It was a 2005 briefing by U.S. Ambassador James Pardew on the state of organized crime in Bulgaria and its extraordinarily cozy ties to government. But after the memo's redactions by WikiLeaks' partners at *The Guardian,* it contained no specific names of Bulgarians. *The Guardian* had used the cable to construct a story on Russian influence in Bulgaria's mafia world, but hadn't been able to confirm any of the allegations against Bulgarians themselves. So the paper simply snipped huge portions of the text, mostly from a section titled "Who's Who in Bulgarian Organized Crime." Of the cable's original 5,226 words, all but 1,406 were missing.

Luckily for Tchobanov and Yordanov, WikiLeaks' control of the cables was itself beginning to spring leaks. One of the group's erstwhile partners, a freelance journalist and controversial Holocaust denier named Israel Shamir, had obtained a portion of the unredacted cables and was using them to write stories for the Moscow magazine *Russian Reporter.* Tchobanov wrote him an e-mail in February asking about the contents of the Bulgarian cable. To his surprise, Shamir responded with the full text. A few days after *The Guardian*'s Bulgaria story, the Norwegian newspaper *Aftenposten* announced that it had also inexplicably gained access to the full set of cables. So Tchobanov wrote to *Aftenposten,* asking the papers' editors to verify the text that Shamir had sent him. They wrote back, confirming that Shamir's slice of the megaleak was the real deal.

The unredacted cable was an encyclopedia of Bulgarian organized crime, with entries for every major group: gangs with names like Multigroup, Intergroup, TIM, the Union of Former Commandos, and the Amigos. It cataloged their involvement in all flavors of crime from tax fraud to smuggling, extortion to sexual slavery. It followed the flow of money to every major political party, and named government officials who openly consorted with the groups or had made the transition from mafioso to politician. The cable named towns like Svilengrad and Velingrad that were controlled entirely by mafia-cum-government.

Bivol published a story on the report, titled simply "Bulgarian Organized Crime, Uncensored." Other Bulgarian newspapers picked up on the story. One, the paper *Capital,* headlined it simply "Black and White"; the cable had confirmed in stark terms all the corruption that had been suspected for years. As usual, no one was indicted, perhaps the strongest evidence of all of the government's symbiosis with criminals.

For Bivol, the most important reaction came from WikiLeaks itself. The group published the unredacted version of the cable on its site rather than the version of the cable that had been gutted by *The Guardian,* and accused the newspaper on its Twitter feed of "cable cooking." Tchobanov wrote to WikiLeaks again, suggesting that instead of *The Guardian,* the group hand all of its Bulgarian cables to Bivol. This time WikiLeaks' staff wrote back, asking for time to look into Bivol's background and to learn more about Tchobanov and Yordanov.

Three weeks later, Tchobanov received an e-mail from his contact at WikiLeaks. He and Yordanov were invited to Ellingham Hall for a meeting with Julian Assange.

Tchobanov and Yordanov's first hours in England went badly. Yordanov left his laptop in an overhead bin on the airplane and they spent hours trying to retrieve it from the airline. The Bulgarian pair got lost on the drive from London to Norfolk after Tchobanov's GPS stopped working. And on one of the roundabouts, Tchobanov forgot to drive on the left and caused a minor collision with an oncoming car.

When they finally reached Ellingham, they found the WikiLeaks founder dressed in a gray suit and in a dour mood. He seemed preoccupied, Tchobanov and Yordanov remember, with his legal fate and the financial industry's ongoing blockade choking donations to WikiLeaks. Assange also worried that the pair, like WikiLeaks' rogue partner Israel Shamir, might redistribute the cables willy-nilly, and had prepared a contract that held them responsible for redacting names of sensitive State Department sources before publishing the cables. It also stipulated that they only access the unredacted files from a computer with no Internet connection.

But Assange also praised BalkanLeaks, Yordanov and Tchobanov told me. He said he had looked over the submission site's security and approved of its simple rigor. And he seemed to enjoy the homemade rakija that Yordanov had presented him as a gift. "By the time we opened the second bottle, I knew that he would give us the documents," says Yordanov with a grin. They made arrangements to hand over the Bulgarian embassy files securely, and returned home.

When they accessed the full documents a month later, they found the wealth of scandals they had hoped for. One cable showed that Bulgarian officials in the United States had accumulated parking tickets totaling more than four hundred thousand dollars, so many that the United States had threatened to withhold nearly half a million dollars in aid until they were paid. One cable listed all the Bulgarian banks that engaged in money laundering and corrupt loans.

And then they came upon the greatest prize of all, a cable that dealt with the same subject Yordanov had first tackled sixteen years earlier: Boyko Borisov, Bulgaria's prime minister.

It was a 2006 memo from the U.S. ambassador in Sofia, John Beyrle, on the subject of Borisov, predicting his run for the prime minister post and titled "Bulgaria's Most Popular Politician: Great Hopes, Murky Ties."

The cable began by describing Borisov as "implicated in serious criminal activity" and maintaining "close ties to Lukoil and the Russian Embassy." It then tells Borisov's entire life story, starting with his youth as a "neighborhood tough" in a gang on the edges of Sofia, how he founded a private security firm "and built it into one of the biggest in the country at a time when 'private security' was synonymous with extortion and strong-arm tactics," as the cable reads. As chief secretary, he reportedly paid cash for positive press coverage and threatened journalists who criticized him.

Then the cable comes to another section labeled "The Dirt."

> Accusations in years past have linked Borisov to oil-siphoning scandals, illegal deals involving LUKoil and major traffic in methamphetamines. . . . Borisov is alleged to have used his former position as head of Bulgarian law enforcement to arrange cover for criminal deals, and his common-law wife, Tsvetelina Borislavova, manages a large Bulgarian bank that has been accused of laundering money for organized criminal groups, as well as for Borisov's own illegal transactions. Borisov is said to have close social and business ties to influential Mafia figures, including Mladen Mihalev (AKA "Madzho"), and is a former business partner of [organized crime] figure Roumen Nikolov (AKA "the Pasha").

"We should continue to push him in the right direction," the cable concludes. "But never forget who we're dealing with."

If a single document could ever be Bulgaria's Watergate, this was it. And two journalists from a news website that no one had ever heard of were about to publish it.

A year after WikiLeaks released its Collateral Murder video, the first fruits of IMMI appeared. Inspired by Jónsdóttir's lobbying, the Icelandic parliament passed a new media law that legally protected the anonymity of journalists' sources just as strongly as in Sweden. Under the law, Icelandic reporters aren't simply exempt from investigations that might reveal their sources. They're legally forbidden from identifying them.

But even as IMMI's information fortifications rose, Jónsdóttir discovered just how tough it's become to escape the long reach of the American government's war on anonymity. In early 2011, Jónsdóttir received a letter from Twitter, Inc., informing her that a government investigation had requested access to all of her data from the service—both public and private.

In a sense, nothing about this was particularly unusual. Any Internet service's data is fair game for law enforcement. In 2006, for instance, AOL revealed to *The New York Times* that it received about one thousand such requests for its users' information from the government every month. Three years later, when Facebook was still less than a third of the size it is now, one of its staffers told *Newsweek* that it was receiving ten to twenty requests for data from law enforcement every day. Google, the only major technology company to formally publish statistics on those requests, reports that in the first half of 2011 alone, the government asked it to hand over user data 5,950 times, and that the company complied in 93 percent of those cases.

The only fact that set Jónsdóttir's case apart from those thousands of others was that Twitter had even bothered to notify her about the government's snooping instead of silently acquiescing.

Jónsdóttir contacted the lawyers at that cyberlibertarian stalwart, the Electronic Frontier Foundation, who agreed to represent her in the legal fight to keep her private data private. Soon it was apparent she wasn't alone: the online information of Jacob Appelbaum, the Dutch WikiLeaks associate Rop Gonggrijp, and likely Julian Assange and Bradley Manning were all caught up in the same dragnet. The U.S. Department of Justice was searching for any scrap of incriminating communications related to WikiLeaks; conversations between any of the group and Manning might be used to build a conspiracy case. And though Twitter had the courage to speak up about the government's probe, Jónsdóttir's lawyers learned that four other unnamed companies had also quietly received requests for her data without alerting her.

Together with Appelbaum and Gonggrijp, Jónsdóttir would spend the next year fighting the data requests in court, demanding that a judge unseal the rest of the secret investigation of their online activities. But in appeal after appeal, the courts ruled against them, declaring that users have no expectation of privacy on services like Twitter even as they kept the investigation's own inner workings shrouded. Eventually they would lose the legal battle, and their Twitter data, along with their personal information from several other unidentified services, would be handed over to investigators.

When I speak to Jónsdóttir about the case in the fall of 2011, she's surprisingly cheery. "I'm quite happy the American government has chosen to violate my privacy and make this an international diplomatic issue," she says. Better to go after a public figure and bring attention to the problem than let the cherry-picking of private individuals' data by the American government continue in secret, she says.

Even so, the legal threats that have obtained her private data and prevented Jónsdóttir from traveling to the United States since the investigation began represent a problem for IMMI too. The Internet doesn't reside in some abstract "cyberspace" of John Perry Barlow's gospel and Tim May's sci-fi imagining. Much of it, like Jónsdóttir's Twitter data, resides in the United States. And until it physically moves to Iceland, it won't be protected by IMMI's laws.

As legal blogger Arthur Bright pointed out when IMMI first surfaced, a media or technology company would have to relocate *all* of its staff and assets to Iceland or face the reality that its people and property back at home would be subject to the same archaic media laws as always. "Even if Iceland's laws offer the best protections in the world, they're still a Maginot Line," Bright wrote.

Jónsdóttir is undeterred. Moving their entire staff and assets to Iceland, she argues, is exactly what companies ought to do. "I don't see why that's not a possibility," she muses, disregarding the sunless winters and relative isolation from the rest of humanity. But she helpfully offers another option. "The United States could also repeal the Patriot Act and try democracy instead of tyranny."

Changing the rest of the world's media laws isn't outside of Jónsdóttir's endless ambition. She and Smári McCarthy, IMMI's other champion, have been holding up Iceland as a proof of concept for the rest of the world, meeting with free information advocates in Reykjavík and elsewhere to spawn nascent movements like the Irish Modern Media Initiative, the Italian Modern Media Initiative, and even one American Indian woman in Berkeley, California, who hopes to use an Indian reservation's legal protections as the basis for a data transparency haven within America's own borders.

Like WikiLeaks before it, Jónsdóttir sees IMMI as just another piece of a grander, global "alchemy of change."

"These things are just drops in one big wave. That wave is just one wave in a river," she says. "And I don't know where that river is going to take us."

In December 2010, just as the first rounds of WikiLeaks' State Department Cables were metastasizing around the Internet, I spoke with Evgeny Morozov, a Belarusian academic and writer with a famously pessimistic attitude toward the Internet's ability to democratize global politics. Instead, he believes digital tools have only tightened governments' control over their citizens.

I ask him about WikiLeaks, and whether it might be an exception to his rule. He thinks not. "Information can embarrass governments, but you have to look at the nature of governments as well as the nature of information to measure this embarrassment factor," he answers.

In Russia or China, he specifies, corruption is already an open secret. "Just go and take photos of their villas and the summer houses they buy with their state salaries," he says. "It's already in the open, but exposure by itself in these countries doesn't lead to democratic change."

And what about BalkanLeaks, the Bulgarian site that at that time was just starting to get its hands on some juicy documents? Bulgaria is a subject Morozov knows well: He studied for several years at the country's American University in Blagoevgrad.

"I don't know what information you could publish to embarrass the Balkans. It's a tough one," he says. "There's an environment that's so suffused with cynicism toward politicians that to me it's hard to imagine what kind of stuff would need to be leaked."

In May 2011, BalkanLeaks put that cynicism to the test. It published the words of the U.S. ambassador that labeled Bulgaria's prime minister a criminal several times over. The news reverberated around the country's blogs and was written up in several newspapers.

And then, as Morozov predicted, very little happened.

In a display of frantic backpedaling, the U.S. embassy in Sofia released a statement backing Borisov. "While we cannot comment on the content of alleged classified materials which may have been leaked, we would like to underscore that the U.S. and Bulgaria share an excellent relationship and that our high level of bilateral cooperation speaks for itself."

Borisov himself angrily told one reporter who asked about his ties to Lukoil that "I do not read WikiLeaks," and "will not comment on yellow press publications."

Soon the usual politics kicked in. The opposition party demanded a probe into the accusations. Borisov's own party emphasized that the report's release was an underhanded move timed ahead of upcoming elections. The country's top prosecutor, Boris Velchev, refused to pursue the case. "If we allow an investigation to be opened on mere allegations, can you imagine what country we would be turning into?" he asked rhetorically.

Borisov, it seemed, had emerged with hardly a scratch.

A few months after that miniscandal, I ask Tchobanov if he's satisfied with the results of his leaks. "Yes, I am quite satisfied with the impact," he answers without hesitation. Several judges have been pushed out by various means since BalkanLeaks' reports on bribery and the Masonic lodge, what he sees as internal housecleaning. And since the cable publication on the country's prime minister, Borisov hasn't been invited to meet with any other European leaders one-on-one, he says—they don't want to be seen shaking hands with an "Armani-clad tough guy," as the U.S. ambassador once secretly described him in a memo.

The former minister of defense and two other officials exposed in Balkan-Leaks' early wiretapping transcripts have been charged with bribery, and their prosecution is ongoing. Others, like the prosecutor blackmailed by Angel Donchev, and another who pressured a witness to change his testimony in a real estate case, haven't been charged with crimes.

On a larger scale, the leaks may have also contributed to a decision by the Netherlands and Finland to veto Bulgaria's accession to the EU's visa-free Schengen travel zone based on concerns about organized crime—a clear sign from Bulgaria's neighbors that it must clean up its mafia taint.

But didn't Tchobanov hope that the cable about Borisov would lead to his resignation? The soft-spoken Bulgarian asks for patience. He says that the full influence of the report still isn't clear. "It's a slow process. With the Pentagon Papers, nothing happened at first. But eventually there was Watergate," he says. "First they ignore it, then they fight it, then they finally accept it as evidence."

I offer the adage attributed to Mahatma Gandhi: "First they ignore you, then they laugh at you, then they fight you, then you win."

"No," Tchobanov responds without looking at me. "Sometimes you lose."

On my last day in Varvara, Tchobanov, Yordanov, and a group of friends invite me to go sailing in the Black Sea on a small boat with *Moby Dick* written on its side in Cyrillic. We drop anchor in a shallow cove with an isolated beach in the distance, populated by only a single tent and a pirate flag planted in the sand.

As Tchobanov plays with his two squealing children, I swim over to an outcropping of volcanic rock fifty feet away, and Yordanov follows me. We admire a few of the dead medusa jellyfish floating in the tidal pools. "Very beautiful," Yordanov says.

Then he points off in the distance to a complex of unfinished four-story buildings on a cliff beside the beach, modern structures with diagonally expanding floors that lean out over the sea, with a round, bare concrete tower at their center.

Yordanov explains that a story he wrote for *Politika* exposed what would have been a luxury apartment development there as illegal construction, part of the series of investigations that led to the knife attack on him in Burgas. The news resulted in a government order to halt the construction we're looking at. If not for that story, he says, the beach below would have been developed as private land.

"I'm very proud my investigations can save this beach," says Yordanov. "I'm very proud of my work."

Since Yordanov's exposé, the apartments' massive concrete skeleton has been left to rot. No one is allowed to finish building it, but no one has bothered to remove its carcass either. It stands instead as an enormous concrete Acropolis, a monument to a country caught between its impulse to develop and the corruption it can't escape. As we climb back into the *Moby Dick* and sail toward Varvara, the newly constructed ruins loom over us from the cliff face and then recede into the distance.

CHAPTER 7

THE ENGINEERS

The fifty-year-old Soviet biplane lurches, banks hard to the left, and nearly pitches me and the nine hackers aboard into the port-side windows. I resist the urge to vomit as my stomach floats into my chest. The fluffy-bearded young man sitting behind me doesn't, and pukes generously into a paper bag.

A few thousand feet below the fuselage of steel in which we're riding is a German landscape covered with trees, rivers, windmills, and suddenly a field populated with a patchwork of multicolored tents and strips of pavement. Our pilot, a tall Berliner with a sadistic smile, pushes the Antonov An-2 into an alarmingly steep descent, testing my nervous system's accelerometers again. And then, with unexpected grace, the landing wheels connect with the tarmac and we glide to a stop.

As the plane's Shvetsov engine sputters to a halt and passengers tumble out dazedly, two men approach, one with long purple hair and the other with a brown military hat, a thick black beard, and a suit and tie. They welcome us to the Chaos Communication Camp.

The CCC, or simply Camp, as it's called by the transnational hackers who regularly attend, occurs every fourth summer at an airfield in Finowfurt, a tiny town in former East Germany an hour outside of Berlin. For five days, a distinct hacker-hippy culture takes shape in a village of tents, veined with power cords and Ethernet and permeated with Wi-Fi. The three thousand or so hackers hold research presentations in underground hangars on code-breaking, government surveillance, and insanely ambitious DIY projects. (One talk at the latest Camp set a new goal for the CCC: Put a hacker on the moon by 2034.) At night, they build elaborate light-shows and sculptures around the remains of the Soviet aircraft and tanks that litter the terrain. The result is something like a colder, wetter Burning Man for the radical geek elite.

I spend my first two hours at the Chaos Communication Camp wandering in the dusk around the surreal ruins: past a statue of Lenin with headphones and turntables added to convert him into a socialist DJ, a rusting fighter jet with elaborate rainbow-knitted caps for its pointed engines and nose. Hackers have bivouacked in the shelter of defunct missiles and helicopter engines, like survivors of the apocalypse who have rebuilt a simpler digital society amid the remains of the military-industrial complex.

It's only after nightfall that I find Daniel Domscheit-Berg standing in the dark at the edge of the airfield, wearing a long reflective yellow coat, his face looking rather forlorn as it's lit by another hacker's headlamp. I call out his name and he turns and greets me with a wide-eyed smile and a handshake. The thirty-three-year-old engineer is Assange's darkened doppelgänger, nearly as tall and slim but with dark short hair, dark-rimmed glasses, dark beard. I ask him how it's going. "Everything's going wrong," he says, without dimming his innocent, slightly gap-toothed smile. "We're a full two days behind."

By "we," Domscheit-Berg means OpenLeaks, his nascent spin-off from WikiLeaks. Birgitta Jónsdóttir, who flew in to support the group, is sick in a hotel, he tells me. Her young son tripped on a tent stake, twisted his ankle, and is in the hospital. And ninety-mile-per-hour winds have been pummeling the two-room army tent OpenLeaks has set up as a headquarters, strong enough that the hackers have spent most of the last forty-eight hours trying to prevent it from collapsing. "This afternoon we were helping to set up the marquee tent," he says in a plaintive German accent, pointing to a dome fifty yards away. "Then the storm hit, and ten minutes later it ended up looking like some kind of modern art installation."

Domscheit-Berg invites me into the tent, an orangish structure with what looks like a small Tibetan shrine in one corner, an antinuclear poster, couches, and cases piled on cases of Club-Mate, the sugary, highly caffeinated tea favored by nocturnal German hackers. He hands me a bottle, sits down on the couch, picks up his laptop, and then, without apology, gets back to work.

For Domscheit-Berg, after all, tomorrow is a big day: For the first time, he plans to open OpenLeaks' leak submission platform to the world.

With this launch, Domscheit-Berg and the other young men milling around the OpenLeaks tent and buried in computer screens don't merely expect that their newly coded system will be attacked. They're asking for it. "We will open the system for ninety-six hours to a penetration test," Domscheit-Berg wrote to me by instant message a month before the Camp. "We want people to break it."

OpenLeaks, in other words, aims to harden its code in the fire of three thousand hackers simultaneously probing it for vulnerabilities and leaks. "If it still works, and is not compromised, I think we are in a good position to go live," he wrote.

Going live has been a long time coming. Domscheit-Berg left WikiLeaks in an epically messy divorce in September 2010. He announced OpenLeaks three months later. He planned to launch his first test with the site's media partners, four small European newspapers and the nonprofit Foodwatch, in January 2011. Then April. Now it's August, and OpenLeaks has yet to even launch its submissions website, fueling the frustration of its supporters and the schadenfreude of Domscheit-Berg's former colleagues at WikiLeaks.

"It's not just putting up a website," Domscheit-Berg counters patiently when I interrupt his typing to ask about this long delay. "We're working on an end-to-end environment that takes into regard the whole process. What kind of material you get. What the requirements are to access that material to make sure there's no security breach. How to allow lots of people to work on the material and redact it. How to encrypt it so that only the partners can decrypt it and we can't. Adding checks in the system so that if there's a maintenance window nothing is exposed. We're working on a seriously engineered solution."

The long-gestating system is designed to allow the same anonymous whistleblowing as WikiLeaks, but unlike the parent project where Domscheit-Berg spent three years of his life, OpenLeaks isn't designed to actually make anything public. Instead, it aims to securely pass on leaked content to partnered media organizations and nonprofits, avoiding the dicey role of publisher that got WikiLeaks into so much trouble. It will focus, Domscheit-Berg says, on the most technically tricky and crucial link in the leaking chain: untraceable anonymous uploads.

Domscheit-Berg believes he has all the ingredients to build a new WikiLeaks that's more efficient, more democratically organized, and perhaps most important, more legal. He wants to incorporate as a nonprofit, a steadfast, permanent institution that can strike blows for information freedom against the world's governments and corporations without needing to hide from anyone.

But there's another difference from WikiLeaks: Domscheit-Berg believes that merely replicating the previous project's security isn't good enough. Not only because, the former WikiLeaker says, Julian Assange's brainchild never quite reached his ideal standards for data protection. Nor because, despite his denials, the German is still playing out a dark and bitter game of one-upmanship with Assange himself, who once counted Domscheit-Berg a close friend and now publicly casts him as one of the leaking movement's greatest villains. (In a newspaper interview a few months earlier, Assange called Domscheit-Berg a "dangerous, malicious conman.") But also because in the year since WikiLeaks began dropping nuclear data bombs on world superpowers, the stakes have risen considerably.

"WikiLeaks appeared out of nowhere," says Domscheit-Berg. "It caused a lot of new problems no one had thought about before. Now they've thought about this whole thing for a bit. The dust has settled. And it will never be as easy again."

Hence Domscheit-Berg's plan for the entire Chaos Communication Camp to pile on OpenLeaks' data conduit in a massive hackfest starting tomorrow. Better to be attacked by friends first than intelligence agency spooks and state-sponsored hackers later.

"There was a Swiss newspaper that wrote something like, first there's a visionary, and then come the engineers," Domscheit-Berg says. "That's what's happening with us as well. Julian had the vision, paired with the spirit to kick this off. We are the engineers."

In March 2011, while late to a meeting and running down Fifth Avenue in Manhattan, I received a call on my BlackBerry from Sarah Harrison, Julian Assange's personal assistant.

"Julian would like to speak with you," she tells me.

"Great, when?" I ask cheerily, trying to restrain my out-of-shape panting.

Suddenly Sarah's voice has been replaced with Assange's, and he's launched into a critique of my latest blog post, a bit of news about WikiLeaks' reaction to plans for an upcoming film based on two books, one by two reporters at *The Guardian* and one by Domscheit-Berg, neither of which portrays Assange in a flattering light. "This is how bullshit ends up being history," a WikiLeaks staffer had written on Twitter earlier in the day.

On the other end of the phone, Assange is taking issue with how I described Domscheit-Berg in my story, as having "left WikiLeaks in September" 2010 and taking "several" staffers with him. "He did *not* leave. He was suspended," Assange says in a scolding tone. "And he did not take several staffers with him. He took one." (I later spoke face-to-face with several staffers who had left WikiLeaks at the same time as Domscheit-Berg, two of whom had gone on to work for OpenLeaks.)

"What this shows me, Andy," he continues slowly in the manner of a disappointed school headmaster, "is that you're not properly checking your facts."

I can sense the subtext of this one-way conversation: I've quoted

Domscheit-Berg in recent stories. And Assange knows that I and every other journalist covering WikiLeaks have read Domscheit-Berg's just-published memoir, which describes Assange as an arrogant tyrant and a selfish, petty nerd, complete with descriptions of him mistreating his German compatriot's cat, eating his Ovaltine straight from the package, and possessing the table manners of someone "raised by wolves."

I point out that checking facts with him is difficult when Domscheit-Berg returns my phone calls, and Assange doesn't. Then I try to explain that my primary interest in speaking with Domscheit-Berg is not to insert myself into the feud between him and Assange, but rather to learn more about OpenLeaks and what it's doing to continue the work Assange began.

"As far as I can tell, it's doing nothing," Assange says.

"That's true, I suppose. But I'm interested in the ideas behind it and where they're going," I respond lamely.

"Then you should know that every idea in OpenLeaks is my idea," Assange replies without hesitation. "So I'm glad you like my ideas."

I'm not quite sure how to respond to this, and we sit on the phone in silence for a moment.

"I have to go now, Andy," he says. Then he hangs up.

If Assange had violated his house arrest in England, flown to Germany, made a surprise appearance at the Chaos Communication Camp, and personally pegged Daniel Domscheit-Berg with a piece of rotten fruit during the announcement of OpenLeaks' test launch, perhaps the otherwise near-total failure of the day would have been complete.

Domscheit-Berg takes the stage inside one of the Camp's hangars, and within a few minutes, he's delivering bad news, admitting to the packed room of hackers that after months of delay, the test site still isn't yet online. He complains in passive-aggressive terms that the Camp's staff hadn't properly set up their server colocation facility.

He goes on to explain all the massive technical challenges OpenLeaks faces: how, for instance, to set up secure anonymous submissions systems on the websites of media outlets that use widgets and tools that make online anonymity nearly impossible? Tracking tools included in newspapers' Web advertisements collect data on users to better sell them cars and toothpaste. Anonymous leaking sites aren't meant to collect any data at all. Many of the scripts that run in visitors' Web browsers when they visit media sites can even be rigged to gain control of the user's computer. And given that OpenLeaks doesn't plan to run its submissions system exclusively as a Tor Hidden Service—the group sees them as too complex for many users to access—Domscheit-Berg explains that they need to come up with anonymity protections that don't rely solely on popular anonymity tools like Tor.

After listing this litany of problems, Domscheit-Berg neglects to explain how OpenLeaks will solve any of them.

Instead, he jumps right into his call for the Camp's hackers to pile onto the test site as soon as it comes online—he assures the crowd it will be up shortly—and examine it for security flaws. "All of you are so important in determining what the future looks like—the technical side of the future—and what the influence will be on the freedoms in society," he says in a short pep talk. "This goes to the heart of society. If we don't come up with solutions, who else will?"

But when Domscheit-Berg's idealistic speech ends and the floor opens for questions, the crowd's skepticism comes pouring out. The first darkly worded statement is made by a member of the audience that Domscheit-Berg considers a longtime friend: Jacob Appelbaum.

"I think it would be really fantastic if everything you do is free software, and I want to advocate that you make *sure* everything you do is free software," Appelbaum says. To the hackers present, the suggestion carries two shades of meaning: First, free software can be freely used by other organizations with similar aims. But free—as in "open source"—software can also be thoroughly checked for security bugs, both ones included by mistake and others planted for covert spying.

The young activist follows his comment with a question about OpenLeaks' purported association with the Germany Privacy Foundation. "I don't know if it's true, but I've heard those guys are just a front for the defense intelligence agencies of Germany," he says. "My question is, if you have a foundation, how do you avoid being infiltrated by all the bad motherfuckers that want to infiltrate your organization? And how would you take a rumor like that one, that the Privacy Foundation are related to the spooks, and vet it? And if you found out they were spooks, would you stop working with them or not?" A round of tentative applause follows.

"I'm a German, I know this problem," Domscheit-Berg responds with a thin smile. "I know all these rumors, and the problem is that you don't know what to make of that . . . I've been reading about myself that I might be paid by the FBI, which is not the case."

"It was you!" someone shouts from the back of the room, to some sparse laughs. Domscheit-Berg smiles and jokingly puts one finger over his lips.

"We shouldn't be scared just by all these rumors," Domscheit-Berg continues, unflustered. "Because that won't enable us to do anything."

Then Birgitta Jónsdóttir, who has been sitting quietly near the front of the room, pipes up. "Paranoia will kill us," she says loudly and matter-of-factly.

"Yes, I agree with Birgitta," echoes Domscheit-Berg, sounding tired. "Paranoia will kill us."

The jabs continue, many picking up on Appelbaum's open-source critique. "What could possibly justify that every bit of software produced so far is not released as free-speech software?" fumes one young hacker.

"It is free software, it's just not open source right now," Domscheit-Berg responds, arguing that making code open source requires constant time-consuming bug fixes that OpenLeaks can't yet afford to make. "This is due to the overhead—"

"Where's the code? Where's the code?" the critic interjects with controlled anger. Another member of the audience asks that OpenLeaks simply publish the SSH password to its servers so that anyone can get into the computers remotely and see exactly what they're doing.

Domscheit-Berg shakes his head. "You can't run this like a zoo where everyone can go and watch," he says.

Near the end of the line of questioners stands CCC board member

Andy Müller-Maguhn, a pale and wide-bodied German with compact facial features, a tuft of thin hair on his forehead, and clear blue eyes. "I'm trying to find out what's open about OpenLeaks," he says evenly. "I had hoped you would use the principle of openness to ensure the integrity and trustworthiness of the project. For now, you haven't convinced me you're doing that."

Domscheit-Berg can only respond by begging for time again, saying that the group will "probably" open parts of the site's code to the public. "You'll have to take my word as much as that's not optimal," he says weakly. "That's all that I can give."

And then comes the final person in the line of interrogators: John Gilmore, the venerable bearded and ponytailed cofounder of the cypherpunks and the Electronic Frontier Foundation. His mere appearance at a conference east of the Mississippi River is a meaningful event; in 2002, Gilmore filed and lost a lawsuit against the Department of Homeland Security that contested the constitutionality of its practice of asking for his identification before boarding an airplane. Since then, he's vowed never to board a domestic U.S. flight again, so has had to fly directly from San Francisco to Europe.

"I just want to thank you for trying to do this work," Gilmore begins with the calm of an elder statesman. "Because if you succeed at it, we get transparency in other parts of the world that have not had it. And if you fail at it, or if people think that you're lame or whatever, maybe you inspire them to do it better."

It's hardly a glowing endorsement. But the crowd applauds more than it has for any other comment.

Over the next hours it becomes clear that OpenLeaks' immediate problem isn't a debate over open or closed source software, or even a whisper campaign about its supposed cooperation with intelligence agencies. It simply can't get online.

The test platform for OpenLeaks is meant to be a submissions system for the left-leaning newspaper *Die Tageszeitung—Taz* for short. But an hour after Domscheit-Berg's talk, Leaks.taz.de still returns a "Page not found" message. Moving from the camp's facilities to an outside data center is taking OpenLeaks' crew longer than they expected. Two hours pass, with no leak site online. Then three. Then twenty-four.

On the second day of camp, I meet with Reiner Metzger, the editor-in-chief of *Die Tageszeitung,* who has been camping for the first days of the conference in a small tent next to OpenLeaks' temporary headquarters to oversee the launch of Leaks.taz.de. But now he's packing up his things to head back to Berlin, with little to celebrate about his paper's bold step into the future of leaking. In a very restrained, German way, Metzger is extremely pissed off. He opens his laptop to show me a headline on the website of the competing German newspaper *Die Zeit*: "Leaking Sky Prevents OpenLeaks Launch," mocking Domscheit-Berg's excuse that the storm hindered their preparations.

"Here's why this is a PR disaster," he explains as he stuffs his belongings into a bag and rolls up his tent. "We made a big splash. The hackers who come here are still mythical for media people. They're coming here, thrown it into the ring to fight with this server. It's a story that every news shift staffer can get immediately. It was a story that was running in every meaningful German newspaper, millions of people saw it. And now a high percentage tried to get to the website. And then again. And again. Nothing happened. Tomorrow the whole thing goes poof and vanishes from the media."

Metzger had hoped to tout that *Die Tageszeitung*'s OpenLeaks submissions platform had passed the test of three thousand hackers attacking it. He isn't looking forward to explaining to his staff that a launch in which his paper has invested a significant chunk of reputation and a front-page story simply didn't happen.

And he worries the damage may be worse than embarrassment.

"Leak sites have to first have a leak," he says. "But how do you get this leak? For that you need publicity. Now the publicity is there, and the website is not. And maybe some of the leakers are turned off. In the short run, it's a disappointment. But in the long run the issue is the leaks."

"To leak or not to leak," he adds with a grim laugh as he packs up his things and prepares to head into the OpenLeaks tent to meet with Domscheit-Berg. "That is the question."

... -.-- - ....- -.-. --- .-- -.-- -.-- ... - - --..-- .-- .... - --- -- .-- -.

Birgitta Jónsdóttir's warning about the destructive power of paranoia must have rung a special bell for Domscheit-Berg. It was paranoia that introduced the man known then as Daniel Berg to Julian Assange. And it was paranoia that pushed the two into acts of mutual sabotage that would cause each of them more harm than any state intelligence adversary has yet been able to inflict.

Daniel Berg was born in the West German town of Wiesbaden, the son of an engineer who was the son of an engineer. He grew up playing with Fischertechnik mechanical toys—as a small child, he used the plastic motors and gears to build a functional refrigerator and a light sensor on the stairs up to his bedroom. The latter gadget was intended to alert him to his mother's approach so he could pretend to be sleeping and continue reading late into the night.

Berg's family bought a Commodore 64 in 1986, when he was eight years old. It had an interface that allowed him to connect the computer to his Fischer components, and he was amazed to see how the unassuming box of silicon let him program creations like a robotic hand and bring the inanimate plastic to life.

When Berg was thirteen, he bought a copy of Hitler's *Mein Kampf* from a man selling illegal Nazi paraphernalia at a flea market. The book was then banned in Germany, and it fascinated and terrified the teenager. He had heard his grandfathers' World War II stories—one had been stationed on a minesweeping boat in the North Sea, the other in Poland. Both had deserted near the end of the war—one was shot in the leg during his escape and arrived home in Wiesbaden in such a terrible state that his own mother and brother didn't recognize him.

But Hitler's sinister vision pushed Berg to read on about the war and its atrocities, books like *The Diary of Anne Frank*, *The Order of the Death's Head,* about the dreaded Schutzstaffel, and *Hell's Gate*, about the concentration camp in Ravensbrück on the outskirts of Berlin. And he was struck by the foolishness of hiding such a dark piece of the country's history as the memoir of its former Führer.

Soon, his interest in banned words and computers began to mesh. His only friend who owned his own PC set up a bulletin board that allowed them to share files across phone lines. It had a total of about six regular users. But at one point, one of them posted a copy of *The Anarchist Cookbook*—about as exciting a piece of digital contraband as any bored teenager could hope to discover.

Berg and his friends used the virtual tome's recipes to mix their own gunpowder and create homemade firecrackers from common chemicals. "For a few months we were completely crazy about explosives," Domscheit-Berg says. They experimented with melting through various materials, and even obtained a few of the ingredients for plastic explosives. One night they borrowed an antique cannon on wheels from one of the friends' parents who were away on vacation, filled it with homemade gunpowder, and at three A.M. fired it at a neighbor's garage before running gleefully into the dark. (The teenagers hadn't actually inserted a cannonball, so their stunt resulted only in a thrilling bang and a garage door completely blackened by soot.)

Berg was an extremely average, entirely unmotivated student. But he read the books his father, a data center engineer for a German insurance company, left lying around the house. And during his high school summers, he worked for a cabling company, laying four-inch-thick electrical and networking copper lines and connecting them into data centers to keep up with the mid-1990s' nearly infinite optimism about the coming deluge of data.

With that tech boom under way, Berg saw little reason to go to a university. He got a job at a consulting company, building and tweaking networks for corporate customers. In his spare hours he and his friends took an abandoned house owned by one of their parents and turned it into a kind of proto-hackerspace, filling its empty rooms with their computers, networking equipment, and records, and hauling couches up to its flat roof. "It was surrounded by trees so that no one could see what we were doing," he says. "For one summer, we were totally free."

In the earliest days of wireless Internet, Berg's crew would pile into his tiny Renault 5, packing it with five bodies and as many antennas as they could buy or scavenge, and go war driving. Wi-Fi encryption was still rare, so most networks were wide open. At one point they climbed to the highest local point, Mount Neroberg, and used a five-foot antenna to access the Wi-Fi of a university ten miles away. On another war drive, they discovered an office management company's open network, and mapped out its architecture, with its connections to satellite offices in Dresden, Munich, Hamburg. "At the time, it was the most complex network I had ever seen," says Berg. They watched its traffic and studied it for two months, until one of Berg's more reckless friends decided to send a note to every printer in the building that the staff should turn off a light they had left on overnight in an upstairs office. It printed on every printer in the office, again and again, until the machines ran out of paper. "Two days later, the wireless network wasn't there anymore," says Berg. "I think we had freaked them out."

In 2001, a friend told Berg about the Chaos Computer Club, and he attended a local meeting and then later the Chaos Communication Congress in Berlin. The twenty-three-year-old Berg had not only never met so many politically savvy hackers—he had never even been to the capital city. It was a life-altering experience. "The first conference blew me away," he says. "It really got me out of my provincial thinking."

Despite his budding hacktivist tendencies, Berg kept to the trajectory of technically skilled young men. When the heady days of the dot-com boom ended, he went to a technical university in Mannheim to study computer science and upon graduation got a job with the giant IT consultant EDS. Berg made a deal with his manager that he wouldn't work for defense contractors or intelligence agencies, so instead spent his days setting up networks for car manufacturers and airlines.

It was uninspiring work that left Berg with plenty of extra brain matter for CCC-inspired daydreaming. He read and donated to Cryptome regularly and had been intrigued by its megaleaks of intelligence officers' names over the previous decade. So when John Young posted his leak of WikiLeaks' early mail list discussions, including Young's paranoid implication that the site was a CIA front, it caught the German engineer's attention. Berg, who had read Assange's autobiographical *Underground*, was captivated by the twisted notion of a legendary hacker turned government informant creating an elaborate cryptographic honeypot.

Then, in November 2007, WikiLeaks leaked the official handbook of the Pentagon's Guantánamo prison. And it became clear that the site was no honeypot.

Something about WikiLeaks pushed a button in Berg that made him yearn for a mission beyond his daily network admin's grind. He wanted in. "I just didn't want to waste my life helping GM produce more cars anymore," he says. He posted a message on WikiLeaks' IRC chat room, offering to help.

Two days later, he got a response from Julian Assange himself. "Still interested in a job?"

For much of his first year with WikiLeaks, as Daniel Domscheit-Berg tells it, the group functioned as a blowfish—a small piece of sushi puffed up to look as large and dangerous as possible. It claimed to have thousands of active volunteers around the globe, a team of Chinese dissidents among its founders, a legal representative named Jay Lim on retainer, and servers spread across Europe. In fact, it had one server, a fictitious lawyer, and two members responsible for most all of its activities: Julian Assange and Daniel Berg.

They made an odd couple. Assange, the radical, homeless guerrilla hacker and Berg, the quietly subversive engineer with a corporate job, a carefully arranged apartment, and a favorite local organic-foods grocery shop. Much of their interaction took place over instant messages, including the coordination of early bombshells like a collection of offshore account information from the Swiss bank Julius Baer and the secret documents of the Church of Scientology. But they would also attend three Chaos Communication Congresses together—each time with a higher profile talk as WikiLeaks' representatives—embark on a fifteen-hundred-mile road trip across Europe to find safe data centers to house their collection of servers, and even spend two months living together in Berg's Wiesbaden home.

Their personality contrasts occasionally flared into deeper conflicts over their idea of activism. One of the most representative, perhaps, was the issue of suits. Like Philip Zimmermann, Berg subscribed to the Ellsberg strategy of protest. "We had some public appointments where I was convinced we could achieve more in conservative attire than in the normal slacker stuff we wore," he would write later. "Solid in appearance, subversive in performance, that was my motto." Assange agreed in theory. But in practice, his wayward lifestyle as an international subversive meant he dressed in shabby, wrinkled clothes and dirty sneakers. The Australian was deeply annoyed by Berg's occasional suggestions that he wear cleaner clothes or business attire, even when meeting with government officials.

The suit issue represented a fundamental disconnect between Berg's and Assange's vision for WikiLeaks. When donations to the nonprofit group started to trickle in, Berg dreamed of using the money to transform the group into a legitimate nonprofit with permanent infrastructure: state-of-the-art servers, a headquarters in a former military air-raid shelter with a WikiLeaks flag flying above it, a computer center with space for partners to host their own projects. But Assange said he wanted to remain an "insurgent operation." Even in late 2010, he would describe WikiLeaks to me in the same terms as his wandering youth: "We're like a traveling production company; everyone moves somewhere, and we put on a production."

That nomadism, Assange believed, helped WikiLeaks to stay a step ahead of legal and political threats. And Assange saw those threats everywhere. He believed he was constantly being tailed by intelligence services or having his travel plans sabotaged by state agents. When he stayed at Berg's apartment, he insisted they never enter or leave at the same time. He used a multitude of temporary SIM cards and avoided all payment forms other than cash.

Berg believed that Assange simply had a flair for spy-novel sensationalism that served as marketing for WikiLeaks. His greatest mistake, in retrospect, may have been underestimating Assange's capacity for true paranoia, both justified and not.

Personal differences aside, they worked well as a team. They also became close friends—or so Berg believed. In 2009, he quit his job with EDS and went to work with WikiLeaks full-time.

Around the same period, a third central figure appeared within the group. He was an old acquaintance of Berg's and a highly skilled network engineer, one whose caution regarding privacy dwarfed that of even Assange or Jacob Appelbaum. His name has never been publicly linked with WikiLeaks, and many within the group don't know it either. To most, he is simply known as "the Architect."

Berg asked the Architect to help with a specific technical problem, one that Domscheit-Berg wouldn't even describe to me for fear of providing more information on the man's specific abilities. The Architect handled the task with a degree of efficiency that deeply impressed the German WikiLeaker, who praises his skills as superior to any he had ever seen, including Assange's. Birgitta Jónsdóttir calls the Architect "a genius." Smári McCarthy, the Icelandic WikiLeaker who later helped draft the IMMI legislation, described him to me as "frighteningly skilled."

When the newly recruited engineer took a look at WikiLeaks' infrastructure, however, he was horrified. He saw it as a patchwork of hacked-together components with no thought put into its overarching structure. He soon demanded that the site be taken down and completely rebuilt, its tangled code and creaking servers replaced with a network of load-balanced hardware and efficient software with no loose ends that might offer security vulnerabilities. In a sign of both Assange's and Berg's respect for the Architect's judgment, no one argued. The site would be off-line for the next six months.

Pinpointing the moment when Berg and Assange's philosophical differences blossomed into full-out contempt and animosity isn't easy: Perhaps it was after Berg exploded at Assange in a cramped, dark, and stuffy hotel room in Reykjavík. Or maybe it was when Berg began to use the group's funds to pay for systems upgrades without asking Assange for his consent.

But only one event has been publicly cited by both men as a clear spark for their conflict. When I asked Jacob Appelbaum, he summarized it: "Basically, Daniel never should have gotten married."

Berg met Anke Domscheit at a falafel joint in Berlin in February 2010. She was ten years his senior and had a young son. But they connected immediately—Domscheit was a consultant with Microsoft focused on "open government," working on the same issues of transparency as Berg, and he was attracted to her unique style and idealism.

Just nine days later, they decided to wed. They planned to change both of their names to Domscheit-Berg.

Assange's first reaction, when Berg told him about meeting Domscheit, was to suggest that Berg dig up "dirt" on her that would be useful when they separated, a piece of advice that deeply wounded Berg. When Berg moved into Domscheit's apartment shortly after their relationship began, Assange chastised him for putting his full name on the door, a gross display of negligence in Assange's unspoken rules of operational security.

In a written statement Assange would release eighteen months later explaining Domscheit-Berg's expulsion from WikiLeaks, he would mark that violation as the first sign that Berg couldn't be trusted with WikiLeaks' resources and materials. In the same statement, he went on to write that the girlfriend of a Mossad agent attended the Domscheit-Bergs' wedding, and to accuse Daniel Domscheit-Berg of having given "helpful" information to U.S. intelligence agencies. He added that Anke Domscheit-Berg worked with CIA agents during her time at the consulting firm McKinsey.

Daniel Domscheit-Berg flatly denies ever sharing any information with law enforcement or intelligence agents of any nation or hosting any at his wedding. He says he hasn't even dared travel to the United States since his time with WikiLeaks to avoid the possibility of having to answer questions about the group.

For Anke Domscheit-Berg, Assange's charges struck her as absurd and maddening on another level altogether. In a long phone conversation just a few weeks after the Chaos Communication Camp, she explained to me—slowly, with a certain amount of emotional reluctance—just why Assange's words had irked her so deeply.

The older of the two Domscheit-Bergs spent the first twenty-one years of her life in East Germany before the fall of the Iron Curtain. One of her closest friends was a political dissident. In the year before the fall of Communism, he was imprisoned on charges of drinking while driving a motorcycle, but treated as a political prisoner, placed in solitary confinement and often shackled to a radiator. She posed as his fiancée in order to visit him in prison, but all but one of her visitation appointments were canceled by the warden. Domscheit sent letters to him, numbering them so that he could better track which ones were blocked. Eventually she received an anonymous letter saying that a letter-smuggling system her friend had set up had been discovered, and now none of her notes were reaching him. So instead, she began writing to the warden and to editors of local newspapers, demanding his release.

Domscheit was a student of textile art at a technical school in southeastern Germany, and later the same year she won a French language competition for art students with the prize of a three-month fellowship at a studio in Paris. "At the time, stuck behind the Wall, it's hard to describe just what a paradise that sounded like," she says.

Before she could go, however, Domscheit was called to a nearby town's tourist office. Waiting for her was an officer in the East German secret police known as the Stasi. "Were you really so naïve as to think you could take the scholarship without our permission?" she remembers him asking.

"I tried to tell myself 'so what' as my big dream disappeared," she says, her voice shaking with anger as she recounts the conversation. The agent explained that if she wanted to go to Paris, she would need to volunteer as a Stasi informant. She refused. He told her that it might cause problems for her father's livelihood as a doctor if she didn't cooperate. But Domscheit wouldn't budge.

She was let go, but told to meet the same agent the next day in a parking lot. Early the next morning, he put her in a car and drove to a forest near the Czech border, still hung with fog in the early dawn daylight. Domscheit thought perhaps they were going to kill her and dump her body among the trees, as the Nazis had done with Communists in the previous regime. But still she refused his offer to work as an informant. The agent drove her back to town.

The secret police's intimidation tactics had failed, and the hated wall fell just months later. Her friend was released from prison under an amnesty program. But Domscheit wouldn't make it to Paris until years later. "In the end no one got the scholarship. It was too late to give it to someone else," she says bitterly. "What a waste."

Her experiences in that dark last chapter of the Soviet Union, she says, left her with a deep hatred for intelligence agencies and the closed, secretive surveillance society they represented. "I had to deal with the secret police in East Germany, and I'm happy to have survived that," she says, her voice still trembling slightly. "So when Julian Assange tells me that I worked with the secret services, it's like a punch in the face."

One day after OpenLeaks' test launch belatedly comes online, an OpenLeaks staffer at the Chaos Communication Camp who has asked me not to name or even describe him is giving a workshop on anonymous leaking in the group's sand-colored military tent. OpenLeaks' temporary headquarters has filled with a dozen hackers who are volunteering to probe a handful of willing WikiLeaks copycats for security flaws—StateLeaks, KHLeaks, FrenchLeaks, QuebecLeaks, and OpenLeaks itself, among others.

The OpenLeaker is laying down some ground rules: "Be responsible. Break, don't abuse," he says. "And only test the sites we have the OK for. If you start hacking Cryptome or something, John Young will be pretty pissed at us."

Then the hackers get to work, each team of two assigned to audit a different site. "Some music?" the workshop leader offers, pacing around the room as they bury their heads in laptops. "Death metal?" He puts on an instrumental groove album instead.

To my right sits Daniel Meredith, a developer recently hired by Al Jazeera to revamp the news network's own leaking site after its mockery by most of the computer security community. He's a solidly built blond American, with cheeks tinged red by the summer sun of Qatar, the Arab emirate where Al Jazeera has stationed him.

Meredith has taken on the task of testing StateLeaks.org, and he walks me through his reconnaissance. The audit starts simple: a search in the "Whois" database, which publicly tracks ownership of domain names. Domains can be registered with pseudonyms or anonymity services, but this one wasn't. It's registered to an organization called "Geeks Paradox," and specifically to someone named Travis McCrea.

His phone number, e-mail address, and postal address in Chevak, Alaska, are all listed. "If this guy is making an attempt to be anonymous, he's making a very shoddy attempt," says Meredith.

The Al Jazeera developer runs a publicly available test from the computer security firm Qualys on the SSL setup of the site's submission system, and the result is a grade of C. The page doesn't use the latest version of SSL and allows weak encryption schemes.

Next Meredith runs Nmap and Firebug, two scanning tools that can help identify the software StateLeaks is using and vulnerabilities in its code. The servers' visibility to these tools can be obscured with the right settings, but McCrae hasn't bothered. He's running an Apache server application on the Linux operating system. At this point Meredith says he would perform some timing analyses to see if the site is hosted on a single server or rotating among several computers for stability. But the Camp's wireless connection likely isn't steady enough for the test, and he says he's already found plenty of loose ends to work with.

"At this point I could probably take this information, run a simple exploit kit, and own his box," he says. "Luckily I'm a journalist, not a hacker."

It's only then that Meredith takes the usual first step of a reporter and googles Travis McCrea. He immediately finds his MySpace page, complete with a photo of a very young, very sincere-looking shaggy-haired boy in an ill-fitting black suit and a gold tie. "That's him?" Meredith asks himself. "I'm getting the feeling we've been wasting our time looking at some teenager's website."

When the hackers reconvene and start presenting their findings, State-Leaks is hardly the worst off. One site runs its public website on the same server as its submissions system, opening it to attacks that could spill source data. One failed to load at all. They've found flaws in OpenLeaks too: The unprotected informational site at OpenLeaks.org includes contact information without warning leakers not to send sensitive material to the group there. And the site's SSL setup is missing an intermediate certificate, part of the chain of signatures that certify that an encrypted site is not only scrambled but comes from the source it appears to. The oversight might have let an impostor site posing as OpenLeaks lure and identify its leakers.

After the copycat review, the OpenLeaker leading the session starts to ask tricky questions without easy answers. Should you advise leakers to upload from an Internet café or even hand their encrypted data to someone else to upload? Is it acceptable to link to your submissions page from a nonencrypted site, given that hacker tools like "SSL Strip" can remove a Web page's encryption when the user clicks on it? Should you host a chat room on your site, or does it merely open you to criminal accusations of "soliciting" leaks? Is Sweden a good country for hosting a submissions site, or does the 2009 law expanding the surveillance powers of the country's intelligence services mean leakers should move elsewhere?

"Everyone is saying that they have these secure submissions systems, and it means nothing. We need some kind of public standard," he says. "Right now it's like the 1930s on airplanes and everyone is smoking and partying and there are no rules."

When the workshop ends and the hackers file out, I approach the unnamed OpenLeaker and ask why he didn't focus more on Tor and similar anonymity tools to protect whistleblowers. OpenLeaks' test site, I point out, even lets users upload documents without using its Hidden Service, potentially with none of Tor's multilayered identity protection.

The simple answer, he says, is that he doesn't believe Tor alone is enough. "When you force people to use this tool, you put all your trust in it. If someone shows that the circuits are sniffed by the USA or something, it's broken," he says. "You'll have advertised a totally broken system. Tor isn't the golden bullet of anonymity on the Internet."

So how does OpenLeaks plan to protect the identity of sources who don't have the savvy to use Tor or their own choice of proxy server? The OpenLeaker sighs, as if I've asked a question with a very long answer. Then he grabs a Club-Mate and sits down.

WikiLeaks, he recaps, used cover traffic to mask which visitors were simply curious readers and which were leakers. A script on the site would run in their browser, uploading a randomly sized document. OpenLeaks will implement cover traffic, too, he says. But implementing that tool on news organizations' websites won't be as easy, given that a visit to those sites' home pages would look different from visits to the leak submissions page. So they're planning on eventually integrating their submissions page directly into the home pages themselves, a trick that requires coaching their media partners on how to excise security bugs from the most complex portion of their sites.

Once they have what the OpenLeaks engineer calls that "armored car" version of the partner sites set up, they plan to go even further than WikiLeaks, building more convincing cover traffic than has ever existed before, this unnamed engineer tells me. They've statistically modeled the timing and file size of uploads to WikiLeaks and have used it to spoof those submissions with high statistical accuracy. Most submissions to WikiLeaks were between 1.5 and 2 megabytes, for instance. Less than one percent are above 700 megabytes. Their cover traffic aims to follow exactly the same bell curve, making it theoretically indistinguishable from real submissions under the cover of SSL encryption, even when the user isn't running Tor.

"We have over one and a half years of submissions data to analyze. That's something you can model. That's mathematics," he says. "The more submissions we get, the better we model the cover traffic. It's a feedback loop."

I ask how it is that he has access to one and a half years of WikiLeaks submissions. And that's when the man I'm talking to explains to me, without preamble, that he is the Architect.

I'm paralyzed for a moment. Slowly it dawns on me that I've stumbled into the man at the technical center of the leaking movement, one whom I'd never expected to communicate with, let alone meet face-to-face. The Architect, whether or not he notices my tongue-tiedness, speaks without pretension. He has a calm and patient authority. I launch into a long list of questions about his mysterious role in WikiLeaks and OpenLeaks, and he declines to answer most of them. He tells me nothing about his background, his career—beyond being a network engineer—or even his nationality.

But there's one story he will tell: the events of his time at WikiLeaks, and why he decided to leave.

When the Architect was first recruited by Domscheit-Berg, he says, WikiLeaks was essentially a pair of servers, one hosted at PRQ in Stockholm that redirected to another more sensitive server in a data center somewhere else in Europe. "If the authorities had gotten that box, that would have been it," he says. "Game over."

The Architect demanded that the entire project be rethought and redesigned, which took the site off-line for months. He didn't much like the group's organizational architecture either: He warned Berg that Assange had too much control of the project, and that more of the financial and organizational responsibility should be shared. When Berg mentioned this to Assange, Assange accused Berg of plotting a power grab. "Julian warned me that Daniel was trying to control me," the Architect says with a bitter laugh. "In fact, it was my idea."

After the site's downtime, in April 2010, the Architect had most of WikiLeaks' materials ready to put back online, and began pinging Assange to get the go-ahead to relaunch the site. But Assange was in Iceland, busy preparing the Collateral Murder video that would springboard WikiLeaks to stardom. The Architect says that he didn't respond. The video went online while the site was still down, and Assange blamed the technical volunteers working with the Architect for missing an important media opportunity, while the Architect bristled at the insult.

In July, when the group was preparing to publish the seventy-six thousand files known as the Afghan War Diaries, the Architect says he asked Assange to have the index for the release ready two weeks early. In the end, Assange left finishing the index page to the last minute, and it went up four hours late. "That was fine," the Architect says calmly. "But I told him I wouldn't tolerate any more major fuckups."

WikiLeaks had left fifteen thousand files unpublished that the group and its media partners at *The New York Times, The Guardian,* and *Der Spiegel* deemed too sensitive—many contained the names of civilian informants to the U.S. military who might face reprisal if they were exposed. The Architect says he recruited a group of forty trusted volunteers to pore over the files to determine how they could be redacted and published. After four weeks of steady work, the files were edited and ready. Then the Architect learned from Assange that he didn't in fact intend to publish those fifteen thousand documents, and wanted to use the group's momentum with the media to publish the 392,000 Iraq documents instead. "So it was my job to tell all the guys they had spent four weeks reading shit for nothing," he says.

The Architect scrambled to work on a document organization system that the group could use for the Iraq files with double-blind reviews and redactions by volunteers. But instead, Assange simply redacted all names from the files with an automated program that deleted words based on their frequency, what the Architect saw as sloppy overredaction.

By this time, Assange had already developed a deep distrust of Domscheit-Berg and begun to see him as a threat and a rival. In fact, it was the Architect, not Domscheit-Berg, who was fomenting a mutiny, the Architect says. He no longer believed Assange was responsible or careful enough to run the organization, IT resources, and finances, and told Domscheit-Berg as much.

The Architect wasn't the only one turning against Assange. Reporters Without Borders and Amnesty International both issued open letters to

Assange criticizing WikiLeaks for failing to more completely redact sources' names from the Afghan War Diaries. "Indiscriminately publishing 92,000 classified reports reflects a real problem of methodology and, therefore, of credibility," read the Reporters Without Borders statement. "Journalistic work involves the selection of information." Even Birgitta Jónsdóttir's allegiance with the group began to show cracks as WikiLeaks' publications became larger and less discriminate. "We were very, very upset with [the Afghan War release,] and with the way he spoke about it afterwards," Jónsdóttir told *The New York Times*. "If he could just focus on the important things he does, it would be better."

Domscheit-Berg began to raise questions to Assange over instant messages about his lack of transparency as a leader and his singular control. Assange responded by accusing Domscheit-Berg of making comments to a *Newsweek* reporter that Assange should be ousted from the group, and demanded the German confess to his insubordinate statements. "If you do not answer the question, you will be removed," wrote Assange in an instant message to the German.

"You are not anyone's king or god," snapped back Domscheit-Berg. "And you're not even fulfilling your role as a leader right now. A leader communicates and cultivates trust in himself. You are doing the exact opposite. You behave like some kind of emperor or slave trader."

"You are suspended for one month, effective immediately," Assange responded.

A few days later, Assange held a group meeting on an IRC chat room he called "missionfirst" to discuss Domscheit-Berg's behavior and lobby for his expulsion from WikiLeaks.

It was just after the meeting that Domscheit-Berg and the Architect decided to stage a partial shutdown of the site. Just for a day, the Architect—one of the few with access to the group's most sensitive infrastructure—took WikiLeaks' archive and home page off-line, a kind of strike to get the group's attention. Assange responded by shutting down WikiLeaks' Domain Name System entry, blacking out its submissions system, e-mail, and chat rooms in a digital game of chicken. The Architect caved and turned the elements of the site he controlled back on. But he wanted nothing more to do with Assange.

Domscheit-Berg had worked on a system similar to what would become OpenLeaks as part of a failed grant proposal to the American nonprofit Knight Foundation, and the Architect says he developed the idea further in a paper and sent it to Domscheit-Berg, suggesting they leave WikiLeaks to work on it. "The thing between J and Daniel is on a very personal level. But with me, it's simple. If you fuck with me, I fuck with you," he summarizes calmly. "My work comes at a price. Not to be famous. I wanted to do something good. And if someone corrupts that, I'll pull the plug."

Much of the hardware the site ran on belonged to the Architect or Domscheit-Berg, they say, and they had no intention of donating it to Assange's project. The Architect says he gave the remaining WikiLeaks staffers two weeks to migrate their data off the servers they owned. A portion of the files were moved, but Assange had only tasked one developer to the operation. When the two weeks were up, that WikiLeaks volunteer had made little progress assembling a secure setup for the Architect and Domscheit-Berg to transfer the files. They gave Assange's developer another week. When that deadline passed, too, the pair lost patience. So they simply changed the systems' passwords and took control of all of it: the submissions system, the archive of published documents, and the unpublished submissions collection of three thousand leaked files.

Why disembowel WikiLeaks so thoroughly on their way out? The Architect and Domscheit-Berg claim that they didn't trust the group under Assange's leadership to properly protect the material, some of which they say contained data that was sent to Domscheit-Berg personally, and that might identify sources if it wasn't kept secure. For the nearly one year between their departure from WikiLeaks and the Chaos Communication Camp, they kept the files encrypted and left them in the hands of a third party who didn't have the key. ("Best to give them to someone who doesn't even want the shit," says the Architect.) They had no plans to publish the files, and said they'd offered to return them to WikiLeaks. But they claim Assange never offered a secure method of making the handoff.

"I didn't mind that [Assange] likes media attention, or even the thing with the girls," the Architect told me. "But I don't believe he's able to handle the basic law that first, you protect the sources. Before the project, before any of the people in it."

When John Young published a leaked excerpt of Domscheit-Berg's book in January 2011 on Cryptome that revealed he and the Architect had taken the unpublished submissions, Assange sent me a statement through Icelandic spokesperson Kristinn Hrafnsson that described Domscheit-Berg as an unethical, unstable charlatan:

> [Domscheit-Berg] has falsely misrepresented himself in the press as a programmer, computer-scientist, security expert, architect, editor, founder, director and spokesman. He is not a founder or co-founder and nor was there any contact with him during the founding years. He did not even have an email address with the organization until 2008 (we launched in December 2006). He cannot program and wrote not a single program for the organization, at any time.

The statement didn't once mention the Architect.

When I spoke with that unnamed engineer, eleven months after the rupture, WikiLeaks had neither gotten its unpublished submissions back from the OpenLeakers nor built a new submissions system to replace the one that the Architect and Domscheit-Berg took with them.

The Architect says he has no regrets, either about dismantling WikiLeaks' technology or cutting ties with Assange. "WikiLeaks is like jumping from an airplane. It's for the adrenaline junkies," he says. "At some point you have to open the parachute. Some people open it earlier, some later. Some don't get the chance to open it at all."

Only two men have been expelled from the Chaos Computer Club in its thirty-year history. One was a Nazi. The other was Daniel Domscheit-Berg.

On the third day of the Chaos Communication Camp, after OpenLeaks' fumbled launch, CCC board member Andy Müller-Maguhn and three other Club board members approached Domscheit-Berg at three A.M. outside a party a few tents away from OpenLeaks' encampment. They handed him a letter on the official CCC letterhead marked with the Chaos Knot, a bundle of tangled cables that serves as the group's emblem. It explained that his membership had been revoked for "damaging the reputation of the Chaos Computer Club through the public presentation of your talk on the project OpenLeaks," and "creating the impression that the Chaos Communication Camp and its attendees had taken over a security check for your project and the source protection it promised."

When Domscheit-Berg shows me that letter, it's the last day of Camp and he's pacing around the OpenLeaks tent, quickly and mechanically packing things away. "I don't need Andy Müller-Maguhn to give us a permit for this project," he says angrily. "I don't fucking care." He stops for a moment and looks out of the tent flap as the first drops of rain began to fall from the dark sky over Finowfurt. "If I had bothered about everything that everyone said about me since I left WikiLeaks, I would be living on a desert island right now."

He walks back into the tent and asks in an agitated tone if there's any Club-Mate left. To Domscheit-Berg's visible relief, it turns out his young stepson has hidden a case under a table as a backup supply. As he opens a bottle, Domscheit-Berg explains what he believes is the real story behind his excommunication. Andy Müller-Maguhn has been asked by Julian Assange to retrieve the submissions that he and the Architect took from WikiLeaks. The fact that the OpenLeakers still haven't handed the materials over, as Domscheit-Berg tells it, is prejudicing the CCC's decision making against him.

And why exactly hasn't he handed those materials over to Müller-Maguhn? The Architect, who is sitting on a couch nearby, answers. "There's a network of trusted people who handle stuff," he says nonchalantly, "and he's not one of them."

"Besides, this is the guy who is already responsible for the biggest data-handover fuckup of all time," Domscheit-Berg adds. "He's not capable of anything serious."

What does that mean? I ask the pair, confused. They decline to explain.

"Just imagine the worst-case scenario you can think of," Domscheit-Berg offers after a moment, "and then add a little to it."

After this foreboding statement, he walks out of the tent and into the rain, closing the flap behind him.

"The more secretive or unjust an organization is, the more leaks induce fear and paranoia in its leadership and planning coterie," Julian Assange wrote in his "Conspiracy as Governance" essay in 2006. Five years later, that maxim wholly applied to WikiLeaks and Assange himself.

The Architect's and Domscheit-Berg's departure from the group with three thousand unpublished submissions represented the first major breach of the organization's security. In the months that followed, the spillages continued: Rogue WikiLeaks partner Israel Shamir allegedly gave unredacted cables to the repressive government of Belarus, including information that may have been used against the Belarusian political opposition. The freelance journalist Heather Brooke extracted a copy of the cables from the Icelandic WikiLeaker Smári McCarthy and passed them on to *The Guardian* newspaper, allowing the paper to publish the cables entirely without WikiLeaks' control and infuriating Assange.

After the OpenLeakers' departure with WikiLeaks' submission system and files, Assange began contacting former WikiLeakers and other common associates to beg, cajole, and threaten them into helping him resolve what he called "the hostage situation." By early 2011, Assange was publicly vowing to sue both *The Guardian* and Domscheit-Berg, lawsuits that never materialized. As his Nixonian anxiety grew, he went so far as to demand every WikiLeaks staffer sign a nondisclosure agreement that levied a twenty-million-dollar fine for distributing a WikiLeaks document, or even revealing the existence of the NDA itself.

Inevitably, the contract itself leaked. When the document showed up on the *New Statesman*'s website, *Guardian* reporter and former WikiLeaker James Ball admitted he was the source. "WikiLeaks is not democratically accountable," Ball wrote in an editorial for the paper. "It has no board, or no oversight. If any organization in the world relies on whistleblowers to keep it honest, it is WikiLeaks. In such circumstances, silencing dissent is not just ironic, it's dangerous."

Like the institutions Assange had once described as his targets, WikiLeaks was compromising its cause in an effort to contain its own employees' impulses to spill the organization's guts. And the biggest leak was yet to come.

In retrospect, Andy Müller-Maguhn may not have been the ideal judge of whether the Chaos Computer Club should lend its support to WikiLeaks' most prominent spin-off group. Long before the CCC board member had expelled Domscheit-Berg from the Club, he already considered the German ex-WikiLeaker a traitor to hacker principles and a possible government informant. "I've been a member of the CCC for twenty-six years," he says as he picks at an arugula salad at an Italian restaurant near the hacker group's headquarters in Berlin. "Perhaps I have seen too many people's intelligence files."

After WikiLeaks' three megaleaks and Domscheit-Berg's departure from the group in late 2010, while the U.S. government was coiling into counterattack mode, Müller-Maguhn says Domscheit-Berg began behaving strangely. He was so nervous when Müller-Maguhn ran into him around the Chaos Computer Club headquarters that the younger German's body shook and he couldn't complete a sentence, Müller-Maguhn recounts.

After WikiLeaks and OpenLeaks split, Müller-Maguhn was tasked by Assange as mediator in the two groups' digital custody dispute. Around the same time, as the CCC board member tells it, Domscheit-Berg seemed to suddenly and spontaneously regain his calm composure. "Some people in the CCC believed that he made a deal that would ensure his safety from prosecution," Müller-Maguhn says knowingly. "I can't tell you what happened. Maybe I'm a conspiracy theorist. But I imagine this is true."

And adopting this conspiracy theory, what does Müller-Maguhn think of OpenLeaks? "If we step back and look at this from very far away, from outer space," he says thoughtfully, "it looks like an intelligence agency's dream. To control the infrastructure itself."

(When I give Domscheit-Berg a chance to respond to these accusations, he laughs and says again that he has never cooperated with intelligence agents. He reminds me of Assange's claim that government spies attended his wedding; in fact, Domscheit-Berg says, the only person at the event with ties to intelligence agencies was Müller-Maguhn himself, whose CryptoPhone company sells to government customers.)

But regardless of their motives, as Müller-Maguhn tells the story, Domscheit-Berg and the Architect seemed determined to make the handover of WikiLeaks' files as difficult as possible.

Müller-Maguhn had been asked by Assange to retrieve three items from the OpenLeakers: the archive of already-published documents, the submissions system software, and the three thousand unpublished leaks. The CCC president went after the submissions system first, contacting the Architect over encrypted chat. To his surprise, the Architect immediately said he had no intention of giving back the submission system he had created under any circumstances. "He called it his *intellectual property,*" says Müller-Maguhn, pronouncing the two words with evident disgust. "I couldn't believe it. To me, those were words from a different culture. That was the language of the enemy."

The already-published documents were more easily retrieved. Domscheit-Berg sent them to Müller-Maguhn, and Müller-Maguhn relayed them to a WikiLeaks volunteer, who posted them in a downloadable format on WikiLeaks' Twitter feed so that they would be mirrored around the world and could never again be removed from the Internet.

But when Müller-Maguhn asked for the as yet unpublished files, WikiLeaks' eighteen-gigabyte collection of unrevealed secrets, Domscheit-Berg and the Architect seemed to respond with an endless stream of roadblocks and excuses. First, they said the files had been given to someone else and needed to be retrieved before they could be handed over. Then Domscheit-Berg reconsidered and said he would need to sort out the files that were addressed specifically to him from those addressed to WikiLeaks at large. At each step, whichever of the two OpenLeakers Müller-Maguhn managed to contact would say that he needed more time to discuss with the other, further stalling the process. "My mood toward Daniel was changing," he says. "I was getting the feeling he was playing bullshit games. But there was nothing I could do."

A few months into this game of tag, Domscheit-Berg committed what Müller-Maguhn considers a mortal sin against the unwritten hacker code. He published a tell-all book, one that detailed the group's warts-and-all history and even included his bitter private chat logs with Assange. "Why did he print internal chat protocols, private correspondence that had no context in philosophical or political disputes?" asks Müller-Maguhn. "I decided from that moment that my trust in Daniel must be reduced."

At the Chaos Communication Camp, Müller-Maguhn was dismayed to see Domscheit-Berg touting a penetration test of his systems by the Chaos Computer Club, even as he declined to make the site's full code available. And then, when he asked one, final time for the OpenLeakers to hand over WikiLeaks' data, they gave him what he describes as an entirely new excuse: that WikiLeaks couldn't be trusted with *any* sensitive data, and that the pair owed it to sources to fully vet and redact the files before returning them.

Müller-Maguhn called a meeting of the Club's board at ten P.M., and five hours later the five members had unanimously decided to oust Domscheit-Berg from the group. Officially, the decision was based on OpenLeaks' abuse of the CCC's name at the Camp. But for Müller-Maguhn, his anger toward Domscheit-Berg and the Architect had been building for nearly a year.

Eleven months of diplomacy between OpenLeaks and WikiLeaks had ended in failure. A few days after the Camp, Domscheit-Berg and the Architect decided that there was no way they would ever give WikiLeaks back its files, and that there was no use in holding on to them and endangering sources.

So they deleted their keys, rendering the files permanently, irrevocably encrypted.

When the news emerged that the OpenLeakers had essentially destroyed three thousand submissions, WikiLeaks sent out a stream of angry comments on Twitter, listing the contents of files it claimed were lost to history: internal communications of twenty neo-Nazi groups, sixty thousand e-mails from the ultra-right-wing NPD party in Germany, a video of an airstrike in the Afghan town of Granai that allegedly killed 140 civilians, surveillance policies by over a hundred Internet companies, the entire U.S. No-Fly List, and, most significantly to me after a year of leakless waiting, five gigabytes of internal data from Bank of America.

Domscheit-Berg later told me that WikiLeaks trumped up most of those claims: Of the files WikiLeaks listed, only the No-Fly List was included in the encrypted cache and hadn't been published because it was already available elsewhere online. (Sites like No-fly-list.com do offer some version of the list.) The others, he says, had been stored by WikiLeaks elsewhere, or didn't exist. Both he and the Architect admitted the encrypted files did likely include some data from Icelandic financial institutions, but wouldn't provide details. As for the Bank of America files, Domscheit-Berg claims that WikiLeaks simply lost them, a victim of the site's mess of creaking servers and failing hard drives before its 2010 reorganization.

Just what files became collateral damage in the dispute between WikiLeaks and OpenLeaks will likely never be completely known. Domscheit-Berg says he and the Architect used the Department of Defense standard for data erasure for all existing copies of their secret keys, the most secure practice for eradicating information short of demolishing the hard drive that stores it. They wrote over the keys' data seven times with pseudorandom patterns to cover all possible forensic traces. In a few minutes, the three thousand documents submitted by anonymous leakers to the world's most successful whistleblowing site over the course of eight months were permanently reduced to eighteen gigabytes of chaos that would require longer than the history of civilization to decipher.

By early 2011, WikiLeaks had experienced the full eviscerating effects of disgruntled insiders—from Domscheit-Berg's book to Heather Brooke's transmission of the State Department Cables to *The Guardian* to James Ball's leaked NDA contract. But WikiLeaks' most damaging leak would result from a more mundane phenomenon: simple human carelessness.

When a WikiLeaks staffer received the archive of already-published leaks recovered by Andy Müller-Maguhn at the end of 2010 and posted it online, the collection was uploaded to the Pirate Bay within days. What better outlet to prevent the next Domscheit-Berg from undoing the group's work, after all, than that Swedish bastion of uncensorable file-sharing? "Now you can have your very own copy of the WikiLeaks archive! How cool is that?" wrote the unnamed user who first uploaded the document collection.

Any curious visitor who downloaded the file might have noticed a strange folder among the CIA memos, Bilderberg meeting reports, lists of words banned from the Internet by the Chinese government, and stolen e-mails from Sarah Palin's Yahoo! account. It came last in alphabetical order, and hardly attracted attention. It was called, simply, "xyz."

Opening it revealed four files: x, y, y-docs, and z, each encrypted with PGP and thus unreadable. And they would have remained unreadable if it weren't for another simple mistake, this one committed by David Leigh, the reporter from *The Guardian* who first engineered the partnership with WikiLeaks to release the Cablegate files. In January 2011, *The Guardian*'s reporters published their own tell-all book about their work with WikiLeaks. And there, in the heading to the eleventh chapter, were printed the words that to Julian Assange must have jumped off the page with horrifying significance:

"AcollectionOfDiplomaticHistorySince_1966_ToThePresentDay#—Julian Assange's 58-character password."

It was the full passphrase to WikiLeaks' copy of the encrypted, unredacted cables. To a technological muggle like Leigh, the PGP password must have seemed like a harmless historical detail to add intrigue to his cloak-and-dagger story. He later claimed that Assange had told him the password would soon be changed, and saw no harm in publishing it a few months later. But to Assange and any other hacker, revealing a password represented a glaring security breach. Those familiar with PGP know that when a file is encrypted to a certain key, the private key will always open a copy of that encrypted file and thus can never be revealed. Secret keys remain secret for life.

This was no minor operational security slipup. If someone curious about the archive's mysterious "xyz" folder—and Web forums of WikiLeaks-watchers were already buzzing about the folder's mysterious contents—tried testing the printed password out on the four files, one by one, the result would be an incredible and terrible discovery: When he or she reached "z," the final file would open to reveal the entire, unredacted set of State Department Cables, complete with every sensitive source's name, from Chinese dissidents to African journalists, every innocent informant to the State Department in every repressive regime around the world. As Bradley Manning had described it, "world-wide anarchy in CSV format."

WikiLeaks had accidentally published an encrypted copy of the cables in a form that it couldn't unpublish. And now *The Guardian* had published the key.

For six months, the data breach was kept below the radar. If WikiLeaks was aware of its leak, it didn't comment on it. On file-sharing sites like the Pirate Bay and Torrent.net, it seemed that at least a few users had put together the password with the "z" file, accessed the cables, and had noted the inclusion of the full cables in their description of the archive. Whether the cables were found and decrypted by foreign intelligence agencies who might use the information for their own purposes is less clear.

One person, at any rate, was both well aware of WikiLeaks' cable breach and quite willing, it seemed, to talk about it: Daniel Domscheit-Berg.

In late summer of 2010, the small German newspaper *Freitag,* an Open-

Leaks partner, published a story with the unassuming headline, "Leak at WikiLeaks." It was a peculiar article, making the shocking claim that WikiLeaks' security had failed and that it had lost control of the entire cable database, but carefully leaving out all details that might help someone find or decrypt it.

It was, nonetheless, the only hint that the Internet needed. Soon Twitter users were making the connections between the printed password and the "xyz" folder. Finally, it was John Young, the "spiritual godfather of online leaking," who helpfully decrypted the entire database and posted it, entirely unredacted, to Cryptome. "Mediation of this disclosure is not needed in a democracy," he explained in his Twitter feed. "That the unreconfigured cables have become public is to be applauded and not condemned."

WikiLeaks found itself in the embarrassing position of holding back portions of files that anyone could already read online. So it soon followed Cryptome's lead and published in unredacted form the remainder of the quarter million cables it hadn't yet released. The metaleak was complete.

Then the recriminations began: WikiLeaks blamed *The Guardian* for having negligently published the password. *The Guardian*'s David Leigh pointed the finger at WikiLeaks for having published the encrypted file, even insinuating that Assange had wanted the full cables published all along and had purposefully tricked Leigh into printing the password so that the fiasco could be blamed on him.

In fact, it was Domscheit-Berg who, advertently or not, had caused WikiLeaks' leak to be sprayed across the Internet. He later told me that it was indeed he who tipped off Steffen Kraft, the editor at *Freitag* who publicized the breach.

Domscheit-Berg claims that he had long known about the cable spillage, and believed it demonstrated exactly why he and the Architect couldn't safely return WikiLeaks' unpublished submissions. As for Andy Müller-Maguhn, Domscheit-Berg blamed him for having uploaded the archive file to the Web, what he had elliptically described to me at the Camp as the "biggest data-handover fuckup of all time." (Müller-Maguhn denies any role in uploading the file.)

"I've been shutting up about this for months. I've been taking all the blame and all the heat from people who say my concerns for WikiLeaks' operation security are just made up. That I'm just a liar. That I'm trying to make them look bad, because I'm not giving anyone proof," he says. "So I pick one reporter that I trust at *Freitag* and told him the detail so he could verify I had a concern. I didn't want him to spread the story. That was his choice. . . . I'm not interested in these cables leaking at all. It's completely irresponsible, and it's not the consequence of what I've done."

But by alerting the mainstream media, hadn't he screamed into a megaphone a secret that until then had only been whispered around the Web? "You think that would have gone on forever?" he asks angrily. "It was only a matter of time until one and one were put together. If that's not communicated publicly, then the people implicated in the cables will never find out they need to be careful. That was the most important thing."

Domscheit-Berg wasn't alone in thinking that the covers of the State Department's informants were already blown. P. J. Crowley, the former spokesperson for the State Department who had resigned after criticizing the military's treatment of Bradley Manning, commented that "any autocratic secret service worth its salt" had already accessed the cables.

Nonetheless, after the *Freitag* story, new damage from the leak was already beginning to surface. Two Zimbabwean generals whose names had been marked "strictly protected" in the cables had met secretly with State Department officials to criticize the leader of the country's armed forces, calling him an inexperienced leader in the sway of corrupt president Robert Mugabe's political party. With their names exposed, they faced a possible court-martial on charges of treason. The names of Chinese dissidents exposed in the leak were passed around on nationalist Web forums, with some calling for manhunts and violence against them. Nine Iraqi Jews in Baghdad who were named in the cables were advised by the U.S. embassy and the Iraqi Anglican church to leave the country for fear of violent reprisal. After one Ethiopian journalist who communicated with the embassy in Addis Ababa was exposed as having met with a confidential informant in the government's communication office, he was interrogated by officials who gave him twenty-four hours to reveal his source. Instead, he fled to Uganda. "It's very sad, within a week leaving your home without any preparation," he told the BBC. "I love my country and I love my job and it's a big loss for me."

WikiLeaks, to be fair, had never promised its sources it would redact or edit the information it received from them—only that it would maximize that information's impact. It hadn't vowed to protect the people mentioned in its leak, but rather the identity of the leaker himself, a promise the group has never violated.

But when that mission came up against the practical, humanitarian necessity of keeping some secrets secret while revealing others, WikiLeaks had tried to resist the natural tendency of *all shared information* to leak. And when it inevitably failed to control that tendency, it put at risk some of the very truth-tellers and whistleblowers it had sought to empower. The secret-killing machine had turned upon itself.

... - . --- -.. -.- ... -. .--- ..-. ... .- .-.. -- ---

Fifty-five miles north of Berlin, on the north edge of a group of picturesque lakes, stands a cluster of single-story buildings inside a brick-walled compound: the remains of the Ravensbrück Nazi concentration camp. From 1939 to 1945, the all-female camp imprisoned more than 130,000 women from across Europe: Jews, gypsies, lesbians, political activists, resistance fighters, and a small contingent of children who had been in the victims' care when they were captured. More than 100,000 women of all ages were gassed, shot, lethally injected, buried alive, murdered in inhuman medical experiments, or marched to death as their captors moved them westward to hide from the invading Soviet army. Almost all of the children died from starvation. Most of the victims' remains are buried in a mass grave covered in stones facing a lake that contains the ashes of thousands of cremated bodies.

Across that body of water, just two miles away, inside a white, three-story house in a sleepy German town that he asks me not to name, Daniel Domscheit-Berg invites me into his home and the future headquarters of OpenLeaks.

Domscheit-Berg didn't intend to move his family and his organization next to the site of one of the twentieth century's darkest atrocities, he explains as he shows me around the house. But he got a very good deal on the property.

The OpenLeaks founder's office on the ground floor is strewn with random computer paraphernalia. Unused servers are stacked waist-high in the corner. Near his desk lies an enormous, 160-watt megaphone he recently used in a protest against European Union data retention laws. A length of four-inch-diameter copper cabling that he took as a souvenir from his high school summer job laying electrical lines rests at the foot of a couch. He recently purchased a four-foot-tall, fourteen-hundred-pound steel safe he plans to install in the basement to hold his family's and OpenLeaks' most sensitive files.

Despite the maelstrom of anger and blame swirling around the test launch of OpenLeaks, the irretrievably lost WikiLeaks submissions, and the leak of the unredacted cables, Domscheit-Berg seems utterly relaxed, sitting with me and munching on an apple from the century-old tree in his backyard. "We felt like Frodo in *Lord of the Rings,*" he says of the files he and the Architect scuppered. "People kept finding reasons why we should give them the data. In the end, we knew we had to destroy it. And since we did, life is good. I'd rather take the shit storm and be everyone's scapegoat than go against my best knowledge and risk compromising sources."

Five months after this meeting and half a year after Domscheit-Berg's expulsion from the Chaos Computer Club, his hacker credibility would be partially redeemed. A special meeting of the group in February 2012 reinstated Domscheit-Berg's membership, and Andy Müller-Maguhn lost his board position in a reproach of his hasty and biased decision to expel the OpenLeaker. ("We decided that if we evicted people based only on suspicions and doubt, it would become very easy to destroy us with rumors," one CCC member later told me.)

But at the time of my meeting Domscheit-Berg in his home, his reputation among his hacktivist cohorts has reached a nadir. I ask the obvious question: Doesn't his role in WikiLeaks' setbacks and crises bode ill for the future of OpenLeaks? When even many of his fellow hackers see him as a traitor, how does he expect leakers to trust him? "If this depends only on my reputation, it won't work anyway," he responds calmly. "We can only do this by proving the technology works and slowly building up trust."

Domscheit-Berg seems to be in a chatty mood; we talk about his plan to turn the third floor of this house into a workshop for activists, about the concentration camp across the lake, and then about Domscheit-Berg's early obsession with World War II and the Holocaust. As the conversation meanders, he brings up the White Rose movement, a resistance group that attempted to distribute underground newspapers during the Nazi era, and we discuss whether WikiLeaks-style megaleaks might have prevented Hitler's rise to power—sitting so geographically close to the site of so many Nazi atrocities that remained secret for far too long, the question hangs in the air. Domscheit-Berg admits it's probably impossible to answer.

Instead, he brings up a German-language book he recently read, titled *Soldiers,* cowritten by two professors who gained access to 150,000 pages of transcribed, secret recordings made of German prisoners of war in British and American camps. Domscheit-Berg was fascinated by the cavalier way the soldiers discussed killing civilians and raping women with professional dispassion in the book's pages. The last chapter deals with WikiLeaks' Collateral Murder video, with its American helicopter gunners firing on Iraqi civilians as if in a video game.

Both wars' recordings demonstrate the quintessential act of leaking, Domscheit-Berg says: They take an immoral act out of some special, secret culture where it seems acceptable and expose it to the world of normal human relationships, where it's exposed as obviously horrific. "Within a certain frame of reference, what they're doing seems professional or even cool," he says. "But if you get rid of that secrecy, it seems crazy. If you make it all transparent, their own mothers would call them and ask, 'What the hell are you doing? That's not how I raised you!'"

Just as Domscheit-Berg is articulating that ultimate definition of a leak's value, he receives a phone call and has a tense German conversation. He tells me he needs to get to Berlin. On the train a few minutes later, I ask him if he hopes OpenLeaks will spill entire wars' histories and huge caches of diplomatic documents the way WikiLeaks has. He initially dodges the question, saying that the decision would fall to the group's media partners. But after a pause, he answers.

"That stuff isn't going to happen again," he says, looking at the German countryside rolling by. Bradley Manning's treatment and improved government security measures, he believes, have scared off any near-term megaleakers of high-level government secrets on the scale of the WikiLeaks 2010 releases.

But that doesn't mean some sort of megaleak isn't in the works, he warns. "Some leak will very harshly damage people's privacy. Some large amount of health care data, perhaps. Something where the whole world will agree that it never should have happened."

It all sounds like a very dark vision for a transparency advocate, I point out, and one that's very different from that of Julian Assange. He nods. "Julian wrote this really lame piece of philosophy in 2006," he continues, referring to the "Conspiracy as Governance" essay. "He sees everything as a conspiracy that must be taken down. I don't see the world in these black-and-white terms. I think there's a valid reason for some things to be secret. You can't solve the entire Middle East's problems in public."

So what should be secret, then? "Every situation is different," he answers. "Drawing the line is the toughest question in this field."

I can forgive Domscheit-Berg for his reluctance to answer the impossible questions of the leaking movement. Unlike Assange, he is, and has only claimed to be, an engineer, not a philosopher. And for an engineer, things were clearer before 2010, during the period when WikiLeaks was engaged in smaller, targeted, high-frequency leaking. Before the megaleaks, the redactions, the risk of leaked leaks, the need to sort out good secrets from bad on a massive, terrifying scale. Back when WikiLeaks was, for the most part, two idealistic young men exposing wrongdoing from a steadier moral high ground.

As we arrive in Berlin, I ask him if he has any message he'd like me to pass on to Assange, given that the two haven't spoken in nearly a year. "I guess tell him to stop lying about me," he says quickly. "That's the least I can ask from someone who talks about telling the truth so much."

Then he thinks for a moment and brightens slightly, as if he's remembering a different person altogether and another time. "And also tell him good luck."

CONCLUSION

THE MACHINE

In New York's Zuccotti Park, the epicenter of a global anticapitalist and anticorruption movement that began in the fall of 2011 under the name Occupy Wall Street, protesters adopt the same tactics of angry, confrontational nonviolence that Birgitta Jónsdóttir used in the Icelandic Revolution of 2009, that Daniel Ellsberg and Phil Zimmermann used in their Cold War protests for nuclear disarmament, that John Young used in the Columbia University Occupation of 1968. They chant slogans, acquiesce to arrest without resistance, and carry signs: "We are the 99%," "Robin Hood Was Right," "Free Assange," and "Free Bradley Manning."

And they also carry cell phones, almost all of which contain a video camera.

Video clips that have emerged from the protests on websites like YouTube and LiveLeak include one of police pushing into crowds of demonstrators on the Brooklyn Bridge, grabbing protesters seemingly at random, and dragging them out to be arrested as the crowd chants, "The whole world is watching." Others show unresisting protesters violently thrown to the ground, and a group of young women surrounded with plastic mesh police barricades and then, after they've been penned in, doused with Mace and left blinded and screaming. (Based on videos of that last incident, the policeman responsible was later publicly identified by members of Anonymous as Anthony Bologna, and John Young posted a 2001 Indymedia report to Cryptome that described the senior officer as "notorious for his previous treatment of protesters." Bologna was fined six thousand dollars by the department and faced a further inquiry by the Manhattan district attorney.)

The tiny cell phone cameras that filmed those incidents are the tools Rich Jones believes represent the next stage of the transparency movement. Jones, a gaunt twenty-three-year-old Boston software developer with hair that flops over his ears, is the creator of a suite of simple smartphone apps with names like OpenWatch and Cop Recorder. The programs run on Android and iPhone, and allow users to press a button and start invisibly recording audio and video. That content is uploaded to Jones's servers, where Jones and his collaborators strip out any identifying information and post the file with a transcript. More than a hundred thousand users have already downloaded the apps, and they upload more than fifty videos a day. The goal, Jones says, is to create millions of "reverse surveillance cameras" that constantly keep tabs on authority figures.

"Since September eleventh, the government's rhetoric has been that if you have nothing to hide, you have nothing to worry about," says Jones with just a hint of righteous anger in his voice. "I say if those are the rules of the game, play them across the board. Show us what goes on."

A few of the recordings Jones has obtained are disturbing, if not quite explosive. One audio file uploaded to the site captures a cop calling a detained suspect in a Durham, North Carolina, courthouse an "old-school pimp," denying his request to use the bathroom and asking that the detainee rap for him and flash gang signs. Another video file shows a San Diego policeman pull over a driver for a DUI check and then illegally search his car against the driver's wishes, flipping through the driver's wallet after he's alone in the vehicle. The video sparked a minor scandal in San Diego and was aired on the local news station. When I spoke to Jones, he was looking for volunteers to help him listen to hours of recordings from the Occupy Wall Street protests, and he and his two developers had just been commissioned to build protest-focused apps for the National Lawyers Guild and the American Civil Liberties Union.

"I'd be surprised if we ever had our own Collateral Murder," says Jones. "But we have a hundred thousand people who now see their phone as a weapon against corruption. It's not spies versus spies, and megaleaks. It's about giving everyone a way to be subversive."

Jones has no intention of rebuilding WikiLeaks. But he does say he was directly inspired by Julian Assange. He sees himself as part of the next generation of Assange's Bourbaki media movement, enabling "scientific journalism" that uncovers complete primary source materials for the audience and brings the public inside private, corrupt worlds.

"The idea is to create a more active WikiLeaks, one that isn't just receiving these documents, but actively capturing new data from secret places," he says. "Here's a technology you already have. Here's a way to apply it to create a transparent society by force. I want to build technologies that make it possible for everyone to be part of leaking information."

In 1999, a nineteen-year-old named Shawn Fanning, working in the office of his uncle's Internet start-up Chess.net, launched a music file-sharing service called Napster. Using the service, practically any MP3 file could be downloaded from another user's computer, and music, in its new, discless form, became essentially free. At its peak, more than twenty-six million people used the service, at a time when only about five hundred million people had access to the Internet.

By late 2001, Napster had been effectively shut down. The company ran afoul of the Digital Millennium Copyright Act, was hit with a twenty-billion-dollar lawsuit by the Recording Industry Association of America, and went bankrupt in 2002. Aside from blatantly ignoring intellectual property law, Napster had made the mistake of running its peer-to-peer file-sharing index on a single central collection of servers—every search for a song required that central hub to connect the uploading user and the downloading user. The service that made enemies of some of the world's most powerful industries had a single point of failure.

Around the same time Napster was being legally dismantled, however, a twenty-six-year-old coding savant and former contributor to the Cypherpunk Mailing List named Bram Cohen released a new peer-to-peer file-sharing protocol called BitTorrent. BitTorrent assembled downloads piecemeal from hundreds of users at once, and kept its index of which user had which file available for upload on multiple "tracker" servers. Anyone could run a tracker server, making them far harder to shut down. More fundamentally, BitTorrent was a protocol, not a company. It couldn't be sued.

Today, thanks in part to outlaw index sites like the Pirate Bay, BitTorrent now accounts for somewhere between a quarter and a third of the entire traffic volume of the global Internet. Due largely to the free file-sharing BitTorrent makes possible, the RIAA claims, music industry revenue has been cut in half since 1999, from $14.6 billion to $7.6 billion.

For a pair of Italian hackers hoping to reshape the future of leaking, there are worse models for changing the world.

Fabio Pietrosanti and Arturo Filastò, the cofounders of GlobaLeaks, say they aim to create the BitTorrent to WikiLeaks' Napster. Where WikiLeaks was a single, vulnerable target, GlobaLeaks aims to create what they've called a "worldwide, distributed leak amplification network."

Pietrosanti is a thirty-year-old security engineer who looks like a twenty-one-year-old actor, small, with big eyes and Tom Cruise hair. Filastò, on the other hand, is an actual twenty-one-year-old former actor, who spent two years playing the gangly, long-haired teen geek heartthrob on a popular Italian soap opera before leaving the TV industry to study mathematics and become a Tor developer.

The software the two Italians and a few other coders have been working on—and the group merely aims to offer software, not run an active leaking service like WikiLeaks or OpenLeaks—is designed to allow anyone to set up a leaking conduit in minutes, using Tor's Hidden Services to offer a submissions system that's both secure and untraceable. Unlike OpenLeaks, GlobaLeaks won't limit who uses its software, and has posted its source code online for all to see, tweak, and use. Although the pair's work had yet to produce a leak when I spoke with them, they were busy meeting with any group who might consider deploying their software to host a niche whistleblower site: two left-wing Italian political parties, a Serbian newspaper, an Italian energy utility that wants to facilitate internal whistleblowing, a British leak site called BritiLeaks, and even Atanas Tchobanov and Assen Yordanov at BalkanLeaks.

Their end goal, Pietrosanti says, is to expand the leaking movement from the current fifty or so WikiLeaks copycats to a network of hundreds or thousands of "leak nodes," run by everyone from U.S. corporations that are legally mandated to run an internal whistleblowing outlet to radical activists that hope to pass their materials on to publishers while using Tor to remain completely anonymous. Like BitTorrent, GlobaLeaks aims to disperse the risk of handling sensitive material over an army of individuals rather than one vulnerable group of intermediaries. "Some people may be like Assange, and say, OK, we'll publish and fight and whatever," says Pietrosanti. "But lots of people want to fight corruption without taking that much responsibility. If the risk profile of everyone who runs a leak node is reduced, there will be a lot more leak nodes."

"WikiLeaks taught us something. And it brought the word *whistleblower* back into the awareness of the public," adds Filastò. "But GlobaLeaks is the next logical step."

My time in the orbit of WikiLeaks and the inchoate movement it represents began with Assange's challenge to the American financial system in November 2010: a promise to "take down a bank or two." Less than a year later—and just five years after Assange had vowed in a letter to Daniel Ellsberg that he would "place a new star in the political firmament of man"—the finance giants had taken their revenge, and seemingly dragged WikiLeaks down to earth.

In a halting statement at the Frontline Club in London in October 2011, Assange explained that Visa, MasterCard, PayPal, and Bank of America had successfully starved WikiLeaks of the cash it needed to survive. The financial embargo on the group had reduced the group's funding from donations of more than three hundred thousand dollars in the twenty-four hours before the embargo to a trickle of less than ten thousand dollars a month. "If WikiLeaks does not find a way to remove this blockade, we will simply not be able to continue by the turn of the New Year," he told the crowd.

Money, of course, was only one of the growing number of forces paralyzing WikiLeaks. Assange himself remained chained by an electronic manacle to Ellingham Hall, the mansion where he had already spent 322 days under house arrest while appealing extradition to Sweden for questioning regarding his alleged sex crimes. Meanwhile, an American grand jury secretly debated whether he should be charged in the United States and extradited for trial. Many of his most ardent supporters had abandoned his cause after WikiLeaks' publication of the entire unredacted cables. And the group's defectors within OpenLeaks had—with whatever intentions—critically damaged both WikiLeaks and the reputation of the system they had hoped would replace it.

Shortly after Assange's speech about WikiLeaks' financial problems, I contacted one of the group's technical volunteers—perhaps the youngest to work with WikiLeaks at the time—by encrypted instant message. Like the Architect, he had never told me his real name, and in publishing this interview he asked that I not even use his pseudonym.

The young engineer was, understandably, demoralized. "I think WikiLeaks is at an all-time low," he wrote, calling the group "stagnant" and "broke." "It's not the WikiLeaks that came out with Collateral Murder. It's like a decaying New York City metro station."

"I feel like an old-timer talking about the good old days when I remember what WikiLeaks was. It was fucking amazing a year or two years ago. It was the most beautiful thing ever," he wrote, unloading his feelings without my prompting. Assange, he said, had wasted WikiLeaks' enormous political capital and substantial donations. "I love him. He's awesome. But I just wish he hadn't thrown it all away."

But then his tone changed. And he expressed the message that has kept the ideals behind WikiLeaks progressing for generations.

"Maybe one day, in a couple decades, when I'm forty, I'll have my own go," he wrote. "And maybe I won't fail."

The cypherpunk drive to destroy institutional secrecy hasn't ended, any more than it ended when Tim May shut down his BlackNet experiment, when Julf Helsingius caved to the Scientologists and killed Penet, when Mendax and the International Subversives were arrested by the Australian Federal Police, when Bradley Manning was thrown into a military brig, or when the Anonymous hackers allegedly connected to the HBGary hack were arrested. Today, the leaking movement is no longer WikiLeaks, or even OpenLeaks, Anonymous, or any one of the copycat experiments that are sprouting up around the world. As Jónsdóttir had predicted, WikiLeaks has morphed into "two things or ten," and then again into the "thousand WikiLeaks" that Domscheit-Berg had once demanded. With all their variation in goals and means, OpenLeaks, IMMI, BalkanLeaks, GlobaLeaks, and even Jones's OpenWatch smartphone apps are all stepchildren of a movement that stretches back to the cypherpunks two decades earlier and the Pentagon Papers two decades before that. And with its greatest successes in just the last few of those forty years, its work is only starting.

After WikiLeaks lost control of the full, unredacted State Department Cables, John Young posted a statement in the comments of an article on the website of *The Economist* newspaper. It was a carefully written passage, and it echoed the short speech he gave to the students occupying the Columbia architecture building forty-three years before, the pep talk that energized the protesters in their moment of crisis. It read as follows:

> WikiLeaks has undergone several transformations during its short history. Some quite wrenching and near fatal. It has surpassed them with renewed energy, as it will this latest chal-

lenge. What is admirable is how it manages to become more resilient and creative when the pressure is greatest. It will likely continue to face ever greater tests of its capabilities, which, for me, is a good prospect, for without the need to grow stronger it will succumb to laziness and braggardy about the glory days. That may be inevitable as Assange and his invention age into the senescence awaiting us all. Some of [us have] reached that point earlier than he, but also paid our dues as he is having to do.

Why not join him in paying your dues, take risks greater than you can handle, ride not his bandwagon but build and drive your own, welcoming the ridicule, praise and condemnation. If as persistent, courageous and lucky as he you just might become rich and famous as a reward for being admirable.

Or you might be an utter failure, but better that than middling.

. .--- -.. -.-. ... --. -. --. --- -... - --.- .--. -. -.-- ..

The Architect, when I met him at the Chaos Communication Camp, gave me no form of contact information. When I asked how I would find him again, he merely laughed and said that I should reach out to him through Domscheit-Berg. "Daniel is my proxy," he quipped. A bit of cypherpunk humor. The follow-up questions I e-mailed to the secretive engineer via his German associate were never answered.

For now, the Architect's pure pseudonymity remains intact. Somewhere, he's building, testing, and tweaking a new, sleeker, more powerful version of the machine that kills secrets. If Assange ends up in a Swedish or American prison, if Daniel Domscheit-Berg's tarnished reputation takes him out of the leaking game, if BalkanLeaks gives up on influencing a hopelessly corrupt government, or GlobaLeaks and the other idealistic heirs of the leaking movement fail, or even if the next Bradley Manning is caught by law enforcement and faces a similarly chilling punishment, the Architect will move on. Perhaps he'll take a different pseudonym, different partners, a different strategy.

Or even if this Architect retires, somewhere, another nameless, faceless architect is coding another antisecrecy weapon. Perhaps another one is reading the archives of the Cypherpunk Mailing List. Or studying GlobaLeaks' source code. Or watching the archived video of Daniel Domscheit-Berg's talk at the Chaos Communication Camp and learning from his mistakes, as John Gilmore suggested future leaking advocates ought to.

We don't yet know the names of the architects who will build the next upgrade to the secret-killing machine. But we'll know them by their work.

AFTERWORD

"For every machine that kills secrets, there are at least two that keep them alive," wrote the digital critic Evgeny Morozov to conclude his review of the first edition of this book in *The New York Times.* Indeed, for many watching the cat and mouse game between the free information movement and the government, the year following the release of *This Machine Kills Secrets* became the cats' turn to control the story.

The Obama administration's "war on leaks" that I described in the fifth chapter of this book has only intensified. In January 2013, ex-CIA agent and waterboarding whistleblower John Kiriakou was convicted of giving classified documents to a freelance reporter and sentenced to thirty months in prison, making him the first CIA official to be judged a criminal for leaking to the media. In a letter from the Loretto, Pennsylvania, Correctional Institution, he's described working as a janitor for $5.25 a month and enduring guards who tear apart his six-man prison cell in arbitrary searches.

Around the same time, the FBI filed an affidavit later published by *The Washington Post*, describing Fox News journalist James Rosen as a possible "aider and abettor and/or co-conspirator" in the Espionage Act indictment of State Department staffer Stephen Kim, accused of giving Rosen information about a nuclear test in North Korea. That attack on Rosen, used to gain access to his Gmail account and confirm his source, blurs the distinction between leakers of secrets and the publications that release them. The threat goes beyond radical leak portals like WikiLeaks: Any solicitation of classified material comes into the crosshairs, essentially outlawing the daily practice of hundreds of mainstream media reporters.

But the events most widely marked as signs of the pendulum swinging back against the world's leakers came in May and June of 2013, starting with the Associated Press's revelation that the Department of Justice had obtained two months of phone records for twenty of its reporters. In a probe to find an insider that revealed a bomb plot foiled in Yemen by an embedded CIA informant, prosecutors had cast out the widest and most intrusive dragnet of the media in recent history. In the process, they also destroyed any illusion the press may have had of the privacy of its traditional lines of communication with government insiders.

That AP surveillance scandal would turn out to be a mere preamble to a far wider one. Just a month later, a leaked top-secret order revealed that Verizon had been giving the NSA millions of Americans' call records, perhaps the greatest exposure of the U.S. government's domestic surveillance since the Bush administration's warrantless wiretapping scandal. Within days, AT&T and Sprint were revealed to be participating in that data collection, too, and another leaked document exposed a powerful Internet spying mechanism known as PRISM, giving the NSA access to information stored by Google, Microsoft, Apple, and Facebook. Yet another leaked document showed that the NSA's internal rules allow for analysis of data "inadvertently" eavesdropped from Americans if it's relevant to "the unauthorized disclosure of national security information."

In late June, the source of those NSA leaks surfaced in Hong Kong, where he identified himself as twenty-nine-year-old Edward Snowden, an analyst working for contractor Booz Allen Hamilton—the same firm Bank of America hired to root out its own potential leak in 2011. As of this writing, Snowden has taken refuge in a Moscow airport and is seeking asylum in Ecuador and Iceland, accompanied and aided by WikiLeaks' staffer Sarah Harrison.

After initially communicating with reporters under the pseudonym "Verax"—the Latin antonym of Assange's Mendax—Snowden chose to reveal his real name, knowing that he may be extradited and prosecuted under the Espionage Act, just as six other leakers have been prosecuted during Obama's tenure. "I understand that I will be made to suffer for my actions," he told *The Guardian*. "My sole motive is to inform the public as to that which is done in their name and that which is done against them."

In many ways, Snowden proves the assertions I made in the prologue: He shows that any of the hundreds of thousands of Americans with access to the government's swelling collection of top-secret information—more than 250,000 of whom work for private contractors—can become the source of a megaleak. Glenn Greenwald, the *Guardian* reporter who first received Snowden's leaks, says Snowden gave him thousands of files. It's also worth noting that anonymous leaking remains possible. The source of the AP's leak, unlike Snowden, hasn't been identified by the Department of Justice's dragnet as of this writing.

But the government's actions in the last year and the vast surveillance revealed by Snowden's documents show that technology also allows fierce new methods of rooting out leakers, and the Obama administration hasn't hesitated to use them. One by one, the fingers that the press once extended into the government's files are being snapped.

For the media in America and around the world, I count three ways to react to the growing leak crackdown: The press can give up on providing any real check against the government's power; it can fight for shield laws that protect its reporting, a worthwhile strategy, but one that's still bound to lag behind new surveillance technologies and leaves less democratic nations entirely vulnerable; or it can adopt the tools of the cypherpunks and build a different sort of Internet in the shadows of the existing one, where cryptography, not law, keeps the promise it makes to its sources and to the public.

For the last two years of his life, the freedom of information activist and coding savant Aaron Swartz worked to make that third path possible. Swartz, who helped code a widely used version of the RSS protocol at age fourteen and later developed much of the social news site Reddit, found himself working at the magazine giant Condé Nast when Reddit was acquired by the company in 2006.

The then-twenty-year-old hacker hated the office environment, which he later described as "dullening, full of gray pillars and fluorescent lighting, drones tapping at computers and talking about synergizing." He soon left and eventually cofounded Demand Progress, an influential activist group that fought successfully against overbroad Internet regulation like the Stop Online Piracy Act, and campaigned on behalf of bank whistleblowers and Bradley Manning.

Around the time that WikiLeaks was hitting the peak of its megaleaks, Swartz was also attempting a leak of his own. Over the course of several months, according to an indictment later filed against him in a federal court, Swartz used a computer planted in a closet of MIT's library to download millions of academic papers from the online service JSTOR, which he planned to release to the public. In January 2011, he was arrested on MIT's campus, and between July of that year and September 2012 was hit with thirteen felony charges, including wire fraud and computer fraud. Facing a maximum of thirty-five years in prison and suffering from depression, the twenty-six-year-old hung himself in his Crown Heights, Brooklyn, apartment in January 2013.

It was only four months later that Condé Nast revealed the final piece of code that Swartz had built on its behalf. Kevin Poulsen, a former hacker turned editor at *Wired* magazine, had hired Swartz to create a WikiLeaks-like submission system for *Wired*, and Swartz had returned to the media company's offices from time to time as an outside contractor in the years leading up to his suicide. Eventually *Wired* dropped the project during a management shake-up following the departure of its editor in chief. But another Condé Nast publication, *The New Yorker*, took on Poulsen and Swartz's leak system and launched it with the name Strongbox.

Strongbox followed all the best practices of anonymous leaking, and invented some new ones, too. Sources are required to run Tor and upload their files or tips to a Tor hidden service, run from a server stashed in a data center far away from *The New Yorker*'s own systems. When a source first visits the site, he or she is asked to create a pseudonymous account that allows a leak's recipients to send messages back to the source in a two-way anonymous conversation.

Anything the source uploads is immediately encrypted, and only two reporters are assigned to access those enciphered files, downloading them over a protected connection and then decrypting them only on a separate computer kept entirely disconnected from any other network. For added security against spyware, that "review" machine has no hard drive. It's booted from an unalterable CD, and the private keys used to read the leaked materials would be kept on a separate thumb drive.

In his work for Condé Nast, Swartz insisted on one final condition: that his system be free and open source. That code would be called DeadDrop, available to any other organization that wished to set up its own anonymous leaking conduit.

A few weeks after *The New Yorker* revealed its anonymous leak system, I suggested to my editors at *Forbes* magazine that we should build one, too, using that same freely available code. By the time you're reading this, *Forbes* will have followed in the footsteps of BlackNet, Cryptome, and WikiLeaks, providing state-of-the-art cryptographic protections to anonymous sources.

You can find a link to our anonymous leak system at http://www.thismachinekillssecrets.com/contact.

I don't know what will result from the mainstream media's adoption of WikiLeaks' methods. It may not produce bombshell megaleaks of the kind Assange received, but perhaps will bring about a more modest outcome: the mere ability to continue the watchdog media's investigative work under the growing scrutiny of the government.

As *Wired*'s Kevin Poulsen describes it, a system like DeadDrop is no longer a radical hacker trick so much as a wheelchair ramp at the entrance to a restaurant: a necessary consideration on behalf of its most vulnerable patrons. "This isn't like playing a slot machine and hoping for a big jackpot," Poulsen says. "That's exactly the wrong way to think about it. This is about fixing an architectural deficiency that virtually all news organizations suffer from."

Meanwhile, Daniel Domscheit-Berg's and the Architect's OpenLeaks project has pivoted to focus on something similar. In December 2012, more than a year after OpenLeaks' failed test run with *Die Tageszeitung*, Domscheit-Berg posted an update on its website titled "State of the Leak." The statement announced that OpenLeaks would no longer be seeking to create a product for media companies to implement, but will rather serve as something closer to security consultants, sharing the know-how they gained as WikiLeakers with the wider world. "We want to see any organisation seriously interested in harnessing the potential of whistleblowers in the digital world to have the skills for it," Domscheit-Berg wrote. "We can contribute by providing expertise, and by fostering a collaborative effort towards the best possible solution. Not the least for the sake of a technically more savvy fourth estate of the future."

The leaker's tool kit, meanwhile, remains as strong as ever. Despite constant doubts about Tor's security, no real-world user of the anonymity network has yet been publicly identified by cracking Tor's protections. On the contrary, the FBI in June 2012 revealed that it had given up on a child pornography case because the user had employed Tor to cover his or her tracks. In another case, the drug-selling site Silk Road has amassed around 60,000 visits a day to its Tor hidden service, where they can use the cryptocurrency Bitcoin to buy any drug imaginable. The site's business has exploded over two years, with no sign that the Drug Enforcement Agency can locate the site's owners or shut down the servers that run it.

Tor's anonymity isn't merely being used for crime, either. Just two years after BalkanLeaks' first scoop, WikiLeaks' Bulgarian offshoot demonstrated again that anonymity can still be used for truth telling, too.

In February 2013, Atanas Chobanov and Assen Yordanov received a document through their Tor submission system that has come to be known as the "Buddha" file. The 1997 memo from Bulgaria's federal police referred to the future Prime Minister Boyko Borisov by the code name "Buddha," and suggested using him as an informant against his connections in the country's mafia, noting his "criminal orientation."

Following BalkanLeaks' earlier publication of the State Department cable on Borisov's alleged criminal activities, the confirmation of that dirty history from within Bulgaria's own government struck home. When Bulgarians took to the streets later that month protesting energy prices, they also chanted slogans about corruption like "Buddha, nie ne sme budali," a pun that translates to "Buddha, we're not idiots."

"For one week, this was the biggest story in Bulgaria," says Atanas Chobanov. "There was a period when no one called him Borisov. Everyone called him Buddha."

Eighteen days after BalkanLeaks' "Buddha" leak, Borisov resigned.

Chobanov holds no illusions that BalkanLeaks was solely responsible for that coup, or that it achieved total victory. In the ensuing election, Borisov won back a seat in the Bulgarian parliament, but without enough votes to become prime minister; a coalition of opposition parties now controls the government. And as in Tunisia, the leaked document only fed a spark that had emerged from economic concerns and popular frustration. But Chobanov believes that BalkanLeaks' well-timed publication "proves that we really can change things," he says. "We are not saying the Buddha file was the reason for his resignation. But it certainly helped."

And what about the protagonist of this book and the world's most famous cypherpunk? In May 2012, Julian Assange was denied an appeal in his extradition case, an outcome that threatened to send him from London to Stockholm for questioning on suspicion of sex crimes, and, he claims, on from Sweden to the United States to face still-secret charges related to his publications.

Shortly after that decision was announced, Assange responded with the kind of unexpected gambit that has become his trademark: He took refuge in London's Ecuadorian embassy, applied for asylum, and refused to leave. Assange had hosted Ecuadorian president and WikiLeaks fan Rafael Correa on his talk show months earlier, and in Assange's moment of need, Correa's friendly administration granted his refugee request. Since then, Assange has been locked in a stalemate with the London police who surround the Ecuadorian compound, waiting to arrest him if he makes a break for the airport. He's spent more than a year trapped in the embassy's two rooms, living the life of an eccentric celebrity, receiving guests including Lady Gaga and Oliver Stone, and running for a Senate seat in his native Australia.

But while Assange's high jinks have held the media's attention, it's his most important source who has proven to be the true prisoner of conscience. In February 2013, Bradley Manning pleaded guilty to charges that he had given WikiLeaks the hundreds of thousands of classified files related to the war in Iraq, the war in Afghanistan, and the State Department database of cables. Later that month, a recording of the full, hour-long statement he read in court was leaked online, despite the military's ban on recording devices at his hearings.

In that contraband audio file, Manning reads his statement in a clear and confident voice, the first time he'd spoken in public since he'd been outed as the world's most prolific leaker. Countering speculation that he might blame the violation of his secret clearances on Assange or others within WikiLeaks to lessen his sentence, he carries the weight of his data crimes entirely on himself. "The decisions that I made to send documents and information to the [WikiLeaks organization] were my own decisions," he says. "I take full responsibility for my actions."

He doesn't apologize for those leaks, but instead attempts to justify them:

> I believed that if the general public, especially the American public, had access to the information contained within the [Iraq and Afghanistan files], this could spark a domestic debate on the role of the military and our foreign policy in general as well as it related to Iraq and Afghanistan. I also believed the detailed analysis of the data over a long period of time by different sectors of society might cause society to reevaluate the need or even the desire to engage in counterterrorism and counterinsurgency operations that ignore the complex dynamics of the people living in the affected environment every day.

Later, he describes his motive for leaking the Apache helicopter footage that WikiLeaks would title "Collateral Murder," and expressed his satisfaction at the public response to the leaked video.

> I hoped that the public would be as alarmed as me about the conduct of the aerial weapons team crew members. I wanted the American public to know that not everyone in Iraq and Afghanistan are targets that needed to be neutralized, but rather people who were struggling to live in the pressure-cooker environment of what we call "asymmetric warfare." After the release I was encouraged by the response in the media and general public, who observed the aerial weapons team video. As I hoped, others were just as troubled—if not more troubled—as I by what they saw.

In his statement, Manning doesn't mention what possible harm his spilled secrets, including the full, unredacted State Department database, may have caused. But throughout his testimony, it struck me that very little, if any, of Manning's official account contradicted the motives he'd described to Adrian Lamo in their private chats years earlier, when he'd said that he hoped his releases would result in "worldwide discussion, debates, and reforms."

If leaked information gains its power by showing a disconnect between public appearances and private conduct, Manning's behavior should serve as a reminder that one antidote to leaks is simple consistency in ethics: In the end, Manning's moral reasoning was the same in public and in private, unlike so many of the figures exposed by his breaches of secrecy.

As of this writing, Manning's court martial is ongoing. His army prosecutors continue to charge him with twenty-one offenses—including the most serious crime of "aiding the enemy"—and to seek a life sentence in prison.

Andy Greenberg
July 2013

SOURCES

This is a book, in a sense, about primary source documents. E-mails, chat logs, memos, and manuals are the currency of the leaking movement, and like the book's subjects, I've sought to use them whenever possible to underpin this story.

In this age of overflowing, recorded digital communications, my task in writing several chapters was to carve a narrative out of hundreds or thousands of pages of text—often leaked themselves—whether it be Adrian Lamo's and Bradley Manning's instant message logs, the decade-plus archive of the Cypherpunk Mailing List, or the hacked e-mails of HBGary Federal. If I had adhered to Julian Assange's doctrine of scientific journalism, which demands that the reporter publish the entire source document of a story along with his or her interpretation, this book would have been many thousands of pages long.

But for many sections of the book I also resorted to the usual method of a reporter: hundreds of hours of interviews, conducted face-to-face whenever possible, and when necessary by phone, e-mail, instant message, and letters. I interviewed every person included in the character list at the front of this book, with the exception of Bradley Manning, who for the duration of my reporting has been in a military jail or a courtroom. I'm especially grateful to many sources who spent hours with me, speaking under the condition of anonymity with no direct personal benefit.

The very few bits of dialogue in the book that I didn't personally hear were recounted to me by witnesses who were present, and thus may not be recorded exactly verbatim. I've edited some quoted texts' punctuation and capitalization for readability. With the exception of any stray facts that may have been missed in my efforts to note all sources, everything I've written that's not cited below can be attributed to my own reporting.

Primary sources and interviews aside, I'm particularly indebted to a few prior books and articles as instructive signposts for my reporting and primary sources in their own right. They include Daniel Ellsberg's memoir *Secrets,* Suelette Dreyfus and Julian Assange's *Underground,* Steven Levy's *Crypto,* Daniel Domscheit-Berg's memoir *Inside WikiLeaks,* Robert Manne's "The Cypherpunk Revolutionary: Julian Assange" in Australia's *The Monthly,* Nathaniel Rich's "The Most Dangerous Man In Cyberspace" in *Rolling Stone,* and Raffi Khatchadourian's spectacular *New Yorker* article "No Secrets."

PROLOGUE: THE MEGALEAK

trick companies' employees into revealing their passwords over the phone Suelette Dreyfus and Julian Assange. *Underground: Hacking, madness and obsession on the electronic frontier.* First published by Mandarin, a part of Reed Books, Australia, 1997, available at http://suelette.home.xs4all.nl/underground/Underground.pdf

speculation that WikiLeaks' target would be Bank of America shaves off $3.5 billion from the company's total value Dan Fitzpatrick. "Bank's stock declines on WikiLeaks Anticipation." *Wall Street Journal,* November 29, 2010.

Many of them cited WikiLeaks' revelations about the U.S. State Department's disdain for Tunisian president Ben Ali Sami Ben Hassine. "Tunisia's youth finally has revolution on its mind." *The Guardian*, January 13, 2011.

"WikiLeaks, which publishes information written by lying ambassadors in order to create chaos" Robert Mackey. "Qaddafi Sees WikiLeaks Plot in Tunisia." *The New York Times,* January 17, 2011.

WikiLeaks had cratered negotiations that might have kept them there longer CNN wire staff. "Obama: Iraq war will be over by year's end; troops coming home." CNN.com, October 22, 2011.

choking it to the point of paralysis Will Oremus. "Almost Broke, WikiLeaks Suspends Operations." Slate, October 24, 2011.

actively coached the young Army private, potential grounds for his own indictment Kim Zetter. "Jolt in WikiLeaks Case: Feds Found Manning-Assange Chat Logs on Laptop." Wired.com, December 19, 2011.

94 percent of the world's recorded information Martin Hilbert and Priscilla Lopez. "The World's Technological Capacity to Store, Communicate, and Compute Information." *Science,* February 2011.

five times as many pages being added to the world's classified libraries as to its unclassified ones Peter Galison. "Removing Knowledge." *Critical Inquiry,* Autumn 2004.

76.7 million documents were classified in 2010, compared with 8.6 million in 2001 and 23.4 million in 2008 Information Security Oversight Office Annual Report, April 15, 2011.

Of those, about 1.2 million have top-secret clearance Greg Miller. "How many security clearances have been issued? Nearly enough for everyone in the Washington area." WashingtonPost.com, September 20, 2011.

"These Days the Web Unmasks Everyone." Brian Stelter. *The New York Times,* June 20, 2011.

as the *New Yorker* cartoon caption reads Peter Steiner. *The New Yorker,* July 5, 1993.

"a series of unfortunate events" Clay Shirky. "WikiLeaks has created a new media landscape." *The Guardian,* February 4, 2011.

CHAPTER 1: THE WHISTLEBLOWERS

only other analyst who knew about and sympathized with Ellsberg's leaking plans Daniel Ellsberg. *Secrets* (London: Penguin Books, 2002), p. 295.

Was that peculiar green color some kind of radiation? Ibid., p. 302.

comb through the encyclopedia-size pile to excise them Ibid., p. 370.

nonchalantly consume a sweet roll and a cup of coffee over the course of several hours Ibid., p. 332.

greet the policemen politely, and carry on his work as soon as they left Ibid., p. 301.

understand exactly what he had done, and why Ibid., p. 305.

aide hastily rescinded the offer Ibid., p. 333.

"Pretty simple and unglamorous" Evan Hansen. "Manning-Lamo Chat Logs Revealed." Wired.com, July 13, 2011.

devoured the books and looked up to their author Tom Wells *Wild Man: The Life and Times of Daniel Ellsberg* (New York: Palgrave, 2001), p. 38.

"It was hard for me to understand people who were willing to burn children like that. It still is." Ellsberg, p. 23.

hiding his books to keep him at the keyboard Wells, p. 43.

shook the faith his parents had tried to instill in him Ibid., p. 49.

His sister never did Ibid., p. 72.

"I guess I don't have to play the piano anymore" Ibid., p. 73.

"Then I realized: I felt *free*, for the first time in my life" Ibid., p. 81.

Ellsberg was handed his first top-secret security clearances Ibid., p. 28.

"couldn't help one another to find their way home" Ellsberg, p. 239.

one stop sign and fifteen churches Denver Nicks. "Private Manning and the Making of WikiLeaks." *This Land*, September 23, 2010.

won the top prize at his school's science fair three times Hansen.

described him as "demeaning," another as simply "a dick" Nicks.

he had announced to friends that he was gay Ibid.

"basically really into America" Ibid.

leave them largely isolated Interview with Brian Manning. PBS *Frontline*, published on Frontline.com, March 29, 2010.

vodka in her morning tea Ellen Nakashima. "Bradley Manning is at the center of the WikiLeaks controversy. But who is he?" *Washington Post Magazine*, May 4, 2011.

basics of Web servers and Internet routing Hansen.

"quirky as hell" David Leigh and Luke Harding. *WikiLeaks: Inside Julian Assange's War on Secrecy* (New York: Public Affairs), p. 25.

"I have been telling him he needs to get a job and he won't get a job!" PBS *Frontline*, "*Frontline* Exclusive: The Bradley Manning 911 Call." Available at http://www.pbs.org/wgbh/pages/frontline/wikileaks/bradley-manning/bradley-manning-911-call/

hiding in the bedroom from Davis's father until he could find a bare-bones apartment in town Denver Nicks. "Manning in the Making." *This Land*, March 7, 2011.

finally moving in with his aunt near Rockville and enrolling in a local community college Ibid.

"twisted his arm" Interview with Brian Manning, PBS *Frontline*.

In October 2009, he shipped out to Iraq Kevin Poulsen. "An Interactive Timeline of Bradley Manning's Alleged Leaking." Wired.com, March 7, 2011. http://www.wired.com/threatlevel/2011/03/manning-timeline/

spent practically every waking moment digesting thousands of pages Ellsberg, p. 37.

a rifle in his hand and a grenade in his lap Ibid., p. 110.

Ellsberg Paradox "Risk, Ambiguity, and the Savage Axioms." *Quarterly Journal of Economics* 75 (4), 1961.

within weeks he was in the field, accompanying troops on operations Ellsberg, p. 11.

justify President Lyndon Johnson's moves to slowly widen the war in Vietnam Ibid., p. 68.

even as he took notes and photographs as an analyst Ibid., p. 152.

POW in a cramped bamboo cage for the next seven years Ibid., p. 113.

In fact, many of the other officers felt the same way Ibid., p. 148.

we were not going to defeat them Ibid., p. 156.

pessimistic comments regarding Vietnam fell on deaf ears Ibid., p. 183.

it was simply "a crime" Ibid., p. 157.

Even if it meant going to prison Ibid., p. 272.

"smart enough to know what's going on, but helpless to do anything" Hansen.

demoted for hitting another soldier and shouting down a superior Hansen.

the two words *I want* carved into a wooden chair Nathan L. Fuller. "In-depth notes from the art. 32 courtroom." Bradley Manning Support Network. Published at Bradleymanning.org

"a double life" Hansen.

"Bradley Manning is in the barracks, alone. I miss you, Tyler!" Greg Mitchell. "From Boston to Baghdad." TheNation.com, March 25, 2011.

He would hand it over to WikiLeaks, where it would become the prologue for a classified exposé to dwarf all others in history. All the uncited facts in the section above come from Wired.com's Lamo-Manning chat logs.

"ridiculous, counterproductive, and stupid" Amy Davidson. "Ridiculous, Counterproductive, and Stupid." New Yorker.com, March 11, 2011.

use their computers for marathon hacking sessions Jennifer Kahn. "The Homeless Hacker v. *The New York Times*." *Wired*, December 2004.

sometimes responded by spitting out change or food Ibid.

three hundred thousand dollars in searches on the paid research service Lexis-Nexis Ibid.

pay sixty-five thousand dollars in fines and spend six months under house arrest at his parents' home Ibid.

"a very dangerous precedent for the government the way it wants to operate today" Sam Bozzo. "Hackers Wanted." Available on YouTube http://www.youtube.com/watch?v=cLJbMP2S5sA

"If you had unprecedented access to classified networks fourteen hours a day seven days a week for eight plus months, what would you do?" Hansen.

"Isn't it after all only history?" Ellsberg, p. 357.

"I'm sorry, I can't do it." Ibid., p. 363.

sneak into the Cambridge apartment, have the papers photocopied in a nearby shop, and return them Ibid., p. 375.

Vietnam Archive: Pentagon Study Traces 3 Decades of Growing U.S. Involvement Neil Sheehan. "Vietnam Archive: Pentagon Study Traces 3 Decades of Growing U.S. Involvement." *The New York Times,* June 13, 1971.

Gelb immediately fixated on Ellsberg as the source Wells, p. 407.

"Ellstein" as Nixon called him Ibid., p. 426.

Boston Globe,* the *L.A. Times, The Christian Science Monitor,* the *St. Louis Post-Dispatch Ibid., p. 396.

the one who had offered Ellsberg her photocopier—testified to the bureau's agents too Ibid., p. 404.

"The culture fed opportunities" Hansen.

"Resources are strained." Ibid.

"That truly baffles me" Senate Homeland Security Committee hearing, March 10, 2011. Originally broadcast on C-Span, available on YouTube: http://www.youtube.com/watch?v=w_VZ4GANG1o

"Frankly, most of our focus was on the outside intruder threat, not the inside threat" Ibid.

Manning described to Lamo how he used a combination of security tools Hansen.

"Lie to me," he had told Manning Ibid.

"Have a good day" "Court told of Bradley Manning 'link to WikiLeaks.'" BBC News, December 20, 2011.

"That's all there is to it!" Ellsberg, p. 426.

Try him in the press Ibid., p. 432.

The plan was scrapped G. Gordon Liddy. *Will: The Autobiography of G. Gordon Liddy* (New York: St. Martin's Press, 1980), p. 170.

"totally incapacitate" "Nixon White House Counsel John Dean and Pentagon Papers Leaker Daniel Ellsberg on Watergate and the Abuse of Presidential Power from Nixon to Bush." DemocracyNow.com, April 27, 2006.

unlucky protesters at the event's edges Ellsberg p. 451.

"The bizarre events have incurably infected the prosecution of this case" Wells, p. 556.

had himself been indicted on charges of conspiracy, obstruction of justice, and perjury Ellsberg, p. 456.

"enjoy a modicum of legal protection" Hansen.

"They touch my life, I touch their life, they touch my life again . . . full circle" Ibid.

Only a life sentence in a military prison "Court martial sought for suspected WikiLeaks leaker." Reuters, published on MSNBC.com, January 12, 2012.

protesting Manning's inhumane confinement in a Quantico, Virginia, military prison Video available on YouTube: http://www.youtube.com/watch?feature=player_embedded&v=Gq0CpWhVag4

Outside the base there, he staged another sit-in and was arrested again Ibid.

"I was Bradley Manning" Ashley Fantz. "Pentagon Papers leaker: 'I was Bradley Manning.'" CNN.com, March 19, 2011.

The president turns away, and the conversation is over Video available on YouTube: http://www.youtube.com/watch?feature=player_embedded&v=IfmtUpd4id0

The materials that Ellsberg leaked were actually of a *higher* top-secret classification Glenn Greenwald. "The intellectual cowardice of Bradley Manning's critics." Salon.com, December 24, 2011.

"I can't tell you how much that affected me." Fantz.

CHAPTER 2: THE CRYPTOGRAPHERS

one unit of data switching from a one to a zero or vice versa seemingly of its own accord Daniel S. Morrow. "Craig R. Barrett, Ph.D. Oral History." Computerworld Honors Program International Archives, October 24, 2002.

"He went off and did something wonderful" Ibid.

"Anonymous networks, digital pseudonyms, reputations, information markets, black markets, collapse of governments" Tim May. "The Crypto-Anarchist Manifesto." In Peter Ludlow, ed. *High Noon on the Electronic Frontier* (Cambridge: Massachusetts Institute of Technology, 1996), p. 239.

long-bearded hermit, living in a well-fortified redoubt in the mountains Thomas Fischermann. "Die Piraten des 21. Jahrhunderts." *Die Zeit,* December 4, 2003.

covering them with the detached doors of their homes Robert Scheer. *With Enough Shovels* (New York: Vintage Books, 1983), p. 23.

"We are on strike, we, the men of the mind" Ayn Rand. *Atlas Shrugged* (New York: Random House, 1957).

one rebel group allows anyone to anonymously spill their secrets over the phone lines Jon Brunner. *The Shockwave Rider* (Ballantine Books, 1976).

a history of the National Security Agency and its shadowy work James Bamford. *The Puzzle Palace* (New York: Penguin Books, 1983).

only weakness is the identity that ties them to their frail bodies Vernor Vinge. "True Names." In *True Names and the Opening of the Cyberspace Frontier* (New York: Tor, 2001), first published in Dell Binary Star #5, 1981.

M. T. Graves and the Dungeon Steven Levy. *Crypto* (New York: Penguin Books, 2001), p. 187.

Herbert Zim's *Codes & Secret Writing* Ibid.

produce a solution in minutes Levy, p. 188.

remove the pad's random noise, breaking the ciphers "The Vernon Story," published by the Center for Cryptologic History, NSA.gov, available at http://www.nsa.gov/about/_files/cryptologic_heritage/publications/coldwar/venona_story.pdf

"Poe's dictum will be hard to defend in any form" Martin Gardner. *Penrose Tiles to Trapdoor Ciphers—and the Return of Dr. Matrix* (New York: W. H. Freeman, 1989).

In fact, that was a few zeroes too many Levy, p. 104.

"Security without Identification: Transaction Systems to make Big Brother Obsolete" David Chaum. "Security without Identification: Transaction Systems to make Big Brother Obsolete." *Communications of the Association of Computing Machinery*, October 1985.

"the most gee-whiz-whoopie enthusiastic character I had run into" Simson Garfinkel. *PGP: Pretty Good Privacy* (Sebastopol, Calif.: O'Reilly & Associates, 1994).

MIT was running the program on a mainframe using LISP Levy, p. 189.

the two men spent a week at his whiteboard hashing out crypto-programming Garfinkel, p. 90.

ITAR was choking his business Garfinkel, p. 88.

It is the sense of Congress that providers of electronic communications services Levy, p. 195.

Uncrackable encryption will allow drug lords, spies, terrorists, and even violent gangs to communicate Statement of Louis Freeh, Senate Judiciary Committee Hearing, July 9, 1997, available at the website of the Federation of American Scientists: http://www.fas.org/irp/congress/1997_hr/s970709f.htm

stock up on crypto gear while you can still get it Levy, p. 196.

using pay phones to log on and upload copies of the program to message boards without revealing the program's source Levy, p. 197.

Phil, I wish you to know: let it never be . . . Statement of Philip Zimmermann, Senate Committee on Commerce, Science, and Transportation, June 26, 1996, available on Philip Zimmermann's website: http://www.philzimmermann.com/EN/testimony/index.html

A specter is haunting the modern world, the specter of crypto anarchy May in Ludlow, p. 237.

Users of a Mix network . . . David Chaum. "Untraceable electronic mail, return addresses, and digital pseudonyms." *Communications of the Association of Computing Machinery*, February 1981.

"Cypherpunks write code" Eric Hughes. "A Cypherpunk's Manifesto." As printed in *Crypto Anarchy, Cyberstates, and Pirate Utopias*, Peter Ludlow ed. (Cambridge: Massachusetts Institute of Technology, 2001), p. 81.

Even laws against cryptography reach only so far as a nation's border and the arm of its violence Ibid., p. 83.

"It was the worst day" Philip Zimmermann's talk at the University of Illinois at Champaign-Urbana, October 24, 2004, available on Philip Zimmermann's website at http://www.philzimmermann.com/EN/audiovideo/index.html

cut-rate criminal lawyer that Zimmermann had hired in Boulder Ibid.

A cease-and-desist letter from Intel threatening a suit for trademark infringement eventually kiboshed that guerrilla sticker campaign Levy, p. 252.

"Not ninety-nine percent. One hundred point zero percent" Zimmermann's University of Illinois talk.

strapping a copy of PGP to a missile and shooting it at Mexico, just to prove a point Ibid.

"When they got that one, I can imagine the blood draining from their faces" Ibid.

Karn sued them in a federal court Ibid.

"I'd like you to also publish the source code to PGP" Ibid.

By 1996, Clipper was sunk Levy, p. 268.

Your name has come to our attention Tim May. "Introduction to BlackNet," in Ludlow's *High Noon,* p. 241.

report any contact with the shadowy organization Tim May. "Untraceable Digital Cash, Information Markets, and BlackNet." Talk at the Computers Freedom and Privacy conference, 1997.

"Classified classifieds," so to speak. "No More Secrets" Tim May. "BlackNet Worries," in ibid., p. 245.

CHAPTER 3: THE CYPHERPUNKS

"was in heaven" Stephen Muirhead. "MUMS the Word: Julian Assange, Wikileaks, and the Fight to End Government Secrecy." *Paradox,* August 15, 2010.

insisting that it be replaced with an image of an alien Ibid.

most physicists pathetically lugged about with pride and ignorance Julian Assange's blog at IQ.org, July 12, 2006 **(no longer online but mirrored at** http://aworldbeyondborders.com/research-raw-materials/julian-assange-writings/).

inaccurately, according to the department's staff Muirhead.

rolling over them and burying them alive Nicki Barrowclough. "Keeper of Secrets." *The Age,* May 22, 2010.

Assange invented a game: The Puzzle Hunt Muirhead.

Another conundrum involved factoring large numbers into primes Melbourne University Mathematics Society Puzzle Hunt 2004 Puzzles, available at http://www.ms.unimelb.edu.au/~mums/puzzlehunt/2004/puzzles.html

a secret about a secret that is veiled by a secret. Ibid.

"when you have to do something or you'll lose the game" Barrowclough.

"standing around looking pretty, even making tea" Muirhead.

Hello Puzzle Hunters Ibid.

a political version of the Puzzle Hunt, with great social implications Ibid.

"homemade nitroglycerin in the old cypherpunks blast shack has gone off" Bruce Sterling. "The Blast Shack." Webstock.org.nz, December 22, 2010

archival footage of Hiroshima Cryptome.org, April 2011 archive, available at http://cryptome.org/cryptomb29.htm

immigration papers for Barack Obama Sr. Ibid.

Wau Holland Foundation Ibid.

"Don't believe anything you see there" Cryptome.org privacy policy, available at http://cryptome.org/other-stuff.htm

maneuvers by Microsoft to remove his site from the Internet in 2010 Ryan Singel. "Microsoft Takes Down Whistleblower Site, Read the Secret Doc Here." Wired.com, February 24, 2010.

"Well, I'm actually looking for that information right now" Michael Crowley. "Let's Shut Them Down. These websites are an invitation to terrorists." *Reader's Digest*, March 2005. Reproduced at http://cryptome.org/Web-threats.htm

all while periodically stomping around the room Dreyfus and Assange, *Underground.*

***splendide mendax*, the "nobly untruthful" in Horace's Odes** Raffi Khatchadourian. "No Secrets." *The New Yorker,* June 7, 2010.

Assange was determined to access Minerva Dreyfus and Assange.

"Yes, it's L-U-R-C-H—full stop." All the above comes from ibid.

"living in a bikini" and "going native" "Julian Assange's Mother Recalls Magnetic." *Magnetic Times*, August 7, 2010.

opossums ran across their beds in the dark George Hirst. "Christine Assange Recalls Her Magnetic Island Days." *Magnetic Times*, August 31, 2011.

"There was a sense of safety and security" Ibid.

"I wasn't sorry to leave when presented with the dental bills of my tormentors" Assange, blog at IQ.org, July 18, 2006.

fifteen different towns and at least as many schools, when he attended school at all Dreyfus and Assange.

"get out of politics" or risk being seen as an "unfit mother" Hans Ulrich Olbrist. "Interview With Julian Assange, Part I." *E-Flux,* May 2011.

"Chess is very austere, in that you don't have many rules, there is no randomness, and the problem is very hard" Khatchadourian.

Therefore its readership remained at three Dreyfus and Assange.

"to enter the depths of the Pentagon's Eighth Command at the age of seventeen was a liberating experience" Hans Ulrich Obrist.

"and share information" Dreyfus and Assange.

hide his location and identity by routing his modem's phone traffic through that intermediary Ibid.

Mendax's career was over All the above in this passage comes from ibid.

"a cross between a mutter and the Oracle of Delphi" Richard Rosenkranz. *Across the Barricades* (New York/Philadelphia: J.B. Lippincott, 1971), p. 179.

"the Avery Commune was once again a functioning organism" Ibid.

"I approached a condition of human relationships that can usually be found only in the realm of ideas" Ibid., p. 44.

"I think my childhood was just great" Ibid.

"We're prepared to start right now" John Cook. "Secrets + Lies." *Radar*, August 2007.

before he could call his fellow hackers to warn them that he had tipped off the telecom's security Dreyfus and Assange.

"I am not concerned about using my skills there" All the above in this passage from ibid.

Scientologists believed in communication with plants Andrew Fowler. *The Most Dangerous Man in the World* (Melbourne: Melbourne University Press, 2011), p. 26.

"True belief only begins with a jackboot the door" Assange's blog at IQ.org, July 17, 2006.

one demanding user a "dummy" and tells him to "get a life" E-mail from Julian Assange to the Cypherpunk Mailing List, December 24, 1995.

"some research is in order before you go shooting off your mouth" E-mails from Julian Assange to the Cypherpunk Mailing List, January 14, 1996.

"afterschool Tupperware get-together" Ibid., December 30, 1995.

"Your testical, [sic] again Nancy?" and "National Gay Secrecy Unit" Ibid., February 3, 1996.

"The Internet is, by its very nature a censorship free zone" Ibid., December 17, 2003.

Eleven people showed up Fowler, p. 26.

one user with the Penet pseudonym "an144108" Sabine Helmers. "A Brief History of anon.penet.fi, The Legendary Anonymous Remailer." *Computer-Mediated Communication Magazine*, September 1997.

"All of them," answered Jim Jim Bell. "Assassination Politics," available at http://cryptome.org/ap.htm

botched a series of deals "How DigiCash Blew Everything." *NEXT*, January 1999, available in translation from Dutch here: http://cryptome.org/jya/digicrash.htm

It would be an encrypted, anonymous, digital dead pool Bell.

No military? Ibid.

put out anonymous hits on criminals just as easily as politicians Ibid.

murder those who annoy us sufficiently E-mail from anon-remailer@utopia.hacktic.nl to the Cypherpunk Mailing List, January 27, 1996.

"Others won't" E-mail from Jim Bell to the Cypherpunk Mailing List, January 26, 1996. (The seeming date discrepancy between Bell and the anonymous cypherpunk is caused by time zone differences.)

"I am out to 'get' the government" Ibid., January 29, 1996.

by resorting to violence you are no better than the ones you purport to protect us against E-mail from Jim Choate to the Cypherpunk Mailing List, February 6, 1996.

Are you a statist? E-mail from Jim Choate to the Cypherpunk Mailing List, February 10, 1996.

the e-mail that followed his BlackNet experiment more than three years earlier May in "BlackNet Worries."

leaked data in all directions Wim van Eck. "Electromagnetic Radiation from Video Display Units: An Eavesdropping Risk?" *Computer & Security*, December 1985. Republished at http://cryptome.org/jya/emr.pdf

water pipes and sprinkler system around a computer might propagate its electric field and spill its data even further E-mails from Jim Bell and Julian Assange to the Cypherpunk Mailing List, May 29, 1996.

"knowing that reasonable people will think you're a nut seeking celebrity martyrdom" E-mail from John Young to the Cypherpunk Mailing List, February 11, 1996.

"I may be one of the system's first victims" E-mail from Jim Bell to the Cypherpunk Mailing List, February 11, 1996.

federal agents who seized his computers, his car, three assault rifles, and a .44 Magnum handgun "Criminal complaint against Jim Bell," May 16, 1997, available at http://cryptome.org/jya/jimbell3.htm

find its way into the building's computers and short out their wiring Ibid.

dumping a chemical called mercaptan on the rug outside an IRS office in Vancouver, Washington Ibid.

"They are all either crooks or they tolerate crooks or they are aware of crooks among their numbers" Declan McCullagh. "Crypto-Convict Won't Recant." Wired.com, April 14, 2000.

where he spent his days demolishing computer monitors for forty-six cents an hour Declan McCullagh, "Jim Bell Update." Wired.com, May 25, 2002.

a groundbreaking work in "government accountability systems" Letter from John Young to Vikki Hardy, July 11, 1998, available at http://cryptome.org/jya/chrysler98.htm

"Jim Bell . . . lives . . . on . . . in . . . Hollywood!" E-mail from Julian Assange to the Cypherpunk Mailing List, January 9, 1998.

He called it Marutukku E-mail from Julian Assange to Firewalls Mail List, June 4, 1997.

would soon rename it, simply, "Rubberhose" Suelette Dreyfus. "The Idiot Savant's Guide to Rubberhose," available at http://namcub.accela-labs.com/pdf/maruguide.pdf

"Our motto is 'let's make a little trouble'" Ibid.

"Alice certainly isn't in for a very nice time of it. (Although she's far more likely to protect her data.)" E-mail from Julian Assange to mgraffam@mhv.net, March 27, 1998, available at http://cryptome.org/0001/assange-cpunks.htm

In 1999, he registered Leaks.org Barrowclough.

"one to be cherished and the other to be destroyed" E-mail from Julian Assange to cypherpunk@minder.net, March 23, 2002, available here: http://cryptome.org/0001/assange-cpunks.htm

posted it to his blog with the name "Conspiracy as Governance" Available here: http://cryptome.org/0002/ja-conspiracies.pdf

create powerful incentives for more humane forms of governance. Ibid.

"the result of mental inclinations honed for the preliterate societies in which our species evolved" Ibid.

resulting in decreased ability to hold onto power as the environment demands adaption. From Julian Assange's blog at IQ.org, Available here: http://cryptome.org/0002/ja-conspiracies.pdf

"secretive or unjust systems are nonlinearly hit relative to open, just systems" Ibid.

"Man is least himself when he talks in his own person. Give him a mask and he'll tell you the truth." Dreyfus and Assange.

The NSA first denied his request but gave in on appeal Letter from William Black to John Young, December 18, 2000, available at http://cryptome.org/nsa-foia-app2.htm

listed 116 names of MI6 officials sent to the newsweekly, along with locations and dates showing their movements across the globe Available at http://cryptome.org/mi5-lis-uk.htm

the source, a PSIA agent named Hironari Noda, revealed his identity within days Available at http://cryptome.org/psia-lists.htm

a trove of files by an ex-CIA agent to be published at his death Available at http://cryptome.org/cia-2619.htm

". . . Will you be that person?" E-mail from Julian Assange to John Young, October 4, 2006, http://cryptome.org/wikileaks/wikileaks-leak.htm

Then he unsubscribed John Young from the list All the above quotes from ibid.

Jim Bell was scheduled for release from prison on March 12, 2012 Federal Bureau of Prisons Website http://www.bop.gov/iloc2/LocateInmate.jsp

CHAPTER 4: THE ONION ROUTERS

those are the systems required or used by the current government oppressors Jacob Appelbaum writing on Twitter, February 19, 2011.

"the Arab dictator's favorite uplink" Ibid.

"I wanted to meet interesting and stimulating people of an ancient culture . . . and own them" Ibid.

"It's ethical to own them" Ibid., February 18, 2011.

"if you've got them, I'll track them" Ibid., January 28, 2011.

"Good luck with that, you son of a bitch!" Ibid.

"Jake has been a tireless promoter behind the scenes of our cause" Nathaniel Rich. "The American WikiLeaks Hacker," RollingStone.com, December 1, 2010.

hard drugs and weapons, or one of several sites that claim to offer untraceable contract killings Some examples available at the Tor Hidden Service kpvz7ki2v5agwt35.onion/wiki/index.php/main_page (must be running Tor to access this site).

and then extrapolate the addresses of others Stevens Le Blond, Pere Manils, et al. "One Bad Apple Spoils the Bunch: Exploiting P2P Applications to Trace and Profile Tor Users," March 2011, available at https://db.usenix.org//events/leet11/tech/full_papers/LeBlond.pdf

recognize and analyze Tor Hidden Services based on fingerprinting those timing differences Steven J. Murdoch. "Hot or Not: Revealing Hidden Services by their Clock Skew," available here: http://www.cl.cam.ac.uk/~sjm217/papers/ccs06hotornot.pdf

and some in-between actors whose truth-telling is utterly unpredictable Raymond Smullyan. *What Is the Name of This Book?* (Englewood Cliffs, N.J.: Prentice Hall, Inc., 1978).

crawling the entire Chinese-language Web looking for Tor node addresses and blocked nearly all of them Andrew Lewman. "Tor partially blocked in China." Tor Project blog, available at https://blog.torproject.org/blog/tor-partially-blocked-china

"My hatred of authority was pretty much solidified" Jacob Appelbaum. "Personal experiences bringing technology and new media to disaster areas." Speech at the Chaos Communication Congress, December 2005, available here: http://events.ccc.de/congress/2005/fahrplan/events/478.en.html

installed a red lightbulb in his bedroom in an effort to regulate his sleep Barrowclough.

activists who would crash in the house rent-free in exchange for working on Assange's project Khatchadourian.

accept unencrypted documents by post and even scan in reams of paper submissions and convert them to text files E-mail from Julian Assange to WikiLeaks developer list, December 13, 2006, available at http://cryptome.org/wikileaks/wikileaks-leak.htm

"Yes, the guy running the exit node can read the bytes that come in and out there" Bruce Schneier. "Lesson from Tor Hack: Anonymity and Privacy Aren't the Same." Wired.com, September 20, 2007.

a member of the project who ran a Tor exit node had noticed Chinese hackers using the relay to hide their tracks Khatchadourian.

"Somewhere between none and a handful of those documents were ever released on WikiLeaks" John Leyden. "Wikileaks denies Tor hacker eavesdropping gave site its start." TheRegister.co.uk, June 2, 2010.

"When they pull, so do we" E-mail from Julian Assange to John Young, January 7, 2007, available at http://cryptome.org/wikileaks/wikileaks-leak2.htm

thirty times the size of every text article stored on Wikipedia Wikipedia: Database download, available at http://en.wikipedia.org/wiki/Wikipedia:Database_download

"let it flower into something new" Julian Assange to John Young, January 7, 2007, available at http://cryptome.org/wikileaks/wikileaks-leak2.htm

spreading free software like a hacker Johnny Appleseed Jacob Appelbaum. "Personal experiences bringing technology and new media to disaster areas." Speech at the Chaos Communication Congress, December 2005, available here: http://events.ccc.de/congress/2005/fahrplan/events/478.en.html

"As an American, I found myself feeling pretty awful about what we'd contributed to" Ibid.

grabbed the remote, turned up the volume, and refused to change the channel Ibid.

A man beaten in the shower. Nightly curfews, women raped. Xeni Jardin interview with Jacob Appelbaum. "Katrina: 'Rape, murder, beatings' in Astrodome, say evacuees." BoingBoing.net, September 7, 2005.

"The same thing, over and over again. The disconnection. The lack of humanity." Jacob Appelbaum. "Personal experiences bringing technology and new media to disaster areas." Speech at the Chaos Communication Congress, December 2005, available here: http://events.ccc.de/congress/2005/fahrplan/events/478.en.html

transfer the equivalent of $50,000 from a bank to the CCC's accounts Steve Kettman. "Tribute to Hippie Hacker Holland." Wired.com, July 31, 2001.

even when authorities are standing over the user, rubber hose in hand, demanding the key Jacob Appelbaum. "A discussion about modern disk encryption systems." Speech at the Chaos Communication Congress, December 2005, available here: http://events.ccc.de/congress/2005/fahrplan/speakers/165.en.html

"Justice was just too slow to catch you" Ibid.

The handbooks of secret rituals for nine different fraternities All of these are available at the WikiLeaks.org archive: http://www.wikileaks.org/wiki/Category:Analyses.

"smearing and stinging by governments, corporations, persons of all demonics" E-mail from John Young to the WikiLeaks developer mail list, December 20, 2006, http://cryptome.org/wikileaks/wikileaks-leak.htm

"Or is it a clever smear by US intelligence?" "Inside Somalia and the Union of Islamic Courts." WikiLeaks.org, available at http://wikileaks.org/wiki/Inside_Somalia_and_the_Union_of_Islamic_Courts

reports of currency counterfeiting by the regime's organized crime connections Xan Rice. "The looting of Kenya." *The Guardian*, August 30, 2007.

indiscriminate police killings of thousands of young men "Oscar Foundation letter to Minister for Internal Security over extra-judicial killings in Kenya." WikiLeaks.org, October 14, 2008, available here: http://wikileaks.org/wiki/Oscar_Foundation_letter_to_Minister_for_Internal_Security_over_extra-judicial_killings_in_Kenya,_14_Oct_2008.

tax shelters administered by the Swiss Bank Julius Baer "Bank Julius Baer." WikiLeaks.org, available here: http://wikileaks.org/wiki/Bank_Julius_Baer

dumping in the Ivory Coast that had been legally prevented from appearing in British media "Ivory Coast toxic dumping report behind secret Guardian gag." WikiLeaks.org, October 13, 2009 available here: http://wikileaks.org/wiki/Ivory_Coast_toxic_dumping_report_behind_secret_Guardian_gag

Icelandic banking documents that would catalog the country's financial meltdown "Financial collapse: Confidential exposure analysis of 205 companies each owing above EUR45M to Icelandic bank Kaupthing." WikiLeaks.org, September 26, 2008 available at http://wikileaks.org/wiki/Financial_collapse:_Confidential_exposure_analysis_of_205_companies_each_owing_above_EUR45M_to_Icelandic_bank_Kaupthing,_26_Sep_2008

And a collection of pager messages from September 11, 2001 "9/11 tragedy pager intercepts." WikiLeaks.org, available here: http://911.wikileaks.org/

would catch the attention of one young analyst in a dusty base in Iraq Hansen.

"Wikileaks will release several thousand additional pages of Scientology material next week" "Scientology threatens WikiLeaks over secret cult bibles." WikiLeaks.org, April 7, 2008. No longer online but available at http://Web.archive.org/Web/20080704235334/https://secure.wikileaks.org/wiki/Scientology_threatens_Wikileaks_over_secret_cult_bibles

one of the largest collections of the church's internal documents stored anywhere in the world. WikiLeaks archive: http://www.wikileaks.org/wiki/Category:Analyses

CHAPTER 5: THE PLUMBERS

Note: Much of the material for this section regarding HBGary Federal and Aaron Barr came from AnonLeaks, a website created to publish the hacked e-mails of the employees of HBGary and HBGary Federal. The site no longer exists, and given that I no longer consider the documents taken from that site to be public, I've treated them as my own reporting and haven't cited them below.

it put the first five GPS satellites into orbit Duncan Graham-Rowe. "Fifty years of DARPA: Hits, misses and ones to watch." New Scientist.com, May 15, 2008.

developed and flew the first stealth planes Ibid.

organized a series of races of robotic, driverless cars through the desert Ibid.

driven between San Francisco and Los Angeles with no human assistance "Google Cars Drive Themselves, in Traffic" *The New York Times,* October 9, 2010.

build flying Humvees Clay Dillow. "DARPA's 'Flying Humvee' Is Moving Ahead, Ready for Prototype." Popsci.com, October, 25, 2011.

mechanical bats that can suck electricity from power lines Jonathan Fahey. "How to Build a Spy Bat." Forbes.com, June 26, 2009.

cyborg cockroaches Travis Korte. "Cyborg Insect Breakthrough: Generating Power Through Body Chemistry." HuffingtonPost.com, January 8, 2012.

roving robots that can switch between liquid and solid form Anne-Marie Corley. "iRobot's Shape-Shifting Blob 'Bot Takes Its First Steps." IEEE Spectrum, October 13, 2009.

roving robots that can feed themselves with grass and twigs Noah Shachtman. "Company Denies Its Robots Feed on the Dead." Wired.com, July 17, 2009.

Iron Man–like exoskeletons that multiply human strength by a factor of ten Larry Greenemeier. "Real-Life Iron Man: A Robotic Suit That Magnifies Human Strength." *Scientific American,* April 30, 2008.

surveillance systems designed to watch every moving object in entire cities Noah Shachtman. "Darpa's Far-Out Dreams on Display." Wired.com, March 15, 2004.

"might already have on their hands the blood of some young soldier" Adam Levine. "Top military official: WikiLeaks founder may have 'blood' on his hands." CNN.com, July 29, 2010.

said that the exposure hadn't led to any documented casualties Ellen Nakashima. "Pentagon: Undisclosed Wikileaks documents 'potentially more explosive.'" Washingtonpost.com, August 11, 2011.

another fifteen thousand civilian deaths that hadn't been previously documented "Iraq War Logs: What the numbers reveal." Iraqbodycount.org, October 23, 2010.

Nouri al-Maliki used "detention squads" in the Iraqi army to harass political rival groups Gregg Carlstrom. "Nouri al-Maliki's 'detention squad.'" Al Jazeera, October 24, 2010.

claiming it violated the company's terms of service David Leigh and Rob Evans. "WikiLeaks says funding has been blocked after government blacklisting." *The Guardian,* October 14, 2010.

"Saudi Arabia Urges US Attack on Iran to Stop Nuclear Programme" Ian Black and Simon Tisdall. *The Guardian,* November 28, 2010.

"China leadership 'orchestrated Google hacking'" BBC.co.uk, December 4, 2010.

"Did Pfizer Bribe Its Way Out of Criminal Charges in Nigeria?" Walter Armstrong. TheAtlantic.com, December 27, 2010.

"Texas Company Helped Pimp Little Boys To Stoned Afghan Cops" John Nova Lomax. HoustonPress.com, December 7, 2010.

"China 'ready to abandon North Korea'" Simon Tisdall. *The Guardian.* November 29, 2010.

"WikiLeaks cables on Afghanistan show monumental corruption" Tim Lister. CNN.com, December 2, 2010.

"Iraqi Children in U.S. Raid Shot In Head" Matthew Schofield. McClatchy Newspapers, August 31, 2011.

"U.S. Bombs Yemen in Secret" Justin Elliott. Salon.com, November 29, 2010.

"US diplomats spied on UN leadership" Robert Booth and Julian Borger. *The Guardian*, November 28, 2010.

one out of every two issues of *The New York Times* in 2011 cited a document published by WikiLeaks Caitlin Dickson. "Nearly Half of 2011's *New York Times* Issues Rely on WikiLeaks." Theatlanticwire.com, April 25, 2011.

"closer to being a hi-tech terrorist than the Pentagon Papers" Ewen MacAskill. "Julian Assange like a hi-tech terrorist, says Joe Biden." *The Guardian*, December 19, 2010.

"pursued with the same urgency we pursue al-Qaeda and Taliban leaders" "Assange lawyer condemns calls for assassination of WikiLeaks' founder." MSNBC.com, December 2, 2010.

undermine the ability of our government and our partners to keep our people safe and to work together to defend our vital interests" "LIEBERMAN CONDEMNS NEW WIKILEAKS DISCLOSURES." Lieberman .senate.gov, November 28, 2010.

Amazon, which had hosted some WikiLeaks Web servers, banned the group Rachel Slajda. "How Lieberman Got Amazon to Drop WikiLeaks." Talking Points Memo, December 1, 2010.

Another woman said he had begun having sex with her in her sleep Juha Saarinen. "Documents in Julian Assange Rape Investigation Leak Onto Web." Wired.com, February 2, 2011.

once housed the writer of his favorite quote on the power of anonymity: Oscar Wilde David Allen Green. "An interview with Julian Assange's lawyer." Jack of Kent blog, December 14, 2010.

five gigabytes of data from the megabank Dan Nystedt. "WikiLeaks plans to make the Web a leakier place." Computerworld.com, October 9, 2009.

"I think it's great. We have all these banks squirming, thinking maybe it's them" *60 Minutes*, CBS News, January 30, 2011, available at http://www.cbsnews.com/video/watch/?id=7300034n

the bank documents lacked the punch of WikiLeaks' previous three megaleaks Mark Hosenball. "Assange suggests bank documents are a snore." Reuters, February 9, 2011.

review millions of possible documents in its archive that might damage the firm if they were leaked Nelson D. Schwartz. "Facing Threat from WikiLeaks, Bank Plays Defense." *The New York Times,* January 2, 2011.

Brianmoynihanblows.com and Brianmoynihansucks.com, references to its CEO "Bank of America Wants You to Know Its Executives Don't Suck." Domainnamewire.com, December 20, 2010.

included the Tea Party and its billionaire corporate supporters the Koch brothers Clare O'Connor. "FBI Hunting Hackers Who Took Down Koch Brothers' Websites." Forbes.com, July 26, 2011.

the antihomosexual extremist Westboro Baptist Church Catharine Smith. "Anonymous Attacks Westboro Church Website During Live Interview." Huffingtonpost.com, February 25, 2011.

Sony Corporation after it sued a hacker who reverse-engineered the PlayStation 3 Lawrence Latif. "Anonymous takes down Playstation website and Playstation Network." TheInquirer.net, April 6, 2011.

Anguilla, Australia, Brazil, Egypt, Israel, Sweden, Tunisia, Turkey, the United States, Venezuela, and Zimbabwe, among others Dean Wilson. "Anonymous hacks Anguilla, Brazil, Zimbabwe and Australia governments." TheInquirer.net, June 28, 2011.

Paul Wagenseil. "Anonymous 'hacktivists' attack Egyptian Websites." MSNBC .msn.com, January 26, 2011.

Sean-Paul Correll. "'Tis the Season of DDoS—WikiLeaks Edition." Panda Labs blog, December 4, 2010, available at http://pandalabs.pandasecurity.com/tis-the-season-of-ddos-wikileaks-editio/

Daren Butler. "Turkish websites attacked by Anonymous before vote." *Reuters,* June 9, 2011.

Max Read. "Anonymous Attacks Tunisian Government over Wikileaks Censorship." Gawker.com, January 3, 2011.

Anshel Pfeffer and Oded Yaron. "Israel government, security services websites down in suspected cyber-attack." *Haaretz,* June 11, 2011.

"Swedish prosecutor's website under cyber attack." Agence France Presse, December 7, 2010.

"GET YOUR ASS BEHIND A PROXY AND JOIN THE RAID!" Available at http://xo-whs.wikispaces.com/file/view/Anonymous_Propaganda_by_raithesheep.jpg/35922471

leaked video of scientologist star Tom Cruise extolling the church's virtues Nick Denton. "The Cruise Indoctrination Video Scientology Tried to Suppress." Gawker.com, January 15, 2008.

nihilistic pranks like hacking an online epilepsy forum to display blinking lights intended to cause seizures Mattathias Schwartz. "The Trolls Among Us." *New York Times Magazine*, August 3, 2008.

Hello, Scientology. We are Anonymous. Available here: http://www.youtube.com/watch?v=JCbKv9yiLiQ

harmless wheat germ and cornstarch—mailed to dozens of the church's addresses "'Anonymous' stalks Church of Scientology." UPI, February 5, 2008.

"The first serious infowar is now engaged. The field of battle is WikiLeaks. You are the troops." Sitara Nieves. "Morning Wrap: Mastercard and 'Anonymous' Hacker Group—Technological Warfare?" The Takeaway, WNYC, December 8, 2010. www.thetakeaway.org/blogs/takeaway/2010/dec/08/morning-wrap-mastercard-and-hacker-group-anonymous-technological-warfare

spent hundreds of millions of dollars acquiring companies in the so-called Data-Leak Prevention (DLP) industry Brian Prince. "McAfee Buys Out Data Loss Prevention Specialist Reconnex." *eWeek*, July 31, 2008.

implementing leak-focused software, and another third were considering the option Andrew Jaquith. "The Forrester Wave: Data Leak Prevention Suites." Forrester Research, October 12, 2010.

60 percent of employees admit to taking sensitive data before leaving a job Brian Prince. "Survey: Axed Employees Often Walk Out with Corporate Data." *eWeek,* February 2, 2009.

how physical media like CDs could be used on SIPRNet machines Noah Shachtman. Military Bans Disks, Threatens Courts-Martial to Stop New Leaks. Wired.com, December 9, 2010.

"But to me this is putting an ax to a problem that requires a scalpel" Senate Homeland Security and Governmental Affairs Committee hearing, March 10, 2011. Originally broadcast on C-Span, available on YouTube: http://www.youtube.com/watch?v=w_VZ4GANGlo

"dimensions of the mission," any of which could be strung together and add up to a data leak DARPA-BAA-10-84, Cyber Insider Threat (CINDER) Program, August 25, 2010, available here: https://www.fbo.gov/index?s=opportunity&mode=form&id=cf11e81b7b06330fd249804f4c247606&tab=core&_cview=0

he had once received an informal warning from a "three letter agency" Bruce Gottlieb. "HacK, CouNterHaCk." *New York Times Magazine,* October 3, 1999.

"Freak out and beg Microsoft to make the bad man stop" E-mail from Dildog to Bugtraq Mail List, November 10, 1997, available here: http://seclists.org/bugtraq/1997/Nov/79

sniffing the net like an anteater on Dexedrine Pamela Ferdinand. "'White Hat' Hackers Probe Pores in Computer Security Blankets." *The Washington Post*, April 4, 1998.

But the thieves themselves hid behind layers of proxies that kept them altogether anonymous Nathan Thornburgh. "The Invasion of the Chinese Cyberspies (And the Man Who Tried to Stop Them)." *Time*, August 29, 2005.

"You were only going to wait half an hour?" Richard A. Clarke. *Your Government Failed You* (New York: Harper Perennial, 2009), p. 299.

significant fraction of the Internet through China for eighteen minutes in April of 2010 James Cowie. "China's 18-Minute Mystery." Renesys blog, November 18, 2010.

where he sat two seats away from the president Mark Small. "Other Paths." *Berklee Today*, Fall 2007.

a price low enough that it didn't affect the antivirus giant's accounting enough to be disclosed. Stephen Shankland. "Symantec acquires @stake." CNET.com, September 17, 2004.

"providing us with the ability to identify such covert activities" Mudge. "Insider Threat: Models and Solutions.": *login*, December 2003.

reverse tunnels are symptoms of actions initiated from internal machines that are already compromised Ibid.

combed the site and found a critical flaw in the code Peter Bright. "Anonymous speaks: the inside story of the HBGary hack." Ars Technica, February 2011.

it had scrambled them with a type of encryption called cryptographic hashes Ibid.

HBGary didn't use salting Ibid.

So once the attackers owned his account, they owned all of them Ibid.

"Aaron was peddling fake/wrong/false information leading to the potential arrest of innocent people?" Chat logs between HBGary employees and Anonymous, February 7, 2011, available at http://pastebin.com/x69Akp5L

"we are kind of pissed at him right now" Ibid.

"PLEASE KEEP IN MIND WE HAVE ALL YOUR EMAILS" Ibid.

permaculture expert whose anarchist activities only extended as far as home gardening Dan Tynan. "Who is Anonymous' Commander X? Not this guy." ITWorld.com, February 16, 2011.

severing relations with HBGary Federal Robert McMillan. "Hacked and now vandalized, HBGary pulls out of RSA," IDG News, February 16, 2011.

Hoglund canceled a talk of his own at the simultaneous RSA conference in San Francisco Ibid.

excoriating essays on the military-industrial complex's dirty tactics in the digital realm Glenn Greenwald. "The leaked campaign to attack WikiLeaks and its supporters." Salon.com, February 11, 2011.

***The Colbert Report* aired a segment mocking Barr.** "Corporate Hacker Tries to Take Down WikiLeaks." ColbertNation.com, February 24, 2011.

he resigned from his position at HBGary Federal Andy Greenberg. "HBGary Federal's Aaron Barr Resigns After Anonymous Hack Scandal." Forbes.com, February 28, 2011.

"Anonymous should be as cold as ice and get on to the next operation" Ibid.

"At least we destroyed him in anonymous style" Ibid.

HideMyAss, which some Anons had used in lieu of Tor, admitted it turned over data to law enforcement Mathew Schwartz. "LulzSec Suspect Learns Even HideMyAss.com Has Limits." InformationWeek.com, September 27, 2011.

a twenty-four-year-old man in Doncaster Steve Ragan. "FBI says Anonymous is a potential threat to national security." TheTechHerald.com, September 9, 2011.

He had infiltrated and identified Anonymous' inner circle. Jana Winter. "Infamous international hacking group LulzSec brought down by own leader" FoxNews.com, March 6, 2012.

"Or are you still doing what you believe in and trying to put a dent in the universe?" Mudge's keynote talk at the Black Hat 2011 conference, available here: http://www.youtube.com/watch?v=IWGjWYIToFU

"nothing to do with humans" Ibid.

"you're still remaining true to the cause" Ibid.

"Tomorrow is zero hour," and "The match begins tomorrow" Jane Mayer. "The Secret Sharer." *The New Yorker*, May 23, 2011.

By the time the project was canceled in 2006, it had become a $1.2 billion boondoggle Ibid.

no one acted to rein in the program Ibid.

including one that focused on Trailblazer Ibid.

a team of armed FBI agents arrived at his home Ibid.

"send a message to the silent majority of people who live by secrecy agreements." Jesselyn Radack. "Judge Has Choice Words for Justice Department's Prosecution of Drake."Whistleblower.org, July 18, 2011.

"unconscionable" Ibid.

Jeffrey Sterling, an ex-CIA analyst who gave information to author James Risen Scott Shane. "Judge May Order Reporter to Testify Against Ex-CIA Officer Accused of Leaks." *The New York Times,* June 28, 2011.

Shamai Leibowitz pleaded guilty to leaking classified transcripts of bugged conversations Richard Silverstein. "Why I Published US Intelligence Secrets About Israel's Anti-Iran Campaign." Truth-out.org, October 14, 2011.

Stephen Kim, an arms expert for the State Department, the military, and Lawrence Livermore National Lab, was prosecuted for leaking Scott Shane. "U.S. Pressing Its Crackdown Against Leaks." *The New York Times,* June 17, 2011.

John Kiriakou, who had at times defended and criticized the Bush administration's use of waterboarding, was indicted John Rudolf. "Arrest of Ex-CIA Official, John Kiriakou, for Leaks About Detainee Torture Is Criticized." HuffingtonPost.com, January 25, 2012.

"should be encouraged rather than stifled" President Obama's website Change.gov, available at http://change.gov/agenda/ethics_agenda/

CHAPTER 6: THE GLOBALIZERS

spontaneously ejected a twelve-mile high mushroom cloud of steam and ash into the sky Ian Sample. "Grimsvötn volcano's worst eruption may be over, but concerns remain." *The Guardian,* May 23, 2011.

"There are technical problems and no one to take care of them" Marcel Rosenbach and Holger Stark. "'The Only Option Left for Me Is an Orderly Departure.'" *Der Spiegel,* September 27, 2010.

"in the end, there must be a thousand WikiLeaks." Ibid.

ScienceLeaks, TradeLeaks, UniLeaks All the leaking sites listed at Leakdirectory.org

threatened legal action against each other over the rights to the name Claudia Parsons. "WikiLeaks, OpenLeaks, GreenLeaks and more leaks." Reuters, January 28, 2011.

only one thing was missing from this newborn leaking movement. Leaks. Greg Mitchell writing on Twitter, March 30, 2011.

"even planted a tracking cookie file in the user's browser" Hanni Fakhoury. "WSJ and Al-Jazeera Lure Whistleblowers with False Promises of Anonymity." Electronic Frontier Foundation Deeplinks Blog at EFF.org, June 7, 2011.

"Pro tip: if you're going to create a document leaking Website—have a clue!" Jacob Appelbaum writing on Twitter, May 5, 2011.

"They reserve the right to sell you out" Fakhoury.

It was an agreement from the Bulgarian Department of Energy outlining the construction of a nuclear power plant "Memorandum of Belene prepared by Bogomil Manchev?" BalkanLeaks.eu, December 8, 2010, available here: http://www.balkanleaks.eu/en/memorandum.html

"a member of the Masonic lodge, has an answer to this question" "Information on the Masonic Lodge in the judiciary." BalkanLeaks.eu, December 10, 2010, available here: http://www.balkanleaks.eu/en/masoni.html

"a true guide to the methodology of bribery in the judiciary" "Special Investigation Methods Santirov-Petrov-Popov." BalkanLeaks.eu, December 11, 2010, available here: http://www.balkanleaks.eu/en/legal-srs.html

BalkanLeaks had arrived: a lone beacon of success in the leaking diaspora All the above-mentioned leaks are available at BalkanLeaks.eu

a raid by the dreaded antimafia police known as the "berets." "A Tale with Freemason-Mafia Aftertaste and Bulgarian Homebred Prosecution." BalkanLeaks.eu, September 6, 2011, available at http://www.balkanleaks.eu/en/angeldonchev.html

the country has the least freedom of the press of any in the European Union "WORLD PRESS FREEDOM INDEX 2011-2012" Reporters Without Borders, available at http://en.rsf.org/IMG/CLASSEMENT_2012/C_GENERAL_ANG.pdf

No one was charged in any of the three cases "Bulgaria: Website editor beaten with hammers in Sofia." Committee to Protect Journalists, UNHCR.org, September 23, 2008.

he died in a hospital three days later "Ricin and the umbrella murder." CNN.com, October 23, 2003.

He points instead to an agreement made at the end of World War II between the intelligence agencies Clay Shirky, speaking at the Personal Democracy Forum Conference, January 24, 2011, available here: http://personaldemocracy.com/pdf-presents-symposium-wikileaks-and-internet-freedom-ii

they traded off Ibid.

"obviously superior from the point of view of the leaker to any previous system" Ibid.

"that is the struggle we're going to see today" Ibid.

"please go sodomize yourself with retractable batons" E-mail from Gottfrid Svartholm to Dennis L. Wilson, August 21, 2004, available at http://static.thepiratebay.org/dreamworks_response.txt

suggest a specific model of baton to Apple's attorneys, the Asp twenty-one-inch E-mail from Gottfrid Svartholm to Ian Ramage, April 21, 2005, available at http://static.thepiratebay.org/apple_response.txt

Sealand refused to sell to them "Piratebay's sovereign ambitions blasted." TheRegister.co.uk, January 17, 2007.

allegedly defaming the prosecutor of 2011's Amanda Knox murder trial Candace Dempsey. "Sweden rescues Italian Amanda Knox blog. Google, are you watching?" SeattlePI.com, May 13, 2011.

took pictures, and published the story Assen Yordanov. "Illegal cigarettes factory near Burgas." *Standard,* March 31, 1995.

"A scent of death bleeds into the scent of Christmas" Birgitta Jónsdóttir. *The Chameleon's Diary* (Radical: Reykjavík, 2005), p. 5.

published in the newspaper *Helgarpósturinn* Birgitta Jónsdóttir. "Svartar Rosir." *Helgarpósturinn,* May 21, 1982.

"I have erected an iron raft in my back, it will not bend" Jónsdóttir, p. 10.

"I was being prepared for the times we are facing on my nearly bankrupted island" Birgitta Jónsdóttir. "Living in suspense." Birgitta Jónsdóttir's official blogspot, October 7, 2008, available at http://joyb.blogspot.com/2008/10/living-in-suspense.html

so we never forget/ the true horror of war Birgitta Jónsdóttir. "The Horror of War," available here: http://this.is/birgitta/poems/peace/horror.html

100 percent of the country's gross domestic product to 1000 percent CIA World Factbook entry on Iceland, available here: https://www.cia.gov/library/publications/the-world-factbook/geos/ic.html

The stock market value of Icelandic companies fell 90 percent Peter Gumbel. "Iceland: The country that became a hedge fund." CNN.com, December 4, 2008.

had been forced to pay in its crippling Treaty of Versailles after World War I "Cracks in the crust." *The Economist,* December 11, 2008.

"SMS terrorism" "Lawmakers hailed last night by text messages." Vesti.bg, February 29, 2008.

the "Crusade Against Strandzha" Maria Nikolaeva and Assen Yordanov, *Politika,* September 2, 2007.

"you know what happens to curious journalists. They get acid thrown at them." "Acid threat against journalist." Reporters Without Borders, February 23, 2007.

Her left eye was so badly damaged that it had to be surgically removed "Chronicles of courage." GlobalJournalist.org, July 1, 2001.

"the unacknowledged legislators of the world" Bruce Sterling. *The Hacker Crackdown: Law and Disorder on the Electronic Frontier.* (New York: Bantam Books, 1992), p. 235.

led to everything from the Thirty Years' War to the Spanish Inquisition John Perry Barlow speaking at the Reykjavík Digital Freedoms Conference, July 5, 2008, available here: http://www.youtube.com/watch?v=snQrNSE1T7Y

"it could become like the Switzerland of Bits" Ibid.

billion dollars, for instance, went to the bank's main owners "Financial collapse: Confidential exposure analysis of 205 companies each owing above EUR45M to Icelandic bank Kaupthing." WikiLeaks.org, September 26, 2008 available at http://wikileaks.org/wiki/Financial_collapse:_Confidential_exposure_analysis_of_205_companies_each_owing_above_EUR45M_to_Icelandic_bank_Kaupthing,_26_Sep_2008

would eventually be arrested in London and Reykjavík Cahal Milmo. "Billionaire brothers Vincent and Robert Tchenguiz arrested in Fraud Office raid." *The Independent*, March 10, 2011.

Afterward, strangers on the street offered them hugs and bought them drinks in bars Daniel Domscheit-Berg. *Inside WikiLeaks* (New York: Crown, 2011), p. 117.

"You mentioned to me this idea that in Iceland we should become a vanguard of publishing freedom" Silfur Egils, November 29, 2009, available here: http://www.youtube.com/watch?v=FBzyPB5eEuI&feature=player_embedded

"Why not pull all this together, and become *the* center for publishing in the world?" Ibid.

"a principled, holistic, and modern set of laws fit for the digital age" Heather Brooke. *Assange Agonistes.* Amazon Kindle Single, location 24

Of the cable's original 5,226 words, all but 1,406 were missing Full cable at WikiLeaks.org: http://www.wikileaks.ch/cable/2005/07/05SOFIA1207.html

"US embassy cables: Organised crime in Bulgaria." *The Guardian* December 1, 2010. http://www.guardian.co.uk/world/us-embassy-cables-documents/36013

"Bulgarian Organized Crime, Uncensored" Bivol.bg, October 17, 2011.

"cable cooking" WikiLeaks Twitter feed, September 8, 2011.

the wealth of scandals they had hoped for The full Bulgarian WikiLeaks cables are available at http://www.balkanleaks.eu/wikileaks-balkans.html

withhold nearly half a million dollars in aid until they were paid "WikiLeaks: Diplomats' Unpaid Parking Tickets Threatened US Aid to Bulgaria" Novinite.com, August 27, 2011.

"Bulgaria's Most Popular Politician: Great Hopes, Murky Ties" BalkanLeaks.eu, available here: http://www.balkanleaks.eu/en/06sofia647.html

receiving ten to twenty requests for data from law enforcement every day Christopher Soghoian. "The Law Enforcement Surveillance Reporting Gap," University of Indiana, April 10, 2011, available at http://papers.ssrn.com/sol3/papers.cfm?abstract_id=1806628

hand over user data 5,950 times, and that the company complied in 93 percent of those cases Google Transparency Report, January to June 2011, available at: http://www.google.com/transparencyreport/governmentrequests/US/?p=2011-06

"Even if Iceland's laws offer the best protections in the world, they're still a Maginot Line" Arthur Bright. "Fortress Iceland? Probably Not." Arthur Bright, Citizen Media Law Project blog, citmedialaw.org, February 16, 2010.

our high level of bilateral cooperation speaks for itself "US Embassy in Sofia Downplays Information from Wikileaks Cables." Novinite.com, May 26, 2011.

"will not comment on yellow press publications" "Bulgarian PM Dismisses 'WikiLeaks'-Alleged Ties to Lukoil, Russia." Novinite, May 26, 2011.

"Armani-clad tough guy" "Bulgaria's PM—'Armani-Clad Tough Guy' in WikiLeaks Cable—Report," Novinite.com, August 18, 2011.

veto Bulgaria's accession to the EU's visa-free Schengen travel zone "Bulgaria, Romania's Schengen Applications Formally Vetoed" Novinite.com, September 22, 2011.

CHAPTER 7: THE ENGINEERS

"dangerous, malicious conman" "Julian Assange live," L'Espresso, March 30, 2011.

"raised by wolves" Daniel Domscheit-Berg, *Inside WikiLeaks* (New York: Crown, 2011), p. 64.

"Leaking Sky Prevents OpenLeaks Launch" Anna Sauerbrey. *Die Zeit*, August 12, 2011.

"Still interested in a job?" Domscheit-Berg, p. 8.

two members responsible for most all of its activities Ibid., p. 22.

even spend two months living together in Berg's Wiesbaden home Ibid., p. 60.

even when meeting with government officials Ibid., p. 157.

"insurgent operation" Ibid., p 131.

temporary SIM cards and avoided all payment forms other than cash Ibid., p. 40.

"a genius" Andrew Fowler. "WikiLeaks site in limbo without architect" abc.net.au, October 4, 2011.

worked with CIA agents during her time at the consulting firm McKinsey Julian Assange. "Statement by Julian Assange on the reported destruction of WikiLeaks source material by Daniel Domscheit-Berg," August 20, 2011.

a real problem of methodology and, therefore, of credibility "OPEN LETTER TO WIKILEAKS FOUNDER JULIAN ASSANGE: 'A BAD PRECEDENT FOR THE INTERNET'S FUTURE.'" Reporters Without Borders website, August 12, 2010.

"We were very, very upset with [the Afghan War release,] and with the way he spoke about it afterwards" John Burns and Ravi Somaiya. "WikiLeaks Founder on the Run, Trailed By Notoriety." *The New York Times*, October 23, 2010.

"If you do not answer the question, you will be removed" Domscheit-Berg, p. 226.

"You behave like some kind of emperor or slave trader" Ibid., p. 226.

information that may have been used against the Belarusian political opposition "WIKILEAKS, BELARUS AND ISRAEL SHAMIR," Indexoncensorship.org, February 5, 2011.

extracted a copy of the cables from the Icelandic WikiLeaker Smári McCarthy Kim Zetter. "WikiLeaks Volunteer Hacked a Reporter, Assange Autobiography Reveals." Wired.com, September 23, 2011.

$20 million fine for distributing a WikiLeaks document, or even revealing the existence of the NDA itself. Kevin Poulsen. "WikiLeaks Threatens Its Own Leakers With $20 Million Penalty." Wired.com, May 11, 2011.

In such circumstances, silencing dissent is not just ironic, it's dangerous James Ball. "WikiLeaks, get out of the gagging game." *The Guardian*, Thursday, May 12, 2011.

five gigabytes of internal data from Bank of America WikiLeaks Twitter feed, August 21, 2011.

have your very own copy of the WikiLeaks' archive! How cool is that? Comment by user 5X32C54B, PirateBay.se, December 8, 2010.

AcollectionOfDiplomaticHistorySince_1966_ToThePresentDay#—Julian Assange's 58-character password David Leigh and Luke Harding *WikiLeaks* (New York: Public Affairs, 2011), p. 135.

"Leak at WikiLeaks" Steffen Kraft. *Der Freitag*, August 25, 2011.

"That the unreconfigured cables have become public is to be applauded and not condemned" John Young statement on Twitlonger.com, September 2, 2011.

***The Guardian*'s David Leigh pointed the finger at WikiLeaks for having published the encrypted file** David Leigh, comment on "Swept up and away," Economist.com, September 9, 2011.

"any autocratic secret service worth its salt" Christian Stöcker. "A Dispatch Disaster in Six Acts" *Der Spiegel,* September 1, 2011.

inexperienced leader in the sway of corrupt president Robert Mugabe's political party Alex Bell. "Army generals face possible treason charge after WikiLeaks revelations." *The Zimbabwean,* September 13, 2011.

with some calling for manhunts and violence against them Mark Mackinnon. "Leaked cables spark witch-hunt for Chinese 'rats.'" *The Globe and Mail,* September 14, 2011.

Iraqi Anglican church to leave the country for fear of violent reprisal Billy Hallowell. "JEWISH IRAQIS MAY BE IN DANGER FOLLOWING THE RELEASE OF WIKILEAKS CABLES." TheBlaze.com, October 11, 2011.

"I love my country and I love my job and it's a big loss for me" "Ethiopian journalist ID'd in WikiLeaks cable flees country." Committee to Protect Journalists website, September 14, 2011.

murdered in inhuman medical experiments Rochelle G. Saidel. "Ravensbruck Women's Concentration Camp." Jewish Women's Archive.

CONCLUSION: THE MACHINE

"the whole world is watching" Posted to LiveLeak October 2 , 2011, available at http://www.liveleak.com/view?i=c11_1317570746

doused with Mace and left blinded and screaming Posted to YouTube September 24, http://www.youtube.com/watch?v=moD2JnGTToA

"notorious for his previous treatment of protesters" Cryptome.org, September 26, 2011, available at http://cryptome.org/info/bologna-abuser/bologna-abuser.htm

Bologna was fined six thousand dollars by the department and faced a further inquiry by the Manhattan district attorney "'I'd do it again,' says police commander filmed pepper spraying the faces of women at Occupy Wall Street protest." *Daily Mail,* October 21, 2011.

A few of the recordings Jones has obtained are disturbing All OpenWatch recordings are available at http://openwatch.net/all/

twenty-six million people used the service Benny Evangelista. "Napster files for bankruptcy." *San Francisco Chronicle,* June 4, 2002.

working in the office of his uncle's Internet start-up Chess.net Farhad Manjoo. "A file-trading ship of fools." Salon.com, April 21, 2003.

twenty-billion-dollar lawsuit by the Recording Industry Association of America Rich Menta. "RIAA Sues Music Startup Napster for $20 Billion." MP3Newswire.net, December 9, 1999.

bankrupt in 2002 Evangelista.

single point of failure Anthony J. Howe. "Napster and Gnutella: a Comparison of two Popular Peer-to-Peer Protocols." University of Victoria, February 28, 2002.

cut in half since 1999, from $14.6 billion to $7.6 billion Record Industry Association of America website, RIAA.org/faq

"we will simply not be able to continue by the turn of the new year" Associated Press, October 24, 2011.

ACKNOWLEDGMENTS

If I listed the people who helped me write this book in either chronological order or order of importance, my wife, Malika Zouhali-Worrall, would come first. From the night I kept her up imagining Julian Assange on the cover of *Forbes* magazine, to my last moments of panic trying to meet my publisher's deadlines fifteen months later, Malika offered endless ideas, advice, support, and close, smart editing, even as she codirected and produced a documentary film over the same time frame that was just as all-consuming—if not more so—than any book.

My editor, Stephen Morrow, has been one of the most pleasant editors I've ever had the opportunity to work with, and put enormous enthusiasm, imagination, and energy into shaping my manuscript. Both he and my literary agent, Eric Lupfer, were patient guides through the tortuous process of writing a first book.

I owe a large debt of gratitude to the staff of *Forbes* magazine, and particularly Lewis Dvorkin, who has offered me a level of freedom, resources, and support that any journalist would envy. Randall Lane has matched that generosity since his arrival at the magazine. Dan Bigman saw the full potential for this story within seconds of my walking into his office to pitch it in September 2010, and served as its best advocate among the magazine's editors. Tom Post polished that cover story with care and skill. My colleagues on *Forbes*'s tech reporting team ably and patiently filled in the gaps left in our coverage while I worked on this book. Eric Savitz, as my direct editor, gave me enormous flexibility to both take time off and to work while traveling. (Often without even asking which country I was in while filing stories.) Susan Radlauer and Kai Falkenberg offered me endless research and legal assistance well beyond their duties at *Forbes*, and Coates Bateman and Elizabeth Woyke both gave me valuable advice.

Other people who helped make this book possible include Alby Alkalay, Georgia Cool, Nick Fara, Sam and Lauren Greenberg, Maria Guineva, Kenza and Alex Hagon, Julie Hazan, Stephanie Hitchcock, Birgitta Jónsdóttir, Moxie Marlinspike, Gregory Muccio, Michael Noer, LeeAnn Pemberton, Atanas and Maria Tchobanov, and Assen Yordanov. I'm also particularly grateful to my parents-in-law, Naima Zouhali and Steve Worrall, for their support and for offering me ideal places to live and work at several points during my travel, reporting, and writing.

Finally, I'd like to thank my father, Gary Greenberg, for helping me to find this book's direction in endless phone conversations, for his close editing of the manuscript, for making my career in journalism possible, and for his tireless and good-natured critical attention to my writing, even if he likes to remind me that my talents as a writer peaked in the sixth grade.

THE PUZZLE CONTAINED IN THIS BOOK

I am grateful for the expertise and generosity of G. Mark Hardy who created the puzzle that is integrated into this book. For more information go to www.thismachinekillssecrets.com.

Congratulations to the first three readers to successfully solve the puzzle: Timo Hirvonen, Alexandre Girard, and David Schuetz.

INDEX